# WOMEN AND THE CIRCULATION
# OF TEXTS IN RENAISSANCE

During the Italian Renaissance, laywomen and nuns could take part in every stage of the circulation of texts of many kinds, old and new, learned and popular. This first in-depth and integrated analysis of Italian women's involvement in the material textual culture of the period shows how they could publish their own works in manuscript and print and how they promoted the first publication of works composed by others, acting as patrons or dedicatees. It describes how they copied manuscripts and helped to make and sell printed books in collaboration with men, how they received books as gifts and borrowed or bought them, how they commissioned manuscripts for themselves and how they might listen to works in spoken or sung performance. Brian Richardson's richly documented study demonstrates the powerful social function of books in the Renaissance: texts-in-motion helped to shape women's lives and sustain their social and spiritual communities.

BRIAN RICHARDSON is Emeritus Professor of Italian Language at the University of Leeds. He is the author of *Manuscript Culture in Renaissance Italy* (Cambridge University Press, 2009), *Printers, Writers and Readers in Renaissance Italy* (Cambridge University Press, 1999) and *Print Culture in Renaissance Italy* (Cambridge University Press, 1994).

# WOMEN AND THE CIRCULATION OF TEXTS IN RENAISSANCE ITALY

BRIAN RICHARDSON

*University of Leeds*

CAMBRIDGE
UNIVERSITY PRESS

# CAMBRIDGE
## UNIVERSITY PRESS

Shaftesbury Road, Cambridge CB2 8EA, United Kingdom

One Liberty Plaza, 20th Floor, New York, NY 10006, USA

477 Williamstown Road, Port Melbourne, VIC 3207, Australia

314–321, 3rd Floor, Plot 3, Splendor Forum, Jasola District Centre, New Delhi – 110025, India

103 Penang Road, #05–06/07, Visioncrest Commercial, Singapore 238467

Cambridge University Press is part of Cambridge University Press & Assessment, a department of the University of Cambridge.

We share the University's mission to contribute to society through the pursuit of education, learning and research at the highest international levels of excellence.

www.cambridge.org
Information on this title: www.cambridge.org/9781108702539

DOI: 10.1017/9781108774482

First published 2020
First paperback edition 2022

*A catalogue record for this publication is available from the British Library*

*Library of Congress Cataloging-in-Publication data*
NAMES: Richardson, Brian (Brian F.), author.
TITLE: Women and the circulation of texts in Renaissance Italy / Brian Richardson, University of Leeds.
DESCRIPTION: Cambridge, United Kingdom ; New York, NY : Cambridge University Press, 2020. | Includes bibliographical references and index.
IDENTIFIERS: LCCN 2019039810 (print) | LCCN 2019039811 (ebook) | ISBN 9781108477697 (hardback) | ISBN 9781108774482 (epub)
SUBJECTS: LCSH: Women in the book industries and trade – Italy – History. | Women – Books and reading – Italy – History. | Transmission of texts – Social aspects – Italy – History. | Women – Italy – History – Renaissance, 1450–1600.
CLASSIFICATION: LCC Z340 .R534 2020 (print) | LCC Z340 (ebook) | DDC 028/.90820945–dc23
LC record available at https://lccn.loc.gov/2019039810
LC ebook record available at https://lccn.loc.gov/2019039811

ISBN    978-1-108-47769-7    Hardback
ISBN    978-1-108-70253-9    Paperback

# Contents

# Illustrations

# Preface

One of the most fertile developments in book history in recent years has been the study of the connections between books and the social contexts in which they originated and were used. This social turn is linked closely with the inaugural Panizzi Lectures given in the British Library by Don McKenzie in 1985. In this landmark series, entitled 'Bibliography and the Sociology of Texts', McKenzie challenged a traditional view that bibliography is concerned only with signs written or printed on paper or vellum, and not with their meaning. Rather, he proposed, bibliography should comprehend 'not only the technical but the social processes' of the transmission of texts, 'the human motives and interactions which texts involve at every stage of their production, transmission, and consumption'. In short, it should take account of 'the role of human agents'.[1] As far as early modern culture is concerned, a few examples of the varied ways in which awareness of the social and human faces of bibliography and palaeography has shed new light from around the 1970s onwards are: Armando Petrucci's studies of modes of written transmission; Natalie Davis's essay on books as gifts; Harold Love's groundbreaking book on scribal publication; Roger Chartier's studies of how the forms that transmit texts help to create meaning in conjunction with the 'rebel inventiveness' of readers and listeners; Margaret Ezell's work on social authorship in relation to manuscript and print; Diana Robin's investigations into the print publication of verse by sixteenth-century Italian women; and Antonio Castillo Gómez's research into the social history of written culture in Spain.[2] As a further

[1] D. F. McKenzie, *Bibliography and the Sociology of Texts* (Cambridge University Press, 1999), pp. 13, 15, 16. The lectures were first published by the British Library in 1986.

[2] Armando Petrucci, *Writers and Readers in Medieval History: Studies in the History of Written Culture*, ed. and trans. by Charles M. Radding (New Haven: Yale University Press, 1995), and other studies; Natalie Zemon Davis, 'Beyond the Market: Books as Gifts in Sixteenth-Century France', *Transactions of the Royal Historical Society*, 5th ser., 33 (1983), 69–88; Harold Love, *Scribal Publication in Seventeenth-Century England* (Oxford: Clarendon Press, 1993); Roger Chartier, *Forms and Meanings: Texts, Performances, and Audiences from Codex to Computer* (Philadelphia:

demonstration of the vitality of books after their manufacture, along the dimensions of both space and time, there have been a number of studies of annotations made by readers.[3]

The last few decades have also seen a flourishing of new approaches to the study of the lives of women during the Renaissance. In an essay first published in 1977, the American feminist historian Joan Kelly asked the challenging question, 'Did women have a Renaissance?' Using a sample of evidence drawn primarily from courtly culture, she herself answered with a negative: 'there was no renaissance for women – at least, not during the Renaissance'. The period, she argued polemically, saw a relative contraction of the powers of secular women of the courtly and patrician elite as measured by certain criteria, so that the relation of the sexes became for the most part 'one of female dependency and male domination'.[4] Since Kelly's essay, we have learned more about the nature and extent of the social and legal constraints imposed on women's lives across all social classes, from childhood to adulthood, in the patriarchal society of this period. We are now also aware that Kelly's partial, blunt and pessimistic assessment needs to be nuanced considerably in view of all that women achieved in spite of their subordination to men and their relative lack of opportunities in public life. From the perspective of historians of Italian culture, it is particularly striking that, as Virginia Cox has commented in one of her outstanding studies of this topic, secular women emerged in the sixteenth century 'as cultural protagonists in a quantity and with a prominence unprecedented in the ancient or medieval world'. This shift, Cox argues, was accompanied by positive new male and female attitudes towards the merits of women, including their capacity for erudition, and it was enabled and promoted by a flow of pro-feminist discourses.[5]

University of Pennsylvania Press, 1995), quotation from p. 1; Margaret J. M. Ezell, *Social Authorship and the Advent of Print* (Baltimore, MD: Johns Hopkins University Press, 1999); Diana Robin, *Publishing Women: Salons, the Presses, and the Counter-Reformation in Sixteenth-Century Italy* (University of Chicago Press, 2007); Antonio Castillo Gómez, *Dalle carte ai muri: scrittura e società nella Spagna della prima Età moderna*, trans. by Laura Carnelos (Rome: Carocci, 2016), and other studies.
[3] For instance, Roger Stoddard, *Marks in Books, Illustrated and Explained* (Cambridge, MA: Houghton Library, 1985); Robin C. Alston, *Books with Manuscript* (London: British Library, 1994); William H. Sherman, *Used Books: Marking Readers in Renaissance England* (Philadelphia: University of Pennsylvania Press, 2007).
[4] Joan Kelly, 'Did Women Have a Renaissance?', in *Becoming Visible: Women in European History*, ed. by Renate Bridenthal and Claudia Koonz (Boston, MA: Houghton Mifflin, 1977), pp. 137–64 (quotations from pp. 139 and 140). The essay was republished in *Women, History, and Theory: The Essays of Joan Kelly* (University of Chicago Press, 1984), pp. 19–50.
[5] Virginia Cox, *Women's Writing in Italy, 1400–1650* (Baltimore, MD: Johns Hopkins University Press, 2008), pp. xi–xxii (quotation from p. xiii). See also Cox, *The Prodigious Muse: Women's Writing in*

The intersections between the study of the book in society and the study of women's lives in the Renaissance can shed light on each area of research. On the one hand, the evidence of book history can tell us more about the private and social lives of women: how their writings and those of men were disseminated to others in their own circles and beyond them; their agency in the manufacture and even the commerce of books; what and how they read; and what the places of texts were in women's lives. On the other hand, to look specifically at women's involvement in the production and circulation of books can broaden our understanding of these processes, which have tended to be considered in terms of the predominant and much more visible roles of men. We can ask how activities related to books looked through the eyes of the women of the period. How and how far was it possible for them to participate in making and distributing books, and to do so for their own ends? How far, in concerning themselves with the circulation of books, did they act independently and how far did they collaborate with men, in supporting or leading roles?

Some important recent studies have addressed such questions. To take just two examples concerning Italy, Luisa Miglio has written on the uses that women across all social classes made of handwriting during the fourteenth and fifteenth centuries, and Tiziana Plebani's study of the 'gender' of books includes an informative chapter on women's diverse involvement in book production.[6] There have been several investigations into women's roles in the circulation of texts in other countries of Europe, and some of these will be mentioned in the Conclusion. The present work shares many of the broad aims and methods of such research. Its focus is on texts on the move: especially texts that were embodied in the tangible forms of the manuscripts and printed books that contained them, but also, in the third chapter, those that were transmitted, at least in part, orally. The texts studied include poetry and literary, historical and religious prose works, as well as correspondence that was not intended only for a single reader, but they do not include practical writings such as account books.

---

*Counter-Reformation Italy* (Baltimore, MD: Johns Hopkins University Press, 2011); *Lyric Poetry by Women of the Italian Renaissance*, ed. by Virginia Cox (Baltimore, MD: Johns Hopkins University Press, 2013); and Cox, *A Short History of the Italian Renaissance* (London: I. B. Tauris, 2016), chapter 6. A brief survey is Guillaume Allonge, 'Le scrittrici nella prima età moderna', in *Atlante della letteratura italiana*, ed. by Sergio Luzzatto and Gabriele Pedullà, 3 vols (Turin: Einaudi, 2010–12), II, 119–26.

[6] Luisa Miglio, *Governare l'alfabeto: donne, scrittura e libri nel medioevo* (Rome: Viella, 2008); Tiziana Plebani, 'Le donne nei mestieri del libro', in *Il 'genere' dei libri: storie e rappresentazioni della lettura al femminile e al maschile tra Medioevo ed età moderna* (Milan: Franco Angeli, 2001), pp. 164–85.

In order to study the circulation of texts from person to person, it has been very helpful to make use of the communications circuit first proposed in 1982 by Robert Darnton (Figure 0.1).[7] Communication through books, in Darnton's scheme, begins with the nexus of interactions between the author, as the creator of the text, and the publisher – in other words, the person or the set of persons responsible for managing the creation and diffusion of the resulting book. It then moves clockwise to encompass printers and their suppliers, shippers, booksellers and finally readers. The circuit is closed by a broken line returning to the author, because authors may well be influenced by the favourable or unfavourable reactions of past readers, and by their anticipation of the reactions of future readers.

Writing some years later within a collection of essays that sought to describe 'the mutual and interdependent exchange between the press and the society that feeds and depends upon it',[8] Thomas R. Adams and Nicolas Barker proposed an alternative 'model for the study of books considered as historic artefacts and as a function of social history'. They felt that Darnton's scheme was 'well adapted to the needs of the history of the book in general, allowing as it does for the interplay between external forces and the various processes through which it goes'. However, 'from the point of view of serving the history of the book', it had in their view a weakness, 'that it deals with people, rather than the book'. They proposed a scheme that shows 'the whole socio-economic conjuncture'. At its centre lies a cycle, not of six persons or groups, but of 'five events in the life of a book – publishing, manufacturing, distribution, reception and survival'. Four separate 'indirect forces' act on all these stages: intellectual influences; political, legal and religious influences; commercial pressures; and social behaviour and taste. These forces are placed outside rather than inside the cycle. In this scheme, '[t]he text is the reason for the cycle of the book: its transmission depends on its ability to set off new cycles'.[9] Robert Darnton, in turn, commented that the circuit of Adams and Barker is more adaptable to conditions after the early nineteenth century, whereas he had in mind primarily publishing between 1500 and

---

[7] Robert Darnton, 'What Is the History of Books?', in *The Kiss of Lamourette: Reflections in Cultural History* (London and Boston: Faber and Faber, 1990), pp. 107–35 (figure on p. 112); first published in *Daedalus*, III.3 (Summer 1982), 65–83.

[8] Nicolas Barker, 'Introduction', in *A Potencie of Life: Books in Society*, ed. by Nicolas Barker (London: British Library, 1994), pp. 1–4 (p. 2).

[9] Thomas R. Adams and Nicolas Barker, 'A New Model for the Study of the Book', in *A Potencie of Life*, ed. by Barker, pp. 5–43 (pp. 5, 10, 12, 13–15).

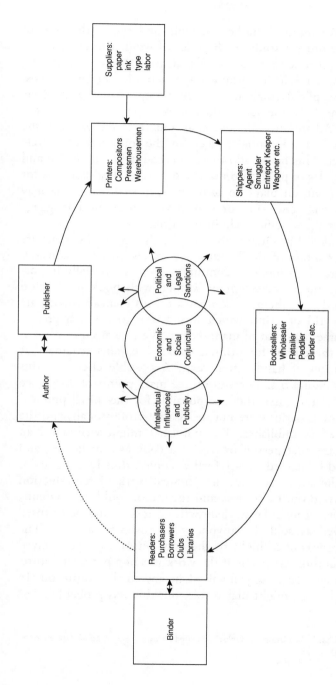

Figure 0.1 Robert Darnton's communications circuit. From Robert Darnton, 'What Is the History of Books?', *Daedalus*, 111.3 (Summer 1982), 65–83 (p. 68). Reprinted courtesy of The MIT Press

1800, and that Adams and Barker's circuit underplays the role of authors.[10] For the present study of the roles of women in the circulation of texts, it is sensible to make use of Darnton's model as a starting point precisely because it foregrounds the activities of individuals; indeed, Darnton explicitly includes women alongside men as subjects of book historians.[11] At the same time, it is important to note the point, made by Adams and Barker, that the text, rather than the author in person, is the essential trigger for the initiation of a cycle of communication. This factor allows us to account for successive and possibly diverse cycles of publication of the same text. It also allows for cycles in which an author plays no active part; indeed, he or she may belong to a previous generation or may have written in a language other than that of the specific cycle in question.

Darnton intended his circuit to apply only to books that are printed.[12] In the context of the Renaissance we also need to consider manuscript culture. This mode of communication is especially important in evaluating the involvement of women with book production because it was harder for them, in comparison with men, to participate actively in the world of print, which was driven to a much greater extent by commerce than that of manuscripts. We thus need to have in mind, alongside the circuit for printed books, a parallel scheme that maps the circulation of handwritten texts. A possible circuit of this kind is shown in Figure 0.2. There are three main points of difference from Darnton's circuit. First, those responsible for the initial publication of works in manuscript were not necessarily professionals, and the author often acted as publisher. The publisher might well select an individual to be the first person to receive a copy as a dedicatee, and this person would be named in any further copies, thus lending his or her prestige to the work. Second, the physical work of reproduction was of course carried out by scribes, and they, too, could be amateurs, including perhaps authors. Third, handwritten texts could be diffused informally, as well as sold, by anyone who possessed a copy. The dedicatee, if there was one, might be the only person to have received a copy from the author, especially if the work was of a personal nature, and he or she might be closely involved in any further diffusion. In this process, booksellers might play a role, but this was probably a less

[10] Robert Darnton, '"What Is the History of Books?" Revisited', *Modern Intellectual History*, 4 (2007), 495–508 (pp. 502–04).
[11] Ibid., pp. 496, 502.   [12] Ibid., p. 502.

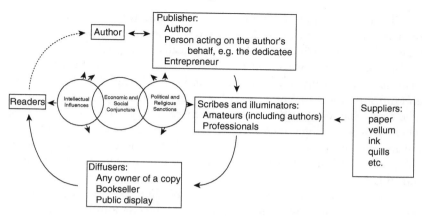

Figure 0.2 A communications circuit for manuscript culture

important one than that of networks and communities.[13] Certain kinds of texts, whether libellous, seditious or official, might be diffused in copies, handwritten as well as printed, that were displayed in public places.[14] The three general sets of influences at the centre of the circuit can be seen as broadly similar to those suggested by Darnton, except that publicity in support of sales is of negligible importance and that, in the period with which we are concerned, we need to take account of sanctions imposed by the Church.

The three chapters of this book look at Italian women's involvement at key points in the communications circuits from around the mid-fifteenth to the mid-seventeenth century. The first chapter focuses on the earliest stage: the nexus of the publisher and the author, or at least of the publisher and the author's text, if the author was deceased or not involved in the process of circulation. The chapter considers the extent of women's agency

[13] On the Italian context, see Brian Richardson, *Manuscript Culture in Renaissance Italy* (Cambridge University Press, 2009). Key studies of the scribal circulation of texts in early modern Britain include Love, *Scribal Publication in Seventeenth-Century England*; Arthur F. Marotti, *Manuscript, Print, and the English Renaissance Lyric* (Ithaca, NY: Cornell University Press, 1995); H. R. Woudhuysen, *Sir Philip Sidney and the Circulation of Manuscripts 1558–1640* (Oxford: Clarendon Press, 1996); Peter Beal, *In Praise of Scribes: Manuscripts and their Makers in Seventeenth-Century England* (Oxford: Clarendon Press, 1998); Ezell, *Social Authorship and the Advent of Print*, pp. 21–44.

[14] For examples, see Richardson, *Manuscript Culture in Renaissance Italy*, pp. 114–26; Castillo Gómez, *Dalle carte ai muri*, pp. 197–242; Castillo Gómez, 'Writings on the Streets: Ephemeral Texts and Public Space in the Early Modern Hispanic World', in *Approaches to the History of Written Culture: A World Inscribed*, ed. by Martyn Lyons and Rita Marquilhas (Basingstoke: Palgrave Macmillan, 2017), pp. 73–96.

xvi                                    *Preface*

in diffusing texts that were in their possession, whether composed by themselves or by men, and it then asks to what extent and for what reasons women played distinctive roles as dedicatees of published texts. In the second chapter, we move to the next two points in the circuits of manuscript and print and look at the hands-on participation of laywomen and nuns in producing texts, as scribes or as printers, and in selling books. The final chapter considers how women readers gained access to texts, whether by acquiring copies through their social connections or by other means, or by hearing them in performance. In this last context, the chapter will outline a possible third communications circuit that accounts for oral transmission.

A theme that runs through this book, binding together the topics of textual culture and of women's lives, is that of the relationship between the written (and, to some extent, oral) circulation of texts and communities of different kinds. A helpful broad definition of community in the early modern period, offered by Karen E. Spierling and Michael J. Halvorson, is 'a group of people who perceived themselves as having common interests and, thus, a common identity or self-understanding'.[15] The communities with which this book is concerned range from tight-knit organizations whose members knew each other personally, such as a princely court, a religious house or a family, to more open-ended groupings, not bounded by one location, of those who shared kindred interests. In many instances, the members were both male and female, but in the case of religious houses the primary members of the communities considered here were female. All their members interacted with one another, even if they were not always directly acquainted, and they were bonded, to a greater or lesser degree according to the cohesiveness of the groupings, by a sense of shared identity and a solidarity of purpose.[16] Phil Withington and Alexandra Shepard have written that one of the constituent parts of a community, understood as 'something done as an expression of collective identity by groups of people', is 'the acts and artefacts – whether communicative or material – which defined and constituted it'.[17] The circulation of texts in oral or written form

---

[15] Karen E. Spierling and Michael J. Halvorson, 'Introduction: Definitions of Community in Early Modern Europe', in *Defining Community in Early Modern Europe*, ed. by Michael J. Halvorson and Karen E. Spierling (Aldershot: Ashgate, 2008), pp. 1–23 (p. 2).

[16] For the example of the construction of memory within female religious communities, see *Memoria e comunità femminili: Spagna e Italia, secc. XV–XVII*, ed. by Gabriella Zarri and Nieves Baranda Leturio (Florence: Firenze University Press; [Madrid]: UNED, 2011).

[17] Phil Withington and Alexandra Shepard, 'Introduction: Communities in Early Modern England', in *Communities in Early Modern England: Networks, Place, Rhetoric*, ed. by Alexandra Shepard and Phil Withington (Manchester University Press, 2000), pp. 1–15 (p. 12).

belongs to this aspect of the concept. Of course, in the Renaissance written circulation could regularly take place within a market economy, open to anyone with the necessary resources, and this became the norm in the case of print culture. However, the circulation of manuscripts and even of printed books could also take place partially or solely in the contexts of social, cultural and spiritual communities. Books of all kinds both formed part of and enabled social interactions. In manuscript culture, an author often published a text socially, starting with the presentation of a copy to a dedicatee or friend, which could be followed by further social circulation. Authors could present copies of printed editions to specific readers, typically to ones who were prestigious in terms of their rank and social status. Receiving books as gifts and borrowing them were important means of acquiring texts of all sorts, sometimes the only means of doing so. Many texts were published with letters of dedication that had the effect of linking the work, or an edition of the work, with a person who was generally described as playing some kind of social role. Since copies of some texts were rare, perhaps because their circulation was restricted by the author or because their message was contentious, exclusive or near-exclusive possession of them bestowed prestige on their owners in the eyes of others. Such prestige also stemmed from the ownership of finely produced copies of texts in manuscript or print. In short, the circulation of books was influenced in many ways by social as well as by economic factors. This was especially true in the case of women, since their opportunities to exercise financial power were more limited than those of men. Their access to sociable textual culture was also important because they were largely unable to play any significant part in the lives of the academies that were constituted by Italian men from the mid-1520s onwards. As Virginia Cox has written,

> Even in those few cases where women were elected as members, their status was marginal and their presence in the academies tended to be virtual, rather than actual; they were corresponding members, rather than actually attending meetings, which would have raised issues of decorum.[18]

Most of the texts with which this book is concerned were composed in the vernacular or in Latin, but obstacles stood in the way of women's access to forms of language other than their own spoken tongue during the Renaissance. In a politically fragmented peninsula, most works composed

---

[18] Virginia Cox, 'Members, Muses, Mascots: Women and Italian Academies', in *The Italian Academies 1525–1700: Networks of Culture, Innovation and Dissent*, ed. by Jane E. Everson, Denis V. Reidy and Lisa Sampson (Cambridge: Legenda, 2016), pp. 132–69 (p. 132).

in the vernacular made at least some use of a language that was based on the written word: the Florentine used by three great authors of the fourteenth century, Dante, Petrarch and Boccaccio. The linguistic influence of the last two grew markedly stronger during the sixteenth century. However, their variety of the vernacular differed to a greater or lesser extent from the vernaculars of the Renaissance Italian states, even from those of Tuscany. All readers therefore needed to learn to understand the written literary vernacular, and it required close study on the part of those who wished to use it as authors. Latin was predominantly the province of men: it was the language studied in the formal educational curriculum, which was intended mainly to benefit boys. Nevertheless, as we shall see, some women were engaged as scribes or compositors in the diffusion of Latin texts, some became proficient authors in this language and a few of them translated Latin works into the literary vernacular.

***

This book is based on the three Panizzi Lectures delivered at the British Library in London in October 2012. It was a great honour to be invited by the council of the Panizzi Foundation to follow the distinguished scholars who have given these lectures in the past, and I am very grateful to its members and David Pearson for giving me this opportunity. I was closely supported by the late Chris Michaelides of the British Library: he assisted in many practical ways and he acted as a friendly and reassuring guide during the process of planning and giving the lectures. Many others helped me as I prepared the lectures and then wrote this book. Virginia Cox and Helena Sanson offered very valuable advice. I also thank colleagues who generously provided information, especially Bonnie Blackburn, Elena Bonora, Luca Degl'Innocenti, Filippo de Vivo, Cristina Dondi, John Gagné, David and Penny Hartley, the late Anthony Hobson, Francesco Lucioli, Melissa Moreton and Clara Stella. Another version of the section on Isabella d'Este in Chapter 3 was published as 'Isabella d'Este and the Social Uses of Books', *La Bibliofilìa*, 114 (2012), 293–325.

In transcriptions of Renaissance texts and book titles, original spelling has been preserved, except for the distinction between the consonant *v* and the vowel or semivowel *u*, the expansion of abbreviations, the transcription of '&' as 'et' and some changes to word division, punctuation and accentuation in line with modern practice. Translations are mine unless indicated otherwise. In the currency of account of Renaissance Italy, 1 lira = 20 soldi = 240 denari.

# *Abbreviations*

| | |
|---|---|
| Ascarelli and Menato, *La tipografia* | Fernanda Ascarelli and Marco Menato, *La tipografia del '500 in Italia* (Florence: Olschki, 1989) |
| ASF | Florence, Archivio di Stato |
| ASMn | Mantua, Archivio di Stato |
| BAM | Milan, Biblioteca Ambrosiana |
| BAV | Vatican City, Biblioteca Apostolica Vaticana |
| BLF | Florence, Biblioteca Medicea Laurenziana |
| BNCF | Florence, Biblioteca Nazionale Centrale |
| BRF | Florence, Biblioteca Riccardiana |
| *DBI* | *Dizionario biografico degli Italiani* (Rome: Istituto della Enciclopedia Italiana, 1960–) |
| *GSLI* | *Giornale storico della letteratura italiana* |
| *LB* | *La Bibliofilìa* |
| Menato, *Dizionario* | Marco Menato, Ennio Sandal and Giuseppina Zappella, eds, *Dizionario dei tipografi e degli editori italiani: Il Cinquecento*, vol. I (Milan: Editrice Bibliografica, 1997) |

# CHAPTER I

# *Publishing Texts*

This chapter examines the parts that women in Renaissance Italy played, directly or indirectly, in promoting scribal or print publication without their necessarily having a commercial interest in the process. The first section deals with the role in which they were most active, that of self-publisher, investigating the steps that they took to diffuse their own texts, in manuscript or in print. The second section considers two ways in which women contributed to the publication of texts composed by others. In the first of these types of involvement, which was similarly an active one, women occasionally promoted works written by men because they had a personal interest in the writings, out of religious or cultural solidarity. In the second and much more widespread type, individual women were invoked as dedicatees of a work because it was considered, for a variety of reasons, that the publication of the work would benefit from their being connected with it. In most cases a dedicatee's willingness to give consent to a dedication would have been ascertained in advance.[1] Even if a woman's involvement in the publication of a work went no further than according such permission, and her role as patron was thus not necessarily a very active one, the dedicator's decision to select a woman as dedicatee was socially significant for her, and above all it could have a strong influence on the reader's perception of the work.

---

[1] For two examples of preliminary enquiries about a dedication, and an example of an apology for not having made a request for permission, see Richardson, *Manuscript Culture in Renaissance Italy*, pp. 219–20. Paolo Manuzio felt unable to print Silvan Cattaneo's *Dodici giornate* in 1551 because the Venetian patrician Marco Antonio da Mula had not provided a formal 'commissione' (instruction) to state that he would act as dedicatee: Bonnie J. Blackburn, 'Fortunato Martinengo and His Musical Tour around Lake Garda: The Place of Music and Poetry in Silvan Cattaneo's *Dodici giornate*', in *Fortunato Martinengo: un gentiluomo del Rinascimento fra arti, lettere e musica*, ed. by Marco Bizzarini and Elisabetta Selmi (Brescia: Morcelliana, 2018), pp. 179–209 (pp. 197–98).

## Self-Publication

*Self-Publication in Manuscript*

Laywomen who composed works intended for a public readership in the fifteenth century could involve themselves in their circulation in manuscript. Isotta Nogarola (1418–1466), the remarkable humanist from Verona, evidently kept copies of the Latin letters she wrote to public figures,[2] and one of her correspondents, Lauro Quirini, mentions her letters 'iam in volumen redactas' (now collected in a volume).[3] Another, Lodovico Foscarini, talks of '[s]cripta [...] tua edita et data mihi' (your writings, published and given to me) when he was leaving Verona in 1452.[4] Ceccarella Minutolo of Naples made a collection of her letters on love and other topics, written around 1470 in a high-flown vernacular, and addressed it to Francesco Arcella. Dedicating the work, she makes the conventional claim that others wished to 'publicare mei licterule' (publish my little letters) and asks that Arcella, who has encouraged her 'ad tal audace facto' (to such a daring deed) will defend her against criticism.[5]

In the 1530s, Ippolita Clara, a member of the social elite of Alessandria in Piedmont, whose husband had a distinguished political career, published her poetry in copies written in her own hand. Through her verses, she cultivated relationships with other members of the ruling class, female and male, across northern Italy, and in several poems she commented on political and social events of her time, which she managed to follow closely in spite of having (apparently) twenty-four pregnancies. When sending out her correspondence poems to readers, she used a regular but not calligraphic variety of the cultured script known as humanistic cursive or, outside the peninsula, italic.[6] An example is a leaf containing two sonnets addressed to the Duke of Milan, Francesco II Sforza, and signed by Ippolita as his 'Humil serva et fidel suddita' (Humble servant and faithful subject; Figure 1.1). In the second poem, Clara exhorts the duke to return from Vigevano to Milan, where she is writing out her verse: 'et io le carte lieta vergo | vicina a te, de' miei concetti

---

[2] Isotta Nogarola, *Complete Writings: Letterbook, Dialogue on Adam and Eve, Orations*, ed. and trans. by Margaret L. King and Diana Robin (University of Chicago Press, 2004), pp. 93–94.

[3] Isotta Nogarola, *Opera quae supersunt omnia*, ed. by Jenö Ábel, 2 vols (Vienna: Gerold, 1886), II, 10; Nogarola, *Complete Writings*, p. 107.

[4] Nogarola, *Opera*, II, 118.

[5] Ceccarella Minutolo, *Lettere*, ed. by Raffaele Morabito (Naples: Edizioni Scientifiche Italiane, 1999), p. 34.

[6] For a summary of the development of scripts in fifteenth- and sixteenth-century Italy, see Richardson, *Manuscript Culture in Renaissance Italy*, pp. 59–62.

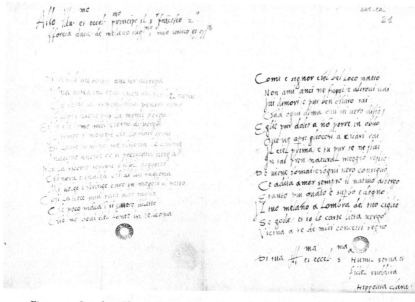

Figure 1.1 Ippolita Clara, two sonnets addressed to Francesco II Sforza. Forlì, Biblioteca Comunale, Raccolte Piancastelli, Sezione Carte Romagna, busta 445 / 21 fronte

segno' (lines 13–14; and I happily copy out my writings on paper, near you, as a sign of my thoughts). This leaf was sent as a letter, with the address on the verso, folded and sealed.[7] In 1533 Clara wrote out and communicated to Duke Francesco, as dedicatee, her verse translation of Virgil's *Aeneid*, Books I–VI. In her letter of dedication, she explains that she has chosen to translate these books, leaving aside the later ones which are full of warfare, for the benefit of women, since they do not understand Latin. Book I, for instance, showed them how one should try to avoid incurring the wrath of the gods:

> tal opera i' fece per essempio alle indotte donne, cioè che non intendano la latina lingua, acciò nel primo de l'*Eneida* vedano come sempre si debbe (quanto si pò) fugir l'ira de li dei, che se ben il fugir in tutto non placa tal ira almeno tal atto di cedere la sminuisse.[8]

---

[7] Forlì, Biblioteca Comunale, Raccolte Piancastelli, Sezione Carte Romagna, busta 445 / 21. See Simone Albonico, 'Ippolita Clara e le sue rime', *in Ordine e numero: studi sul libro di poesia e le raccolte poetiche nel Cinquecento* (Alessandria: Edizioni dell'Orso, 2006), pp. 95–122 (pp. 106, 113).

[8] Madrid, Real Biblioteca del Escorial, MS f-IV-17, fol. III[v]. Albonico published the letter of dedication in 'Ippolita Clara', pp. 120–21.

(I carried out this work as an example to women who are unlearned, that is, who do not understand Latin, so that in the first book of the *Aeneid* they may see how one must always flee the gods' wrath as far as possible; for although fleeing does not placate their wrath completely, at least yielding reduces it.)

At the end of Book VI, Clara again signs her work as the duke's 'Humil serva et fedel suddita'. But in publishing her work through him, Clara was clearly hoping, if possible, to reach and to educate a wide female readership.

An autograph manuscript that at first sight is, in contrast, humble and unprepossessing is an account of seven 'rivelationi' (visions) written in 1544, the last year of her life, by Lucia Brocadelli, born in 1476 and a member of the Dominican tertiary order. Duke Ercole I d'Este of Ferrara had resolved to have Brocadelli brought to his city, and she had been smuggled out of her native Viterbo in a basket of linen in 1499. In Ferrara, she became prioress of a community of tertiaries and held a privileged position there until Ercole's death in 1505. Thereafter she lost her position as prioress and lost respect, even within her own community; she was suspected of feigning sanctity. Brocadelli wrote *Le rivelationi* in an irregular, unskilled hand and without punctuation. However, the making of this copy seems to have helped her fellow tertiaries in Ferrara to change their minds about her. After Lucia's death her manuscript soon came to be considered as a precious object, and it took on the function of strengthening the identity of her community. At a later stage, maybe in the early eighteenth century when Lucia was beatified, it was provided with a cover embroidered with religious symbols.[9]

If an author preferred to make use of a less personalized but more aesthetically pleasing artefact, then she could use the services of a professional scribe. This was the option taken by the noblewoman Vittoria Colonna, the

---

[9] Pavia, Biblioteca Civica, MS II 112. On Brocadelli, see E. Ann Matter, Armando Maggi and Maiju Lehmijoki-Gardner, '*Le rivelazioni* of Lucia Brocadelli da Narni', *Archivum fratrum praedicatorum*, 71 (2001), 311–44; Tamar Herzig, 'The Rise and Fall of a Savonarolan Visionary: Lucia Brocadelli's Contribution to the Piagnone Movement', *Archiv für Reformationsgeschichte*, 95 (2004), 34–60; Herzig, *Savonarola's Women: Visions and Reform in Renaissance Italy* (University of Chicago Press, 2008), pp. 180–83; Herzig, *Christ Transformed into a Virgin Woman: Lucia Brocadelli, Heinrich Institoris, and the Defense of the Faith* (Rome: Edizioni di Storia e Letteratura, 2013). Brocadelli was beatified in 1710. On an eighteenth-century transcription of Lucia's autobiography, of which the original is now lost, see Gabriella Zarri, 'Memoria individuale e memoria collettiva: gli scritti di Lucia da Narni († 1544) e la loro conservazione', in *Memoria e comunità femminili: Spagna e Italia, secc. XV–XVII*, ed. by Gabriella Zarri and Nieves Baranda Leturio (Florence: Firenze University Press; [Madrid]: UNED, 2011), pp. 73–86, and Zarri, 'Blessed Lucia of Narni (1476–1544) between "Hagiography" and "Autobiography": Mystical Authorship and the Persistence of the Manuscript', in *The Saint between Manuscript and Print: Italy 1400–1600*, ed. by Alison K. Frazier (Toronto: Centre for Reformation and Renaissance Studies, 2015), pp. 421–45.

pre-eminent female poet of the sixteenth century, when, in late 1539 or perhaps 1540, she offered to Michelangelo a manuscript of 103 recently composed spiritual sonnets, now BAV, MS Lat. 11539.[10] Having this manuscript made and then presented was an unprecedented act for a woman of Colonna's period. This was very probably the first ever thematically organized collection of lyric verse created by a female Italian poet.[11] Its presentation seems extraordinarily generous and trusting when one considers that Colonna had been extremely reluctant to give out her verse to anyone even in manuscript. Her action has to be explained by the nature of gift-giving within the select group of reform-minded Catholics or *Spirituali* to which she and Michelangelo belonged. For them, the presentation of a work of art or literature by one member to another was free from the economies of the marketplace or of the patronage system, and indeed free from the normal expectation of a reciprocal gift.[12] The manuscript is written elegantly, but is undecorated and sober, in a spirit entirely in keeping with that of Colonna's spiritual verse. A title for the collection, 'Sonetti spirituali', was added later and casually, in another hand, probably that of someone known to both the poet and Michelangelo, since he or she adds 'Della Signora Vittoria' on the next line as an afterthought.[13] The script of the manuscript might have seemed slightly old-fashioned in 1540: the letter shapes are similar to those of one of the typefaces used by Ludovico degli Arrighi while working as a printer in Rome during the 1520s, based on his own humanistic cursive handwriting. The hand that wrote these sonnets is not quite as neat as that of another scribe who was commissioned by the Venetian

[10] Enrico Carusi, 'Un codice sconosciuto delle "Rime spirituali" di Vittoria Colonna, appartenuto forse a Michelangelo Buonarroti', in *Atti del IV Congresso nazionale di studi romani*, ed. by Carlo Galassi Paluzzi, 5 vols (Rome: Istituto di studi romani, 1938), IV, 231–41; Carlo Vecce, 'Petrarca, Vittoria, Michelangelo', *Studi e problemi di critica testuale*, 44 (April 1992), 101–25; Monica Bianco and Vittoria Romani, 'Vittoria Colonna e Michelangelo', in *Vittoria Colonna e Michelangelo*, ed. by Pina Ragionieri (Florence: Mandragora, 2005), pp. 145–64; Claudio Scarpati, 'Le rime spirituali di Vittoria Colonna nel codice vaticano donato a Michelangelo', in *Invenzione e scrittura: saggi di letteratura italiana* (Milan: Vita e Pensiero, 2005), pp. 129–62; Vittoria Colonna, *Sonnets for Michelangelo*, ed. and trans. by Abigail Brundin (University of Chicago Press, 2005); Abigail Brundin, *Vittoria Colonna and the Spiritual Poetics of the Italian Reformation* (Aldershot: Ashgate, 2008), pp. 67–100; Tobia R. Toscano, 'Per la datazione del manoscritto dei sonetti di Vittoria Colonna per Michelangelo Buonarroti', *Critica letteraria*, 45 (2017), 211–37. On this and other manuscripts of Colonna's verse, see Abigail Brundin, 'Vittoria Colonna in Manuscript', in *A Companion to Vittoria Colonna*, ed. by Abigail Brundin, Tatiana Crivelli and Maria Serena Sapegno (Leiden: Brill, 2016), pp. 39–68. For an overview of women's religious writing, see Rita Librandi, *La letteratura religiosa* (Bologna: il Mulino, 2012), pp. 47–69.

[11] A collection made by Ippolita Clara, completed by November 1536, simply follows the order of composition of the poems (written between 1530 and about 1535) and was not intended for presentation: Albonico, 'Ippolita Clara', pp. 98–105.

[12] On the gift of art, see Alexander Nagel, 'Gifts of Michelangelo and Vittoria Colonna', *Art Bulletin*, 79 (1997), 647–68.

[13] Vecce, 'Petrarca, Vittoria, Michelangelo', p. 104.

patrician Pietro Bembo to prepare a gift collection of his verse around this period.[14] However, Colonna was using the same method of publishing a lyric collection or *canzoniere* that was conventionally followed by male authors, that of presenting it in the first place to a contemporary. She would have hoped that, through Michelangelo, it would then have reached those to whom she refers in line 8 of her opening sonnet, 'sì ch'io scriva ad altrui quel ch'Ei sostenne' (so that I may write to others what He endured): the close members of her spiritual community to whom she wishes to express the meaning of Christ's suffering on the cross.

We know that another manuscript collection of Colonna's verse was copied and sent in 1540 to the devout Marguerite de Navarre (1492–1549), sister of the French king François I. It is uncertain, however, whether the poet was involved in making this gift. It has been suggested that the manuscript in question is BLF, MS Ashb. 1153, dated 1540 on the title page.[15] However, it seems unlikely that the collection contained in this Florentine manuscript was put together under the control of Colonna, not only because 8 of the 102 sonnets contained in it are not by her and are not concerned with religious subject matter, but also because of the material presentation of the texts. In strong contrast with the manuscript for Michelangelo, this one is decorated: it has the arms of Marguerite de Navarre facing the title page and coloured initials at the start of each quatrain and tercet of the sonnets. Moreover, the wording of the title page, written all in capital letters, would surely not have been approved by Colonna: 'Sonetti de più et diverse materie della divina signora Vittoria Colonna Marchesa di Pescara con somma diligenza revisti et corretti nel anno MDXL' (Sonnets on several different subjects by the divine lady

[14] London, National Art Library, MS L/1347/1957, illustrated in Joyce Irene Whalley, *The Art of Calligraphy: Western Europe & America* (London: Bloomsbury Books, 1980), p. 120. On the manuscript and its contents, see Alessandro Gnocchi, 'Un manoscritto delle rime di Pietro Bembo', *Studi di filologia italiana*, 60 (2002), 217–36; Daniele Ghirlanda, 'La raccolta Farnese: un piccolo canzoniere di Pietro Bembo', in *Il Petrarchismo: un modello di poesia per l'Europa*, 2 vols (Rome: Bulzoni, 2006), II, ed. by Floriana Calitti and Roberto Gigliucci, 117–31; Pietro Bembo, *Le rime*, ed. by Andrea Donnini, 2 vols (Rome: Salerno Editrice, 2008), II, 548–49, 798, 851–59.
[15] Contributions to the discussion include Domenico Tordi, *Il codice delle Rime di Vittoria Colonna, Marchesa di Pescara, appartenuto a Margherita d'Angoulême, Regina di Navarra* (Pistoia: Flori, 1900); Angela Dillon Bussi in *Vittoria Colonna: Dichterin und Muse Michelangelos*, ed. by Sylvia Ferino-Pagden (Vienna: Skira, 1997), cat. no. II. 36, pp. 202–04; Brundin, *Vittoria Colonna and the Spiritual Poetics of the Italian Reformation*, pp. 101–31; Antonio Corsaro's entry on MS Ashb. 1153 in *Vittoria Colonna e Michelangelo*, ed. by Ragionieri, pp. 129–30, and his 'Manuscript Collections of Spiritual Poetry in Sixteenth-Century Italy', in *Forms of Faith in Sixteenth-Century Italy*, ed. by Abigail Brundin and Matthew Treherne (Aldershot: Ashgate, 2009), pp. 33–56 (pp. 34–39); Toscano, 'Per la datazione del manoscritto'.

Vittoria Colonna, Marchioness of Pescara, revised and corrected with the utmost diligence in 1540). The adjective 'divina' is typical of the title pages of the printed editions of her works, none of them authorized by her, starting with the first edition of 1538. The phrase about diligent revision also belongs to the terminology of print publication, and the poet herself would not have employed it.[16]

A combination of autography and transcription on behalf of the author was used in the case of the verse play *Amor di virtù* by suor Beatrice Del Sera, a Dominican nun of San Niccolò in the Tuscan city of Prato, and a cousin of Michelangelo's. This example of convent theatre, a genre designed for both spiritual edification and entertainment, was composed in 1548 or 1549 and was then transcribed in 1555 in a calligraphic hand for suor Beatrice, who added some corrections and other texts. The occasion for the creation of the copy found in BRF, MS 2932 may have been a performance in the Medici court during the carnival of that year. However, it was probably suor Beatrice who added some stage directions and paratexts, including a sonnet addressed 'Al discreto lettore' (To the discerning reader).[17]

## Self-Publication in Print

When it came to circulation in print, women authors needed to proceed with great caution, for reasons of social propriety and because it was much harder for them to take a direct part in the commercial negotiations that were normally necessary in order to have an edition produced. Nerida Newbigin has suggested that Antonia Tanini Pulci (*c.* 1452–1501) may have been 'the first woman in Western Europe to see her own writings through the printing press' if she played a part in commissioning the first Florentine editions of her sacred plays, attributable to the press of Antonio Miscomini and datable to 1483. Plays by Antonia's husband Bernardo were printed probably by Miscomini around the same time, and she may have acted in conjunction with Bernardo in having her own plays printed: it seems significant that she is identified as 'donna di Bernardo Pulci' (wife of

---

[16] The same phrase is found in contemporary printed Venetian editions such as the *Fior de vertù* (Francesco Bindoni and Maffeo Pasini, 1543); *Libro della regina Ancroia* (Giovanni Andrea Vavassore detto Guadagnino, 1546); Castiglione's *Libro del cortegiano* (Gabriele Giolito De Ferrari and brothers, 1552).

[17] Beatrice Del Sera, *Amor di virtù: commedia in cinque atti, 1548*, ed. by Elissa Weaver (Ravenna: Longo, 1990), pp. 75–82 (the main scribe may have been a certain Bonino: see p. 79); Elissa Weaver, *Convent Theatre in Early Modern Italy: Spiritual Fun and Learning for Women* (Cambridge University Press, 2002), pp. 151–69.

Bernardo Pulci) on the first page of the play of *Santa Domitilla*.[18] Laura
Cereta, daughter of a lawyer of Brescia, apparently had plans to have her
collected Latin correspondence printed around 1488, when she was only
about nineteen years old and already a widow. She writes in a letter to
Sigismondo Bucci of 'Epistolarum grande volumen, quod libraria nunc
elementatim format impressio' (the great volume of letters that printing is
now forming bit by bit).[19] There is no trace of such an edition today, but
Cereta was nevertheless confident that her collection would be widely read.
She addresses her dedicatee, Cardinal Ascanio Maria Sforza, in an extensive
prologue and in an epilogue, and predicts in the latter that, enhanced by his
wit and reputation, 'gratus ibit iste liber in populos' (this book will be
welcomed by the peoples).[20]

A curious example of apparent collaborative authorship and self-
publication by women with a man is the *Opera nuova da insegnar parlar
hebraico et una disputa contra hebrei, approvando esser venuto il vero Christo*,
composed – or purporting to be composed – by three 'hebrei fatti christiani' (Jews converted to Christianity), Giovan Battista, his mother Orsola
and his daughter Isabeta, and printed in Florence at their instance in 1552.
This small volume, a single gathering in octavo, contains a dialogue about
articles of faith between a Jew and his sister, who does most of the teaching,
followed by a list of Hebrew words and a Hebrew prayer with translations
in 'lingua Christiana', that is, Italian. The publication was perhaps part of
a conversion campaign, but it is significant that important roles are
attributed to women, even if they are fictitious.[21]

It was not until the middle of the sixteenth century that a few women
authors began to venture more consistently into the public sphere of the
press. We can identify several stages in this process. The potential for
commercially successful publication of works composed by a living
woman was first demonstrated through a series of unauthorized editions
of poems by Vittoria Colonna, starting with one printed in Parma by
Antonio Viotti in 1538. Filippo Pirogalli nonchalantly acknowledged in his
dedication of this edition to Alessandro Vercelli that he had had this

[18] Nerida Newbigin, 'Antonia Pulci and the First Anthology of *Sacre Rappresentazioni* (1483?)', *LB*, 118 (2016), 337–61 (quotation from p. 337).

[19] Laura Cereta, *Epistolae*, ed. by Jacopo Filippo Tomasini (Padua: Sardi, 1640), fol. A8ᵛ. 'Libraria impressio' was the phrase used by Marcantonio Sabellico when describing the invention of printing in the *Secunda pars enneadum* (Venice: Bernardino Viani, 1504), X. 6, fol. u2ʳ.

[20] Cereta, *Epistolae*, fols A1ʳ–A5ᵛ, P2ʳ–P3ʳ (fol. P3ʳ); Laura Cereta, *Collected Letters of a Renaissance Feminist*, ed. and trans. by Diana Robin (University of Chicago Press, 1997), pp. 36–45.

[21] On the context, see Brian Pullan, 'The Conversion of the Jews: The Style of Italy', *Bulletin of the John Rylands Library*, 70 (1988), 53–70.

collection of sonnets printed without the poet's permission: 'ho preso ardire di mettergli in istampa, anchora che contradicessi al voler d'una sì gran Signora; stimando meno errore dispiacere a una sola Donna (benché rara, e grande) che a tanti huomini desiderosi di ciò' (I have been so bold as to put them into print, even though this goes against the wish of such a great lady, considering it less wrong to displease a single lady, however special and great, than to displease so many men who desire this).[22] Colonna's death in February 1547 seems to have encouraged initiatives to try to raise the verse of other contemporary women to a similar status in print, initiatives taken first by male supporters of female poets and then by the poets themselves. The Venetian printing firm of Gabriele Giolito had already published in 1544–45 two treatises on the status and comportment of women and an anthology of lyric verse that included poems by three women alongside, and on a par with, poems by men.[23] In 1547 the same company brought out two works by the courtesan Tullia d'Aragona (*c.* 1508–1558), then residing in Florence. One was a collection of lyric verse (*Rime della signora Tullia di Aragona; et di diversi a lei*) that gave prominence to broadly social rather than introspective themes: to Tullia's cultural links with Florentine men of letters and especially to her gratitude to the Duke and Duchess of Florence, Cosimo I de' Medici and Eleonora de Toledo, who had recently spared her from the humiliating obligation of wearing a yellow veil in public as common prostitutes had to do. Tullia must at least have consented to, and collaborated in, the printing of these *Rime*, which have a dedicatory letter from her to the duchess. Sonnets addressed to her by male poets outnumber those composed by her. The other work was her *Dialogo della infinità di amore*. This is dedicated by her to Duke Cosimo in terms that recall the dedication of the *Rime*: both use

[22] See Antonio Corsaro's entry on the 1538 edition in *Vittoria Colonna e Michelangelo*, ed. by Ragionieri, pp. 130–31. For an overview, see Tatiana Crivelli, 'The Print Tradition of Vittoria Colonna's *Rime*', in *A Companion to Vittoria Colonna*, ed. by Abigail Brundin, Tatiana Crivelli and Maria Serena Sapegno (Leiden: Brill, 2016), pp. 69–139.

[23] The treatises are Heinrich Cornelius Agrippa von Nettesheim, *Della nobiltà et eccellenza delle donne, nuovamente dalla lingua francese nella italiana tradotto* (1544), and Lodovico Dolce, *Dialogo della institution delle donne secondo li tre stati che cadono nella vita humana* (1545). The anthology is the *Rime diverse di molti eccellentiss[imi] auttori nuovamente raccolte, libro primo*, ed. by Lodovico Domenichi (1545, reprinted in 1546 'con nuova additione'), which included three poems by Vittoria Colonna, eleven by Veronica Gambara and two by Francesca Baffa. See Salvatore Bongi, *Annali di Gabriel Giolito de' Ferrari da Trino di Monferrato stampatore in Venezia*, 2 vols (Rome: Ministero della Pubblica Istruzione, 1890–97), I, 77–78, 88–89, 100–02. Giolito dedicated Francesco Coccio's translation of Agrippa's work to Bona Maria Soarda da San Giorgio in September 1544 and, in a letter addressed to Giolito on 11 November 1544, she described him as 'devoto del sesso donnesco' (a devotee of the female sex): cited in Angela Nuovo and Christian Coppens, *I Giolito e la stampa nell'Italia del XVI secolo* (Geneva: Droz, 2005), p. 121.

the modesty topos of 'la bassezza della condition mia' (the baseness of my condition) contrasted with the 'altezza' (loftiness) of the status of the dedicatee. However, this edition opens with a letter to Tullia from the author Girolamo Muzio, who must have taken the manuscript of the work from Florence to Venice, and who says he has had it printed without her knowledge. Even if this is a fiction intended to protect Tullia from criticism, it seems that the print publication of her texts was organized chiefly not by her but by two of her gentlemen admirers, Muzio and Benedetto Varchi, the second of whom also helped to revise her verse.[24]

The first woman poet who came to take an active and successful part in the print publication of her works was Laura Terracina (1519–1577?), born into a noble family of the Kingdom of Naples but not a leading family of Naples itself.[25] Eight books of verse by her were printed during her lifetime, and her involvement in their production became gradually stronger and more explicit. The first book, which appeared from the Giolito press in 1548 and 1549 and gave prominence to verses addressed to individual members of the community of her acquaintances, was edited by Lodovico Domenichi, a writer from Piacenza. Terracina had probably come to Domenichi's attention around 1546: he had included in his edition of *Rime diverse di molti eccellentissimi auttori nuovamente raccolte* of that year, printed by Giolito, a capitolo in ottava rima in which Terracina writes that she knew him only through his writings and expressed her literary aspirations (fols R4$^r$–R5$^r$). Domenichi claims in his dedication of Terracina's first *Rime* that the decision to print the verse and the choice of dedicatee, Giovanni Vincenzo Belprato, count of Anversa in

[24] Bongi, *Annali di Gabriel Giolito*, I, 150–98 (especially pp. 187–88), 198–99; Francesco Bausi, 'Le rime di e per Tullia d'Aragona', in *Les Femmes écrivains en Italie au Moyen Age et à la Renaissance: actes du colloque international, Aix-en-Provence, 12, 13, 14 novembre 1992* (Aix-en-Provence: Université de Provence, 1994), pp. 275–92. The publication of these editions has been linked with Colonna's death by Bausi (ibid., p. 282) and Virginia Cox (*Women's Writing in Italy*, pp. 80–81). On Varchi's role as linguistic advisor, see also Marco Biffi and Raffaella Setti, 'Varchi consulente linguistico', in *Benedetto Varchi, 1503–1565: atti del convegno, Firenze, 16–17 dicembre 2003*, ed. by Vanni Bramanti (Rome: Edizioni di Storia e Letteratura, 2007), pp. 25–67.

[25] For an overview of her life and works, see Claudio Mutini, 'Bacio Terracina, Laura', *DBI*, 5 (1963), 61–63. Works by Terracina are discussed in Deanna Shemek, *Ladies Errant: Wayward Women and Social Order in Early Modern Italy* (Durham, NC: Duke University Press, 1998), pp. 126–57. On Terracina's editions, see also Bongi, *Annali di Gabriel Giolito*, I, 227–31, 269–70; Tobia R. Toscano, *Letterati corti accademie: la letteratura a Napoli nella prima metà del Cinquecento* (Naples: Loffredo, 2000), pp. 202–03, 208–09, 232–34, 241; Cox, *Women's Writing in Italy*, pp. 80–91, 108–13, 115–18. On her relationships with her editors and publishers, see Amelia Papworth, 'Pressure to Publish: Laura Terracina and Her Editors', *Early Modern Women: An Interdisciplinary Journal*, 12.1 (Fall 2017), 3–24.

the Abruzzi, were his: 'ho meco stesso deliberando preso partito di prove-
dere di dignissimo albergo alle rime della valorosa signora Laura Terracina'
(fol. A2$^r$; I have decided, after some thought, to provide a most fitting
home for the poems of the worthy lady Laura Terracina).[26] Domenichi
argues that Terracina's modesty had not allowed her to publish the poems
herself:

> Nè perciò dubiterò d'havere offeso la signora Laura, publicando le fatiche
> sue sotto il nome vostro: perché io mi rendo certo, che havendole io havute
> in mano per sua cortesia, io habbia anco potuto con tacita licenza di lei farne
> il voler mio. Oltra che io non ho dubbio alcuno, che quando la sua nobil
> modestia le havesse consentito il poter darle in luce, ella non l'havrebbe
> giamai divulgate, se non col titol vostro. (fol. A3$^{r-v}$)

> (Nor will I therefore fear I have offended the lady Laura by publishing her
> labours under your name; for I am certain that, having obtained them
> through her courtesy, I could also do what I wished with them with her
> implicit permission. Furthermore, I have no doubt that, if her noble
> modesty had allowed her to publish them, she would only have given
> them out inscribed to you.)

A woodcut profile portrait of a youthful Terracina appears in the edition,
and its delicacy contrasts strongly with the precedent of the woodcut on the
title page of the 1540 edition of Colonna's *Rime* (Venice: Comin da Trino
for Nicolò Zoppino), in which an elderly lady in a nun's habit prays before
a crucifix.[27] This hints that Terracina, in spite of her 'noble modesty', had
more than a passive part in the process, but that her participation was being
concealed in order to protect her reputation.

In any case, thereafter Terracina's involvement in printing her verse
became, step by step, ever more manifest. Her *Rime seconde* appeared in
Florence in 1549, apparently from the Torrentino press, of which Domenichi
had become a collaborator. The collection was promoted by a German
gentleman, Leonardo Khurz, and edited by members of the Neapolitan
Accademia degli Incogniti, of which Terracina was a member, but it included

---

[26] For an outline of Domenichi's life and works, see Angela Piscini, 'Domenichi, Ludovico', *DBI*, 40 (1991), 595–600, and the bibliography 'Lodovico Domenichi', ed. by Enrico Garavelli, www.nuovorinascimento.org/cinquecento/domenichi.pdf (accessed 24 October 2017). On Belprato, see Romeo De Maio, 'Belprato, Giovanni Vincenzo', *DBI*, 8 (1966), 49. Domenichi's choice of Belprato as his dedicatee was doubtless influenced in part by the count's provenance from a noble family of the Kingdom of Naples and in part by their shared sympathy for the cause of religious reform.

[27] Giuseppina Zappella, *Il ritratto nel libro italiano del Cinquecento*, 2 vols (Milan: Editrice Bibliografica, 1988), I, 69, 152, 195, and II, Figure 335; Antonio Corsaro's entry on the 1540 edition in *Vittoria Colonna e Michelangelo*, ed. by Ragionieri, pp. 132–33.

a letter signed by Terracina that shows she was aware of the edition and grateful for it. She herself then signed the dedicatory letter of her *Discorso sopra tutti li primi canti d'Orlando furioso fatti per la Signora Laura Terracina*, addressed to the scholarly Giovanni Bernardino Bonifacio, Marquis of Oria in Puglia, on 29 April 1549, describing the volume as 'questo terzo libro delle mie, quantunque rocissime rime' (fol. A3ᵛ; this third book of my verse, however hoarse).[28] The work contains a series of reflections on the first stanzas of each of the forty-six cantos of the *Furioso* of 1532, weaving Ariosto's verses into Terracina's own ottava rima. It was first printed by Gabriele Giolito with the dates 1549 on the title page and 1550 in the colophon, but in 1550 Giolito printed a revised edition entitled *Discorso sopra tutti i primi canti d'Orlando furioso fatto per la S. Laura Terracina* [...] *da la medesima riveduti, di nuovo con diligenza ristampati et corretti*. In a new letter of dedication to Bonifacio, dated 1 August 1550, Terracina explains that she had hoped that the Venetian man of letters Lodovico Dolce, who had been working as an editor for Giolito since the early 1540s, was going to correct the work before it reached the dedicatee: 'volendola mandar fuori, desiderai che prima si bagnasse nel dolce fonte di M. Lodovico, a tal che più baldanzosamente, lasciata da canto la rovidezza, non s'havesse ad offrire così impolita et mal composta, nel cospetto di V[ostra] S[ignoria] Illustrissima' (wishing to publish it, I wanted it to be bathed first in the sweet spring of messer Lodovico, so that it could offer itself to the sight of your excellency not unpolished and poorly written but with more self-confidence, having put coarseness aside).[29] In the context of this edition printed by Giolito, Terracina could not criticize Dolce too harshly for the way in which he had then treated her work, but she makes it clear, with a further ironic allusion to his surname, that he had let her down badly and she had had to make her own revisions:

> non me riuscì il disegno; che oltra stette in suo potere per spacio d'uno anno, non solamente nulla gustò di dolcezza, ma bevette tanto d'amaro tosco, che ben è stata cagione ad altrui [di] pena, et a se stessa havria dato la morte, se non che l'hanno da quella difesa i fulgenti et vivi raggi de la vostra eterna gloria, i quali per tutto il mondo traluceno come le stelle in cielo. Ond'io, generoso Signore, ho voluto senza altrui correttione porla sotto la mia leggiera emenda, et solamente purgarla delli più biasmevoli errori, ritro[v]- andosi ella data in stampa. (fol. A3ʳ⁻ᵛ)

---

[28] See also Laura Terracina, *Discorsi sopra le prime stanze de' canti d'Orlando furioso*, ed. by Rotraud von Kulessa and Daria Perocco (Florence: Cesati, 2017), pp. 347–48. The editions of the *Discorsi* are listed and discussed at pp. 12–15 and 343–45. On the edition of 2017, see the review by Francesco Lucioli in *Archiv für das Studium der neueren Sprachen und Literaturen*, 255 (2018), 468–83.

[29] On Dolce's life, see Giovanna Romei, 'Dolce, Lodovico', *DBI*, 40 (1991), 399–405.

(my plan did not succeed; for apart from his keeping hold of the work for a year, not only did it taste no sweetness, but it drank so much bitter poison that it has caused much suffering to others and it would have brought about its own death if it had not been saved from that fate by the gleaming and bright rays of your eternal glory, which shine throughout the world like the stars in the sky. Thus I, generous lord, have decided to submit it to my own light emendation, without the correction of others, and only to purge it of the most reprehensible errors, now that it is being sent to the press.)

For this revised edition of 1550, Terracina also composed a stanza addressed to the Venetian editor that assertively rubs in the point that she herself has done the work that he should have undertaken:

> Ecco il discorso pur, Dolce gentile,
> in fretta da me visto, e non d'altrui.
> E se la lingua mia fu sì virile,
> perdon vi chieggio; e s'arrogante fui,
> ch'io non sapea se 'l verso feminile
> era sì degno apparir 'nanzi a vui,
> pur ho compito al fin, col mio sudore
> a le vostre promesse, et al mio honore.          (fol. A3ᵛ)

(Here is the pure discourse, noble Dolce, revised in haste by myself and no other. And if my tongue was so manly, and if I was arrogant, I ask pardon of you, for I did not know whether womanly verse was worthy to appear before you; yet with the sweat of my brow I have at last made good your promises and my honour.)

This stanza was followed by her original letter to Bonifacio dated 29 April 1549. During the process of publishing this second edition, another collaborator of Giolito, the Florentine writer Anton Francesco Doni, attached to Terracina's work an appendix of three 'lettere amorose' of his own, dedicating them to Bonifacio (fols L6ʳ–L8ᵛ). Terracina may well have been consulted about this, and she evidently did not disapprove since, as we shall see shortly, she allowed Doni's letters to reappear in an edition of 1567. A further paratextual stanza by Terracina, addressed to the Neapolitan bookseller-publisher Marcantonio Passero and included in this second edition within a series of poems that concludes the volume, suggests that she had links with the book trade of her own city.[30] Its tone suggests a surprisingly close friendship between the author and a man who was well versed in the printing industry:

[30] On Passero, see Angelo Borzelli, *Marcantonio Passero: librario nel 500 napolitano* (Naples: Aldo Lubrano, 1941); Angela Nuovo, *The Book Trade in the Italian Renaissance*, trans. by Lydia G. Cochrane (Leiden: Brill, 2013), pp. 419–20; Toscano, *Letterati corti accademie*, pp. 192–93, 208–09, 269, 281.

> Amico, io so, che tu m'hai posta in voce,
> et a me, mi convien ponerti in cima,
> e quanto posso con la debil voce,
> alzarti insino al ciel, con la mia rima,
> e quando non potrà la rocha voce
> dir tanto, quanto la mia mente stima,
> vi mostrarò, col core, e col desio,
> che quanto amar si può tanto v'amo io.        (fol. K2<sup>r</sup>)

(Friend, I know that you have given me a voice, and so I need to place you at the summit, and raise you to the skies with my verse as far as my weak voice is able; and when my hoarse voice cannot express all the esteem my mind feels, I shall show you with my heart and desire that I love you as much as anyone can love.)

The edition of Terracina's *Quarte rime* appeared in Venice in 1550 from another printer, Giovanni Andrea Valvassori, and was protected not just by a dedication to a prince, Pietro Antonio Sanseverino, but also by an opening exchange of letters between Terracina and the poet Giovanni Alfonso Mantegna, who testified that her writing did not need his correction. In her letter to Mantegna, Terracina now complained openly that 'messer Lodovico Dolce' had made her *Discorso* less correct than her original. With another play on the Venetian's surname, she commented that he was:

> dolce forse ad altrui a me amarissimo, perciò che havendomi per più sue lettere offerto, voler egli haver pensiero di correggere la mia terza opera data in luce sopra i canti de l'Ariosto, non solo non l'ha punto corretta ma Dio il volesse (con sua pace parlando) che fusse almeno di quel medesimo modo ch'io la mandai et non di peggiore stampata, che non si scorgerebbeno in essa tanti errori. (fol. A2<sup>r</sup>)

(sweet to others, maybe, but most bitter to me. After showing, in several letters of his, his willingness to take on the correction of my third published work on the cantos of Ariosto, not only did he not correct it at all but I wish to God (with due respect) that it was at least as I sent it and not printed worse, for then there would not be so many errors to be seen in it.)

A further increase in Terracina's self-confidence is apparent in her *Quinte rime*, printed by Valvassori in 1552. This time the collection is dedicated by her to another woman, Sanseverino's wife Henrina (or Erina or Irene) Skanderbeg. The edition includes another exchange of letters with Mantegna, but this time the correspondence is placed at the end of the volume, it puts less emphasis on her supposed need for his correction of the verse, and it even includes a claim that a certain Luigi

Valvassori, probably a brother of the printer Giovanni Andrea, was assiduously seeking to print her work: 'la continua sollecitudine di M. Loigi Valvassorio, persona honorevole, et di conosciuta bontade, il quale nelle sue lettere sempre mi ricerca delle mie compositioni per farle imprimere' (fol. H5$^{r-v}$; the continuous solicitude of Luigi Valvassori, a person who is honourable and known for his goodness, who in his letters is always seeking my works to have them printed).[31] This was an outspoken advertisement of Terracina's perception of the prestige she had by now acquired in the world of print publication.

Terracina was able to take a more overtly assertive approach when she had her *Seste rime* printed in 1560. In her edition she recounts that, when she had completed the collection, she was persuaded by Passero and her husband Polidoro Terracina to send it to Vincenzo Arnolfini, a merchant of Lucca. This must have been in about 1556 or 1557, since she says that Arnolfini had kept the text to himself for a year and a half before having it printed in Lucca in 1558 by Vincenzo Busdraghi, and also dedicating it in the poet's name, but without her knowledge, to Isabetta della Rovere Cibo, Marchioness of Massa.[32] Arnolfini had cheated Terracina, and to make matters worse the marchioness had shown the poet no gratitude for the dedication. In 1560, therefore, an angry Terracina organized the printing of another edition of the same work, this time by Raimondo Amato in her native Naples, with a letter of dedication addressed to Colantonio Caracciolo in which she explained how she had been 'defraudata' by Arnolfini. She also included in this Neapolitan edition (fols S2$^v$–S3$^r$) a copy of a letter from herself to the marchioness Isabetta that openly laments that the Busdraghi edition had caused her the loss of two kinds of tangible rewards, the profits from sales and a gift from her dedicatee: 'me ne sono nondimeno hora grandemente doluta, veggendo delle mie fatiche arricchire i librai, et della gratia di vostra Eccelentia rimanerne altri lieti, et io essere dell'un premio, et dell'altro priva' (nevertheless I have now lamented it greatly, seeing booksellers grow rich from my labours and others become happy as a result of Your Excellency's grace, while I am deprived of both these rewards).

---

[31] The correspondence between Terracina and Mantegna is also published in Giovanni Alfonso Mantegna, *Le rime*, ed. by Maria Rosaria Bifolco (Salerno: Edisud, 2001), pp. 173–92.
[32] On the links between Busdraghi and the court of Massa, see Simonetta Adorni Braccesi, '"Telifilo Filogenio [Girolamo Borro] sopra la perfectione delle donne": un libro, un editore e il controllo sopra la stampa nella Lucca del Cinquecento', in *La fede degli Italiani: per Adriano Prosperi*, vol. I, ed. by Guido dall'Olio, Adelisa Malena and Pierroberto Scaramella (Pisa: Edizioni della Normale, 2011), 223–35.

Terracina's *Settime rime sovra tutte le donne vedove di questa nostra citta di Napoli, titolate et non titolate*, printed in 1561 at the Neapolitan press of Mattio Cancer, consisted of a collection of verses addressed to individual widows of her city. As Terracina explained in her dedication to one of them, Maria Anna de la Cueva, Princess of Ascoli, she was writing not just to Maria Anna but also 'per che tutte le altre Signore ancho, et gentil donne private, che io conosco in questa nostra Città dolersi per la morte de' loro mariti, qual che refregerio ne' loro dolorosi ramarichi sentissero per mezzo delle mie voci' (fol. A4ʳ; so that all the other ladies and private gentlewomen that I know are grieving through the death of their husbands in this city of ours can feel some relief in their painful laments through my words).

In 1567 Giovanni Andrea Valvassori printed Terracina's *Discorso* on Ariosto, retitled *La prima parte de' discorsi sopra le prime stanze de' canti d'Orlando furioso*, together with a new series of verses based on the second stanza of each canto, *La seconda parte de' discorsi sopra le seconde stanze de' canti d'Orlando furioso*. The *Discorso*, as we saw, had appeared in 1549 and in 1550 as her third book of verse, but the new edition constituted her eighth and final book to be printed.[33] Terracina's introductory paratexts show that this edition, too, was published with her participation. The first part reused, with slight corrections, the letter of dedication dated 1 August 1550, but it was now addressed to Colantonio Caracciolo rather than to Bonifacio, while the second part was dedicated to a wealthy Genoese banker, Franco Larcari (or Lercari). The first part still included the stanza addressed to Dolce, as a way of recalling Terracina's unfortunate experience with him.[34] Doni's letters were still appended to the *Prima parte*. The concluding selection of poems retained the stanza addressed to Passero, with minimal changes. In the *Seconda parte*, Terracina presents herself, as in the *Quinte rime*, as an author sought after by the Venetian printing industry: Luigi Valvassori, she now claims, had come to Naples and begged her husband Polidoro to entreat and, if necessary, force her to follow her poems on the first stanzas of the cantos of the *Furioso* with a set of discourses on the second stanzas. She was obliged to follow Polidoro's wishes, 'essendo, sapete, le preghiere de gl'huomini espressi comandamenti alle lor donne' (fol. AA3ʳ; since, as you know, the requests of men are

---

[33] The ninth book remained in manuscript: see Luigi Montella, *Una poetessa del Rinascimento: Laura Terracina. Con un'antologia delle None rime inedite* (Salerno: Edisud, 2001).

[34] Terracina took the opportunity to correct the punctuation of line 1, which becomes 'Ecco il Discorso, pur Dolce gentile' (so that 'pur[o]' clearly refers to Dolce), and to introduce a subjunctive and to alter punctuation in lines 6–7, which now read: 'fosse degno apparir dinanzi a vui. | Pur sodisfatto ho al fin col mio sudore'.

express orders to their women). Terracina names Passero as the person who, when she was seeking a dedicatee, pointed out to her that Larcari was visiting Naples, and she mentions Passero as a friend in one of the sonnets that conclude the volume (fol. KK2$^v$).

Terracina was well ahead of her time in her use of dedications. Virginia Cox points out that, in the period 1538–60, only seven out of seventeen editions of works written by living women have dedications signed by the author, and four of these are by the precociously 'commercial' Terracina. At this point, it was more normal for a male intermediary to present the work to the public on a female writer's behalf, claiming that the decision to publish was his, while the author was modestly reluctant to publish in print. But in due course other women followed Terracina's example. In 1580–1602, twenty-three of twenty-six editions of works by women have letters of dedication signed by the female author, and there is a growing tendency for them to address female dedicatees.[35]

At least two other female poets participated in the print publication of their own works in this period. Chiara Matraini, who came from a modest family of Lucca that had been disgraced politically, prefaced her *Rime et prose* (Lucca: Busdraghi, 1555) with a letter addressed to a man, identified only as 'M. L.', perhaps Messer Lodovico Domenichi, in which she defends her spending her time in study and writing even though she is 'non de' più alti sangui nata' (not born of the noblest blood) and although her subject is amorous.[36] Matraini's publication of her translation of the treatise by Isocrates on the conduct of young men may have taken place initially in manuscript. The edition of the *Oratione d'Isocrate a Demonico* that was printed by Lorenzo Torrentino in Florence in 1556 included a dedicatory letter from her to Giulio de' Medici, illegitimate son of the late Duke Alessandro (fols A3$^v$–A4$^v$), but this was preceded by a letter addressed to her in which Torrentino explains that he received the text from Domenichi and has resolved to print it 'per far conoscere agli animi generosi, e amatori di virtù, quanto virtuosamente può operare lo spirito Donnesco, quando sia ben cultivato, come è il vostro' (fol. A2$^{r-v}$; to make generous spirits who love virtue aware of how virtuously the womanly spirit can operate, as long as it is well cultivated, like yours). Although Domenichi acted as an agent in this case as in others, it is conceivable that Matraini was aware of this

---

[35] Cox, *Women's Writing in Italy*, pp. 154–57, 247–53.

[36] Chiara Matraini, *Rime e Lettere*, ed. by Giovanni Rabitti (Bologna: Commissione per i testi di lingua, 1989), pp. 93–99 (p. 93), and Matraini, *Selected Poetry and Prose*, intro. by Giovanna Rabitti, ed. and trans. by Elaine Maclachlan (University of Chicago Press, 2007), pp. 102–05 (p. 102). See also Giovanna Rabitti, 'Matraini, Chiara', *DBI*, 72 (2008), 128–31.

edition but that this letter was intended to avoid any accusation of immodesty on her part. In any case, the process of publication and dedication was initiated by the author.

In 1560, Laura Battiferri, originally from Urbino, took a prominent and controlling role in the organization of an edition of her *Primo libro dell'opere toscane* printed in Florence by the heirs of Bernardo Giunti, prompted, she states in her dedicatory letter to the Duchess of Florence, Eleonora de Toledo, by the fear that others were about to publish her verse. She is careful to say that she has asked her husband's 'licenza' (permission) before going into print and has sought the advice of friends. However, the fair copy that Battiferri wrote out in her neat hand shows how she herself had prepared the text for the printers, polishing it and sometimes adding instructions on the layout of the sonnets.[37]

The exact circumstances of the print publication of the poet Veronica Franco's *Lettere familiari a diversi* are unclear, but she was certainly involved in the process. The edition opens with a letter of dedication addressed to Cardinal Luigi d'Este, signed by her in Venice and dated 2 August 1580. This is followed by a letter addressed to Henri III and two sonnets in which Franco recalls how the French king had visited her humble house and taken away a portrait of her. She also thanks him for '[le] sue benigne, et gratiose offerte fattemi nel proposito del libro' (your kind and gracious gifts to me in the project of [this] book).[38] This suggests an expectation of financial support on his part, perhaps for the printing of her *Terze rime*; however, in the event she dedicated this work around 1575 to Guglielmo Gonzaga, Duke of Mantua. Franco made sure that at least one distinguished French visitor to Venice received her *Lettere*: on 7 November 1580 Montaigne was presented with a gift copy by her messenger and gave two écus in return.[39]

Maddalena Campiglia of Vicenza included a personal *impresa* (an image and a motto that, together, expressed an individual's salient characteristics) in two of her three works printed during her lifetime: in one issue of the edition of her pastoral drama *Flori* (Vicenza: heirs of Perin libraro and Tomaso Brunelli, 1588), where it is found together with an explanatory sonnet written in the first-person singular, and in her pastoral eclogue

[37] Victoria Kirkham, 'Laura Battiferra degli Ammannati's *First Book* of Poetry: A Renaissance Holograph Comes Out of Hiding', *Rinascimento*, 2nd ser., 36 (1996), 351–91; Laura Battiferra degli Ammannati, *Laura Battiferra and Her Literary Circle: An Anthology*, ed. and trans. by Victoria Kirkham (University of Chicago Press, 2006).

[38] Veronica Franco, *Lettere familiari a diversi* ([Venice?]: n. pub., [1580?]), fol. A3ʳ.

[39] Michel de Montaigne, *Journal de voyage*, ed. by François Rigolot (Paris: Presses Universitaires de France, 1992), p. 68.

*Calisa* (Vicenza: Giorgio Greco, 1589). Her *impresa* represented a phoenix with the motto 'Tempore sic duro' ('Thus in adversity', from Ovid, *Tristia*, I. 5. 26). This gesture represented a very bold statement of selfhood, since such emblems were associated chiefly with a small number of aristocratic women.[40]

In Venice, Moderata Fonte (the pen name of Modesta Pozzo) signed the dedicatory poems or letters of her verse works: *Tredici canti del Floridoro* (1581), *La passione di Christo* (1582) and *La resurretione di Giesù Christo* (1592).[41] Her uncle by marriage, Giovanni Niccolò Doglioni, claimed in his biography of Fonte to have played a part in the use of the press to make her writings known: 'cominciai, come amico della virtù ad essercitarla a comporre, et insieme publicando le cose sue, fui principio di farla conoscer al mondo per unica, o rara' (I began, as a lover of outstanding ability, to encourage her to compose and at the same time, by publishing her works, I instigated her being known to the world as unique or rare).[42] Lucrezia Marinella promoted two of her works through the bookseller-publisher Giovanni Battista Ciotti in the same city. In 1595 he issued her epic poem on a Christian martyr, *La Colomba sacra*; Marinella dedicated this to Margherita Gonzaga d'Este, Duchess of Ferrara, and received from her the gift of a ring. Ciotti published Marinella's treatise *Le nobiltà, et eccellenze delle donne: et i diffetti, e mancamenti de gli huomini*, first in 1600 and then with revisions in 1601, with a dedication by her to the doctor Luigi Scarano, who may have introduced her to Ciotti. She mentions in the first edition that, as Ciotti was aware, she had completed it in just two months (fol. B8ᵛ), which suggests she was trying to meet a publication deadline.[43] Marinella signed the dedicatory letters of all but one of her printed works, and behind the scenes she busied herself with correspondence to ensure that her dedications worked effectively.[44] Another author

[40] Maddalena Campiglia, *Flori: A Pastoral Drama*, ed. by Virginia Cox and Lisa Sampson, trans. by Virginia Cox (University of Chicago Press, 2004), pp. 306, 308–10. On the *imprese* of some Renaissance noblewomen, see Monica Calabritto, 'Women's *imprese* in Girolamo Ruscelli's *Le imprese illustri* (1566)', in *The Italian Emblem: A Collection of Essays*, ed. by Donato Mansueto in collaboration with Elena Laura Calogero (Glasgow: Glasgow Emblem Studies, 2007), pp. 65–91.

[41] Sarah Gwyneth Ross, *The Birth of Feminism: Woman as Intellect in Renaissance Italy and England* (Cambridge, MA: Harvard University Press, 2009), pp. 206–09.

[42] Moderata Fonte, *Il merito delle donne* (Venice: Domenico Imberti, 1600), fol. A2ᵛ.

[43] Stephen Kolsky, 'Moderata Fonte, Lucrezia Marinella, Giuseppe Passi: An Early Seventeenth-Century Feminist Controversy', *Modern Language Review*, 96 (2001), 973–89 (p. 975); Paolo Zaja, 'Marinelli (Marinella), Lucrezia', *DBI*, 70 (2008), 399–402.

[44] Rossella Lalli, 'Scrivere per le Gonzaga: Lucrezia Marinella e la promozione a corte delle sue opere (1595–1618)', in *Donne Gonzaga a corte: reti istituzionali, pratiche culturali e affari di governo*, ed. by Chiara Continisio and Raffaele Tamalio (Rome: Bulzoni, 2018), pp. 405–16.

who rushed to meet a deadline in one of her many printed works was Margherita Costa, also renowned as a singer: she excused 'l'imperfezione' of her verse collection *Il violino*, dedicated to Grand Duke Ferdinand II de' Medici, on the grounds both of her poor health and of her desire to present it as a gift on the feast of John the Baptist (24 June), patron saint of Florence.[45] Costa appears to have been directing the publication process with precision.

Margherita Sarrocchi's epic poem *Scanderbeide*, which recounts the war waged by the Albanian prince George Scanderbeg against the Ottoman sultanate, was the first such work composed by a woman. The partial version printed in 1606 appeared, according to the dedicatory letter signed by a man, 'senza saputa di lei' (without her knowledge) and in the expectation that she would be displeased because the work was unfinished.[46] It seems unlikely that Sarrocchi was completely unaware of this edition, but she did not supervise it. The mathematician Luca Valerio confirmed in 1609, when he sent a copy to Galileo Galilei, that she had not checked the proofs. However, Sarrocchi set about completing and polishing her poem for another edition. By 1610 Valerio could write to Galileo that Sarrocchi 's'apparecchia a dare in luce la sua Scanderbeide' (is preparing to publish her *Scanderbeide*).[47] In a correspondence of 1611–12, she asked Galileo's advice about revision and a possible dedicatee, stressing her awareness of the double-edged power of print: 'sì come la stampa mostra il saper de gli huomini, così alcuna volta mostra il poco giudicio' (just as print displays men's knowledge, so it sometimes displays their poor judgement).[48] The full *Scanderbeide* was printed in 1623, six years after Sarrocchi's death.

By the first half of the seventeenth century, even cloistered nuns might occasionally use print publication as individuals. Angelica Baitelli, of the Benedictine convent of Santa Giulia in Brescia, paid the costs for an edition of one of her historical works intended to support the cause of her institution, the *Vita, martirio e morte di S. Giulia cartaginese crocifissa* (Brescia: Antonio Rizzardi, 1644).[49] A Benedictine of Venice, Arcangela Tarabotti, was closely involved with the printing of her works. Her first

[45] Printed in 1638 with the false imprint 'Frankfurt: Daniel Wastch', fol. A3$^r$.

[46] Margherita Sarrocchi, *La Scanderbeide* (Rome: Lepido Faci, 1606), fol. +2$^{r-v}$.

[47] Meredith K. Ray, *Margherita Sarrocchi's Letters to Galileo: Astronomy, Astrology, and Poetics in Seventeenth-Century Italy* (New York: Palgrave Macmillan, 2016), p. 44, n. 12; p. 48, n. 42.

[48] Galileo Galilei, *Le opere*, ed. by Antonio Favaro, 20 vols (Florence: Barbèra, 1890–1909), XI, 164; Ray, *Margherita Sarrocchi's Letters*, p. 70, and compare p. 74.

[49] Silvia Evangelisti, 'Angelica Baitelli, la storica', in *Barocco al femminile*, ed. by Giulia Calvi (Rome and Bari: Laterza, 1992), pp. 71–95; Gabriella Zarri, *Libri di spirito: editoria religiosa in volgare nei secoli XV–XVII* (Turin: Rosenberg & Sellier, 2009), p. 229.

printed work, *Paradiso monacale* (Venice: Guglielmo Oddoni, '1663' [but
1643]), dedicated by her to Cardinal Federico Cornaro, contains a letter
from the printer Oddoni, addressed to the reader, that suggests
a collaborative relationship with the author. He apologizes for errors in
Latin quotations that would not have occurred 'se chi ha composto havesse
potuto assistere all'impressione' (if the writer had been able to be present
during printing), and he announces works forthcoming from the same pen
that are 'forse più piccanti' (perhaps more biting), beginning with *La
tirannia paterna* (fol. π4$^{r-v}$). One of the functions of Tarabotti's collection
of *Lettere familiari e di complimento*, first printed in her city in 1650, is to
chronicle and justify her involvement with the print publication of her
works. A letter to her noble dedicatee, Giovan Francesco Loredan, thanks
him for encouraging her to print her letters but also rebukes him for failing
to support her to the extent that he had promised. Letters addressed to
Vittoria Medici della Rovere, Grand Duchess of Tuscany, to an anonymous gentleman and to Bertucci Valier concern her requests for help in
obtaining licences from Venice and other states to print works of hers.
Tarabotti even envisaged an audacious but unsuccessful scheme to have *La
tirannia paterna* printed in Paris, making requests about details of production: 'ch'il libro sia stampato in dodici e ben corretto, che il carattere sia
grandetto ma bello' (that the book should be printed in duodecimo format,
carefully proofread, in a typeface that is quite large but elegant).[50]

## The Publication of Texts by Others

### Writings by Men

As well as publishing their own works, women might promote the circulation of manuscript and printed texts composed by others, mainly by men.
In some cases, elite women had privileged possession of texts that they had
acquired either directly from authors or indirectly through their social

---

[50] Arcangela Tarabotti, *Lettere familiari e di complimento*, ed. by Meredith Kennedy Ray and Lynn
Lara Westwater (Turin: Rosenberg & Sellier, 2005), especially letters 18, 58, 70, 87, 94, 112, 131–35,
148–49, 164–66, 174, 176, 207, 250; quotation from letter 58, p. 115. See also Beatrice Collina,
'Women in the Gutenberg Galaxy', in *Arcangela Tarabotti: A Literary Nun in Baroque Venice*, ed. by
Elissa B. Weaver (Ravenna: Longo, 2006), pp. 91–105; Meredith K. Ray, *Writing Gender in Women's
Letter Collections of the Italian Renaissance* (University of Toronto Press, 2009), pp. 184–213.
A Venetian decree of 1562 designated three representatives of the Church and the state who had
to grant licences to print: Horatio F. Brown, *The Venetian Printing Press 1469–1800* (London:
Nimmo, 1891), pp. 127–28, 213–14; Paul F. Grendler, *The Roman Inquisition and the Venetian Press,
1540–1605* (Princeton University Press, 1977), pp. 151–54.

connections, and they may have seen themselves as outright owners of these texts.

The first edition of a vernacular translation of the letters of St Jerome was printed in Ferrara by Lorenzo Rossi in 1497, richly decorated with woodcuts. The costs of production would have been considerable. The copies must have been intended in large measure for devout female readers, not only because the text was in the vernacular but also because the volume concluded with rules for nuns drawn from the saint's writings and translated by fra Matteo of Ferrara. Variant versions of fol. a1$^v$, dated 1494 or 1495, indicate that the edition was prepared over at least four years and that three subsets of copies were linked with prominent figures. One group has a dedication to the doge, senate and people of Venice. Two others acknowledge support from local sources. The copies were produced in one case 'felici auspicio ac liberalitate maxima' (with the propitious help and greatest generosity) of Duke Ercole d'Este of Ferrara, and in the other case with help from two women, Ercole's wife and one of her daughters. The copies sponsored by these two have a full-page statement in capital letters (with careful use of diacritics), in the form of an inscription: 'Eleonorae Estensis Ducis. Ferr. ac Lisabellae eius filiáe Mantuáe regináe munificen. ac liberalitate divi Hieronÿmi divinum hoc opus in lucem prodiit ann. MCCCC.LXXXXV' (This divine work of St Jerome was published in the year 1495 through the munificence and generosity of Eleonora, Duchess of Ferrara, and her daughter Isabella, Princess of Mantua).[51]

Isabella d'Este became an exceptionally avid collector of texts and a shrewd diffuser of them within her social circle. She had privileged access, as most consorts would have had, to works of court poets, sent directly to her or obtained from relatives or acquaintances, all of whom were members of a group that was simultaneously a social community and a literary community. We shall return to Isabella's means of acquiring texts at the end of Chapter 3, but here we can consider her role in their initial diffusion. The first two examples involve manuscript circulation. On 17 September 1500, one of Isabella's brothers, Cardinal Ippolito d'Este, asked her to provide him with some short poems by Antonio Tebaldeo of Ferrara, a courtly poet closely associated with her. She had lost her copy and thus had to ask the author for another, as she explained in a letter to Ippolito when she responded to his request:

---

[51] *Catalogue of Books Printed in the XVth Century Now in the British Museum*, 9 vols (London: British Museum, 1909–49), VI, 614.

Mando a V[ostra] S[ignoria] li stramotti del Thebaldeo che la mi ha rechesto. Per haver io smarito li mei è stato necessario haverli da epso autore qual da tri infora che non piaceno a lui, volontera me ni ha compiaciuto: mando quelli ho potuto havere et a lei di continuo me raccomando.[52]

(I am sending your lordship the strambotti by Tebaldeo you asked me for. Since I had lost mine, I had to get them from the author himself, who was glad to provide them apart from three he does not like. I am sending those I was able to get, with my continued good wishes.)

A Piedmontese nobleman who was also a poet, Galeotto Del Carretto, sent several poetic compositions to Isabella, and in January 1497 he wrote to ask her for the settings that one of her court musicians, Bartolomeo Tromboncino, had composed for four of them. She seems to have made such pieces available to collectors of music both outside and within her court circles. Two of them, settings of 'Se gran festa me mostrasti' and 'Lassa, donna, i dolci sguardi', found their way into collections of *frottole* printed in Venice by Ottaviano Petrucci in 1505 and 1506, perhaps using a manuscript collection made in that city.[53] The same two settings were transcribed within a collection that was probably put together in Milan. William Prizer has plausibly suggested that it was made for a nephew of Isabella's, Massimiliano Sforza, between late 1512 and 1515, after his return to Milan or more specifically during the carnival of 1513, when Isabella was in the city.[54] Massimiliano was evidently determined to enjoy life to the full, even though his position as Duke of Milan was precarious. It thus appears likely that Isabella was still the primary publisher of Tromboncino's settings of Del Carretto's poems in their scribal form.

On at least one occasion, Isabella made some contribution towards the expenses that an author would have incurred when having a work printed. She wrote in November 1513 to thank Lelio Manfredi for a manuscript copy of the *Carcer d'amore*, his translation of the *Cárcel de amor* by Diego de San Pedro, dedicated to her and sent to her through Manfredi's nephew, adding: 'per hora acceptareti da esso vostro nepote questi pochi denari che per lui vi mandamo acciò habbiati melio il modo di mettere l'opera in stampa, insieme con quell'altra lettera vostra' (for the moment you will

[52] Antonino Bertolotti, 'Varietà archivistiche e bibliografiche', *Il bibliofilo*, 7 (1880), 26–27.
[53] Giuseppe Turba, 'Galeotto Del Carretto tra Casale e Mantova', *Rinascimento*, 2nd ser., 11 (1971), 95–169 (p. 104). Tromboncino's setting of 'Se gran festa' was printed by Ottaviano Petrucci, *Frottole libro quinto* (Venice, 1505), no. 42; an anonymous setting of 'Lassa, donna' is in Petrucci's *Frottole libro sexto* (Venice, 1505/06), no. 26. See Stanley Boorman, *Ottaviano Petrucci: Catalogue Raisonné* (New York: Oxford University Press, 2006), pp. 288–91, 611, 616.
[54] Florence, Biblioteca del Conservatorio di musica 'Luigi Cherubini', MS Basevi 2441, fols 24ᵛ–26ʳ. See William F. Prizer, 'Secular Music at Milan during the Early Cinquecento: Florence, Biblioteca del Conservatorio, MS Basevi 2441', *Musica Disciplina*, 50 (1996), 9–57.

accept from this nephew of yours this small sum of money that we are sending you through him, to help you to have the work printed together with that other letter of yours). In March 1515, Manfredi sent her a printed copy of his translation, regretting that it could not be one of the twelve vellum copies that he had had made, because these had been packed tightly before the ink had dried.[55] However, in 1519–20 the marchioness did not go as far as to subsidize the printing of Marco Girolamo Vida's Latin poem on silkworms, *De bombyce*. 'Facemoli stampare proprio como il volume che la Ex[cellentia] V[ostra] ha mandato' (We are having [the *Bombici*] printed just like the volume Your Excellency sent us), she claimed in a letter to the poet on 15 December 1519. All she did, however, was to send the manuscript to the Mantuan ambassador in Venice with a note that expressed the hope that it would be published in the style of an Aldine octavo: 'Mandamovi il libro de' Bombici del nostro Vida, che se stampe in quella bella forma, characteri et modo che è stampato il Vergilio che fece m[aestr]o Aldo' (We are sending you the book on silkworms by our Vida, for it to be printed in the fine format, types and manner in which the Virgil made by master Aldo is printed). The printer Filippo Pincio or Pinzi, a Mantuan subject now based in Venice, reported to her that nobody else wanted to put up the money 'per essere auctor novus et opus novum' (since the author is new and the work is new), but that he was willing to do so. Isabella, however, did not wish him to suffer a loss on her account. Instead, she planned to send the work to Milan where she had heard that someone wanted to print it. But this project came to nothing.[56]

One author expressed in print his vexation on finding that a woman had allowed a draft copy of a work of his to circulate without his permission. Baldassarre Castiglione wrote in the dedicatory letter of *Il libro del corte-giano*, first printed in 1528, that Vittoria Colonna had had transcribed much of the text that he had sent her to read some years previously, and that 'quella parte del libro si ritrovava in Napoli in mano di molti' (the part of the book concerned had found its way into the hands of many people in Naples).[57]

---

[55] Stephen Kolsky, 'Lelio Manfredi traduttore cortigiano: intorno al "Carcer d'Amore" e al "Tirante il Bianco"', *Civiltà mantovana*, 3rd ser., 29, no. 10 (1994), 45–69 (p. 64, n. 13); see also p. 48 and Alessandro Luzio and Rodolfo Renier, *La coltura e le relazioni letterarie di Isabella d'Este Gonzaga*, ed. by Simone Albonico (Milan: Bonnard, 2005), p. 135. The letter to which Isabella refers, a description of an ancient villa called the *Pallazzo di Lucullo*, was also dedicated to her but was apparently not printed: Kolsky, 'Lelio Manfredi traduttore cortigiano', pp. 48–50.

[56] Luzio and Renier, *La coltura*, pp. 152–55 (quotations from p. 154).

[57] Baldesar Castiglione, *Il libro del cortegiano con una scelta delle opere minori*, ed. by Bruno Maier, 2nd edn (Turin: UTET, 1964), pp. 68–69; Castiglione, *The Book of the Courtier*, trans. by George Bull

The support of two aristocratic women lay behind the printing of the *Libro de vita contemplativa* by the Augustinian friar Antonio Meli of Crema (Brescia: Giovanni Antonio Bresciano, 1527), a substantial volume adorned with fine woodcuts. Meli had composed the work at the request of Lucrezia Borgia (1480–1519), Duchess of Ferrara, and dedicated it to her in 1513. At this stage the work probably did not circulate further in manuscript, but after the duchess's death a copy came into the hands of Giovanna Orsini Gonzaga, Marchioness of Bozzolo. The edition of 1527 opens with an exchange of letters between her and Adeodata Martinengo, abbess of the wealthy convent of Santa Giulia in Brescia, which was mentioned earlier. Orsini asks the abbess to arrange to have the work printed in Brescia (the nearest centre with active presses in that period), at Orsini's expense if necessary:

> sappendo che la felice vostra città di Bressa [. . .] ha peritissimi artifici dell'arte impressoria, e che vostra colendissima signoria e rara virtù, del honore di Dio e della salute de' fideli è zelatissima, i' ho pigliata confidentia de dirizar a quella questo libro pecculiare, pregandola che, per mezzo de' suoi agenti, se digna farlo stampare, offerendomi a pagare le spese per quello contingenti. (fol. $3_1^v$)

> (knowing that your happy city of Brescia [. . .] has craftsmen most skilled in the art of printing, and that you, a person highly revered and of rare virtue, are most fervently devoted to the honour of God and the salvation of the faithful, I have ventured to send you this singular book. I ask you to be kind enough to have it printed, through your agents, and I offer to pay the expenses incurred.)

Martinengo responds that 'quello [libro] mi son ingegnata destinare a publica impressione' (fol. $3_4^r$; I have managed to direct that book for public printing).[58] The costs of printing thus seem to have been taken on by Orsini, perhaps with some contribution from Martinengo or her family.

Ludovica Torelli, countess of the small northern state of Guastalla, was one of the elite women who, like Vittoria Colonna, associated themselves with the movement of reform within the Catholic Church in the first half of the sixteenth century. By 1530, Torelli had taken as her confessor

---

(Harmondsworth: Penguin, 1976), p. 31. See Amedeo Quondam, '*Questo povero Cortegiano*': *Castiglione, il libro, la storia* (Rome: Bulzoni, 2000), pp. 67–73.

[58] Danilo Zardin, 'Mercato librario e letture devote nella svolta del Cinquecento tridentino: note in margine ad un inventario milanese di libri di monache', in *Stampa, libri e letture a Milano nell'età di Carlo Borromeo*, ed. by Nicola Raponi and Angelo Turchini (Milan: Vita e Pensiero, 1992), pp. 135–246 (pp. 191–92); Gabriella Zarri, *La 'religione' di Lucrezia Borgia: le lettere inedite del confessore* (Rome: Roma nel Rinascimento, 2006), pp. 86–99, and Zarri, *Figure di donne in età moderna: modelli e storie* (Rome: Edizioni di Storia e Letteratura, 2017), pp. 87–99.

a heterodox Dominican friar, Battista da Crema, and she claimed to have inherited some of his spiritual writings after his death in 1534. One of fra Battista's works still in manuscript was the *Specchio interiore: opera divina per la cui lettione ciascuno devoto potrà facilmente ascendere al colmo della perfettione* (Inner mirror: Divine work through reading which every devout person can easily rise to the peak of perfection). He had sent a copy to Venice in the 1520s for the use of a group of patrician women who governed a recently founded hospital for incurables. In 1529 the twice-widowed countess had been granted the right to carry out commercial transactions without needing to seek approval from a male relative, as would have been the normal practice under the legal system of her state. This power enabled her to have the *Specchio* printed in Milan in 1540 by Francesco Minizio Calvo. In her letter of dedication, she explained that fra Battista:

> [a]ppresso al fine della sua candida vita lasciò a me, come herede delle sue caritative fatiche, diverse spirituali operette fatte da lui per instruttione della CHRISTIANA VITA, delle quali ne sono già state pubblicate alcune, et alcune altre sono ancora appresso di me. (fol. ℯ3ᵛ)

> (near the end of his blameless life left to me, as heir of his charitable labours, various short spiritual works written by him to teach the Christian life; some of these have already been published, and some others are still with me.)

As well as organizing the printing of the *Specchio*, and probably underwriting its costs at least in part, the countess arranged to have the language of the work revised for the benefit of educated readers: as she put it, 'temperata prima alquanto dalla peritia dello impressore la nativa lingua dello Autore, per non tanto offendere le dotte et delicate orecchie' (fol. ℯ5ʳ; first having had the author's natural language tempered somewhat by the skill of the printer, so as not to offend learned and delicate ears so much).[59]

Another widowed noblewoman who came to control the posthumous circulation of writings by a heterodox author was Giulia Gonzaga, a relative of Vittoria Colonna's by marriage. She decided in 1535, at the age of about twenty-two, to take up residence in the convent of San Francesco delle

---

[59] See also Orazio Premoli, *Fra' Battista da Crema secondo documenti inediti: contributo alla storia religiosa del secolo XVI* (Rome: Desclée, 1910), pp. 113–14; Zarri, *Libri di spirito*, pp. 131–33; P. Renée Baernstein, 'In Widow's Habit: Women between Convent and Family in Sixteenth-Century Milan', *Sixteenth Century Journal*, 25 (1994), 787–807 (pp. 795–98); Baernstein, *A Convent Tale: A Century of Sisterhood in Spanish Milan* (New York: Routledge, 2002), pp. 29–34; Elena Bonora, *I conflitti della Controriforma: santità e obbedienza nell'esperienza religiosa dei primi barnabiti* (Florence: Le Lettere, 1998), pp. 121–200, especially pp. 124–25, 130–33, 150–52.

Monache in Naples.[60] In this city she became a key member of the aristocratic circle of the Spanish theologian Juan de Valdés. The manuscript originals of the spiritual writings of Valdés came into Gonzaga's possession, and after his death in 1541 she became their main publisher, in the sense that she oversaw a selective and duly cautious scribal distribution among those whom she considered enlightened followers of the Spaniard's doctrines.[61] Thus in 1541 Vittoria Colonna wrote from Viterbo to thank Gonzaga for sending Valdés's exposition of St Paul (a work not printed until 1556) which she said was eagerly awaited, especially by her – implying that others awaited it, too: 'Ho inteso che V[ostra] S[ignoria] ha mandato la espositione sopra San Paulo, ch'era molto desiderata, et più da me, che n'ho più bisogno, però più ne lla ringratio, et più quando la vedrò, piacendo a Dio' (I have heard that you have sent the commentary on St Paul, which was much desired, and more by me who needs it more; therefore I thank you for it more and [will do so] more when I see it, God willing).[62]

In the early 1540s, Giulia Gonzaga sent works of Valdés to another member of the community of Spirituali, Marcantonio Flaminio. Her purpose was to have them translated from Spanish into Italian, according to the testimony of Pietro Carnesecchi during his trial for heresy in 1566–67:

> il Flaminio haveva seco una parte delli scritti di Valdés, et credo che fussero il libro delle considerationi et il commento sopra li psalmi, et che andava traducendoli di spagnolo in italiano per compiacere alla sudetta signora che n'haveva ricerco.[63]

[60] Camilla Russell, *Giulia Gonzaga and the Religious Controversies of Sixteenth-Century Italy* (Turnhout: Brepols, 2006), pp. 19–28; Susanna Peyronel Rambaldi, *Una gentildonna irrequieta: Giulia Gonzaga fra reti familiari e relazioni eterodosse* (Rome: Viella, 2012), pp. 125–31.

[61] Benedetto Nicolini claims, but without citing evidence, that Valdés bequeathed his manuscripts to Gonzaga: see his *Ideali e passioni nell'Italia religiosa del Cinquecento* (Bologna: Libreria antiquaria Palmaverde, 1962), p. 84. Valdés named Giovan Tommaso Minadois as heir of his property in Naples, with instructions to pass the greatest share to one of Valdés's nephews: see Giovanni di Valdés, *Alfabeto cristiano: dialogo con Giulia Gonzaga*, ed. by Benedetto Croce (Bari: Laterza, 1938), pp. 173–78.

[62] Vittoria Colonna, *Carteggio di Vittoria Colonna marchesa di Pescara*, ed. by Ermanno Ferrero and Giuseppe Müller (Turin: Loescher, 1889), letter CXLII (1541), pp. 238–40; *I processi inquisitoriali di Pietro Carnesecchi (1557–1567)*, ed. by Massimo Firpo and Dario Marcatto, 2 vols (Vatican City: Archivio segreto vaticano, 1998–2000), II, 1032–34; Marcantonio Flaminio, *Apologia del 'Beneficio di Christo' e altri scritti inediti*, ed. by Dario Marcatto (Florence: Olschki, 1996), pp. 202–03; Russell, *Giulia Gonzaga*, pp. 95–96, using *Opuscoli e lettere di riformatori italiani del Cinquecento*, ed. by Giuseppe Paladino, 2 vols (Bari: Laterza, 1913–27), I, 94.

[63] *I processi inquisitoriali di Pietro Carnesecchi*, ed. by Firpo and Marcatto, II, 1031; Flaminio, *Apologia*, p. 8. On Gonzaga's relationships with Valdés and his works and with Carnesecchi, see Peyronel Rambaldi, *Una gentildonna irrequieta*, especially pp. 95–105, 118–22, 149–50, 223 and 232–56.

(Flaminio had with him some of Valdés's writings, and I think that they
were *Le cento e dieci divine considerazioni* and the commentary on the
Psalms, and that he was translating them from Spanish to Italian at the
desire of the above-mentioned lady who had asked him to do so.)

Gonzaga's purpose at this stage was evidently to make Valdés's works better
known in the Italian peninsula. By the 1560s, in her last years, it was too risky
for her to continue to diffuse these works, but she did at least manage to keep
them out of the hands of the Holy Office. An indication of Gonzaga's
continuing control over the majority of Valdés's writings, which remained in
manuscript, comes from Carnesecchi's testimony. In order to prove that the
Church had put the works of Valdés on Indexes of Prohibited Books without
proper scrutiny of them, he argued that the authorities could not possibly
have read them because they were 'in potere della quondam signora donna
Iulia Gonzaga' (in the power of the late Giulia Gonzaga), 'havendo lei la
maggiore parte di essi sotto le soe chiave' (since she had most of them under
lock and key).[64] She considered sending them to Venice in 1559 after Pope
Paul IV's Index of that year had prohibited them,[65] but she decided to keep
them in Naples on Carnesecchi's advice. In the same year, Carnesecchi and
Gonzaga discussed having some of Valdés's works printed in Venice, or
elsewhere, but not in Protestant lands. One possibility was for her to send
them to Carnesecchi in Venice by a secure route: for example, addressed to
the Florentine merchant Pandolfo Attavanti.[66] Paolo Simoncelli has noted
that Attavanti had in 1547 been elected consul of the 'nation' of Florentine
residents in Venice 'with the concurrence of a majority of Florentines who
were at the limits, if not beyond, of political orthodoxy', in terms of their
allegiance to the Medicean regime.[67] Gonzaga considered sending the works
to Venice again in 1563 because the situation in Naples had become danger-
ous. Carnesecchi testified that her purpose then was not to have them
printed, something she had contemplated up to 1558–59, but to free herself
from danger and to preserve them. He said that 'sonno extincti insieme con

[64] *I processi inquisitoriali di Pietro Carnesecchi*, ed. by Firpo and Marcatto, II, 74, 454.

[65] J. M. de Bujanda, *Index de Rome: 1557, 1559, 1564. Les Premiers Index romains et l'Index du Concile de
Trente* (Sherbrooke: Centre d'études de la Renaissance, 1990), p. 546. The Venetian Index of 1554
had already condemned Valdés's writings: J. M. de Bujanda, *Index de Venise, 1549; Venise et Milan,
1554* (Sherbrooke: Centre d'études de la Renaissance, 1987), p. 305.

[66] *I processi inquisitoriali di Pietro Carnesecchi*, ed. by Firpo and Marcatto, II, 51, 71, 128–33, 476,
481–82, 987, 1370, 1367–68.

[67] Paolo Simoncelli, 'The Turbulent Life of the Florentine Community in Venice', in *Heresy, Culture,
and Religion in Early Modern Italy: Contexts and Contestations*, ed. by Ronald K. Delph,
Michelle M. Fontaine and John Jeffries Martin (Kirksville, MO: Truman State University Press,
2006), pp. 113–33 (p. 128).

la vita di detta signora' (they have passed away together with that lady's life),[68] and after her death in 1566 copies did indeed disappear; they may have been removed or destroyed by someone close to her.

Giulia Gonzaga was seen as the best person to contact even when a printed work of Valdés was sought after in France. In 1548 the French queen, Catherine de' Medici, asked Carnesecchi (who was at the French court between October 1547 and 1552) to obtain a copy of Valdés's *Alfabeto cristiano* in Italian; she had already read it in French, she said, presumably in manuscript. He replied that he would write to ask Gonzaga to provide 'qualche altra operetta' (some other work), meaning the *Considerationi*, which Mario Galeota, a follower of Valdés from the Kingdom of Naples, had translated at Gonzaga's request in the 1540s and which had been printed in Basel in 1550. There were printed editions of the *Alfabeto*: one brought out in Venice by Niccolò Bascarini at the instance of Marco Antonio Magno, 1545, and two others of 1546.[69] However, in order to speed things up, rather than write to Gonzaga in Naples, Carnesecchi turned to Lattanzio Ragnoni in Venice to ask for his help in obtaining both books.[70]

Just as Giulia Gonzaga sent works to Flaminio, so he sent writings from Viterbo to her in Naples, carried by a trusted messenger, the priest Apollonio Merenda. In January 1542, for example, Flaminio humbly sent her some discourses on the Gospel of St Matthew:

> Pur venendo il nostro messer Apollonio, ho voluto far forza alla mia superbia contentandomi di darli tre ragionamenti fatti sopra san Mattheo, li quali prego Dio che dispiaciano tanto a Vostra Signoria et a quelli altri signori che, in luogo di sollecitarmi allo scrivere, di commune consenso mi comandino ch'io taccia, il che però ogn'hora più mi risolvo di voler fare.[71]

> (Yet, since our Apollonio is coming, I have wanted to overcome my pride, contenting myself with giving him three discourses on St Matthew, which

---

[68] *I processi inquisitoriali di Pietro Carnesecchi*, ed. by Firpo and Marcatto, II, 74.

[69] On Magno and these editions, see Massimo Firpo, 'Nota al testo', in Juan de Valdés, *Alfabeto cristiano, Domande e risposte, Della predestinazione, Catechismo*, ed. by Massimo Firpo (Turin: Einaudi, 1994), pp. cli–clxxviii (pp. cli–clx).

[70] *I processi inquisitoriali di Pietro Carnesecchi*, ed. by Firpo and Marcatto, II, 218–19. On the French translation, see Massimo Firpo, 'Pietro Carnesecchi, Caterina de' Medici e Juan Valdés: di una sconosciuta traduzione francese dell'*Alphabeto christiano*', in *Dal Sacco di Roma all'Inquisizione: studi su Juan de Valdés e la Riforma italiana* (Alessandria: Edizioni dell'Orso, 1998), pp. 147–60.

[71] Colonna, *Carteggio*, letter CXLII (1541), pp. 238–40; *I processi inquisitoriali di Pietro Carnesecchi*, ed. by Firpo and Marcatto, II, 1032–34; Flaminio, *Apologia*, pp. 202–03. On Merenda, see Achille Olivieri, 'Merenda, Apollonio', *DBI*, 73 (2009), 639–43.

I pray God that you and those other gentlepersons will dislike so much that, instead of urging me to write, you will agree to order me to be silent; which in any case I am ever more determined to do.)

Again, the writings were not intended for one reader's eyes alone: Gonzaga was evidently expected to pass them on to other followers of Valdés.

Another well-known supporter of reform, Renée de France (1510–1575), the second daughter of Anne of Brittany and Louis XII of France and wife of Duke Ercole II of Ferrara, appears to have given financial assistance for the print publication of works of which she approved. Innocenzio Ringhieri, one of the heterodox members of Renée's circle, wrote in a letter of 1553, according to a summary record of her correspondence, 'de libri sacri che Madama fa stampare in Venetia per il Giulitto' (about sacred books that my lady [the duchess] is having printed in Venice by [Gabriele] Giolito). It could be that Renée's reputation for expenditure of such kind led the scholar Francisco de Enzinas (known as Dryander) to approach her in 1552, just a few months before his death in December of that year, with a request to help him have his translation of the New Testament printed: according to the summary of another letter of Ringhieri's, 'Francesco Driander per lettera di 20 settembre 1552 latina scrive a Madama che li dii aiuto per far stampare la Sacra Scrittura tradotta in Augusta in lingua spagniuola' (Francesco Dryander in a letter in Latin of 20 September 1552 writes to ask my lady for help in having the Holy Scripture translated in Strasbourg into Spanish).[72]

Caterina Barbaro, a Venetian noblewoman, lent support over several years to Iacopo Coppa, a Modenese charlatan (itinerant seller of remedies) and performer, and she may have facilitated his activities as a publisher of short texts in Venice, perhaps by providing a financial investment but without her being named as publisher. Coppa dedicated to her the first edition of Ludovico Ariosto's *Erbolato* (Giovanni Antonio and Pietro Nicolini da Sabbio, 1545), as publisher of the volume, calling her his only consolation in his travails (fol. A2ʳ). It is very possible that Barbaro helped Coppa to obtain the book-privilege that protected the Venetian edition of

---

[72] Chiara Franceschini, '"Literarum studia nobis communia": Olimpia Morata e la corte di Renata di Francia', *Schifanoia*, 28–29 (2005), 207–32 (p. 216). On Ringhieri and the duchess, see Eleonora Belligni, *Renata di Francia (1510–1575): un'eresia di corte* (Turin: UTET, 2011), pp. 320–21, and Chapter 3 below. On Renée's support for Reformers, see also Salvatore Caponetto, 'Renata di Francia e il calvinismo a Ferrara e Faenza', in *La riforma protestante nell'Italia del Cinquecento* (Turin: Claudiana, 1992), pp. 279–90; Kirsi Stjerna, 'Renée de France, 1510–1575: A Friend of the Huguenots', in *Women and the Reformation* (Oxford: Blackwell, 2009), pp. 175–96; Belligni, *Renata di Francia*, pp. 96–97, 299–326.

Ariosto's *Rime* published by him in 1546 against competition from other printings; the dedicatory letter is signed in her name and addressed to another member of her city's nobility, Lodovico Foscarini.[73]

An edition of a verse translation of Virgil's *Georgics* by Antonio Mario Nigrisoli (or Negrisoli) of Ferrara, together with poems of his own, was printed in Venice by Melchiorre Sessa in 1543 at the instigation of Fulvio Pellegrino Morato. However, the edition was judged to be unsatisfactory. From 1550 to 1555, Nigrisoli worked in Poland as secretary of Bona Sforza, second wife of the Polish king Sigismund I, and the queen decided to initiate and control the publication of a new edition. Her letter reveals the authoritative manner in which she went about this:

> Bona, Dei gratia, Regina Poloniae, Magna Dux Lithuaniae Barrique, Princeps Rossani, Russiae, Prussiae Masoviaeque etc. Domina etc.
>
> Magnifici syncere nobis dilectissimi. Havendoci il Magnifico Antonio Mario Negrisoli, gentilhuomo nostro carissimo, compiaciuto della Georgica di Vergilio già molti anni sono fatta et corretta dallui in lingua Thoscana, et con altre sue compositioni accompagnata; le quali opere, perché oltra che a noi hanno molto sodisfatto et da molti nobili intelletti le havemo sentite ancho molto lodare et approvare, desiderando di non mancare in quel che dovemo allo honor di lui, et d'haverne appresso di noi alcune copie in bona et bella lettera espresse, con questa nostra vi la mandiamo, accioché senza fallo la facciate stampare quanto più presto potete con l'intitulatione, lettere et ordine che vi ne sarà mandato, il che esseguito, poi ci ne manderete in fino a venticinque copie, accioché noi et altri possiamo accommodarne. Di Varsovia il dì 27 di gennaio del 1551. Bona Regina etc.
>
> Magnificis viris Thomae et Ioannimariae Iuntis, agentibus nostris Venetiis syncere nostris dilectissimis. Venetiis.

(Bona, by the grace of God Queen of Poland, Grand Duchess of Lithuania and Bari, Princess of Rossano, ruler etc. of Russia, Prussia, Mazovia etc.

Most dearly beloved. Antonio Mario Negrisoli, our most dear gentleman, has pleased us with Virgil's *Georgics*, translated and corrected by him in Tuscan already many years ago and accompanied by other compositions of his. These works have satisfied us greatly, and we have also heard them much praised and approved by many noble intellects. Since we wish not to fall

[73] Salvatore Bongi, 'Le Rime dell'Ariosto', *Archivio storico italiano*, 5th ser., 2 (1888), 267–76 (pp. 272–74); Bongi, *Annali di Gabriel Giolito*, II, 32–35; Giorgio Busetto, 'Coppa, Iacopo, detto Iacopo Modenese', *DBI*, 28 (1983), 584–86; Alberto Casadei, 'Sulle prime edizioni a stampa delle "Rime" ariostesche', *LB*, 94 (1992), 187–95 (pp. 187–92); David Gentilcore, *Medical Charlatanism in Early Modern Italy* (Oxford University Press, 2006), p. 69; Rosa Salzberg, *Ephemeral City: Cheap Print and Urban Culture in Renaissance Venice* (Manchester University Press, 2015), pp. 112–13; Eugenio Refini, 'Reappraising the Charlatan in Early Modern Italy: The Case of Iacopo Coppa', *Italian Studies*, 71 (2016), 197–211 (pp. 199, 201–02).

short in our duty towards his honour and to have with us some copies printed in a fair and attractive font, with this letter of ours we send it to you, so that without fail you may have it printed as quickly as you can, with the dedication, types and order that will be notified to you. Once you have done this, you will then send us up to twenty-five copies so that we and others may make use of them. From Warsaw, 27 January 1551. Queen Bona etc.

To the magnificent Tommaso and Giovanni Maria Giunti, our most dearly beloved agents in Venice. In Venice.)

Tommaso and Giovanni Maria were sons of the powerful publisher Lucantonio Giunti. The edition was duly printed in February 1552 by Niccolò Bascarini, presumably at the instance of the Giunti brothers, and the queen's letter was included on fol. A5$^r$.[74] It was followed by another letter, from one of her courtiers, Prospero Provana, to her confessor, fra Mario Francesco Lismanino (fols A5$^v$–A7$^v$), which explains that the first translation had been 'mal trattata et scorrettamente impressa' (badly treated and incorrectly printed), but that the queen has 'per sua cortesia fatto opra di mandare in publico la di lui poi corretta' (graciously taken steps to publish the version later corrected by [Nigrisoli]). Pietro Aretino states that the queen paid for the costs of this edition in a letter of April 1552 to the translator's son Ercole, in which he writes that the book is 'in vero degno che la serenità di lei l'abbia fatto per mezzo de la propria pecunia imprimere' (truly worthy that her serene highness has had it printed by means of her own money).[75]

In 1592, Maddalena Campiglia heard that a comedy, *Gli inganni*, by Curzio Gonzaga, a Mantuan friend and a relation by marriage, was about to be printed in Venice and that he was planning to dedicate the edition to her. At this point, she claims to have intervened in order to have the work presented to the public in a different way, with a dedication to Marfisa d'Este, illegitimate granddaughter of Duke Alfonso I of Ferrara, that came from herself and not from the author of the play, as one might have concluded from the mention of the dedicatee after the author's name on the title page. The source of the dedication is revealed in a letter in which

[74] *La Georgica di Vergilio con sciolti versi traddutta in lingua toscana dal magnifico m. Antonio Mario Negrisoli nobile ferrarese.* [. . .] *Rime et altre cose del medesimo con sue risposte ad altre rime allui scritte.* On Nigrisoli, see Caterina Brandoli, 'Nigrisoli, Antonio Maria', *DBI*, 78 (2013), 565–66. On the Giunti brothers, see Paolo Camerini, *Annali dei Giunti*, vol. I, 2 parts (Florence: Sansoni, 1962–63), I.1, 293–99. On Bascarini's editions, see Conor Fahy, 'The Venetian Ptolemy of 1548', in *The Italian Book, 1465–1800: Studies Presented to Dennis E. Rhodes on his 70th Birthday*, ed. by Denis Reidy (London: British Library, 1993), pp. 89–115 (pp. 110–11).

[75] Pietro Aretino, *Lettere*, ed. by Paolo Procaccioli, 6 vols (Rome: Salerno Editrice, 1997–2002), VI, letter 113, p. 118.

Campiglia explains that she wanted Gonzaga's work printed according to her own will: 'sentendo io ch'era per stamparsi in Venetia, et ch'egli con una sua dedicatoria in essa, ne havea fatto a me particolare et publico dono; subito ordinai che fosse stampata secondo il disegno, et desiderio mio' (when I heard that it was about to be printed in Venice and he had made a particular and public gift of it to me with a letter of dedication, I ordered straight away that it should be printed according to my plan and desire). Campiglia explains that she had been waiting for an opportunity to dedicate a work to Marfisa, and has chosen to present this comedy rather than one of her own unpolished compositions.[76] If this account is true, it indicates that a determined woman could take over the print publication of a man's work and use it for her own purposes.

Eleonora de' Medici, daughter of Grand Duke Francesco I de' Medici and married in 1584 to Vincenzo Gonzaga, who became Duke of Mantua in 1587, concerned herself with the publication of works in more indirect ways, by using her influence to promote the cause of writers who desired favours from the court in Florence. On 10 August 1585, she wrote from Revere, near Mantua, to ask her father to accord a favour to Orazio Diola of Bologna in relation to the publication of a work of his, doubtless the translation of Marcos de Lisboa's chronicle of the life of St Francis and of his order (*Croniche degli ordini instituiti dal padre s. Francesco*):

> Ms. Horatio Diola m'ha fatta pregare ch'io voglia intercedere per lui con Vostra Alt[ezz]a perché gli conceda la gratia contenuta nell'alligato memoriale in materia di stampare certo suo libro, et perché io ho giudicato la richiesta sua giusta et solita a concedersi da tutti i principi, vengo a supplicarla che per rispetto mio voglia favorirnelo.[77]

> (Orazio Diola has had a request made to me that I should intercede on his behalf with your highness to grant him the favour contained in the attached memorandum on the subject of printing a certain book of his. Since I consider his request reasonable and of the kind that is granted by all princes, I beseech you kindly to favour him concerning it for my sake.)

The first part of Diola's translation had been published at his own expense and without the protection of book-privileges in 1581 (Parma: Erasmo Viotti), but several other editions soon appeared elsewhere in northern Italy (Casalmaggiore, Venice, Brescia). In 1585, however, the Giolito press

[76] (Venice: Giovanni Antonio Rampazetto, 1592), fols A2$^r$–A7$^v$ (quotation from fol. A5$^v$). On Campiglia and Gonzaga, see Campiglia, *Flori*, pp. 4, 46–48.
[77] ASF, Mediceo del Principato, vol. 2939, unfoliated.

in Venice brought out an edition of the second part of the *Croniche* that was protected by book-privileges granted by all the major Italian states including Tuscany.[78] Eleonora's intervention in support of the devout author had evidently been successful.

On another occasion, Eleonora helped to get a book published in Mantua. Torquato Tasso asked her in a letter of 2 January 1587 to write to the Tuscan ambassador in the city 'perché non sia impedita la stampa d'un libro di mio padre, il quale è dedicato al Serenissimo Signor Duca suo suocero' (so that there should be no obstacle to the printing of a book by my father, which is dedicated to your father-in-law the duke).[79] The work in question was the narrative poem *Il Floridante*, which Bernardo Tasso had left unfinished on his death in 1569, but which his son Torquato had now completed and polished. This work was duly issued in Mantua in 1587 by the ducal printer Francesco Osanna, with a dedication by Torquato to Guglielmo Gonzaga dated 6 July.[80]

Another instance of behind-the-scenes influence by a noblewoman concerns the first two editions of all twenty canti of Torquato Tasso's *Gerusalemme liberata*, both of which were printed in 1581, one in Parma in duodecimo, the other in the nearby town of Casalmaggiore in quarto. At that point, the author was imprisoned in the hospital of Sant'Anna in Ferrara. Both editions include a dedicatory letter signed by Angelo Ingegneri, addressed to Carlo Emanuele, Duke of Savoy, and dated 1 February 1581, which suggests that Isabella Pallavicino Lupi, Marchioness of Soragna, near Parma, played a part in persuading Alfonso II d'Este, Duke of Ferrara, to allow the work to be printed:

> Et è V[ostra] A[ltezza] Sereniss[ima] pure, cui tocca protegerla e favorirla; da che, per mandarla in luce, non è mancato chi l'habbia in raccomandation ricevuta: ché la Signora Marchesana di Soragna [...] s'è presso a questo saggio Principe così felicemente interposta, ch'ogni difficoltà superata, io l'ho pure, dopo quattro mesi, ridotta a segno che posso mandarla all'Altezza Vostra Serenissima.[81]

---

[78] Bongi, *Annali di Gabriel Giolito*, II, 400–01; Nuovo and Coppens, *I Giolito e la stampa*, pp. 253–54, and p. 440 for the Venetian book-privilege granted to Giovanni Giolito the Younger and Giovanni Paolo Giolito in September 1585. On Diola's translation and its reception, see Federica Dallasta, 'Orazio Diola traduttore delle "Croniche de gli ordini instituiti da padre San Francesco" di Marcos de Lisboa (1581–1591) e la sua biblioteca', *Collectanea Franciscana*, 85 (2015), 523–93.

[79] Angelo Solerti, *Vita di Torquato Tasso*, 3 vols (Turin: Loescher, 1895), II.1, 42, no. LXVII. The same favour was requested in a letter of 27 January 1587: ibid., II.1, 45, no. LXXIII.

[80] Ibid., I, 511–12.

[81] *Gerusalemme liberata del sig. Torquato Tasso* (Parma: Erasmo Viotti, 1581), fol. +3$^{r-v}$; *Gerusalemme liberata del sig. Torquato Tasso* (Casalmaggiore: Antonio Canacci and Erasmo Viotti, 1581), fols +2$^v$–+3$^r$.

(And it is your most serene highness who must also protect and favour [the work], since, in order to publish it, there were some who took it under their protection; for the Marchioness of Soragna [. . .] intervened so successfully with this wise ruler [Alfonso] that, once every difficulty was overcome, I have even, after four months, brought [the work] to a state in which I can send it to your most serene highness.)

In the Parma edition alone, this letter is followed by another, addressed by Ingegneri to the marchioness herself and dated 1 March 1581. Here, too, Ingegneri's wording is unclear in some respects, but he implies that her intervention was crucial in persuading Duke Alfonso to allow these two editions to appear:

Hebbero finalmente le cortesi fatiche di V[ostra] S[ignoria] Illustriss[ima] quella ventura ch'era al valor dovuta di sì prudente negotiatione. Il Sig. Duca di Ferrara, a' preghi di questo,[82] si contentò, che la GERUSALEMME LIBERATA fosse stampata qui in Parma; et io, con tutto l'irrevocabile accordio, già fermatone a Casalmaggiore, volontieri mi rivolsi a questa doppia spesa, per non malusare d'un favore tanto degno e tanto importante. Di queste mille trecento copie adunque, ch'ei ne potrà legger di più, e 'n forma così gratiosa, habbia tutto l'obligo il Mondo a V[ostra] S[ignoria] Illustriss[ima]. La quale per sangue chiara e per beltà risplendente, è ben ragion che, per virtù incontemplabile, co 'l lume dell'infinita sua cortesia mostri all'altre principali Dame la strada, ond'esser da ogni cuore riverite, e celebrate da tutte le lingue.[83]

(Your courteous efforts finally met with the fortune deserved by the worthiness of such a prudent negotiation. The Duke of Ferrara, at your request, was pleased that the *Gerusalemme liberata* should be printed here in Parma. In view of the firm agreement already reached at Casalmaggiore, I was glad to undertake this double expense, in order not to abuse a favour so worthy and so important. Let everyone be therefore completely obliged to you for these 1300 further copies that they can read, and in such an elegant form. Since you are of high lineage and resplendent beauty, it is natural that, through a virtue above understanding, with the light of your infinite courtesy you should show other leading ladies the way to be revered by every heart and celebrated by every tongue.)

Lucrezia Marinella gave practical assistance to the printer-publisher Barezzo Barezzi when in 1606 he brought out an edition of Luigi

---

[82] I assume that 'questo' is intended to refer to the dedicatee; it may be an error for 'questa'.

[83] Parma edition, fol. +6ʳ. See also Solerti, *Vita di Torquato Tasso*, I, 331, for his interpretation of the marchioness's involvement, and II.2, 154–55, doc. CXLV, for the letter addressed to her; Stefano Andretta, *La venerabile superbia: ortodossia e trasgressione nella vita di suor Francesca Farnese (1593–1651)* (Turin: Rosenberg & Sellier, 1994), p. 56.

Tansillo's poem *Le lacrime di san Pietro*. As Barezzi explained in his letter to readers, she provided at his request verse summaries of the content of each canto (*argomenti*), prose summaries of their religious significance (*allegorie*) and an *allegoria universale* for the entire work.

## Dedications to Women

The most frequent way in which women, normally from the social elite, could contribute to the initial diffusion of texts on the part of male authors and publishers was through the mediating role that they might play as dedicatees when a text was presented to the public. Of course, this kind of involvement was of a different nature from the instances discussed so far: there, women were involved in publication at first hand, while in the case of dedications their support was being invoked by others who had the principal responsibility for publication.

In Renaissance Italy, most newly composed works and some older ones were sent out into the world, both in manuscript and in print, prefaced by a form of dedicatory address, 'To so-and-so', usually followed by a letter to the dedicatee that set out the reasons for which he or she had been chosen by the author, publisher or editor who signed the letter. The importance attached to the process was reflected increasingly, as the sixteenth century went on, by the advertising on title pages of the name of the person who was being honoured, and sometimes through the incorporation of his or her coat of arms, which of course demonstrated the person's nobility. An example is the title page of Laura Battiferri's *Primo libro dell'opere toscane*, mentioned above, of which over half is taken up by the name and arms of Eleonora de Toledo.

The framing of a work by means of a dedication was intended, in the first place, to form part of a social transaction between the dedicator and the recipient. Jason Scott-Warren has observed that 'Dedications are performative: their words, like the words of a promise or a bet, are deeds'.[84] One of the purposes of the deed was often to consolidate a relationship of patronage, or to seek to establish a new one, with a person of higher social status. A Paduan poet, Antonio Ongaro, summed up neatly the reasons for dedicating a work in his *Alceo favola pescatoria*, addressed to the brothers Girolamo and Michele Ruis:

> Per tre cause principali si sogliono dedicar l'opere, o per speranza di dover
> per mezo di essa dedicatione conseguir qualc'utile, o per render ricompensa

---

[84] Jason Scott-Warren, *Sir John Harington and the Book as Gift* (Oxford University Press, 2001), p. 2.

de' beneficii ricevuti, o per procacciare, per dir così, tutore ad esse opere. (Venice: Francesco Ziletti, 1582, fol. a2$^r$)

(Works are usually dedicated for three main reasons: either in the hope of obtaining some profit through the dedication, or to reward for benefits received, or to appoint a guardian, so to speak, for these works.)

To dedicate might indeed be a means of suggesting that patronage would be welcome, or it might be a means of showing gratitude to someone who had already provided support for the dedicator, including perhaps a subvention towards the costs of printing. Naturally, any hopes of reward were not to be mentioned openly in a dedicatory letter, lest the act of giving should seem self-seeking. However, such hopes might be mentioned in a private context.[85] A renowned author such as Torquato Tasso might even suggest how his dedicatee could best reciprocate. After offering the second volume of an edition of his *Rime* to Eleonora de' Medici, now Duchess of Mantua, with a letter dated 1 January 1593, he wrote to her again on 14 April to say that he had heard that she wanted to give him turquoises, but that he would prefer different jewels:

> Mi è stato detto, che Vostra Altezza disidera di donarmi due turchine. Io la ringrazio, quanto debbo, del buon animo, come farò d'ogn'altro favore che le piacerà di farmi: ma veramente le sarei più obligato se mi donasse un rubino ed una perla legata in oro; perché s'avenisse mai ch'io dovessi prender moglie, non mi mancherebbono con la sua grazia anella da sposarla: e senza questa occasione, sarebbono quasi un remedio a la maninconia.

> (I have been told that Your Highness wishes to give me two turquoises. I am duly grateful for your kindness, as I shall be for any other favour you are pleased to show me; but in truth I would be more obliged to you if you gave me a ruby and a pearl set in gold. If I were ever to take a wife, I would not lack, with your grace, rings to wed her; and if I did not have this opportunity, they would be like a cure for melancholy.)

---

[85] A frank reference to a male author's expectation of a contribution towards the cost of printing is found in a letter of Bernardino Daniello to Nicolò Guidiccioni, dated 13 October 1547, in which he writes of Duke Cosimo de' Medici: 'vedendo questo principe tutto rivolto a favorir le cose delle lettere, et a premiar le fatiche altrui, deliberai farli un presente di queste mie sopra Dante. [. . .] Ma avvertite, S[ign]or mio, che quello che io fo, lo fo con speranza di premio, per non haver io il modo di farlo imprimere, s'io non ne sono da S[ua] E[ccellentia] accommodato' (seeing this prince completely intent on supporting letters and rewarding the labours of others, I decided to present to him these labours of mine, [my commentary] on Dante. But take note that what I am doing, I do in the hope of reward, since I do not have the means to have it printed myself unless I have an arrangement with His Excellency). See the *Miscellanea letteraria pubblicata nell'occasione delle nozze Riccomanni-Fineschi*, ed. by Cesare Riccomanni (Turin: Vercellino, 1861), pp. 110–11.

The tone is light-hearted: the comment about marrying is, of course, made tongue in cheek. But a poet of Tasso's status could, in effect, name his price; and after some months, it seems, his wish was granted.[86]

A dedication of a work, especially in a printed edition, was, however, not only a private transaction: it was also a 'public gift', as we saw Maddalena Campiglia called it, and as Natalie Davis has observed in relation to France in this period.[87] Girolamo Ruscelli addressed the first of his many dedications in 1551 to a count, Vinciguerra di Collalto, but also through him to others: 'a Vostra Signoria, o più tosto al mondo sotto il suo nome' (to Your Lordship, or rather to the world under your name).[88] Scott-Warren, writing of early modern books-as-gifts and the use of the familiar letter in book presentation, comments perceptively on the 'complex, triangular relationships' between writers, dedicatees and other readers:

> Gift-books and epistles both furnish occasions for self-accounting which, because they are produced between seeming intimates, make special claims to authenticity and evidentiality. [. . .] [S]uch books enable their writers to impress an audience beyond their recipients with statements which appear disinterested and therefore encourage assent.[89]

Dedications to individuals, and the endorsements that they seemed to imply on the part of those individuals, had wider and longer-term persuasive functions in the eyes of the potential and actual readers placed at the third vertex of the triangle. Acts of dedication could enhance the prestige and authority of the work and of its author through association with the prestige and the authority of the dedicatee, which in turn the dedication helped to publicize.

As Ongaro pointed out in identifying his third reason for dedicating, authors often expressed a hope that the protection of their patron would have an apotropaic power, shielding them from potential critics.[90] Thus

---

[86] Torquato Tasso, *Delle rime*, 2 vols (Brescia: Pietro Maria Marchetti, 1592–93), II, fols +2ʳ–+3ᵛ. See Tasso, *Lettere*, ed. by Cesare Guasti, 5 vols (Florence: Le Monnier, 1852–55), V, letter 1453 (14 April 1593), p. 146; letter 1470 (10 July 1593), pp. 156–57; letter 1476 (20 November 1593), pp. 160–61.

[87] Davis, 'Beyond the Market: Books as Gifts in Sixteenth-Century France', pp. 73–81. On dedications in Italy, see Marco Paoli, *La dedica: storia di una strategia editoriale (Italia, secoli XVI–XIX)* (Lucca: Pacini Fazzi, 2009); Richardson, *Manuscript Culture in Renaissance Italy*, pp. 198–225; Antonella Orlandi, 'Donne nelle dediche', in *La donna nel Rinascimento meridionale: atti del convegno internazionale (Roma 11–13 novembre 2009)*, ed. by Marco Santoro (Pisa and Rome: Fabrizio Serra, 2010), pp. 383–92.

[88] Girolamo Ruscelli, *Dediche e avvisi ai lettori*, ed. by Antonella Iacono and Paolo Marini (Manziana: Vecchiarelli, 2011), p. 2.

[89] Scott-Warren, *Sir John Harington and the Book as Gift*, p. 17.

[90] The definition of *dedicare* in the first edition of the *Vocabolario degli Accademici della Crusca* (Venice: Giovanni Alberti, 1612) alludes to this latter motive in its concluding phrase: 'offerire,

the young Rinaldo Corso, presenting his *Dichiaratione fatta sopra la seconda parte delle Rime della divina Vittoria Collonna* in 1542 to the poet Veronica Gambara, addressed this envoy to his writings:

> voi fatiche mie per le man de gli huomini andate secure da gli empi morsi dell'altrui invidie, portando in fronte dipinto il nome, ch'io sempre nel core porto con somma riverenza scolpito, di VERONICA Gambara da Correggio chiarissimo splendore del femminil sesso, e dell'età nostra.[91]

> (you, my labours, go through men's hands safe from the cruel criticisms of the envy of others, bearing on your forehead the name that I ever bear engraved in my heart with the greatest reverence, Veronica Gambara of Correggio, shining splendour of womanhood and of our age.)

Alessandro Piccolomini's *Cento sonetti* (Rome: Vincenzo Valgrisi, 1549) has a long dedicatory letter (fols *4ʳ–A8ʳ) addressed by the author to Vittoria Colonna, niece of the poet of the same name.[92] His main subject is the praise of poetry, but he concludes by explaining why he is sending his sonnets to her. At first Piccolomini says he has no need of any protection, disingenuously adopting the pose of someone entrusting the poems to a single copy, as if this were a case of transmission by manuscript intended only for her, a recipient whose critical judgement is shrewd yet benign. In the end, though, he invokes the protection of Colonna in preference to enlisting the example of great poets in self-defence:

> Vi mando dunque, quali essi si sieno, cento de' miei sonetti; e portator di quelli sarà il molto servitor vostro e amico mio, messer Pavolo de' Ricciardi [...]. Nè penso io di dare a questi miei sonetti arme defensiva contra le calumnie, che qual si voglia maligno osasse voler dar loro. Prima perché io mi persuado che non habbino d'andare in altre mani che di voi, la quale, sì come stimo giuditiosissima a cognoscere ogni loro fallo, così a l'incontro per sua benignità a perdonarlo e scusarlo giudico attissima a maraviglia. Di poi, quando ben per sorte venisser a le mani d'alcuno il quale, o con dire che

e donare altrui qualche opera, e particolarmente chiese, o libri, o statue, ponendovi il nome di colui, a cui ella s'intitola, per onorarlo, e per ottener la sua protezione' (to offer and give to another some work, and especially churches or books or statues, placing on it the name of the person to whom it is dedicated, to honour him and to obtain his protection). Roger Chartier cites a similar definition of *dédicace* from Antoine Furetière's *Dictionnaire universel* of 1690: see his *Forms and Meanings*, p. 29.

[91] Cited from the edition of Bologna: Giovanni Battista Faelli, 1543, fol. A3ᵛ. The work was first published in Bologna by Bartolomeo Bonardo in the previous year: see Sarah Christopher Faggioli, 'Di un'edizione del 1532 della "Dichiaratione" di Rinaldo Corso alle Rime spirituali di Vittoria Colonna', *GSLI*, 191 (2014), 200–10. Gambara may well have supported the printing venture, since Corso was only about seventeen years old.

[92] See also Alessandro Piccolomini, *Cento sonetti*, ed. by Franco Tomasi (Geneva: Droz, 2015), pp. 47–56.

l'intessimento de le rime, così de' terzetti come de' quartetti, o qualche
vocabolo che gli paia nuovo non gli sodisfaccia, o per qual si voglia altro
defetto, mi giudicasse degno di reprensione, io non voglio con l'essempio
o del Petrarca o de la Marchesa di Pescara o del Bembo, come potrei (i quali
tre Poeti stimo io sopra tutti gli altri de' nostri tempi), o in qual si voglia altra
maniera cercar di defendermi; ma solo mi basta, per securezza mia, la
confidanza che tengo che, havendo io fatto dono de' miei sonetti a voi,
e sotto la vostra protettione mandatovegli, non sarà huomo alcuno che
ardisca pur offendergli col pensiero. (fol. A7$^{r-v}$)

(I thus send you one hundred of my sonnets, whatever they are worth; and
they will be brought by your devoted servant and my friend, Paolo Ricciardi
[. . .]. Nor do I intend to give these sonnets of mine a weapon to defend
them from the calumnies that some malicious person might dare to wish to
make against them. First, because I am sure that they will go into no other
hands but yours, and just as I believe you most judicious in recognizing each
of their defects, so on the other hand I judge you marvellously able to
pardon and excuse them through your kindness. Then, even if by chance
they were to come into the hands of someone who judged me worthy of
reprehension, because of the combination of the rhymes in the tercets and
quatrains or because he is dissatisfied by some word that seems new to him,
I do not wish to defend myself, as I could, with the example of Petrarch or
the Marchioness of Pescara [Vittoria Colonna] or Bembo (the three poets
I esteem above all others of our times) or in any other way. For my security,
it is enough that I am confident that no one will dare to harm them even in
thought, once I have made a gift of my sonnets to you and sent them to you
under your protection.)

A further example comes from the dedication of Laura Terracina's *Settime
rime* of 1561, mentioned above, to Maria Anna de la Cueva: 'la supplico, che
come giudiciosa Signora, et di soprema bontà voglia benignamente accet-
tarle, et quella protettione prenderne, che di cosa sua propria farebbe, che
già questa sua è, et non più mia' (fol. A4$^v$; I beg you, as a lady of good
judgement and supreme goodness, to accept [the poems] favourably and
offer them the same protection you would give to something of your own –
for indeed this is now yours and no longer mine).

Another aspect of the relationship between dedicatees and other readers was implied rather than explicit, but was nonetheless of the highest
importance. Dedicatees would have been selected as primary readers who
would establish, in the eyes of the public, a clear link between the work
and the contemporary world and who, within that world, would stand as
the epitome, the ideal living embodiment, of the qualities of the wider
category of secondary readers for whom dedicators intended the work.
From this perspective, the decision to choose a woman, rather than

a man, as the focal point of the readership would have been taken with very careful consideration.

The number of dedicatory letters to women in the sixteenth century is higher than one might expect if one were to consider only the subordinate role that society allotted to most of them. In a sample of 1,400 sixteenth-century editions printed in small formats (octavo, duodecimo and sixteens), nearly 10 per cent of the dedications were addressed to one or more women, mainly from the upper classes of northern and central Italy.[93] Similarly, of 238 vernacular editions printed by Francesco Osanna of Mantua between 1573 and 1600, twenty-four were dedicated to women, principally noble-women associated with the ducal court.[94] Another indication of the ratio of female to male dedicatees can be derived from the anthologies of dedicatory letters composed in the period 1501–1607 that were published by Comin Ventura in no fewer than thirty volumes between 1601 and 1608.[95] Many originate from Ventura's own city of Bergamo, but they provide a broad sample of the genre. Out of 551 letters, 77 (nearly 14 per cent) are addressed to living women. All these samples thus give results similar to an estimate made by Jaynie Anderson that 10 per cent of the patrons of art in Florence and Venice in the fifteenth and sixteenth centuries were female.[96]

Why should women have been chosen as dedicatees in preference to men? It was natural that they were frequently offered works that were expected to appeal particularly to female readers.[97] Prominent among these were works of prayer and spirituality, since women were expected to be especially devout. An example is the *Doi aurei opuscoli* by St Thomas Aquinas (Perugia: Girolamo Cartolari, 1510), whose title page announces its dedication by the translator, the Dominican theologian Gaspare da Perugia, to his niece Teodora, a Dominican tertiary and sister of the printer. Works on the excellence of women lent themselves logically to presentation to a lady who could be seen as a shining

---

[93] Xenia von Tippelskirch, *Sotto controllo: letture femminili in Italia nella prima età moderna* (Rome: Viella, 2011), p. 195; see pp. 194–200 for a survey of dedications to women, their motivation and the problem of assessing their reception by the dedicatees.

[94] Valentina Sonzini, 'Il sistema delle dediche nella produzione degli Osanna: le donne Gonzaga nella storia della stampa cinquecentesca mantovana', in *Donne Gonzaga a corte: reti istituzionali, pratiche culturali e affari di governo*, ed. by Chiara Continisio and Raffaele Tamalio (Rome: Bulzoni, 2018), pp. 417–29.

[95] On these collections, see Gianmaria Savoldelli and Roberta Frigeni, *Comin Ventura: tra lettere e libri di lettere (1579–1617)* (Florence: Olschki, 2017). See also Paoli, *La dedica*, pp. 167–98, 378–90.

[96] Jaynie Anderson, 'Rewriting the History of Art Patronage', *Renaissance Studies*, 10 (1996), 129–38 (p. 131).

[97] For indications of the genres of books dedicated to women and for further examples, see Cox, *Women's Writing in Italy*, pp. 95–96; Brian Richardson, *Printing, Writers and Readers in Renaissance Italy* (Cambridge University Press, 1999), pp. 144–45, 147–48; Richardson, 'Advising on Women's Conduct in Renaissance Paratexts', in *Conduct Literature for and about Women in Italy, 1470–1900: Prescribing and Describing Life*, ed. by Helena Sanson and Francesco Lucioli (Paris: Classiques Garnier, 2016), pp. 225–39.

example of the virtues of her sex.[98] Women were seen as appropriate dedicatees for some works in the vernacular concerning heterosexual love by Petrarch and Boccaccio, the two great authors of the generation after Dante.[99] These works were read by educated men and women alike and were widely imitated as literary and linguistic models. It was also natural to associate women with translations into the vernacular, since these could be conceived in part for a female readership that had little or no knowledge of the original language. Examples include the versions of Virgil's *Aeneid*, Books I–VI, that were made around 1539, with each book addressed by its translator to an individual lady.[100] Some of the books were copied by hand or printed individually, and all of them were dedicated to Aurelia Tolomei by Vincenzo di Pers in a six-volume Venetian edition of 1540, *I sei primi libri del Eneide di Virgilio*, printed by Comin da Trino at the instance of Nicolò Zoppino.[101] Among more practical books, those containing advice on marriage, on bringing up children or on the household were often presented to women.

It was much less common for philosophical or scientific books to be addressed to women, but there are exceptions. One is Ludovico Bonaccioli's

[98] For further examples, see the bibliography of works on the excellence of women in Francine Daenens, 'Superiore perché inferiore: il paradosso della superiorità della donna in alcuni trattati italiani del Cinquecento', in *Trasgressione tragica e norma domestica: esemplari di tipologie femminili della letteratura europea*, ed. by Vanna Gentili (Rome: Edizioni di Storia e Letteratura, 1983), pp. 11–50 (pp. 41–50), and Androniki Dialeti, 'The Publisher Gabriel Giolito de' Ferrari, Female Readers, and the Debate about Women in Sixteenth-Century Italy', *Renaissance and Reformation*, 28 (2004), 5–32.

[99] For example, Giovanni Andrea Gesualdo's edition of Petrarch's vernacular poetry, 1533, dedicated to Maria de Cardona; Tizzone Gaetano's editions of Boccaccio's *Fiammetta*, 1524, dedicated to Dorotea Gonzaga, and of Boccaccio's *Filocolo*, 1527, dedicated to Camilla Bentivoglio (in contrast, his translation of Vegetius, *De l'arte militare*, and his edition of Boccaccio's epic poem *Teseida* were dedicated to Dorotea's brothers); and Francesco Sansovino's edition of Boccaccio's *Ameto*, 1545, dedicated to Gaspara Stampa.

[100] The books are addressed as follows: I, Alessandro Sansedoni to Aurelia Tolomei de' Borghesi; II, Ippolito de' Medici to Giulia Gonzaga; III, Bernardino de' Borghesi to Giulia Petrucci; IV, Bartolomeo Carli Piccolomini to Aurelia Petrucci; V, Aldobrando Cerretani to Girolama Carli Piccolomini; VI, Alessandro Piccolomini to Frasia (Eufrasia) Venturi.

[101] On this enterprise see Luciana Borsetto, *L'"Eneida" tradotta: riscritture poetiche del testo di Virgilio nel XVI secolo* (Milan: Unicopli, 1989), pp. 27–36, 157–58, 180–82; Cox, *Women's Writing in Italy*, p. 96; Marie-Françoise Piéjus, *Visages et paroles de femmes dans la littérature italienne de la Renaissance* (Paris: Université Paris III Sorbonne Nouvelle, 2009), p. 56, n. 16; Lorenzo Baldacchini, *Alle origini dell'editoria in volgare: Niccolò Zoppino da Ferrara a Venezia. Annali (1503–1544)* (Manziana: Vecchiarelli, 2011), cat. nos. 410–15, pp. 321–24; Konrad Eisenbichler, *The Sword and the Pen: Women, Politics, and Poetry in Sixteenth-Century Siena* (University of Toronto Press, 2012), pp. 22–23, 69–71. Scribal publication no doubt preceded or accompanied print publication in some cases: for example, Alessandro Piccolomini's version of Book VI is found in New York, Columbia University, Rare Book and Manuscript Library, MS Lodge 1. Eisenbichler also discusses Alessandro Piccolomini's dedication to Eufrasia Venturi of his translation of Xenophon's *Oeconomicon* (pp. 23–25).

Latin treatise on gynaecology and obstetrics, the *Enneas muliebris* ([Ferrara: Lorenzo Rossi, 1502?]; the title alludes to the division of the work into nine chapters). The author was the doctor of Lucrezia Borgia, and he dedicated the work to her, probably soon after she arrived in Ferrara in 1502 as the bride of Duke Alfonso d'Este. (The duchess had a reading knowledge of Latin.[102]) In the preface addressed to Lucrezia, Bonaccioli praises her fine qualities:

> Etenim uni tibi regia maiestate, maximo rerum usu, incomparabili prudentia, admirabili facundia, promptissimo ingenio, castissima eruditione, suprema gloria, incredibili fœlicitate (dum summo in Alexandro pontifice tui patriaeque patre consenescunt) unice pollere datum est. (fol. A2$^v$)

> (For it is given to you alone to be especially strong in queenly majesty, the greatest experience, incomparable prudence, admirable eloquence, the readiest intelligence, the purest learning, supreme glory, incredible felicity (while these qualities grow old together in the great pope Alexander, father of yourself and of the fatherland).)

Bonaccioli goes on to explain that he has no choice but to entrust his work to the duchess as if it were a patient under her medical care:

> At quanto e vinctis tuis uni causatius iustiusque tu mihi, mulierum decus, litteratorum columen, succenseas, si et re medica tibi devinctus autoratusque et testimonio tuo saepissime venustatus, patrocinio adiutus, auctoritate supra modum servatus, lucubrationes meas subcisivis temporibus curata (qualescumque sint) sine tuo auspicio prodire suamque tibi salutem non commendare commisero? (fol. A3$^v$)

> (But with how much greater reason and more justly would you be angry with me alone, among those bound to you, glory of women and pillar of men of letters, if I – who am devoted and obliged to you in medical matters, frequently enriched by your attestations, helped by your patronage and protected beyond measure by your authority – entrusted my lucubrations, such as they are, that I have cared for in my leisure time, to go forth without your blessing and not to commit their health to you?)

In 1531 Agostino Nifo dedicated his twin Latin treatises *De Pulchro et Amore* (Rome: Antonio Blado) to the young Giovanna d'Aragona, Princess of Tagliacozzo, born around 1502 and the wife of Ascanio Colonna. Giovanna is described as the epitome of beauty in two letters

---

[102] Ferdinand Gregorovius, *Lucrezia Borgia nach Urkunden und Korrespondenzen ihrer eigenen Zeit*, 5th edn (Stuttgart and Berlin: Cotta, 1911), pp. 37–38.

that open the first edition, one addressed to Nifo by Cardinal Pompeo
Colonna, who commissioned the work, the other a briefer letter of
dedication from Nifo to Giovanna. Colonna depicts the princess as
'veluti divinitatis aemula' (like a rival of divinity), endowed with both
physical beauty and exceptional virtues. Nifo also praises her 'pulchri-
tudo' (beauty), 'qua sola inspecta atque adamusim explicata, liber non
modo pulcher, verumetiam admiratione dignus redditur' (by whose
vision and accurate exposition this book is rendered not only beautiful
but also worthy of admiration).[103] Another exceptional 'scientific' dedication, more striking because the recipient is praised not merely for her
beauty, is that of Alessandro Piccolomini's astronomical treatises (1540),
discussed below. The *Discorsi sopra le metheore d'Aristotele, ridotti in
dialogo et divisi in quattro giornate* by Niccolò Vito di Gozze (Nikola
Vitov Gučetić, 1549–1610), printed in Venice by Francesco Ziletti with
the dates 1584 and 1585, is particularly unusual because the letter of
dedication is signed by the author's wife, Maria Gondola (Marija
Gondulić) and addressed to another noblewoman of Ragusa (modern
Dubrovnik), Fiore Zuzori (Cvijeta Zuzorić).[104] Gondola states in this
lengthy letter, dated 15 July 1582 (fols *2ʳ–**4ᵛ), that her husband had
presented the work to her. Zuzori is described as 'non men bella che
virtuosa, e gentil donna' (a lady no less beautiful than virtuous and
noble), and Gondola hopes that this combination of qualities will help
to defend the work against its detractors. She does so, writing,

> avenga che molti potriano maravigliarsi della cagione che mi mosse di far
> uscire questi presenti discorsi sotto la protettione o difesa del sesso feminile,
> credendosi eglino forse che, sì come noi per natura non siamo habili
> all'essercitio dell'armi, così ancora naturalmente siamo prive della capacità
> delle scienze e cognitione delle cose, et che allontanate siamo da i costumi
> delle virtù morali. (fol. *4ʳ)

> (although many may be surprised at my reason for publishing these dis-
> courses under the protection or defence of the feminine sex. Perhaps they
> believe that, just as we are by nature unsuited to carrying arms, so we
> naturally have no capacity for sciences and the knowledge of the world,
> and that we are distanced from the customs of moral virtues.)

---

[103] Agostino Nifo, *De Pulchro et Amore*, ed. and trans. by Laurence Boulègue, 2 vols (Paris: Les Belles
Lettres, 2003–11), I, 2–7. Chapter 5 of *De Pulchro* is dedicated to praise of Giovanna's beauty. Her
education is likely to have included Latin: Nifo, *De Pulchro et Amore*, I, lxix.

[104] On this work, see the catalogue entry by Anna Laura Puliafito in *Venezia e Aristotele (ca. 1450–ca.
1600): greco, latino e italiano*, ed. by Alessio Cotugno and David A. Lines (Venice: Marcianum Press,
2016), pp. 66–67.

This opinion, Zuzori believes, arises only out of long-standing prejudice among men; it is impossible to say that one sex is more perfect than the other. However, she goes on to develop a detailed thesis in favour of the superiority of women, arguing for instance that their physical beauty is a reflection of their spiritual beauty.

The attributes or qualities that were looked for in female dedicatees did not necessarily include financial resources. The women selected were often married, or young and yet to be married, whereas female patrons of art and architecture tended to be widows or nuns, because they had greater freedom than married women to give commissions.[105] The most obvious quality sought after was high, even very high, social rank. Francesco Sansovino offered his collection of *Cento novelle scelte da i più nobili scrittori*, printed by himself (Venice, 1561), to Queen Elizabeth of England ('Isabella', as he calls her), known to all her subjects, he writes, as 'humanissima quanto a Principe si conviene, et affabile quanto si ricerca a valorosa giovane e chiara' (fol. *2ᵛ; as benevolent as befits a ruler, and as good-natured as a valorous and famous young lady should be). Sansovino must have felt that sales of his volume would benefit from its being represented as one that a queen could pick up in her occasional moments of leisure, since 'a i Re posti in altissimo luogo, non si disdice talhora spogliandosi della lor gravità, conversar famigliarmente et discorrere con huomini bassi et particolari per alleggerir qualche volta il peso delle lor importanti faccende' (it is not unfitting for the highest-placed rulers, casting aside their seriousness from time to time, to converse familiarly and talk with those of low and private station, in order to lighten now and then the burden of their important tasks). But Sansovino probably received no thanks or reward from Elizabeth, since the revised edition that he published in the following year has a male dedicatee.

If a female consort was chosen as dedicatee, in many cases she was doubtless seen as a channel through which the dedicator could influence her husband. In a letter addressed to Queen Isabella of Portugal, wife of the Holy Roman Emperor, Charles V, placed at the start of Pietro Aretino's *I quattro libri della humanità di Christo* (Venice: Francesco Marcolini, 1538), the author is

---

[105] Anderson, 'Rewriting the History of Art Patronage', p. 136. For a comparison of commissions for art and architecture originating from wives and widows, see Catherine King, *Renaissance Women Patrons: Wives and Widows in Italy, c. 1300–c. 1550* (Manchester University Press, 1998). See also *Wives, Widows, Mistresses, and Nuns in Early Modern Italy: Making the Invisible Visible through Art and Patronage*, ed. by Katherine A. McIver (Farnham: Ashgate, 2012).

typically frank about using her simply as an intermediary in order to influence
favourably the true dedicatee, the emperor himself.[106] He writes:

> io non per cupidità di fama, non per pompa di virtù, non per isperanza di
> premio, ma per ispiratione divina, per consenso fatale, e perché debbo farlo,
> intitolo i quattro libri de l'humanità di Christo a la christianità del vostro
> omnipotente consorte, e la porgo a voi che sète degna, a voi che sète giusta,
> a voi che sète pia, acciò la sua maestà dignissima, giustissima, e piatosissima
> riceva con più fervore le carte divote che divotamente vi appresento.
> (fol. A3$^r$)

> (Not out of desire for fame, not for an outward show of virtue, not in hope
> of reward, but by divine inspiration, by a fated agreement and because
> I must do it, I dedicate the four books of the humanity of Christ to the
> Christianity of your all-powerful consort. I offer it to you who are worthy, to
> you who are just, to you who are pious, so that his most worthy, most just
> and most pious majesty may receive more fervently the devout pages that
> I devotedly present to you.)

However, consorts of male rulers sometimes achieved a high degree of
political authority in the sixteenth century, acting as interim rulers if their
husbands were absent or if their sons had not yet come of age, and they
could also wield considerable power as cultural patrons; indeed, consorts
often came from families more influential and wealthy than those of their
husbands, who had married 'upwards' in order to increase their political
status. In Torquato Tasso's dedication of the second volume of his *Rime*
mentioned above, Eleonora de' Medici's ancestry is seen as the source of
her grace and authority:

> Vostra Altezza è nata di quella nobilissima progenie, a la quale non hanno
> minor obbligo le Toscane lettere, che l'arme, o l'imperio di Toscana, perché
> l'une, e l'altre dal Gran Duca suo Padre, e suo Avolo, e da gli altri suoi
> antecessori sono state a somma dignità essaltate. Là onde non è alcuna poesia,
> o altra compositione così illustre in questa lingua, che dalla sua gratia, e dalla
> sua autorità non possa esser maggiormente illustrata. (fol. +2$^{r-v}$)

> (Your Highness is born of that most noble lineage to which Tuscan
> literature is no less indebted than the arms or rule of Tuscany, because
> both have been raised to the highest rank by the Grand Duke your father,
> and your grandfather, and by your other ancestors. Hence there is no poetry

---

[106] On this letter, see Élise Boillet, 'L'Arétin et l'actualité des années 1538–1539: les attentes du "Fléau
des princes"', in *L'Actualité et sa mise en écriture dans l'Italie des XV$^e$–XVII$^e$ siècles*, ed. by
Danielle Boillet and Corinne Lucas (Paris: Université Paris III Sorbonne Nouvelle, 2005), pp.
103–17 (pp. 109–10).

or other composition so illustrious in this language that it cannot be made more illustrious by your grace and authority.)

Yet a woman of lower social status might possess personal talent that attracted the attention of a dedicator. To Gaspara Stampa, born into the Paduan middle classes (her father was a jewel merchant), Francesco Sansovino offered three editions in 1545, when she was about twenty-two years old.[107] Stampa's skills as a singer were already well known by then, and she had probably also begun to establish her reputation as a talented and innovative poet. Sansovino describes her as a 'valorosissima Giovane' in his edition of Benedetto Varchi's *Lettura* [...] *sopra un sonetto della gelosia di mons. Dalla Casa fatta nella celebratissima Accademia de gl'Infiammati a Padova* (Mantua: [Venturino Ruffinelli]). He represents Stampa as an arbiter of the excellence of the writing of Varchi and Della Casa, since 'assai sé terranno amendui lodati, quando essi sapranno le cose loro, da voi lodatissima esser et lette, et havute care, conciosia che 'l valore et il purgatissimo giudicio vostro di gran lunga avanzi la lode comune' (fol. A2$^{r-v}$; they will both consider themselves praised greatly when they know that their writings have been both read and appreciated by you, the object of much praise, since your worth and most purified judgement greatly exceeds common praise). The two other editions dedicated to Stampa by Sansovino in this year were a work by the most esteemed vernacular prose writer, Boccaccio's *Ameto, comedia delle nimphe fiorentine* (Venice: Gabriele Giolito),[108] and Sansovino's own *Ragionamento d'amore, nel quale brevemente s'insegna a' giovani huomini la bella arte d'amore* ([Venice: Giovanni Griffio il vecchio]). Although the title of the latter work presents it as an *ars amatoria* intended for the instruction of young men, the author claims in his letter to Stampa that he is sending it to her so that, with its help,

> possiate imparar a fuggir gli inganni che usano i perversi uomini alle candide e pure donzelle, come voi sète. E con questa vi ammaestro e vi consiglio a procedere ne' vostri gloriosi studi, fuggendo ogni occasione che disturbar vi potesse dalla impresa vostra.[109]

(you may learn to avoid the deceits used by wicked men on innocent and pure maidens such as you. And with this I instruct and advise you to proceed

---

[107] Jane Tylus, 'Volume Editor's Introduction', in Gaspara Stampa, *The Complete Poems: The 1554 Edition of the 'Rime', a Bilingual Edition*, ed. by Troy Tower and Jane Tylus, intro. and trans. by Jane Tylus (University of Chicago Press, 2010), pp. 1–45 (pp. 6–8).

[108] Bongi, *Annali di Gabriel Giolito*, I, 90–91; Giovanni Boccaccio, *Comedia delle ninfe fiorentine (Ameto)*, ed. by Antonio Enzo Quaglio (Florence: Sansoni, 1963), pp. xxiii–xxiv.

[109] *Trattati d'amore del Cinquecento*, ed. by Giuseppe Zonta (Bari: Laterza, 1912), pp. 183–84 (p. 184).

with your glorious studies, avoiding any occasion that might distract you from your undertaking.)

Sansovino pays tribute to Gaspara's brother Baldassare, who had died recently, and he did no doubt genuinely wish to praise her as well. At the same time, he seems to be playing a clever game, aiming his work at readers of both sexes and showing sympathy with the viewpoints of both sides. Two years later, the composer Perissone Cambio chose Stampa as dedicatee of his *Primo libro di madrigali a quattro voci* (Venice: Antonio Gardane). He highlighted her musical talent, writing of 'i mille, e mille spirti gentili, et nobili: i quali udito havendo i dolci concenti vostri, v'hanno dato nome di divina sirena' (the thousands upon thousands of honourable and noble spirits who, after hearing your sweet song, have given you the reputation of divine siren), but he also mentioned 'le sue rare virtù et bellezze' (your rare virtues and beauty).

An author could address a woman who did not belong to the highest social class in the hope that she could have influence over a more senior figure whose patronage was sought. The Florentine author Niccolò Martelli makes it clear in his first volume of *Lettere*, printed in 1546, that Maddalena (sometimes known as Elena) Bonaiuti, the young second wife of the exiled Florentine poet Luigi Alamanni, had played a very useful role as an intermediary between himself and her mistress, the Dauphine of France, Catherine de' Medici. His dedicatory letter to Bonaiuti mentions that two years previously she had introduced him to Catherine so that he could present a manuscript work to her; and a letter to Bonaiuti within the collection reveals that Catherine had given him 100 scudi, which allowed him to return to Italy 'più accomodatamente' (in greater comfort).[110]

Yet the authors, publishers and others who dedicated books to elite women, and thus sought to associate them with the diffusion of their books, would often claim that these women were appreciated not merely because of their social prestige or their connections, but also because of the intrinsic qualities that made them models of exemplary behaviour. We have already seen an instance of this kind of praise in the letter to Isabella Pallavicino Lupi mentioned near the end of the previous section. Men's descriptions of virtues such as those attributed to her and others

---

[110] Niccolò Martelli, *Il primo libro delle lettere* (Florence: [Antonfrancesco Doni] for the author, 1546), fols A3ᵛ, I4ᵛ–KIʳ (letter of 30 October 1543). See also Henri Hauvette, *Un exilé florentin à la cour de France au XVIᵉ siècle: Luigi Alamanni (1495–1556). Sa vie et son œuvre* (Paris: Hachette, 1903), p. 133. Brucioli had dedicated to Maddalena the *Decameron* printed by Gabriele Giolito in 1542, using a slightly adapted version of his dedicatory letter of 1538 to Alvisia Gonzaga Pallavicino: see Bongi, *Annali di Gabriel Giolito*, I, 42.

seem to constitute, in part, a means for them to construct an ideal social identity for women. Virtues of the intellect and the spirit could, of course, also be praised in male dedicatees, but dedications to men tend to pay attention to their deeds in the public sphere as well as, or even rather than, to their characters.

One quality that was highly valued in women dedicatees was a reputation for an interest in culture. Isabella d'Este's secretary Mario Equicola wrote, in the autograph dedicatory letter of an Italian translation of the *Imagines* of Philostratus, of how the marchioness was promoting the study of both Latin and Greek literature: 'Tu per più prompta retornare alli debiti officii dai per ocio alle lettere latine intensa opera [...] et hora per publica utilità di fare interpretare le cose greche procuri' (In order to return more promptly to your duties, you study Latin literature intensely in your leisure; [...] and now you are having Greek works translated for the public benefit).[111] Nicolò Liburnio praised Isabella for cultivating poetry when dedicating the printed edition of his *Selvette* in 1513. She was of course 'd'alta chiarezza di sangue uscita' (descended from high lineage), but moreover:

> Per via [...] tale di salire al Cielo instruitati, o che 'l fusse magisterio della secreta natura, o ver de' tuoi gloriosi maggiori singulare institutione, possesse l'opere al sesso più infermo pertinenti, per insino già da gli anni più teneri cominciasti la divinità di Poesia coltivare, et di cadauna altra liberale disceplina gli aurei frutti cupidissimamente abbracciare. Dindi è che in terra d'Italia, huomo alcuno ben dottrinato non ce ne sia, il quale non ricorra per disio di contemplarti, et con merite riverenze salutarti.[112]

> (Having educated yourself in the path that leads up to heaven, whether it was through the teaching of your inner nature or the singular ordainment of your glorious ancestors, you passed over the works that belong to the weaker sex and already from your tenderest years you started to cultivate the divinity of poetry and to embrace with the greatest eagerness the golden fruits of every other liberal discipline. Hence there is no learned man anywhere in Italy who does not repeatedly desire to contemplate you and greet you with deserved reverence.)

Some dedications invite participation in the correction of a work, and very occasionally such invitations are addressed to women.[113] An example is

[111] Cambridge, University Library, MS Add. 6007. See Cesare Foligno, 'Di alcuni codici gonzagheschi ed estensi appartenuti all'abate Canonici', *Il libro e la stampa*, n.s., 1, fasc. 3 (1907), 69–75; Michael Koortbojian and Ruth Webb, 'Isabella d'Este's Philostratos', *Journal of the Warburg and Courtauld Institutes*, 56 (1993), 260–67, Plate 43b.
[112] (Venice: Giacomo Penzio, 1513), fol. A1ʳ.
[113] Richardson, *Manuscript Culture in Renaissance Italy*, pp. 211–14. Rosangela Fanara has shown that Sannazaro's dedication of his verse to Cassandra Marchese probably related to the printed edition of

an edition of Boccaccio's *Fiammetta* printed in Venice by Bernardino
Vitali in 1524. Tizzone Gaetano, who prepared the text for publication,
offered it to Dorotea Gonzaga, a member of the aristocracy of northern
Italy by birth and married to a nobleman from the Kingdom of Naples,
Gianfrancesco Acquaviva. In his letter to Gonzaga, Gaetano seeks, at least
ostensibly, to involve her both practically and intellectually as instigator of
the edition and co-editor. In return for his gift, he asks just two things of
her: that she might say in public that 'Io come quella che commandar li
poteva, quel che ha fatto gli ordinai' (As she who could command him,
I ordered him to do what he has done), and that she might make up 'col
vostro ingegno' (with your intelligence) for what is lacking in his.
Nevertheless, just in case she does not grant his wishes, he says he is leaving
wide margins so that expert readers can bring the text back 'al pristino
luogo suo' (to its original state).[114]

Alessandro Piccolomini chose to dedicate the edition of his two astronomical treatises, *De la sfera del mondo* and *Le stelle fisse* (Venice: Giovanni
Antonio and Domenico Volpini for Andrea Arrivabene, 1540), to the
Sienese poet Laudomia Forteguerri chiefly because she stood out as
a shining example to men and women alike on account of her intellectual
curiosity, although she is also praised for her beauty.[115] In his letter to her
(fols +3ʳ–+4ᵛ), Piccolomini recounts that he has heard of Forteguerri's
unhappiness at the fact that, as a woman, she has been unable to devote
her time to the study of knowledge and to learn Latin, still an essential tool
for learning. This leads him to burst into a tribute to her that is in effect an
exhortation to all readers to follow the example of her thirst for knowledge:

> O Nobilissimo e ben purgato Spirto di Donna, Animo veramente saggio,
> e sol degno di così honorata veste quanto le più rare bellezze che mai fusser
> viste lo cingon dattorno: questa si può chiamar Donna senza alcun dubio
> immortale, che de l'ardente desio del sapere s'infiamma e s'accende, il qual
> desio gli huomini stessi salvo che pochi, con l'acque de l'otio e de la poca
> religione d'ammorzar cercan con ogni studio; però che [. . .] chiudendo gli

1530: 'Sulla struttura del *Canzoniere* di J. Sannazaro: posizione e funzione della dedica a Cassandra
Marchese', *Critica letteraria*, 35 (2007), 267–76.

[114] Elena Cursi, '"Per certo donna Fiammetta veggio voi non havere letto gli *Asolani* del Bembo":
lettere di dedica e postille nelle edizioni del primo Cinquecento dell'*Elegia di Madonna Fiammetta*',
*Studi sul Boccaccio*, 36 (2008), 39–61 (pp. 48–51).

[115] On Forteguerri, see Robin, *Publishing Women*, pp. 124–59; Eisenbichler, *The Sword and the Pen*, pp.
25–26, 101–63. Piccolomini praised her in similar terms in his Paduan *Lettura* on one of her sonnets
(Bologna: Bartolomeo Bonardo and Marcantonio da Carpi, 1541), fols B2ᵛ–B3ʳ; on this work see
Cox, *Women's Writing in Italy*, pp. 106–08, 116.

occhi de la mente, e ne la lor viltà ostinati, nel brutto fango de l'Ignorantia dormono gli anni loro. (fol. +3ʳ)

(O most noble and wholly purified spirit of a lady, mind that is truly wise and alone worthy to be enclosed by such an honoured clothing as the rarest beauties ever seen: she can without any doubt be called a lady who is immortal, she who is inflamed and burns with the ardent desire for knowledge. Men themselves, with few exceptions, seek urgently to extinguish this desire with the waters of idleness and neglect of religion; for [. . .], closing their mind's eyes, and obstinate in their baseness, they sleep out their years in the foul mud of ignorance.)

Among works dedicated to Isabella Pallavicino Lupi were Maddalena Campiglia's pastoral play *Flori*: here the marchioness is described as 'donna eccellentissima a' tempi nostri, non solo per nobiltà di sangue, e per grandezza di stato, ma per magnanimità, e per valore' (a lady outstanding in our day not merely for the nobility of her blood and the greatness of her state, but also for her magnanimity and valour).[116] In 1600, Tiberio Palella dedicated a posthumous edition of the *Rime* of Antonio Ongaro (Farnese: Nicolò Mariani) to the marchioness as 'Prencipessa et institutrice' (princess and founder) of the Roman Accademia degli Illuminati, of which Ongaro was a member.[117] Already in 1584 her daughter Camilla had been the dedicatee of the edition of Angelo Ingegneri's pastoral play *Danza di Venere* (Vicenza: Stamperia Nova, 1584), since she had played the part of the nymph Amarilli when the play was performed before a courtly audience. The author praises Camilla, still an unmarried girl, for her 'sangue, forma e senno' (ancestry, appearance and wisdom) as well as for her 'fortuna' (fol. +4ᵛ).[118]

However, where the choice of a female dedicatee was concerned, more important than the woman's reputation as a cultured person was the possibility of portraying her as a paragon of virtue and piety, and hence

---

[116] Campiglia, *Flori*, pp. 44–47; see also pp. 4, 6, 9, 13, 27–28. The second edition of Giovanni Donato Cucchetti's pastoral play *La pazzia* (Ferrara: Giulio Cesare Cagnacini and brothers for Francesco Mammarello, 1586) was also dedicated to the marchioness: see Carlo Ossola, *Dal 'Cortegiano' all'Uomo di mondo'* (Turin: Einaudi, 1987), p. 113.

[117] Cox, *The Prodigious Muse: Women's Writing in Counter-Reformation Italy*, p. 265, and Cox, 'Members, Muses, Mascots: Women and Italian Academies', p. 145.

[118] On Ingegneri's dedicatory letter and Camilla's performance, see also Lisa Sampson, 'Performing Female Cultural Sociability between Court and Academy: Isabella Pallavicino Lupi and Angelo Ingegneri's *Danza di Venere* (1584)', in *Chivalry, Academy, and Cultural Dialogues: The Italian Contribution to European Culture*, ed. by Stefano Jossa and Giuliana Pieri (Cambridge: Legenda, 2016), pp. 107–22.

an inspiring example to others, and not only to those of her own sex. These qualities were also perceived as setting women above most men. The ideal recipient was thus a woman who combined high birth with an irreproachable character. In the Veronese poet Giovanni Fratta's dialogue on dedications (1590), the character Francesco Porta suggests that '[le] donne nobili' (noblewomen) make appropriate dedicatees; Eugenio, who represents Niccolò Marogna, agrees and adds that 'le Donne, poi che sono arricchite di bellezze interne [. . .], meritano ogni preminenza d'honore' (since ladies are enriched with inner beauties, they deserve honour above all others).[119]

One dedicator succeeded in finding two noble and virtuous ladies to receive the same work. An edition of the *Libro della divina providentia* by St Catherine of Siena (Venice: Matteo Capcasa for Lucantonio Giunti, 17 May 1494) has a woodcut of the saint giving copies of her book to two noblewomen, Isabella d'Aragona, daughter of the King of Naples and wife of Gian Galeazzo Sforza, nominally Duke of Milan, and Beatrice d'Este, wife of Gian Galeazzo's uncle Ludovico, who had effectively usurped power in the city (fol. AA1ᵛ; Figure 1.2). The volume was prefaced by a letter to them from an anonymous Dominican friar of Santa Maria delle Grazie in Milan (fols AA2ʳ–AA8ᵛ). After giving an account of the life of the saint, the friar explains why these two women have been chosen as dedicatees. First, they, like their male relatives, have shown generosity to the Dominican order; their husbands, indeed, have been benefactors of his convent. Why, then, did the friar select these two women and not men such as their husbands as recipients of his public gift? The answer lies in the second reason given for his decision:

> Mi sono mosso a dovere el presente dignissimo libro offerire, attribuire et dedicare ale vostre excelentissime et illustrissime signorie: sì per consolatione di quelle come etiamdio per honore di esso sancto libro, el quale, pieno di santitade e vertude, non debe essere dedicado senone a persone virtuose come sono le excellentie vostre. (fol. AA8ᵛ)

> (I have decided that I must offer, attribute and dedicate this most worthy book to your most excellent and illustrious ladyships, both for your consolation and to honour this holy book; full of holiness and virtue, it can be dedicated only to virtuous persons such as Your Excellencies.)

The friar's precise terminology establishes that the edition is now their possession. Young in years but old in virtue, they are worthy of having this

---

[119] *Della dedicatione de' libri, con la correttion dell'abuso*, in *questa materia introdotto* (Venice: Giorgio Angelieri, 1590), fol. E3ᵛ; see also Marco Santoro, *Uso e abuso delle dediche: a proposito del 'Della dedicatione de' libri' di Giovanni Fratta* (Rome: Edizioni dell'Ateneo, 2006), pp. 83–84.

Figure 1.2  St Catherine of Siena, *Libro della divina providentia* (Venice: Matteo Capcasa for Lucantonio Giunti, 1494), fol. AA1ᵛ. Alamy

work as a mirror before their eyes, and the friar prays that, with Catherine as their teacher, they will achieve perpetual glory in paradise. The dedicator is simultaneously showing appreciation of their support for his order and depicting them with the greatest prominence as illustrious models of how St Catherine's writings could benefit other readers, in particular female readers. We should also note the term 'consolation', which we shall meet again several times in the context of reading by women as individuals, within families and within convents. In contemporary usage, it usually signified comfort in adversity, but it could also refer to good cheer and joy.[120]

Two further examples of a virtuous female dedicatee's exemplarity come from humanist editions of the early sixteenth century. The scholar-printer Aldo Manuzio dedicated the Latin verse of Tito and Ercole Strozzi to Lucrezia Borgia in 1513 in Venice with a glowing address to the duchess: 'Quid dicam de tua in Deum divosque omneis pietate? quid item de liberalitate in pauperes, de bonitate in tuos, de iustitia in omneis?' (What shall I say of your devotion to God and all the saints, of your generosity toward the poor, of your goodness to your fellow citizens, of your just treatment of all?).[121] Pietro Marso claimed, in dedicating Cicero's *De divinatione* in 1508 to Anne of Brittany, wife of Louis XII of France, that her piety was exemplary and her prudence protected the Church: 'Tua pietas caeteris et fuit et erit specimen. Tua prudentia ecclesiae Christi sedulo consulit' (Your devotion to others both was and will be a model. Your prudence cares diligently for the church of Christ).[122] The page preceding Marso's letter includes a striking woodcut depiction of the act of presentation of the book by the editor, kneeling before the queen (Figure 1.3).

Isabella del Balzo, widow of Federico d'Aragona, former King of Naples, spent her last years in Ferrara, and here, in 1513, she became the dedicatee of a new edition of the *Prediche devotissime et piene de divini mysterii* of the

---

[120] See the *Grande dizionario della lingua italiana*, ed. by Salvatore Battaglia, 21 vols (Turin: UTET, 1961–2002), III, s.vv. *consolare* and *consolazione*.

[121] Aldus Manutius, *Humanism and the Latin Classics*, ed. and trans. by John N. Grant (Cambridge, MA: Harvard University Press, 2017), pp. 220–21. See also the terms of the dedication by Ludovico Bonaccioli, mentioned above, and compare the dedicatory 'Proemio' of Iacopo Caviceo's *Libro del peregrino*, in which Lucrezia is described as 'Savia, docta, accostumata, et bella' (wise, learned, well mannered and fair) and praised on account of her ancestry (first edition, Parma: Ottaviano Saladi, 1508; quoted from the edition of Venice: Bernardino Viani, 1520, fol. A7ʳ).

[122] *Illustria monimenta: M. T. Ciceronis De divina natura et divinatione a Petro Marso reconcinnata castigata et enarrata* (Venice: Lazaro Soardi, 1508), fol. Iʳᵛ. See also Zappella, *Il ritratto nel libro italiano*, I, 75, 173 and II, Figure 222, and Ruth Mortimer, 'The Author's Image: Italian Sixteenth-Century Printed Portraits', *Harvard Library Bulletin*, n.s., 7, no. 2 (summer 1996) (p. 65). On Anne of Brittany's collection of devotional and other manuscripts, see Joni M. Hand, *Women, Manuscripts and Identity in Northern Europe, 1350–1550* (Farnham: Ashgate, 2013), pp. 30–32. *De divina natura* (*De natura deorum*) is dedicated to King Louis.

Figure 1.3 *Illustria monimenta: M. T. Ciceronis De divina natura et divinatione a Petro Marso reconcinnata, castigata et enarrata* (Venice: Lazzaro Soardi, 1508), fol. I1ʳ. Leeds University Library, Ripon Cathedral Library XVIII.H.18 q

Dominican friar Girolamo Savonarola, printed at the press of Giovanni Mazzocchi. The dedicator, Giovanni Brasavola, explained he had chosen her because she was a devotee of the late friar, renowned for his severe preaching on moral and spiritual reform. The edition, thus protected, served to praise God and her together:

> Pensato ho di me et electo, conoscendo (come ho de sopra narrato) vostra Serenissima Maiestà ale cose dela religione inclinata, et devota, et maxime de questo novo propheta, a quella intitulare li già decti volumi, li quali, come havemo predecto, per publica utilitade de' proximi ho facti reimprimere, acioché havendo nel titolo loro et nel fronte il sacro nome de Vostra Serenissima Maiestà inserto et scolpito, procedano più sicuramente in publico, et per tutto vadano munite et corroborate come da uno adamantino scuto in ogni parte animose et sicure, a laude dela divina maiestade et vostra, la quale Dio omnipotente conservi sancta et felice in l'una et in l'altra vita. Amen. (fol. a1ᵛ)

> (I have considered and chosen to dedicate these volumes, which I have had printed again for the public benefit of others, as already mentioned, to you, knowing (as I have recounted above) that your most serene majesty is inclined towards religion, and devout, especially in regard to this new prophet. I have done this so that, with the sacred name of your most serene majesty inserted and engraved in their title and first page, they may go forth more securely in public and may go everywhere as if protected and strengthened by an adamantine shield, bravely and surely, in praise of the divine majesty and your majesty. May all-powerful God keep you holy and happy both in this life and in the next. Amen.)

The reputed moral or spiritual virtues of women who belonged to the house of Medici, as consorts or daughters of dukes, attracted a number of dedications to them.[123] Eleonora de Toledo was seen by Pietro Lauro of Modena as an example of wifely devotion. His translation of Juan Luis Vives's *De l'ufficio del marito, come si debba portare verso la moglie. De l'istitutione de la femina christiana, vergine, maritata, o vedova. De lo ammaestrare i fanciulli ne le arti liberali* (Venice: Vincenzo Valgrisi, 1546) was, in his words, an 'opera tanto più degna che sia dedicata a V[ostra] Eccellentia, quanto più è per voce di tutti manifesto, che quel verace et sincero amore, che tra marito et moglie si ricerca, è con ogni sua qualità espresso tra lei et il suo illustris[simo] consorte' (fol. *1ᵛ; a work all the worthier to be dedicated to Your Excellency in that all accounts make it manifest that that true and sincere love that is desirable between husband

---

[123] On the cultural roles of Medici women from the sixteenth to the eighteenth century, see *Medici Women as Cultural Mediators, 1533–1743*, ed. by Christina Strunck (Milan: Silvana, 2011).

and wife is expressed with all its qualities between you and your most illustrious consort). Anton Francesco Doni portrayed the duchess as combining all women's virtues, when he dedicated to her his anthology of *Prose antiche di Dante, Petrarcha, et Boccaccio, et di molti altri nobili et virtuosi ingegni* (Florence: Doni, 1547):

> essendosi unite nell'animo reale di vostra Eccellenza le infinite virtù, che sparse in tutte l'altre donne ador[n]ano la nobiltà di ciascuna, siamo mossi a credere, che le tante doti dal cielo a quella concedute siano per ornamento della felicissima sua persona. (fol. A3ʳ)

> (since there are brought together in Your Excellency's royal spirit the infinite virtues that, scattered among all other women, adorn the nobility of each, we are led to believe that the many gifts granted to you by heaven are an ornament of your most fortunate person.)

Eleonora was envisaged as the recipient, and probably the dedicatee, of a translation of the Seven Penitential Psalms by Pietro Orsilago of Pisa, a doctor practising in Livorno, who wrote to Duke Cosimo I on 15 December 1540:

> prego che [Dio] liberar vogli l'Ex[cellenti]a V[ostra] da tutti gli occulti suoi nimici, et l'esalti quant'è il desiderio suo et mio, del che per meglio essere esaudito mi son posto a tradurre i sette salmi di Davit, detti penitentiali, per mandarli come saran finiti a l'Ill[ustrissi]ma et Ex[cellentissi]ma S[igno]ra Consorte d[ella] V[ostra] Ex[cellenti]a, li quali dicendo mi rendo certo ch'i suoi devoti prieghi, sì come giusti ancora saranno accettissimi avanti la bontà di Dio.[124]

> (I pray that [God] may free Your Excellency from all his hidden enemies and exalt you as greatly as you and I desire. For the better fulfilment of this prayer I have undertaken a translation of the Seven Psalms of David, called penitential, to be sent on completion to Your Excellency's most illustrious and excellent consort. I am certain that, when she says them, as her devout prayers are just, so they will be most acceptable in the sight of God's goodness.)

When the next grand duchess, Joanna of Austria, daughter of Emperor Ferdinand I, arrived in Florence, the Medici court did not welcome her. Her marriage in 1565 to Eleonora's eldest son Francesco was difficult from

---

[124] ASF, Mediceo del Principato, vol. 343, fol. 131ʳ⁻ᵛ. On Orsilago, see Michel Plaisance, *L'Accademia e il suo principe: cultura e politica a Firenze al tempo di Cosimo I e di Francesco de' Medici* (Manziana: Vecchiarelli, 2003), especially pp. 212–14, 251. Orsilago's translation was printed in the anthology *Salmi penitentiali di diversi eccellenti autori* (Venice: Gabriele Giolito, 1568) and in Venice by Riccardo Amadino in 1595.

the outset, since Francesco already had a mistress who was well established in his affections, the Venetian Bianca Cappello. Yet some Florentine men exalted Joanna, above all for her exemplification of moral probity. In 1566 the scholar Pier Vettori was given the task of composing a speech in her praise. The edition of the original Latin text was dedicated by the author to Grand Duke Francesco, and Vettori pointedly mentions his admiration for the virtue of Joanna, whom he had often seen in church during the recent Easter-time services.[125] A vernacular translation was dedicated by the printer Iacopo Giunti to Joanna's sister-in-law Isabella Orsini de' Medici, daughter of Duke Cosimo and Duchess Eleonora, explicitly 'per ampliare un tanto e sì lodato, e sì prezioso bene allargandolo' (in order to make more accessible, through wider diffusion, a possession so great, so highly praised and so precious).[126] Here Joanna was proposed as an example that Isabella successfully imitated and as a person on whom Isabella could model herself, just as St Catherine had been seen as an ideal for imitation in 1494:

> Ricevete per tanto le lodi di colei, a cui voi sète d'affinità congiuntissima, et la quale voi amate, et osservate, et innanzi ad ogni altra imitate; et in quelle di sua Serenissima Altezza le proprie doti, e virtù di V[ostra] E[xcellentia] I[llustrissima] leggendo riconoscete.[127]

---

[125] *Liber de laudibus Ioannae Austriacae, natae reginae Ungariae, et Boemiae* (Florence: heirs of Bernardo Giunti, 1566), fol. A2ʳ.

[126] On Isabella, see Elisabetta Mori, 'Isabella de' Medici: Unraveling the Legend', in *Medici Women: The Making of a Dynasty in Grand Ducal Tuscany*, ed. by Giovanna Benadusi and Judith C. Brown (Toronto: Centre for Renaissance and Reformation Studies, 2015), pp. 91–127.

[127] *Orazione o vero libro* [. . .] *delle lodi della Serenissima Giovanna d'Austria Reina nata d'Ungheria, e Boemia, in volgar fiorentino nuovamente tradotto* (Florence: heirs of Bernardo Giunti, 1566), fol. A2ᵛ. See Maria Fubini Leuzzi, 'Un'Asburgo a Firenze fra etichetta e impegno politico: Giovanna d'Austria', in *Le donne Medici nel sistema europeo delle corti XVI–XVIII secolo: atti del convegno internazionale, Firenze, San Domenico di Fiesole, 6–8 ottobre 2005*, ed. by Giulia Calvi and Riccardo Spinelli, 2 vols (Florence: Polistampa, 2008), I, 233–56 (pp. 234–35, 236). Editions dedicated to Joanna are mentioned in Lisa Kaborycha, 'Expressing a Habsburg Sensibility in the Medici Court: The Grand Duchess Giovanna d'Austria's Patronage and Public Image in Florence', in *Medici Women as Cultural Mediators*, ed. by Christina Strunck (Milan: Silvana, 2011), pp. 89–109 (pp. 95–96): Eufrosino Lapini, *Institutionum Florentinae linguae libri duo* (Florence: heirs of Bernardo Giunti, 1569), Francesco de' Vieri, *Compendio della dottrina di Platone in quello, che ella è conforme con la fede nostra*, and Girolamo Borro's study of tides, *Del flusso, et reflusso del mare, et dell'inondatione del Nilo* (both Florence: Giorgio Marescotti, 1577). On Borro, see Giorgio Stabile, 'Borri (Borro, Borrius), Girolamo', *DBI*, 13 (1971), 13–17; Simonetta Adorni Braccesi, *'Una città infetta': la repubblica di Lucca nella crisi religiosa del Cinquecento* (Florence: Olschki, 1994), p. 219, n. 280; Adorni Braccesi, '"Telifilo Filogenio"'. On Joanna's position in Florence, see also Sarah Bercusson, 'Giovanna d'Austria and the Art of Appearances: Textiles and Dress at the Florentine Court', *Renaissance Studies*, 29 (2015), 683–700, and Bercusson, 'Joanna of Austria and the Negotiation of Power and Identity at the Florentine Court', in *Medici Women: The Making of a Dynasty in Grand Ducal Tuscany*, ed. by Giovanna Benadusi and Judith C. Brown (Toronto: Centre for Renaissance and Reformation Studies, 2015), pp. 128–53.

(Receive, therefore, the praises of the woman to whom you are very closely related and whom you love, observe and imitate above every other woman; and, while reading, recognize the gifts and virtues of Your illustrious Excellency in those of Her most serene Highness.)

In the following year, 1567, Joanna herself was chosen by a cleric, Antonio Buonagrazia, as the dedicatee of his translation of *Le Bouclier de la foy* by Nicole Grenier: *Scudo della fede, per ribatter i colpi di tutti i nimici della Chiesa catholica* (Venice: Gabriele Giolito). There could be no better person to defend his work, Buonagrazia claimed, citing both Joanna's membership of her family group and her own action as a Catholic: she possessed her father's holiness and goodness, together with the virtues of her other male Habsburg relatives, and she had already opposed false doctrines (fol. *3$^{r-v}$). Moreover, she wishes to learn the Tuscan language, and reading this holy book will provide her with practice.[128] What better reading, Buonagrazia asks, could Joanna – and by implication other readers – find? In 1573 Captain Scipione Vasoli dedicated to Joanna his *La gloriosa eccellenza delle donne, e d'amore*. In the text itself, she is the only modern woman mentioned and praised by name, alongside Vasoli's other mainly classical examples of virtuous women. In his letter, Vasoli argues that, from examples of 'magnanime regine' (magnanimous queens), 'non se ne puote cavare, che divina Eccellenza, e perfetto Amore' (one can derive only divine excellence and perfect love), and that Joanna stands as a supreme example of such qualities. Among such queens,

> hora ho trovato cotanta immortalità esser posta per la Corona, e Manto della Serenissima Altezza V[ostra] che per il poter di tal thesoro hora acquistato mi conviene voltar ogni mio studio verso quella sapienza, e bella gratia, che dalla Natura a Lei è stata concessa tanto adorna di buona Giustitia con altre generose, et incredibile attioni accompagnata, con le quali tutte sono causa, et opera che 'l Monte d'Helicona sia hoggidì fertile, et abondante d'ogni allegrezza, co 'l mondo svegliato al celebrar la sudetta felicità dell'animo divino, e non humano.[129]

(I have now found that such immortality is bestowed by the crown and mantle of Your most serene Highness that, through the power of the treasure I have now acquired, I must turn all my efforts towards that wisdom and fair grace that nature has granted to you who are so adorned with good

---

[128] On Joanna's study of Tuscan and the dedication to her of Lapini's work on Florentine, see Kaborycha, 'Expressing a Habsburg Sensibility in the Medici Court', pp. 94–95, and Helena Sanson, *Women, Language and Grammar in Italy, 1500–1900* (Oxford University Press for the British Academy, 2011), pp. 99, 104–07.

[129] (Florence: Giorgio Marescotti, 1573), fol. ❧2$^{r-v}$.

justice accompanied by other generous and astonishing actions. All together, these are the cause and means that Mount Helicon is today fertile and abounds in all happiness, with the world awake to celebrate this joy of your divine, rather than human, spirit.)

Christine of Lorraine (1565–1637), granddaughter of Catherine de' Medici, was chosen as a dedicatee on several occasions after her marriage to Grand Duke Ferdinando de' Medici in 1589.[130] Maddalena Salvetti Acciaioli dedicated to her some *Rime toscane* that she had composed in her praise, speaking of

quel debito, che l'alto valor suo, e la grandezza del sangue regale, ond'ella discende, quasi per tributo ricchieggono da tutto il Mondo, e maggiormente dalle Donne, per esser V[ostra] A[ltezza] S[erenissima] quella vera luce, che col suo gran lume rende chiarissimo, e lucidissimo il pregio nostro.[131]

(that debt that your lofty worth, and the greatness of the royal blood from which you descend, demand almost as a tribute from the whole world, and especially from women, since Your most serene Highness is that true light that makes our worth most clear and shining with its great illumination.)

Antonio Migliori, a canon from Ascoli Piceno, offered to Christine his prayer in ottava rima to the Virgin Mary in 1593,

non solo per dedicarmele servitore con gli scritti Spirituali, sì come il P[adre] F[ra] Simeone mio fratello serve in cose dello Spirito al Serenissimo suo consorte, ma anchora per servire in parte alla caldissima devotione, con cui V[ostra] A[ltezza] Serenissima serve alla Vergine Regina del Cielo.[132]

(not only to dedicate myself as your servant with my spiritual writings, just as my brother the Rev. Brother Simeone assists your husband in spiritual matters, but also to support in part the most sincere devotion with which Your most serene Highness serves the Virgin Queen of Heaven.)

When the printer Filippo Giunti dedicated to Christine in 1596 an expanded version of Giuseppe Betussi's translation of Boccaccio's Latin lives of famous women, he claimed that she possessed all the virtues displayed in these accounts of women: 'il quale libro ho mandato alla Stampa sotto il felicissimo nome di V[ostra] A[ltezza] S[erenissima] adorna, e ricca di tutte le qualità, ed eccellenze, che leggerà sparte in

[130] Christine was later to be one of Galileo's main brokers in his maintaining of Medici patronage: Mario Biagioli, *Galileo, Courtier: The Practice of Science in the Culture of Absolutism* (University of Chicago Press, 1993), p. 33.
[131] (Florence: Francesco Tosi, 1590), fol. A2[r].
[132] *Priego alla beata vergine Maria* (Rome: Guglielmo Faciotti for Giovanni Martinelli, 1593), fol. A2[r].

molt'altre' (which book I have sent to the press under the most fortunate name of Your most serene Highness, adorned and enriched by all the qualities and excellence that you will read scattered among many other women).[133] Lucrezia Marinella felt encouraged to dedicate to Christine her poem in ottava rima, *Vita del serafico et glorioso s. Francesco* [...] *con un discorso del rivolgimento amoroso, verso la somma bellezza* (Venice: Pietro Maria Bertano and brothers, 1597), in spite of her own humble condition, because of Christine's affable nature and also by '[il] sogetto religioso, et divino, ch'in queste carte io spiego' (fol. A2ᵛ; the religious and divine subject matter that I unfold in these pages).

Stefano Penello translated Erasmus's *De pueris instituendis* (On the Education of Children) at the request of Perinetta Grimaldi, daughter of a doge of Genoa. Dedicating the printed edition to her in 1545, he observes that she is devoted to the upbringing of her only son and has no need of advice on the subject. However, her own fine judgement is, alas, not shared by all noble persons in Italy:

> m'è caduto nell'animo di presentarle una declamatione, D'ERASMO, [...] affinché V[ostra] S[ignoria] leggendola per suo diporto col parere di così grave huomo molto maggiormente nel suo bellissimo giudicio si confermi, del quale giudicio volesse Iddio che fusseno state e fussero tutte le persone nobili, che si vedrebbe in Italia maggiore copia d'huomini virtuosi, e le Republiche più fiorire e molto più bello il mondo.[134]

> (it has occurred to me to present to you a declamation by Erasmus, [...] so that, when you read it for your enjoyment, you may feel much more strongly convinced in your most fine judgement by the opinion of such a serious man. Would God that all noble persons had shared and did share this judgement, for one would see in Italy many more virtuous men, more flourishing republics and a much fairer world.)

Although, Penello continues, the language of his translation does not match the original, its dedication to her will conceal its defects:

> Ben conosco che al suo bello, e figurato dir Latino non ho io col mio poco limato e semplice volgare corrisposto, ma come sogliono alcuni dorare il ferro, perché si dimostri più bello ch'egli non è di sua natura, così io con

---

[133] *Libro di m[esser] Giovanni Boccaccio delle donne illustri tradotto di latino in volgare per m[esser] Giuseppe Betussi, con una giunta fatta dal medesimo, d'altre donne famose, e un'altra nuova giunta fatta per m[esser] Francesco Serdonati d'altre donne illustri antiche e moderne* (Florence: Filippo Giunti, 1596), fol. +2ᵛ.

[134] *Della institutione de fanciulli come di buona hora si debbono ammaestrare alla virtù et alle lettere. Libro di Erasmo Roterodamo tradotto in lingua volgare per Stephano Penello. Ad instanza della molto magnifica Madonna Perinetta Grimaldi* (Venice: Gabriele Giolito, 1545), fol. A2ᵛ.

dedicare questa mia tradottione, mi son persuaso, che dorata et adornata del fino oro del valore e favore suo, facilmente potrà passar per bella. (fol. A3ʳ)

(I know well that I have not matched [Erasmus's] fine and ornate Latin style with my unpolished and simple vernacular. But, just as some gild iron to make it appear more beautiful than it is by its nature, so I am convinced that, by dedicating this translation of mine, it can easily pass as beautiful when it is gilded and adorned with the fine gold of your worth and favour.)

Vittoria Farnese della Rovere (1519–1602), granddaughter of Pope Paul III, became the second wife of Guidobaldo II della Rovere, Duke of Urbino, in 1547.[135] In 1553 Gabriele Giolito dedicated to her a tragic narrative poem, *L'infelice amore de i due fedelissimi amanti Giulia e Romeo: scritto in ottava rima da Clitia nobile veronese ad Ardeo suo*. Giolito claimed that Gherardo Boldieri, who was probably the author, had promised the poem to her but had changed his mind about offering such a minor work. However, to Giolito it seemed best to print the verses under the name of the duchess, 'acciò che escano fuora con lor maggior honore' (fol. A1ᵛ; so that they may be published to their greater honour).[136] For the most part, however, the duchess attracted dedications of works related in some way to the Christian life. She received an Italian translation of Erasmus's *Christiani matrimonii institutio*, the *Ordinatione del matrimonio de' Christiani* (Venice: Francesco Rocca and brothers, 1550). The letter of dedication, signed by Pietro Rocca and dated 26 October 1549, explains that the duchess was chosen for her dynastic connections but also on account of her virtue as a wife:

Ho diliberato publicarla a beneficio, et commodo di quelli che dell'idioma latino poveri, o pure ignudi sono del tutto. Et disiderando, che ella col favore d'alcuno illustre nome uscisse, senza troppo pensarvi, mi si è all'animo apprasentato il vostro [...]. Perché oltre che con Reverendi Cardinali, e illustrissimi principi fratelli habbiate origine da sì gran patria, et tanto illustre famiglia, da sì onorati avoli, e massimamente Paolo terzo [...], et da tanto padre [...], siete poi di sì rara bellezza, et di tante, et sì gran virtù dotata, et compiutamente adorna, che empiete il mondo di maraviglia. Onde acceso l'illustrissimo Signor Guido Ubaldo d'Urbino con ottimo consiglio vi disiderò, et elesse innanzi ad ogn'altra, siché hora congionto in matrimonio, et ogn'hor più amandovi, con voi felicemente si vive. (fol. A2ʳ⁻ᵛ)

[135] Her life is described in Matilde Rossi Parisi, *Vittoria Farnese, duchessa d'Urbino* (Modena: Ferraguti, 1927).
[136] Bongi, *Annali di Gabriel Giolito*, I, 401–03; Gioachino Brognoligo, 'Il poemetto di Clizia veronese', in *Studi di storia letteraria* (Rome and Milan: Società editrice Dante Alighieri, 1904), pp. 135–53.

(I resolved to publish [this work] for the benefit and advantage of those who know little or no Latin. And wanting it to come out with the favour of some illustrious name, yours sprang to my mind after very little reflection [. . .]. Because not only do you come, together with brothers who are reverend cardinals and most illustrious princes, from such a great state and such an illustrious family, from such honoured grandparents, and especially Paul III, [. . .] and from such a father [. . .], but you are also endowed and perfectly adorned with such rare beauty and so many and so great virtues that you fill everyone with amazement. Enflamed by you, the most illustrious Guidobaldo of Urbino very wisely desired you and chose you above all other women, so that, now joined to you in marriage and loving you continually more, he lives with you in happiness.)

Evidently a wife could be seen as a more appropriate dedicatee for such a treatise than a husband. This work was placed on Indexes of Prohibited Books later in the 1550s, but the duchess's orthodoxy does not appear to have been suspect.[137]

In 1554 Giolito dedicated to the Duchess Vittoria a collection of sermons, *Prediche fatte in diversi tempi* by Cornelio Musso, the Franciscan bishop of Bitonto.[138] The British Library holds the presentation copy, bound for Giolito by the Flemish bookbinder Anthoni Lodewijk.[139] Giolito explained in his dedicatory letter that, publishing the sermons 'a utile e consolation delle menti pie et Christiane, per molte cagioni ho giudicato degno di dedicarle a V[ostra] S[ignoria] Illustrissima' (fol. A2$^r$; for the benefit and consolation of pious and Christian minds, for many reasons I have judged it worthy to dedicate them to Your most illustrious Ladyship). Giolito did not hide the fact that his principal reason for selecting the duchess was to please the duke, but he added that her character made her an eminently appropriate dedicatee for such a work:

> parvemi che indrizzando questi dottissimi Sermoni alla più cara cosa, ch'egli [il duca] havesse, io venissi in così fatto modo a dimostrare alcun vivo segno della servitù mia verso di sua Eccellenza. Senza, che essendo egli Gonfaloniere di Santa Chiesa, et havendo consorte non pure ornata d'ogni

---

[137] Grendler, *The Roman Inquisition*, p. 113; Silvana Seidel Menchi, *Erasmo in Italia 1520–1580* (Turin: Bollati Boringhieri, 1987), p. 187; Bujanda, *Index de Venise*, p. 268, and Bujanda, *Index de Rome*, p. 431; Laura Battiferri degli Ammannati, *I sette salmi penitenziali di David con alcuni sonetti spirituali*, ed. by Enrico Maria Guidi (Urbino: Accademia Raffaello, 2005), p. 12. Erasmus had dedicated his work in 1526 to Catherine of Aragon, for whom it was written, taking the opportunity to praise the virtues of both the queen and her mother and to look forward to the perfection that would be shown in turn by her daughter Mary.

[138] Bongi, *Annali di Gabriel Giolito*, I, 429–33.

[139] Shelfmark C.69.f.8. See Anthony Hobson, *Renaissance Book Collecting: Jean Grolier and Diego Hurtado de Mendoza, their Books and Bindings* (Cambridge University Press, 1999), pp. 129, 260 and Plate 80.

virtù, ma di santi costumi, e di splendida e real vita, era altresì convene-
vole, che un'opra ripiena di santità, et adorna di ogni eloquenza, si
collocasse in sì degno luoco. (fol. A2$^{r-v}$)

(it seemed to me that, by addressing these most learned sermons to the
duke's dearest possession, I was thus showing some clear sign of my devotion
to His Excellency. Further, since he is a Gonfalonier of the Holy Church,
and having a consort who is adorned not only with every virtue but also with
holy manners of conduct and a splendid and royal style of life, it was also
fitting that a work full of sanctity and adorned with every eloquence should
be set in such a worthy place.)

In 1557 the duchess became once again the primary reader, in the public's
eyes, of another edition related to religion when she was chosen as dedicatee of a translation of Latin works of devotion by García de Cisneros, the
*Esercizio de la vita spirituale con il Direttorio de le hore canoniche* (Venice:
Michele Tramezzino, 1557).[140]

We saw earlier that Laura Battiferri dedicated her first book of lyric
verse, *Il primo libro dell'opere toscane*, to Eleonora de Toledo in 1560; she
explained in her letter to the duchess that she was grateful for '[i] benifizii,
che ella, e l'Illustrissimo Signor Duca hanno fatto' (the favours that you
and the most illustrious Lord Duke have shown). In 1564, Battiferri, who
was a native of Urbino, chose to dedicate to Vittoria Farnese her second
book of verse, which was devotional and spiritual in nature: *I sette salmi
penitentiali del santissimo profeta Davit tradotti in lingua toscana* [...]
*insieme con alcuni suoi sonetti spirituali* (Florence: heirs of Bernardo
Giunti). The poet wrote of the joy she would feel if the work were to
please someone as pure as Vittoria:

Ben è vero che, se il Signore Iddio, per essere nata questa mia fatica da un
puro e sincero volere, mi facesse mai degna che un'anima tanto chiara
e purgata, quanto è quella dell'Eccellenza Vostra Illustrissima, ne prendesse
in qualche parte consolazione ed allegrezza, perciò doppio me ne verrebbe
contento, poco curando di quello che ad altrui ne paresse.

(It is certainly true that, since this labour of mine was born of a pure and
sincere desire, if God ever made me worthy that a soul as limpid and purified
as that of Your most illustrious Excellency were to receive some consolation
and good cheer from it, I should receive double happiness from it, caring
little of what others thought.)

[140] Anselmo M. Albareda, 'Intorno alla scuola di orazione metodica stabilita a Monserrato dall'abate Garsias Jiménez de Cisneros (1493–1510)', *Archivum historicum Societatis Iesu*, 25 (1956), 254–316 (pp. 287–88).

The edition was further set under the sign of the holiness of living women through individual dedications of the seven psalm translations to single nuns in convents in Florence or to pairs of nuns in convents in Urbino, one of them perhaps a relative of the poet, Cassandra Battiferri.[141] Vittoria's own reputation for piety also led to the dedication to her by Giovanni Giolito, son of Gabriele, of Lodovico Dolce's translation of a work by an Augustinian canon addressed to Christians running the race to the goal of eternal life: Antonio Ulstio, *Stadio del cursore christiano, il quale sotto al lieve peso di Christo c'indirizza alla meta; cioè al segno e termino della vita eterna*, in two editions, one in quarto and the other in duodecimo (Venice: Gabriele Giolito, 1568).[142]

Doubtless encouraged by the dedication to Vittoria Farnese of Musso's sermons, Battiferri's spiritual verse and Ulstio's *Stadio*, the Augustinian archbishop Gabriele Buratelli offered her his collection of *Prediche* [. . .] *sopra i sette salmi penitentiali di David profeta, accomodate a gli Evangeli quadragesimali secondo l'uso della S. R. Chiesa: opera utilissima a predicatori, et ascoltatori della parola d'Iddio*, which was printed two years after his death (Venice: Francesco and Gaspare Bindoni and brothers, 1573). The preacher states firmly that the sole reason for his choice of Vittoria is that she is already a mirror of the virtuous life to which his sermons encourage the faithful to aspire:

> mi son sforzato d'abbracciare, et d'isprimere tutto quello, che s'appartiene alla vera penitenza, et alla vita virtuosa, et christiana; et prima d'ogn'altra la consideratione di quella vera pietà, et religione, che sin dal ventre materno, et dalla fanciullezza con continovo augumento di fervore, e di devotione a chiarissimi segni ho conosciuto albergarle nel petto, in compagnia di numerosa, et honoratissima schiera di virtù heroiche, e christiane, le quali (sia lontano ogni fumo di gloria mondana, ogni sospetto d'adulatione, ogni stimolo d'invidia ne gli animi dell'altre) la fanno in questo secolo un raro essempio, un specchio, et una norma di vera, et christiana Prencipessa, et la rendono molto più riguardevole, et più illustre (oltra le proprie doti di natura) che l'haver i Fratelli Duchi, et Cardinali, il Prencipe, et l'Avolo Monarca di tutto il Christianesimo: perché la vera, et perfetta nobiltà, et chiarezza consiste non nel sangue, ma nelle virtù, et nell'anima, che è il vero huomo, non nella vana opinione de gli huomini, e nel passare intorno per le bocche del volgo co' nomi, e titoli di grandezze, e d'honori; ma in essere

---

[141] Battiferri degli Ammannati, *I sette salmi penitenziali*, pp. 33–34; Battiferra degli Ammannati, *Laura Battiferra and Her Literary Circle*, pp. 2–3, 45–47, 218–19, 222–27. See also Brundin, *Vittoria Colonna*, pp. 182–83, 185–88, and Jane Tylus, 'Early Modern Women as Translators of the Sacred', *Women Language Literature in Italy*, 1 (2019), 31–43 (pp. 38–43).

[142] Bongi, *Annali di Gabriel Giolito*, II, 270–71.

conosciuto con laude, approvato, et comendato nel conspetto del suo
Creatore, dalle voci de gli Angeli, e de' Santi suoi.[143] (fol. a2ᵛ)

(I have endeavoured to embrace and express everything concerning true
penitence and the virtuous and Christian life; and above any other consideration, that of the true piety and religion that I have seen, from the clearest signs,
dwelling in your heart from your mother's womb and from childhood with
ever-increasing fervour and devotion, accompanied by a copious and most
honoured host of heroic and Christian virtues. Far, I hope, from any empty
worldly glory, any suspicion of flattery or any pang of envy in the spirits of
other women, these virtues make you in this age a rare example, a mirror and
a norm of a true and Christian princess, and they make you much more notable
and more illustrious (in addition to your natural gifts) than having brothers
who are dukes and cardinals, the prince [your husband] and your grandfather
who was the ruler of all Christianity. For true and perfect nobility and renown
consist not in lineage but in virtues and in the soul, which constitutes the true
human being, not in people's empty opinions and in going around in the
common people's mouths with the names and titles of distinctions and
honours, but in being recognized with praise, approved and commended in
the sight of one's Creator, by the voices of His angels and saints.)

It is on account of the duchess's qualities, Buratelli continues, that other
authors have already dedicated sermons and other spiritual works to her. In
doing so, they have shown their good judgement both in offering such
writings to a person who appreciates them, 'sì anco in procurar per questa
via maggior riputatione, e di dottrina, e di pietà alle honorate, et sante
fatiche' (fol. a3ʳ; and also in gaining in this way, for their honoured and
holy labours, a higher reputation for both learning and piety).

An edition of a biography of St Teresa of Ávila translated from the Spanish
of the Jesuit Francisco Ribera and printed in 1599 contains an unusual pair of
dedications, one to a man and another to a woman, and it is instructive to see
how the first relates the text to the man's deeds, while the second relates it to
the woman's character.[144] The translator, Giovanni Francesco Bordini, archbishop of Avignon, announces that he turned the saint's writings 'dalla lingua
Spagnuola nella nostra, per commodità maggiore dell'Italia' (from the Spanish

---

[143] Buratelli also used his dedication to draw attention to his sober manner of preaching (fols a3ᵛ–a4ʳ),
     which contrasted with the style of others; here he was no doubt thinking of Musso. See Élise Boillet,
     'Vernacular Sermons on the Psalms Printed in Sixteenth-Century Italy: An Interface between Oral
     and Written Cultures', in *Voices and Texts in Early Modern Italian Society*, ed. by Stefano Dall'Aglio,
     Brian Richardson and Massimo Rospocher (London: Routledge, 2017), pp. 200–11.

[144] *Vita della m. Teresa di Giesù fondatrice delli monasteri e delle monache, et frati Carmelitani scalzi della
     prima regola. Tradotta dalla lingua spagnuola nell'italiana, dal reverendiss. monsig. Gio. Francesco
     Bordini della Congregatione dell'oratorio, arcivescovo et vicedelegato d'Avignone* (Rome: Guglielmo
     Facciotti, 1599).

language into ours for the greater benefit of Italy). He addresses the writings to Pope Clement VIII, whose coat of arms is given prominence on the title page, because these writings can be of practical use to him: 'gli offero alla Santità Vostra, atteso che ogni mezzo truovato dallo Spirito santo per la pescagione dell'anime, non può non esser gradito sommamente dal successor vero, e legitimo' (fol. *4$^v$; I offer them to your holiness since the true and legitimate successor [of St Peter] can only welcome any means devised by the Holy Spirit for the fishing of souls). Bordini hopes they will bring the pope 'gran conforto' (great comfort), since he approves of 'inventioni' (devices) aimed at increasing the number of servants of God. On the other hand, the letter that follows, signed by the order of Discalced Carmelites and addressed to Maria di Spagna, wife of the Holy Roman Emperor Maximilian II, associates the work with Maria's piety and social status: 'opere sì grandi, et di sì santa donna, di ragione si debbono a V[ostra] M[aestà] la quale è la maggior di tutte l'altre, non meno in santità, che in grandezza' (fol. *8$^v$; it is right that works so great, and of such a holy lady, should be owed to your majesty, who is outstanding among all other women, no less in holiness than in greatness).

While these consorts were seen as staunch supporters of Roman Catholic orthodoxy, other female dedicatees were probably selected because they were thought to sympathize with the cause of renewal within the Church. Their high status seems to have made it easier for them to escape blame for supporting reform. Such a woman was Margherita Paleologo (1510–1566), wife of Federico Gonzaga and Marchioness of Mantua, who at one point tried to attract the Franciscan reformer Bernardino Ochino to her city. Among the spiritual works dedicated to her was a treatise on divine mercy, the *Trattato divoto et utilissimo della divina misericordia* (Brescia: Lodovico Britannico, 1542), ostensibly composed by Marsilio Andreasi, but actually Andreasi's translation of the *De immensa Dei misericordia* by Erasmus. His letter of presentation noted on Margherita's part 'il desiderio [...] di star sempre congiunta con Cristo' (the desire to be always joined with Christ) and described her as an embodiment of the spirit of the work, since she was occupied 'per la maggior parte del tempo nelle opere della Divina Misericordia' (for most of the time in works of divine mercy). Marco Bandarini offered to Margherita his *Opera nuova spirituale* (Mantua: [n. pub.], 1547), a poem in terza rima on the Passion of Christ as recounted by the Virgin Mary, including on the title page a prominent reference to his dedicatee, 'A Madama eccellentissima'.[145] Suor Barbara da Correggio, noble

[145] Seidel Menchi, *Erasmo in Italia*, pp. 163–65. Also dedicated to Margherita was Marco Antonio Natta's *De oratione ad Deum* (Venice: Francesco Portonari, 1557): see Vera Bugatti, 'Orizzonti

daughter of the poet Niccolò da Correggio, was chosen by the twenty-year-old Rinaldo Corso to receive a *Prefatione nella Pistola di san Paolo a' Romani* (Venice: Comin da Trino for Andrea Arrivabene, 1545), attributed to Federico Fregoso, that was in fact a translation of a work by Luther. Anyone who followed in her footsteps would be blessed, wrote Corso; he honoured her 'come angiolo et celeste creatura' (as an angel and heavenly creature); and her authority would shield the work.[146]

Renée de France, Duchess of Ferrara, was known for her willingness to support intellectuals whom she regarded as sympathetic to religious renewal, as we saw earlier. At least three of these men dedicated works to her. In 1545, Pietro Lauro offered her his translation of a work by Erasmus, *Colloqui famigliari* (Venice: Vincenzo Valgrisi), and he addressed to her his *Epistola nella quale con la sola autorità della Scrittura Santa si prova, contro alla ostinatione degli Ebrei, Christo essere il vero Messia, predetto dalla legge, da' psalmi, et da' propheti* (Venice: Alessandro Brucioli and brothers). Here his words of dedication hinted at her practical assistance while underlining her deep religious commitment: 'non havendo al presente come meglio possa fare fede a tutti i Christiani quanto grande sia la pietà di quella verso i servi del Signore' (fol. A2[r]; having no better way now of testifying to all Christians how great is your piety towards the Lord's servants). The Friulian physician Orazio Brunetti presented to the duchess a collection of his letters printed in 1548 by Andrea Arrivabene, who was soon to be interrogated by the Holy Office on account of his suspected sympathies for the Lutheran cause.[147] Brunetti stressed that he had chosen Renée or Renata on account of what he considered her exemplary practice of Christianity, not merely for her royal blood:

> V[ostra] E[xcellentia] essendo grande di nobiltà di sangue, et di beni temporali, nata di Re, anzi di Re nata, et prima Prencipessa d'Italia, ella non di meno è piatosissima christiana, molto lontana da le grandezze humane. Per questo ho eletto V[ostra] E[xcellentia] per mia guida in questo nuovo certame. [. . .] [I]o non le do quelle ambitiose lodi, che da gli altri sogliono darsi a Prencipi mondani, che di ciò si pascono, et vivono: ma io

spirituali nella trattatistica dedicata alla Paleologa', *Civiltà mantovana*, 41, no. 121 (2006), 6–21. Another translation of Erasmus' treatise, printed in Florence by Torrentino in 1554, was dedicated to Virginia Fieschi, Duchess of Piombino: Seidel Menchi, *Erasmo in Italia*, pp. 166–67.

[146] Silvana Seidel Menchi, 'Le traduzioni italiane di Lutero nella prima metà del Cinquecento', *Rinascimento*, 2nd ser., 17 (1977), 31–108 (pp. 81–89, 106).

[147] Grendler, *The Roman Inquisition*, pp. 105–12. On Brunetti's collection, see Anne Jacobson Schutte, 'The *Lettere volgari* and the Crisis of Evangelism in Italy', *Renaissance Quarterly*, 28 (1975), 639–88 (pp. 652, 662, 666–68); Enrica Benini Clementi, *Riforma religiosa e poesia popolare a Venezia nel Cinquecento: Alessandro Caravia* (Florence: Olschki, 2000), pp. 106–08.

essalto in V[ostra] E[xcellentia] una sola mansuetudine, et riverisco una christiana pietà, et singolar caritate verso 'l prossimo, che da Signori mondani suole essere sempre tanto lontana. (fols A7$^r$, A9$^r$)

(Although Your Excellency is endowed with great nobility of birth and temporal goods, born of a king, 'di Re nata' indeed, and the first princess of Italy, none the less you are a most pious Christian, far removed from human glories. Hence I have chosen Your Excellency as my guide in this new contest. [. . .] I do not offer you those praises full of ambition that others usually give to worldly princes, who feed and live on them; instead, I exalt in Your Excellency a simple meekness and I revere a Christian piety and a singular charity towards your neighbour that always tends to be so distant from the lords of this world.)

Another heterodox author, the priest Lucio Paolo Rosello, addressed his *Considerationi devote intorno alla vita e passione di Christo* (Venice: Comin da Trino, 1551) to Renée, 'la cui pietà donatale dal donatore di tutti i beni la fa di maniera riverire, che se le inchinano tutti i buoni' (fol. A3$^r$; whose piety, given you by the giver of all that is good, makes you so revered that all good persons bow before you).

In 1560, a gentleman of Brescia, Giacomo Lanteri, perceived Renée's devout way of life as the basis for her domestic virtues. When he offered her his work on the duties of husbands and wives in managing the household, *Della economica* (Venice: Vincenzo Valgrisi, 1560), he explained that, having completed the work,

altro non mi restava a fare, volendo dare in luce questo mio Trattato (per non mi dilungare dall'usanza antica di tutti li Scrittori), che darlo nobilitato del nome di egregia persona, che lo facesse andare per le mani de gli huomini più accetto, et riguardevole. Da niun'altro Prencipe adunque per grande ch'egli si fosse, tengo io per fermo a questi miei scritti dover venire il favor ch'io desidero, che da V[ostra] E[xcellentia]. Perciochè trattandosi in essi quel tanto, che all'huomo, et alla donna per vivere da Christiani honoratamente fa mestier d'operare, et vedendosi ciò tutto con singolar meraviglia d'ogn'uno espresso nella santissima vita di lei: quando ella haverà accettata questa opera mia sotto la protettione del suo chiaro Nome: qual sarà tanto arrogante, che di quello vedendola ornata si arrischi con invidioso occhio riguardarla, et con maligna lingua lacerarla? Certo niuno. [. . .] Ella nel timor di Dio a tutto il mondo ha dato chiarissimo essempio. (fols *2$^v$–*3$^r$)

(all that remained for me to do in order to publish this treatise of mine, so as not to depart from the ancient custom of all writers, was to present it ennobled by the name of some outstanding person who would make it more welcome and respected as it passed into men's hands. I am certain, therefore, that no ruler, however great, other than Your Excellency could

provide these writings of mine with the favour I desire. They deal with what
man and woman need to do to live honourably as Christians, and everyone
can see, with unique admiration, all this expressed in your most holy life.
Therefore, when you have taken this work of mine under the protection of
your renowned name, who, seeing it thereby adorned, will be so arrogant as
to dare to look on it with an envious eye and tear it with a spiteful tongue?
Certainly no one. [. . .] You have given everyone an outstanding example in
the fear of God.)

Renée's reputation as head of her household was such that two of her
daughters were the object of dedications even while they were still very
young. Antonio Brucioli (1498?–1566), a Florentine exile in Venice who
was very sympathetic to the cause of reform, offered his vernacular translation of the Epistles and Gospels to Anna d'Este (1531–1607) in 1538 and his
translation of the New Testament to her in the following year. His letter
accompanying the Epistles and Gospels begins:

> La fama, Illustrissima Principessa, de' christianissimi et santi costumi di
> vostra eccellentia, ne' giovenili et teneri anni suoi, in modo la rende notabile
> et ammiranda in tutta l'Italia, che ciascuno tanto di bene se ne promette, che
> non pensa che sia altra signora in questi nostri maligni secoli che quella
> superi di pietà verso Iddio et charità verso di quegli che del suo aiuto hanno
> bisogno, oltre alla magnanimità et grandezza dell'animo suo.[148]

> (Most illustrious princess, the renown of Your Excellency's most Christian
> and holy ways in your young and tender years makes you so noteworthy and
> admirable throughout Italy that everyone expects such good to come of you
> that they think no other lady, in these evil times of ours, shows more
> devotion to God and charity towards those who need your help, in addition
> to the magnanimity and greatness of your spirit.)

When Brucioli offers the New Testament to Anna, he writes that 'le cose
sacre' (sacred writings) cannot be dedicated in a better way than to 'quelle
pie anime che le hanno in prezzo, et che pendono tutte dal Signore, come è
la publica fama di vostra signoria, ammaestrata nella via del Signore, da

---

[148] *Epistole lettioni et evangelii che si leggono in tutto l'anno nuovamente tradotti in lingua toscana per
Antonio Brucioli* (Venice: Bartolomeo Zanetti for Giovanni Dalla Chiesa, 1538), fol. [1]2ʳ; praise of
Anna continues on fols [1]2ᵛ–[1]3ʳ. I am grateful to Frédéric Prémartin of the Bibliothèque Méjanes,
Aix-en-Provence, for information on this rare edition. Also dedicated to Anna are another edition
of Brucioli's translation of the *Epistole, lettioni et evangelii* printed in Venice by Claudio Sabini,
datable to 1538, and *Il Nuovo Testamento di Christo Giesù Signore et Salvatore nostro: di greco tradotto
in lingua toscana* (Venice: Francesco Bindoni and Maffeo Pasini, 1539). See Giorgio Spini,
'Bibliografia delle opere di Antonio Brucioli', *LB*, 42 (1940), 129–180 (pp. 147–48, 155);
Edoardo Barbieri, *Le bibbie italiane del Quattrocento e del Cinquecento*, 2 vols (Milan: Editrice
Bibliografica, 1992), I, 274–75.

christianissima et santissima madre' (fol. *2ᵛ; those pious souls who value them and who depend entirely on the Lord, as you are publicly renowned to do, instructed in the way of the Lord by a most Christian and holy mother). He defends his use of the vernacular as a means of access to the Scriptures for all readers, and he places his translation before Anna:

> Onde dovendo tutte le genti, di tutte le lingue, venire a questo santissimo autore et datore della vita, acciò che quegli della Italia che altra lingua non sanno possino gustare questo pane celestiale, con lo aiuto di Dio, al quale vivono tutte le cose, sotto la fidatissima tutela di V[ostra] Illustrissima S[ignoria] avanti alla mensa delle pie menti vulgari lo pongo, a fin che, mangiando di quello, vivino sempre, amonendo tutte le pie menti de' Christiani che venghino a trarsi la sete a questo sacratissimo fonte. (fol. ***6ᵛ)

> (Thus since all people, of all languages, must come to this most holy author and giver of life, so that Italians who know no other language can taste that heavenly bread, with the help of God, in whom all things live, I place [this book] under your most trusted protection before the table of pious minds who use the vernacular, so that, by eating of it, they may live for ever, admonishing all the pious minds of Christians to come to slake their thirst at this most sacred spring.)

Nearly a decade later, in 1548, Brucioli dedicated his edition of Petrarch's Italian verse to Anna's younger sister Lucrezia (1535–1598). According to Brucioli, the renown of her rare virtues had spread well beyond Ferrara. Indeed, Lucrezia was seen as a modern incarnation of the qualities for which Petrarch praised his beloved Laura, and she should 'rendere gratia a Iddio, che di tante alte virtù, vi habbia dotata' (thank God that he has endowed you with so many lofty virtues).[149] Brucioli's image-making on behalf of these two young girls, who in later life both married dukes, would have been appreciated by their mother, Renata.[150] Lucrezia d'Este was also praised for her virtues when she was an adult. Celso Giraldi offered her in 1583 the tragedy *Selene* by his father Giovan Battista Giraldi, pointing out that this was a fitting dedication 'per la innocenza et schiettezza di Selene grande Reina dello Egitto, conforme molto alla bontà et santità de' costumi di lei' (because of the innocence and sincerity of Selene, the great Queen of

---

[149] (Venice: Alessandro Brucioli and brothers, 1548), fol. a8ʳ⁻ᵛ. See also William J. Kennedy, *Authorizing Petrarch* (Ithaca: Cornell University Press, 1994), pp. 73–74, and Davide Dalmas, 'Antonio Brucioli editore e commentatore di Petrarca', in *Antonio Brucioli: humanisme et évangélisme entre Réforme et Contre-Réforme. Actes du colloque de Tours, 20–21 mai 2005*, ed. by Élise Boillet (Paris: Champion, 2008), pp. 131–45 (pp. 133–34).

[150] I am grateful to Elena Bonora for this suggestion.

Egypt, very like the goodness and holiness of your own ways); other queens
could see themselves mirrored not only in Selene but also in Lucrezia.
Chiara Matraini chose Lucrezia as dedicatee of her *Considerationi sopra
i sette salmi penitentiali del gran re, e profeta Davit* (Lucca: Busdraghi, 1586)
because, she said, Lucrezia was an 'imagine di vera virtù' (fol. A2ᵛ; image of
true virtue).

Outside ruling families, too, the intellectual and moral qualities of some
women could lead to their being selected as dedicatees by writers and
others. Among such women, Vittoria Colonna may well have been chosen
most frequently among Italian women of the sixteenth century, for
a number of reasons.[151] It was her intelligence that impressed Ludovico di
Varthema, author of an account of travels to the Far East that may have
been the first work dedicated to her. In 1509, the year in which Colonna
was married at the age of nineteen, Varthema visited her mother Agnese di
Montefeltro in Marino and recounted his travels to them both. It was
probably in the following year that he had a copy of the work made by the
scribe Ludovico degli Arrighi and offered it to Colonna, writing that, when
he met her, he recognized her 'sublime et svelto ingegno, lo excelso et
elevato spirito ultra li anni et sexo meravigliosamente avanzare' (that your
sublime and quick mind, excellent and elevated spirit was marvellously in
advance of your years and sex).[152] In 1519 the poet Girolamo Britonio
praised the good use to which Colonna, the object of his love, had put
her spiritual gifts: 'le nobili et interne doti dal cortese cielo a voi sì
largamente concesse, l'havete non poco sempre con le bellezze de l'animo
accompagnate, et non alla apparenza solo, come molte fanno' (you have
always accompanied to no little extent the noble inner gifts, so generously
granted to you by the kindly heavens, with beauty of the spirit, and not
only for show, as many women do).[153]

Other dedicatory letters praise Colonna's intellectual gifts, her moral
gifts or both. Cardinal Pompeo Colonna, offering a manuscript of his
*Apologiae mulierum libri II* in about 1524–25, calls her 'virtutum omnium

[151] Concetta Ranieri, 'Vittoria Colonna: dediche, libri e manoscritti', *Critica letteraria*, 13 (1985),
249–70.
[152] Emanuele Casamassima, 'Ludovico degli Arrighi detto Vicentino copista dell'Itinerario del
Varthema (cod. Landau Finaly 9, Biblioteca Nazionale Centrale di Firenze)', *LB*, 64 (1962),
117–62 (pp. 134–36).
[153] *Opera volgare intitolata Gelosia del sole* (Naples: 'della stampa di Sigismondo Mair' [Caterina Mayr],
1519), fol. A3ʳ. On this work, see also Raffaele Girardi, 'La scrittura cantabile', in *Modelli e maniere:
esperienze poetiche del Cinquecento meridionale* (Bari: Palomar, 1999), pp. 27–78 (pp. 46–58), and
Mikaël Romanato, 'Per l'edizione della *Gelosia del sole* di Girolamo Britonio', *Italique*, 12 (2009),
33–71.

definiti[o]' (the definition of all virtues).[154] When Giovanni Tommaso Filocalo's *Canzone recitata in Napoli all'illustrissimo s[ignor] don Alfonso Avalo* is printed in Naples by Ioanne Sultzbach and Antonio de Iovino in 1531, the author recalls in his dedicatory letter to Giovanni Antonio Muscettola that he had originally dedicated the poem 'a quella unica Donna de' nostri tempi, Vittoria Colonna, che non solo di stile leggiadro, et bello, et di nobile ingegno, ciascun'altra vince, ma come vedete, ogni dì a se stessa fa guerra, et se medesma avanza' (fol. [1]1ᵛ; to that unique lady of our times, who excels all other women not only in her graceful and beautiful style and her noble mind but, as you see, daily wages war on herself and surpasses herself). Agostino Nifo, around 1531, tells Colonna that 'nostra tempestate sola licterariis muneribus digna es' (in our age you alone are worthy of literary gifts).[155] Bernardo Tasso writes in 1534 that his verse will achieve immortality by association both with Colonna's literary reputation and with her virtues:

> Sperando, che, sì come sola, quell'altissimo grado di perfettione, che in ciascun'arte et in ogni scienza si ritrova occupato tenendo; Sapho, et tutte l'altre nelle bone lettere più famose di gran lunga avanzando, et col volo delle vostre proprie penne sopra le stelle levandovi, havete co' raggi della vostra virtù illustrata questa nostra età, sarete etiamdio contenta, che queste mie egloghe et elegie vivino nel seno della vostra gloria, et col lume de' vostri honori sgombrando le tenebre della loro imperfettione, tanto più volentieri dal mondo lette sieno, quanto più gli ornamenti delle vostre virtù le renderanno belle.[156]

> (You alone – occupying that highest rank of perfection that is found in every art and in all knowledge, far surpassing Sappho and all the other women most famed as literary authors, and rising above the stars with the flight of your own quills – have illuminated this age of ours with the rays of your virtue. I hope that, in the same way, you will be content that these eclogues and elegies of mine may live in the bosom of your glory and that, driving away the shadows of their imperfection with the light of your honours, they may be read by the world all the more willingly as the adornments of your virtues will make them fair.)

---

[154] On Pompeo Colonna's work, see Guglielmo Zappacosta, *Studi e ricerche sull'umanesimo italiano (testi inediti del XV e XVI secolo)* (Bergamo: Minerva Italica, 1972), pp. 159–264, and Brundin, *Vittoria Colonna*, pp. 122–26.

[155] *De vera vivendi libertate*, in BAV, MS Chigi F IV 61: Ranieri, 'Vittoria Colonna', pp. 254–55.

[156] Dedication of the *Egloghe* and *Elegie* within the *Libro secondo de gli amori*, printed together with the *Libro primo* (Venice: Giovanni Antonio da Sabbio, 1534), fols O2ᵛ–O3ʳ. See also Bernardo Tasso, *Rime*, 2 vols (Turin: RES, 1995), I, *I tre libri degli amori*, ed. by Domenico Chiodo, pp. 261–62, and Ranieri, 'Vittoria Colonna', pp. 261–62.

The lawyer Enrico Boccella talks of her in 1539 as a beacon of Christianity: 'ut inter tot Christianae religionis clarissima lumina, plurimum eluceas, atque emineas' (so that you shine out and stand out very strongly among so many bright lights of the Christian religion).[157] Adamo Fumani dedicates to her his version of works by St Basil, as he writes in 1540, at the request of the reforming bishop of Verona, Giovanni Matteo Giberti, who had commissioned the translation. With an allusion to her use of the motif of the sun in her poetry, Fumani tells Colonna:

> acutissimam ingenii tui aciem, dispulsis, si quae erant, quae adhuc officer-ent, humiliorum cogitationum nubibus, ad unum iustitiae solem poenitus contuendum appulisti: haec omnia ita vita ac moribus praestas, ut caeteris non fœminis modo, sed viris etiam, et quidem gravissimis, clarissimum velut e superiore loco ad salutarem vitae portum petendum lumen videaris praetulisse.

> (having dispelled the clouds of lowlier thoughts – if there were such – that might still stand in your way, you applied your very keen intelligence and talent to gazing inwardly upon the one sun of justice; you so surpass all these things by your life and behavior that you seem to have offered a light to everyone else, not only women but even very serious men, a very bright light shining as though from a vantage point, for reaching the harbor of life in salvation.)

Fumani concludes by telling Colonna that Giberti has heard that she lives among women who have consecrated themselves entirely to God – that is, nuns – and that her exhortations will have greater influence if they are supported by her use of St Basil: 'eo maiorem illas cohortationibus tuis fidem tributuras existimavit, si quae cohortandi gratia diceres, ea sanctis-simi ac doctissimi viri authoritate, ac testimoniis confirmasses' (he thought that they would be more likely to trust your exhortations if you had confirmed with the authority and witness of a very holy and learned man what you say by way of encouraging them).[158] In other words, Fumani, writing on Giberti's behalf, sees the dedication of the works of St Basil to Colonna as serving to reinforce her spiritual influence within a specific

[157] *Parastasis id est per testes approbatio, de amore et timore Dei* (Lucca: Giovanni Battista Faelli, 1539): Ranieri, 'Vittoria Colonna', pp. 255–56.
[158] St Basil the Great, *Moralia. Ascetica magna, Ascetica parva, Adamo Fumano interprete* (Lyon: Sébastien Gryphius, 1540), quoted here from *Omnia D. Basilii Magni Archiepiscopi Caesareae Capadociae quae extant opera, a Iano Cornario et Adamo Fumano latinitate donata* (Venice: ad signum Spei, 1548), fol. ***8ᵛ; translations from Barry Collett, *A Long and Troubled Pilgrimage: The Correspondence of Marguerite d'Angoulême and Vittoria Colonna, 1540–1545* (Princeton: Princeton Theological Seminary, 2000), pp. 135–36, with a slight modification.

community of nuns in Rome. Yet surely both men had a wider purpose in mind: they wished to send forth to readers the writings of St Basil under the aegis of probably the most renowned living example of devoutness among lay Italians of either sex. And as it happens, Colonna was generous to her dedicators: she rewarded Fumani for his dedication of Basil's works with fifty gold ducats.[159]

Vittoria Colonna's reputation was used in 1538 in a publication of a work by a very different kind of figure, the itinerant singer and occasional publisher Ippolito Ferrarese. In this year he decided to commission an edition of a popular devotional work called *Opera santissima et utile a qualunque fidel christiano de trenta documenti* (Brescia: Damiano Turlini for Ippolito Ferrarese). The first edition of 1509 had been dedicated by the author, the cleric Pietro da Lucca, to a noble widow of the same city, Caterina Carminiati; Ippolito decided to dedicate the work instead to Colonna, no doubt because of her much wider reputation as a devout widow. He justifies his choice by saying that the work will help her to achieve Christian perfection, and he even adds an admonition that she should read it at least once a month. If read literally, as an exhortation to Colonna alone, Ippolito's words sound presumptuous; but rather, he seems to be using his address to her chiefly as a means of impressing other readers:

> Sapendo io il vostro bon desiderio di volere con la divina gratia attingere a qualche grado di cristiana perfettione e come vera vidoa separata molti anni fa dall'illustre S[ignor] Marchese vostro diletto consorte, e volervi in tutto accostare allo inamorato sposo Cristo Iesu [...] considerando ancora le molte operationi vostre le quale non permettendo che molto tempo abbiate [...] mi è parso con questa mia epistola salutarvi e compendiosamente descrivervi Trenta Documenti ne li quali con brevità di parole si comprende tutta la vita spirituale acciò possiate in poco spacio di tempo studiarla e metterla in memoria e poi essequirla. [...] Non siate adunque pigra ricever e abbracciare questa saluberrima dottrina, la quale almanco ogni mese una volta leggerete con fermo proposito di volerla osservare.

> (I know your good desire to attain, with divine grace, some level of Christian perfection and as a true widow separated many years ago from your beloved consort the marquis [Ferdinando Francesco d'Avalos, Marquis of Pescara], and to draw close in everything to the beloved spouse Christ Jesus. [...] Considering, too, your many activities that leave you little free time [...], I have decided to greet you with this letter of mine and to describe to you in summary Thirty Documents in which are succinctly contained the whole of

---

[159] Ranieri, 'Vittoria Colonna', p. 257, n. 20.

spiritual life, so that you can study it in a short time and memorize it and
then carry it out. [...] Do not therefore delay in receiving and embracing
this most wholesome doctrine, which you should read at least monthly with
the firm intention of following it.)

All this is part of an elaborate façade built up by Ippolito, including the
attribution of the work to an earlier and better-known author, Cherubino
da Spoleto, and the impossible claim made on the title page that
Cherubino, who died in 1484, had passed the work to Ippolito ('donata
per il detto [Cherubino]').[160] The circumstances of the dedication were just
as open to creative manipulation as were the naming of the author and the
alleged circumstances of publication.

A Neapolitan noblewoman related by marriage to Colonna, Maria
d'Aragona d'Avalos (after 1503–1568), receives a similar exhortation in
one of two dedicatory letters addressed to her in Milan in 1540. We saw
earlier that Ludovica Torelli arranged in this year the print publication of
the *Specchio interiore* by fra Battista da Crema. It is significant that her
dedication of this work to Maria d'Aragona is written from the 'Sacred
College of Paul the Apostle', in other words from the religious congrega-
tion co-founded by her in Milan, the Angelic Sisters of St Paul. This had
received a papal constitution in 1535, and by 1539 it comprised thirty-four
professed nuns and seventeen secular women.[161] Torelli uses the name she
had taken in this community, Paula Maria. In her letter to Maria
d'Aragona, she explains why she had chosen her as dedicatee: she is
aware that Maria has already applied herself to 'spiritual studies' and she
wants to assist her in pursuing what she calls her 'chaste desires'. Maria is
therefore urged to look into fra Battista's 'mirror' in order to seek spiritual
perfection (fol. ❧4$^v$–5$^v$), just as Isabella and Beatrice Sforza had been
urged to use St Catherine's dialogue as a mirror in 1494. Of course, if
Torelli had wished to assist Maria d'Aragona alone, she could more easily
have provided her with a manuscript copy of the work; in using print
publication, she is also using Maria's name in order to inspire other readers,
especially women, and to promote her new religious community.

Pietro Aretino, presenting his life of the Virgin Mary (*La vita di Maria
Vergine*) to Maria d'Aragona in 1539, draws a close link between her, in her
position as wife of the governor of Milan, Alfonso d'Avalos, and the

---

[160] Giancarlo Petrella, '"Ad instantia d'Hippolito Ferrarese": un cantimbanco editore nell'Italia del
Cinquecento', *Paratesto*, 8 (2011), 23–80 (pp. 49–54, 72; quotation from p. 52).
[161] Baernstein, 'In Widow's Habit', p. 792, and Baernstein, *A Convent Tale*, pp. 27–55.

Blessed Virgin. What is he to call his dedicatee, he asks? He answers his question in characteristically flamboyant style:

> potrei chiamarvi nutrice de la charità christiana, potrei battezzarvi essecutrice de le opere catholiche, potrei dirvi fautrice de la religion di Giesù: ma perché a le degnità del vostro merito si confà più che altro il cognominarvi erario de le lodi de la madre di Christo; come tale vi saluto, e come a tale ve le presento, et Iddio mi spira a farlo: acciochè gli atti di Maria nata de la stirpe di David siano guardati da Maria discesa del sangue di Aragona.[162]

> (I could call you the wet nurse of Christian charity, I could baptize you executor of Catholic works, I could term you supporter of the religion of Jesus; but since the most fitting name for the dignities of your worth is the treasury of the praises of the mother of Christ, as such I greet you and I present them to you as to such a person. God inspires me to do this, so that the deeds of Mary born of the line of David may be contemplated by Mary descended from the blood of Aragon.)

Here Aretino's starting point is an image of the dedicatee as nurse of the church of Christ, which Jean de Vauzelles had applied to Marguerite de Navarre in his translation (printed in Lyon in 1539) of Aretino's *La humanità di Christo* in three books.[163] Aretino goes on to allude to Maria's powers of intercession to her husband the governor:

> Certo Milano non è più bisognoso, nè servo mentre gli è concesso l'ombra de l'altissima mogliera d'Alfonso Davalos: la providenza del quale non sa, nè può negare pur un minimo de i prieghi di lei, percioché ella tanto pura quanto vaga, e non men religiosa che savia intercede per altri a lui ne la maniera, che Maria vergine supplica per noi a Dio. (fol. A2ᵛ)

> (Certainly Milan is no longer needy or servile as long as it has the protection of the most lofty wife of Alfonso d'Avalos. His providence neither knows how nor is able to deny even the least of her prayers, since she – as pure as she is fair, and no less religious than wise – intercedes to him on behalf of others just as the Virgin Mary supplicates on our behalf to God.)

Aretino wrote to a bishop, Girolamo Verallo, to explain why he chose Maria as dedicatee: she surpasses all other women, 'tal che il Cielo non iscorge petto che alberghi più concetti sacri né più intenzioni sante del suo. Onde io le ho dedicato l'istoria de la Vergine come a creatura che imita il viver de la Reina de gli Angeli, qual si appartiene d'imitarlo' (so that Heaven sees no breast that harbours more sacred thoughts or more holy

---

[162] (Venice: Francesco Marcolini, 1539), fol. A2ʳ.
[163] Boillet, 'L'Arétin et l'actualité des années 1538–1539', pp. 110–11.

intentions than hers. Hence I have dedicated to her the story of the Virgin
as to a creature that imitates the life of the Queen of Angels, as it is fitting to
imitate it).[164] Here again, the dedication to a woman plays a unique role: it
links the work with contemporary realities by connecting the two Marias,
the mother of Christ and her living imitator, an exemplar of spiritual
virtues who in turn should by implication be imitated by Aretino's other
readers.

In an earlier dedication, Aretino had put a typically sly twist on the
notion of presenting a work to a woman whose household had a virtuous
reputation. In February 1533, he dedicated his comedy *Il Marescalco* (The
stablemaster) to Argentina Pallavicino Rangone, daughter of Federico
Pallavicino of Zibello and wife of the soldier Guido Rangone.
A noblewoman was an unexpected choice for any kind of comedy, because
the genre's subject matter was often indecorous, as was the case with this
one. The plot concerns a trick played on a stablemaster who is resolutely
homosexual, but who is told that he is being given a bride. In due course,
however, 'she' turns out to be a page boy in disguise. Aretino argues that
someone such as Pallavicino Rangone was needed in order to give his work
a better reputation. Describing his work as a daughter of his, he fears that
her good reputation is at risk, since she seems to know everyone:

> Onde io, che veggio in pericolo lo onor suo e il mio, poiché non posso
> metterle in core di farsi monica, vedendo la religione in cui allevate le
> nobilissime donzelle poste a i servigi vostri, ve la dono, sperando udire di
> lei qualcuna di quelle qualità che il mondo ode di voi, che avete fatto de la
> casa vostra il tempio di pudicizia; e perché ella è alquanto baldanzosetta,
> insegnatele voi, che sète lo essempio de i gentili costumi, a non passare
> i termini di onestà nel far comedia de la istoria del marescalco, il quale dovea
> consigliarsi di tôr moglie con il gran Cavaliere Guido Rangone, che [. . .] gli
> arebbe aperto gli occhi di maniera che sarebbe corso a pigliarla.[165]

> (I see both her honour and mine in danger; thus, since I cannot persuade her
> to become a nun, and seeing the religion in which you bring up the most
> noble ladies placed in your service, I give her to you. I hope to hear about her
> some of those qualities that the world hears of you, who have made your
> house the temple of modesty. Since she is somewhat bold, teach her, you

---

[164] Aretino, *Lettere*, II, letters 211 and 212 (22 and 25 November 1540), pp. 234–37. The letter to Verallo
is included at the end of the edition of the life of the Virgin. On Maria d'Aragona's role in Milan,
see Robin, *Publishing Women*, pp. 35–38.

[165] Pietro Aretino, *Il Marescalco*, in *Teatro*, II, ed. by Giovanna Rabitti, Carmine Boccia and
Enrico Garavelli (Rome: Salerno Editrice, 2010), 9–152 (p. 25). The first edition was printed in
Venice by Bernardino Vitali. On Argentina Rangone, see Katherine A. McIver, *Women, Art, and
Architecture in Northern Italy, 1520–1580: Negotiating Power* (Farnham: Ashgate, 2006), pp. 21, 143.

who are the example of noble behaviour, not to go beyond the bounds of honour in making a comedy of the story of the stablemaster, who should have asked advice about taking a wife from the great Cavaliere Guido Rangone, who [. . .] would have opened his eyes in such a way that he would have run to wed her.)

A visual paratext that suggests a tacit dedication to Maria d'Aragona seems to present another variation on a convention. It is a woodcut profile portrait that adorns the title page of one of a small group of editions that contain crude parodies of the first canto of Ludovico Ariosto's *Orlando furioso*: the *Rolant furius di mesir Lodovic di Arost stramudat in lengua Bergamascha per ol Zambò de val Brombana indrizat al sagnor Bartolamè Minchió da Bergem so Patró* (Orlando furioso by Ludovico Ariosto changed into the Bergamasque language by Zambò of Valle Brembana, addressed to his patron Bartolamè Minchió of Bergamo).[166] It represents Maria at some point after 1537, since it is inscribed 'Maria Aragonia aetatis suae ann. XXXIIII' (Maria d'Aragona in her thirty-fourth year of age). The portrait had been created for an edition of an entirely different work, the *Lettura di Girolamo Ruscelli sopra un sonetto dell'illustriss[imo] signor marchese della Terza alla divina signora marchesa del Vasto*, printed in Venice by Giovanni Griffio in 1552 and dedicated to her.[167] There is no obvious reason for its inclusion in the *Rolant furius*, but perhaps it was intended as a tongue-in-cheek allusion to the practice of dedicating works to noblewomen, a parody like the text itself.

As mentioned earlier (note 100), Aurelia Petrucci, a member of a leading family of Siena, was the dedicatee of a translation of a book of the *Aeneid*. She also received the dedication of an important vernacular discussion of love, the *Dialoghi d'amore* of the philosopher Leone Ebreo (Judah Abrabanel), printed posthumously in 1535 (Rome: Antonio Blado). The editor, the Sienese nobleman Mariano Lenzi, presents Petrucci as a model for all persons (fol. A2$^{r-v}$): she is someone who will help them to learn 'le vere virtù nell'essempio della vita vostra' (true virtues in the example of

---

[166] ([N. p.]: [n. pub.], [not before 1552].) On the Bergamasque versions, see Luca D'Onghia, 'Due paragrafi sulla fortuna dialettale del "Furioso"', in *'Tra mille carte vive ancora': ricezione del 'Furioso' tra immagini e parole*, ed. by Lina Bolzoni, Serena Pezzini and Giovanna Rizzarelli (Lucca: Pacini Fazzi, 2010), pp. 281–98 (pp. 286–87 on this portrait).

[167] On the portrait, see Benedetto Croce, 'Un sonetto dell'Aretino e un ritratto di Maria d'Aragona, marchesana del Vasto', in *Aneddoti di varia letteratura*, I (Bari: Laterza, 1953), 359–65 (reproduced on p. 363). Ruscelli mentions it in a letter to Aretino datable to May 1551: *Lettere scritte a Pietro Aretino*, ed. by Paolo Procaccioli, 2 vols (Rome: Salerno Editrice, 2003–04), II, 309; Girolamo Ruscelli, *Lettere*, ed. by Chiara Gizzi and Paolo Procaccioli (Manziana: Vecchiarelli, 2010), pp. 28–30.

your life), 'uno specchio, et una Idea del mondo come si convenga vivere alli altri' (a mirror and an ideal of the world as others should live).[168]

It was all too easy to present a noblewoman as an embodiment of virtue when she did not truly deserve this accolade, or at least could not yet have fully deserved it, as in Brucioli's dedications to the young sisters Anna and Lucrezia d'Este. The dedication of Moderata Fonte's remarkable defence of women, *Il merito delle donne*, in the posthumous first edition (Venice: Domenico Imberti, 1600), was addressed to a woman who, it was claimed, was the best person to exemplify the argument that women are much worthier than men. The dedicator was the author's daughter Cecilia Zorzi, and the dedicatee was Livia della Rovere, who had recently become the second wife of the much older Duke of Urbino, her cousin Francesco Maria II. Cecilia argues that, 'sapendosi quanto haveranno questi [huomini] a male un tal concetto; egli è ben giusto destinare a sua difesa Donna tale, al cui sol cenno si sgomentino questi detrattori, et nimici della Donnesca virtù et non ardiscano far parola in contrario' (since it is known how badly these men will receive such an idea, it is certainly right to allocate to its defence a woman at whose gesture alone these detractors and enemies of womanly virtue will be afraid and will not dare to say a word against it). Further, Livia's husband can fortunately be seen as different from the majority of men (fol. a2ᵛ). Yet Livia could hardly have had any opportunity to display her virtues, since in 1600 she was still only fourteen years old.

It is not surprising, then, that one can also find a reaction against the conventional selection of socially powerful laywomen as dedicatees, in favour of a spiritually exemplary member of a religious community. The printer-publisher Orazio Salviani made explicit his rejection of the self-seeking practice of printers when he dedicated his edition of the *Cantici spirituali composti da una religiosa del Ordine di S. Chiara dell'Osservantia* (Naples: Orazio Salviani, 1574) to the Clarissan nun Isabella Revertera: 'Suole esser commune usanza de' stampatori dedicar l'opere, che mandano in luce a qualche persona, dalla quale ne possano ricevere alcuna utilità, o favore, per poter in qualche modo risarcire le spese, et travagli del stampare' (It is the common practice of printers to dedicate the works they publish to some person from whom they can receive some gain or favour, in order to compensate in some way for the expenses and troubles

---

[168] In 1540 Antonio Vignali dedicated to Petrucci his dialogue on love, *Dulpisto*: see the edition of James W. Nelson Novoa at http://parnaseo.uv.es/Lemir/Textos/Dulpisto.pdf (accessed 23 February 2015). On both dialogues, see Eisenbichler, *The Sword and the Pen*, pp. 63–69.

of printing).[169] He wondered to whom to dedicate this work, but could think of no one better than the modest suor Isabella:

> Non già per riceverne utilità, o favori temporali [...]. Ma solo per haver udito per fama le sue rare virtù. Et per esser questa operina composta da una Religiosa del sacro ordine di Santa Chiara, mi parve che non convenisse dedicarla ad altra persona, che a religiosa dell'istesso ordine, come V[ostra] S[ignoria]. Et tanto più che so certo, che non mi mancherà di ciò copioso premio (spirituale però) dignandosi lei per carità, tener memoria di me alle volte nelle sue sante orationi. (fol. A2$^{r-v}$)

> (Not indeed to receive gain or temporal favours from it [...]. But only because I have heard of your rare virtues by renown. And since this little work was composed by a nun of the sacred order of St Clare, it seemed to me that it was not right to dedicate it to any person other than a nun of the same order such as yourself. And all the more since I know for certain that I will not be lacking a rich (though spiritual) reward for this if you deign, out of your charity, to remember me sometimes in your holy prayers.)

Salviani was, however, being somewhat disingenuous, since this sister was a member of a noble family.

Giacomo Lanteri, we saw earlier, wanted to follow the convention of publishing his treatise *Della economica* 'ennobled by the name of some outstanding person who would make it more welcome and respected as it passed into men's hands'. The cases considered in this last section have shown that, in the Italian Renaissance, women were enlisted to fulfil the important role of 'ennobling' texts at the point of publication with some frequency, especially for certain genres. Those selected normally possessed, or were seen to possess, two of the kinds of capital, to use the terminology of Pierre Bourdieu, that also belonged to male dedicatees: economic capital, in the form of financial resources, and social capital, through their membership of an elite community that held political power.[170] (The low number of dedicatees among Venetian patrician women seems to be related to the way in which Venetian society made it hard for women to raise their social and cultural profile, and to the fact that, in general, non-courtly society offered fewer opportunities for women to establish

---

[169] Abigail Brundin, Deborah Howard and Mary Laven, *The Sacred Home in Renaissance Italy* (Oxford University Press, 2018), pp. 92–93, 243–45.

[170] Pierre Bourdieu, 'The Forms of Capital', trans. by Richard Nice, in *Handbook of Theory and Research for the Sociology of Education*, ed. by John G. Richardson (New York: Greenwood, 1986), pp. 241–58.

individual identities.)[171] In choosing women such as Isabella d'Este or Vittoria Colonna, dedicators were also associating their texts with women's cultural capital, their intellectual status or their association with networks of writers, musicians and artists. One particular factor, however, seems to set the image of many women dedicatees apart from that of their male counterparts: they were often described as possessing high *moral* capital in the form of the spiritual and ethical virtues that they were seen to display within their own circles. The figure of the female dedicatee was thus analogous to that of the ideal woman as represented in conduct books intended for women; and of course it suited a male-dominated society to promote the ideal of the chaste and devout female, as a means of main- taining the social and political order.[172] Yet there was also genuine admira- tion for the virtues embodied by real women such as Colonna or Renée de France. In other words, those who opted to dedicate a text to a woman, rather than to a man, could be seeking not just to obtain the conventional rewards that could stem from patronage but also to associate the work with a person whose way of life could be represented as, and indeed often was, a mirror of exemplary conduct held up before the work's other intended readers.

---

[171] An exception is one of the issues of the Petrarch printed by Marcolini in 1539, dedicated to the Venetian noblewoman Laura Badoer, an appropriate choice because of her first name. (See Francesco Marcolini, *Scritti: lettere, dediche, avvisi ai lettori*, ed. by Paolo Procaccioli (Manziana: Vecchiarelli, 2013), no. 8.) Another is the edition of *Il Salterio secondo la Bibbia* (Venice: al segno della Speranza, 1571), dedicated by the bookseller Gasparo Albara to Elena Cappello, noble nun of the convent of Sant'Andrea della Zirada, whom he admits he knows only through her virtuous reputation: see Edoardo Barbieri, 'Di certi usi della Sacra Scrittura condannati: "Il Salmista secondo la Bibbia"', *LB*, 120 (2018), 75–109 (pp. 107–09). Biagioli notes that, for Galileo, 'a republic like Venice (a sort of patrician corporation) could not offer the type of legitimation he sought', in other words the patronage of the absolute prince; he thus left his post as professor in Padua for the Florence of Cosimo II (*Galileo, Courtier*, p. 29).

[172] Nancy Armstrong and Leonard Tennenhouse, 'The Literature of Conduct, the Conduct of Literature, and the Politics of Desire: An Introduction', in *The Ideology of Conduct: Essays on Literature and the History of Sexuality*, ed. by Nancy Armstrong and Leonard Tennenhouse (New York: Methuen, 1987), pp. 1–24 (pp. 5–7).

CHAPTER 2

# Making and Selling Books

## Women as Scribes

### Learning to Copy Texts

In the summer of 1453, a Milanese girl, just eight years old, composed what was probably her first letter to her father. She was living with her mother in Pavia, and she wrote:

> Poi che son tornata a Pavia, avanzandomi tempo in questi dì longhi, ho imparato un poco de scrivere, la qual cosa faccio con summo piacere, acciò che io possa per mie continue lettere parlare con la Ill[ustrissi]ma S[ignoria] V[ostra] et da quella ricevere le gratiose risposte.[1]

> (Since I have returned to Pavia and have some spare time during these long days, I have learned a little handwriting, something I do with the greatest pleasure, so that I can speak with Your most illustrious Lordship through my frequent letters and receive your gracious replies.)

The girl's handwriting is, understandably, still somewhat unsteady, but it is well controlled for someone of her age. Five years later, the same child was set a major task by her tutor: she was to copy out a substantial work of Cicero, the *De senectute*.[2] The opening page (British Library, MS Add.

---

[1] Forlì, Biblioteca Comunale, Raccolte Piancastelli, Sezione Carte Romagna, busta 445/26. Ippolita Maria Sforza, *Lettere*, ed. by M. Serena Castaldo (Alessandria: Edizioni dell'Orso, 2004), letter I (13 July 1453), p. 1, and Sforza, *Duchess and Hostage in Renaissance Naples: Letters and Orations*, ed. and trans. by Diana Robin and Lynn Lara Westwater (Toronto: Centre for Reformation and Renaissance Studies, 2017), letter 1, pp. 61–62. A letter of 1457, busta 445/22, is written in a more regular hand. I am grateful to Dott.ssa Antonella Imolesi for her assistance.

[2] On this manuscript, see Andrew G. Watson, *Catalogue of Dated and Datable Manuscripts c. 700–1600 in the Department of Manuscripts, British Library*, 2 vols (London: British Museum, 1979), I, no. 255; Judith Bryce, '"Fa finire uno bello studio et dice volere studiare": Ippolita Sforza and Her Books', *Bibliothèque d'Humanisme et Renaissance*, 64 (2002), 55–69 (p. 59); Gennaro Toscano, 'Livres et lectures de deux princesses de la cour d'Aragon de Naples: Isabella de Chiaromonte et Ippolita Maria Sforza', in *Livres et lectures de femmes en Europe entre Moyen Âge et Renaissance*, ed. by Anne-Marie Legaré (Turnhout: Brepols, 2007), pp. 295–310 (p. 299); Luisa Miglio, 'Donne e cultura scritta nel

21984, fol. 3$^r$; Figure 2.1) includes an illuminated border with the first syllables of the girl's first names, 'Hip Ma', and her emblem of a palm tree with the motto 'Iustus ut palma florebit et sicut cedrus Libani multi-plicatur' (Psalm 92. 12; The just shall flourish like the palm tree and shall grow like the cedar of Lebanon). The colophon reveals her identity in full: 'Ego Hippolyta Maria Vicecomes filia Ill[ustrissi]mi principis Francisci Sforciae ducis Mediolani exscripsi mea manu hunc libellum sub tempus pueritiae meae et sub Baldo praeceptore anno a natali christiano MCCCCLVIII octavo idus iulias' (fol. 71$^{r-v}$; I, Ippolita Maria Visconti [her mother's surname], daughter of the most illustrious prince Francesco Sforza, Duke of Milan, wrote this little book in my hand around the time of my childhood and under my tutor Baldo, 8 July 1458).

This assignment formed part of what must have been one of the best educations given to a woman in Renaissance Italy.[3] The exercise set by Ippolita Sforza's tutor, the humanist Baldo Martorelli, was partly a moral lesson for a girl who was in due course to become a queen of Naples: copying a work on old age and death even during her childhood, together with an appendix of moral sayings ('sententiae') such as 'Superbia est amor propriae excellentiae' ('Pride is the love of one's own excellence', from St Augustine) and a list of the three parts of penitence (fols 73$^v$–74$^r$). It was also a lesson in the use of the Latin language: Martorelli was doubtless responsible for pointing out the corrections that Ippolita needed to make to her text. On fol. 15$^r$, for instance, an 'a' is inserted in the ending of 'faci(a)t' (line 6) and a word division is indicated in 'A|morte' (line 9) and 'A|rebus' (lines 11–12). On the last full page of text (fol. 71$^r$), just before the colophon, a missing 'u' is inserted in 'uiuendi' (line 3) and four letters are added in 'defatigationem' (line 5). But it is also clear that the exercise had a third function for Ippolita: it formed part of her training in calligraphy, and more specifically in the use of humanistic script, the most elegant and scholarly hand of the period.

Ippolita's education was, of course, exceptionally privileged, and further-more she had the good fortune to share to some extent in the tutoring given to her brother Galeazzo, a year older than her. Yet some training in hand-writing was an integral part of the education of respectable young ladies, even if the results did not always reach such a high level as that achieved by

medioevo: http://edu.let.unicas.it/womediev/', in *Governare l'alfabeto: donne, scrittura e libri nel medioevo* (Rome: Viella, 2008), pp. 207–24 (pp. 216–17). Miglio's essay describes a database of European women scribes from the eighth century up to 1500.

[3] Serena Ferente, 'La duchessa ha qualcosa di dire', in *Atlante della letteratura italiana*, ed. by Sergio Luzzatto and Gabriele Pedullà, 3 vols (Turin: Einaudi, 2010–12), I, 421–26.

Figure 2.1 Cicero, *De senectute*, copied by Ippolita Sforza. © The British Library Board. MS Add. 21984, fol. 3ʳ

Ippolita. A treatise on the upbringing of girls called the *Decor puellarum* or
*Honore delle donzelle* (Honour of Young Ladies), composed by a Carthusian
monk and printed by Nicolas Jenson in Venice in 1471, included a book on
'li exercitii utili et necessari' (useful and necessary exercises), within which
was a chapter on reading and writing 'opere virtuose et devote' (virtuous and
devout works, V. 9).[4] Here the author told girls they could learn to write if
the purpose was good and they were taught by other women, and as long as
they read and wrote only appropriate texts:

> Finalmente vui podete, a bono fin et non altramente, imprender scriver,
> et da qualche vostra sorella, over madre, over qualche vostra honesta
> parente, et non da alchuno maschulo per bona casone; cum questo che
> mai non vogliate ni leger ni scriver cosse vane ni carnale, ni cossa che
> non possiate intender, et recever qualche fructo de virtù, come sonno
> legende de qualche sancte vergine, over de gli sancti padri, dove non se
> nomina cossa de luxuria. Ancora *Fior de virtù*, quello libreto che se
> chiama *Palma virtutum*, et quello che se chiama *Gloria de le donne*,
> *Spechio dela croce* et simel altri utili et virtuosi libri. La Bibia veramente
> a vui donzelle, le quale sète ignorante et senza littere, azò non intresate
> in qualche heresia, non ve conforto che del Testamento vechio legete,
> salvo cha el Genesis, zoè lo primo et lo secundo libro et fin che Moyses
> fece lo tabernaculo, li libri de li Re, la legenda de sam Daniel, de
> Samuel, de Saul etc. Ma più vi conforto lo Testamento novo tutto
> quanto, però che lì non posite errare.

> (Finally you may, for a good purpose and not otherwise, learn to write,
> and from a sister or your mother or some other honourable female
> relative, and not from any male for good reason; as long as you never
> wish to read or write vain or carnal matters or anything you cannot
> understand and derive some fruit of virtue from, for example, lives of
> some holy virgins or of the Holy Fathers, where lust is not mentioned.
> Also the *Fior di virtù* [Flower of Virtues], that little book entitled *Palma
> virtutum* [Palm of Virtues], the *Gloria delle donne* [Glory of Women],
> the *Specchio della croce* [Mirror of the Cross] and other such useful and
> virtuous books. As for the Bible, in truth I advise you young ladies, who
> are ignorant and know no Latin, not to read the Old Testament so that
> you do not enter into any heresy, except Genesis, that is, the first
> and second book and up to Moses making the tabernacle,[5] the Books
> of Kings, the life of St Daniel, of Samuel, of Saul etc. But rather
> I recommend to you the whole of the New Testament, because there
> you cannot go wrong.)

[4] On this work, and the four other devotional tracts printed by Jenson in 1471, see Martin Lowry,
*Nicholas Jenson and the Rise of Venetian Publishing* (Oxford: Blackwell, 1991), pp. 59–60, 240.
[5] That is, to the end of Exodus.

One of the writing masters who made use of print in the sixteenth century was Giovambattista Verini. His career embraced bookselling in his native city, Florence, writing poetry, and teaching handwriting and commercial arithmetic in northern Italy.[6] The colophon of the *Ardor d'amore novamente composto per il morigerato giovane Giovanbaptista Verini fiorentino alla sua diva Cleba* (Vercelli: Giovanni Maria Pellipari, 1534) states that at present the author 'insegnia abacho et scrivere incontro la spetiaria del gallo in Cremona et dallo illustrissimo S[ignor] Ducha di Milano provisionato' (is teaching commercial arithmetic and handwriting opposite the apothecary's at the sign of the cock in Cremona and is salaried by the most illustrious Duke of Milan). He actively sought female students of handwriting, while also wishing to enable them, through his books, to learn to write without the assistance of a teacher. The title page of a writing-book produced by Verini earlier, while he was teaching in Venice, probably between 1526 and 1532, *La utilissima opera da imparare a scrivere di varie sorti lettere di Giovambattista Verini Fiorentino che insegna al Rialto Abbaco et Scrivere*, displays a woodcut of a woman watching her master as he demonstrates writing. A book that Verini had printed in 1538, by which point he was teaching in Milan, offers specimens of various calligraphic hands, as well as an example of how to enter debits and credits in an account book, and the edition is addressed on its opening page to one of the dedicatees mentioned in the first chapter, Maria d'Aragona: *Alla illustra: et eccell[ente] S[ignora] Marchesa del Guasto. Giovanbattista Verini Fiorentino suo dedicatissimo servitore, che insegna Abbacho, et de ogni sorte littre Scrivere al mal Cantone al segno del Ballone i̇ Milano* (Brescia: Lodovico Britannico; Figure 2.2). A woodcut below depicts a master showing a lady how to write capital letters. The words will make up the motto 'Avarum neque parcum numquam di ama(nt)' (The gods never love someone covetous or parsimonious) – perhaps intended to encourage Verini's dedicatee to show generosity to him. The master appears to be Verini himself, since, with his beard and hat, he resembles Verini as portrayed in another woodcut on the following leaf in which he has two young male pupils (fol. A2$^r$). The lady on the first page, who is wearing an

---

[6] Paul F. Gehl, 'The "maiuschule moderne" of Giovambaptista Verini: From Music Texts to Calligraphic Musicality', in *Writing Relations: American Scholars in Italian Archives. Essays for Franca Petrucci Nardelli and Armando Petrucci*, ed. by Deanna Shemek and Michael Wyatt (Florence: Olschki, 2008), pp. 41–70; see also Emanuele Casamassima, *Trattati di scrittura del Cinquecento italiano* (Milan: Il Polifilo, 1966), pp. 27–29. On Verini's verse, see Alessandro D'Ancona, *La poesia popolare italiana*, 2nd edn (Livorno: Giusti, 1906), pp. 459–64. For an overview of handwriting manuals, see Paul F. Gehl, 'Writing Manuals', *Humanism for Sale*, www.humanismforsale.org/text/archives/335 (accessed 18 May 2017).

Figure 2.2 Giovanni Battista Verini, *Alla illustra et eccell[ente] S[ignora] Marchesa del Guasto* (Brescia: Lodovico Britannico for Giovanni Battista Verini, 1538), fol. Ar[r]. Chicago, Newberry Library, Vault Wing ZW 535 .V58

ornate headdress known as a *balzo*, is thus perhaps Maria. Below the woodcut on the second leaf are two strambotti. In the first, Verini urges '[li] spiriti gentili et virtuosi' (noble and virtuous spirits) to study his book if they wish to learn to write, banish ignorance and also gain riches and fame (line 6). The users he has in mind here seem to be chiefly male, but in a second strambotto he turns to women and the benefit they will gain from writing:

Alle fanciulle virtuose et da bene, Giovanbattista Verini Fiorentino

> Donne galante, et voi gentil pulcelle,
>   che virtù seguitate a tutte le hore
> aciò che meglio vi fondate in quelle,
>   composto ho questo sol per vostro amore,
> el qual insegna far littere belle
>   che fia per voi utile, et honore.
> Scrivere impararete bene et presto
>   senza d'avere a star sotto al Maest[r]o.

(To virtuous and worthy girls, Giovanbattista Verini of Florence. Gallant ladies, and you noble unmarried girls, who follow virtues at all times so that you can better base your behaviour on them, I have composed for love of you alone this [book] that teaches how to form beautiful letters, which will bring you profit and honour. You will learn to write well and quickly, without having to be taught by a master.)

Some scripts were considered easier to acquire than others. Even Verini acknowledges within this book that a humanistic cursive hand was particularly hard to write well, and he seems to address his advice on this to men alone, at least in the first instance: 'Littera Cancellerescha per gentil huomini. | Questa littera è molto difficile affarla bene, chi la vuole con tratti, et chi senza tratti' (fol. A2ᵛ; Chancery script for gentlemen. It is very difficult to write this hand well, some want it with strokes, some without), probably meaning with or without serifs. On this leaf, the hand is illustrated by italic printed characters, but he gives a specimen by means of a woodcut later in the book (fol. A6ʳ), plagiarized from a treatise of 1524 by Giovanni Antonio Tagliente.[7]

Towards the end of the sixteenth century, another writing master, Marcello Scalzini or Scalini of Camerino (1555–*c.* 1608), was less optimistic about women's capacity to write 'beautiful letters'; indeed, he took an altogether patronizing view of women as writers. In *Il secretario*, first

---

[7] Casamassima, *Trattati di scrittura*, Figure XXVII.

printed in 1581, his main aim is to teach and publicize what he calls his 'carattere cancellaresco corsivo romano' (cursive roman chancery script). He adds a specimen of it in which the letters are detached, and he suggests that this model will better suit those who are less skilled: 'E se vi sarà alcuno, che si compiaccia di scrivere senza concatenature, come fanno ordinariamente gli oltramontani, le donne et i vecchi potrà usare i medesimi caratteri dell'antiscritta cancellaresca, andando con la mano alquanto leggieri' (And if anyone likes to write without joining letters up, as is usually the case with northern Europeans, women and old people, that person can use the chancery characters mentioned above, moving the hand somewhat lightly). Women, then, are classed in a second division of writers.

The second part of Scalzini's book contains an extended critique of the multiple varieties of often over-elaborate scripts taught by some writing masters. His list of hands includes formal gothic scripts with simple shapes, of the sort used for official documents, and he acknowledges that they have their use for those who cannot read well for one reason or another:

> lettere antiche quadre, tonde staccate, antichette tonde, queste tre servono per Privilegii, Officii, et particolarmente sono commode per quei Vecchi, c'hanno poca vista, o che non vedono senza occhiali, et per quelli, et quelle Donne, che (non sapendo ben leggere) bramano sempre quelle forme di caratteri, che più assimigliano alle stampate, nelle quali hanno imparato a leggere.[8]

> (old [i.e. roman] square letters, separate round ones, old small round ones: these three are used for privileges, [religious] offices, and are especially useful

---

[8] *Il secretario di Marcello Scalzini nel quale si vedono le varie et diverse sorti, et vere forme di lettere cancellaresche corsive romane nuove da secretario al presente usitate, da lui con molto studio ritrovate, prima introdotte; et poi da altri scrittori in Roma, in Venetia, et altre città d'Italia* (Venice: Domenico Nicolini for m[adonna] Helena Moresini, 1585), fol. C2$^{r-v}$, pp. 65–66. See also Paul F. Grendler, *Schooling in Renaissance Italy: Literacy and Learning, 1300–1600* (Baltimore, MD: Johns Hopkins University Press, 1989), p. 329, n. 73; Tiziana Plebani, *Il 'genere' dei libri: storie e rappresentazioni della lettura al femminile e al maschile tra Medioevo e età moderna* (Milan: Franco Angeli, 2001), p. 200. A letter of presentation sent on behalf of Scalzini by Antonio Martinengo to Ferdinando I de' Medici, together with samples of Scalzini's handwriting, in January 1592, just before Scalzini became a gentleman of the Grand Duke, explains that he had worked for the Duke of Savoy from seven years previously until three years ago, and describes him thus: 'huomo dotato di singolari virtù et secreti d'importanza che in opportune occasioni possono essere di grandissimo servitio al Principe et alli stati [ . . . ]. Egli è d'età d'anni 37, di bella presenza, d'honesti costumi, ha buona favella, è ardito, atto a negotii, buon segretario, parla et scrive anco francese mediocremente. È persona di natura patiente, humile et sopratutto fidelissimo et da bene' (ASF, Mediceo del Principato, vol. 831, fol. 90; a man endowed with singular virtues and important secrets that at opportune moments can be of great service to the prince and to states [. . .]. He is 37 years old, personable, of honourable conduct, well spoken, bold, able to conduct business, a good secretary, he speaks and also writes French fairly well. He is a person who is by nature patient, humble and above all very loyal and respectable).

for those old people who have poor sight or cannot see without glasses, and those men and women who, unable to read well, always want those letter shapes that look most like the printed ones with which they have learned to read.)

However, Scalzini is clearly generalizing with uneducated people in mind, and his sweeping statements do not mean that no women had the opportunity to acquire skills with the pen.

An example, although admittedly an exceptional one, of how a young girl of good family might study handwriting in the sixteenth century with the aid of printed writing-books is that of Lavinia Guasco. In the winter of 1585–86, still in her twelfth year, she was sent from Alessandria to Turin by her patrician father Annibale to serve as lady-in-waiting to the infanta Caterina Michaela, daughter of Philip II of Spain and wife of the Duke of Savoy. As a parting gift, Annibale presented his daughter with a treatise so that he could continue to advise on her behaviour and duties. Here he recalled the skills that he himself had already imparted to Lavinia, including that of handwriting. He hoped this ability could be of practical use, since his ambition was for her to become personal secretary of the infanta.[9] He had taught Lavinia chancery script between the ages of six and eleven, not without difficulties for both of them, using as a model one or more of the writing-books composed by the scribe Giovan Francesco Cresci:

> non sai tu che ancora non giugnevi ai sette anni quando io stesso diedi principio ad insegnarti a scrivere, non i caratteri miei, no, ma quelli ch'io non sapeva formare e che con gli esempi del Crescio alla stampa dati ti venni di mano in mano, con quegli avvertimenti ch'io poteva imaginarmi, ammaestrando a formar lettere cancelleresche, delle quali non pur una sapeva io formare? E forse che questa fatica durò due o tre mesi, o cosa tale. Quattro o cinque anni ho io questa difficile opera ogni giorno e talor molte ore in un dì continovata, con quanto travaglio tuo e il mio sappiamo ben noi. Tanto che con l'aiuto di Dio, con la sollecitudine e, dirò anche, importunità mia, e col fastidio tuo bene spesso da lagrime accompagnato, sei finalmente a cotal segno arrivata di poter con la penna te e altrui onorare e servire: cosa che, nella età e nel sesso tuo, forse in altra che in te sì compiutamente non si troverebbe.[10]

---

[9] Annibal Guasco, *Ragionamento a donna Lavinia sua figliuola, della maniera del governarsi ella in corte; andando per dama alla serenissima infante donna Caterina, duchessa di Savoia*, ed. by Helena L. Sanson, *Letteratura italiana antica*, 11 (2010), 61–139 (p. 119, §§ 260–61). The original edition is (Turin: heirs of Niccolò Bevilacqua, 1586).

[10] Guasco, *Ragionamento*, ed. by Sanson, p. 104, §§ 26–29. On Cresci, see James Wardrop, 'The Vatican Scriptors: Documents for Ruano and Cresci', *Signature*, n.s., 5 (1948), 3–28; Casamassima,

(do you not recall how you had not even attained your seventh birthday before I myself set to work to teach you to write, not just in the characters in which I myself write, oh no, but in those that I did not know how to form, and how, with the printed examples of Cresci, you began little by little, and with what assistance I could give you, to master the art of forming chancery script, although I myself did not know how to form a single one of those characters? And, pray, did this labour last for two or three months or thereabouts? No, but rather for four or five years did I continue this difficult task every single day and, sometimes, for many hours at a stretch in a single day, with how much tribulation on both our parts we both know well. But finally, with God's help and my own tireless efforts and, I should say, importunity, and in spite of your vexation, very often accompanied by tears, you finally reached such a degree of excellence that you could do honour and service to yourself and others with your pen. Indeed, it would probably be impossible to find another girl of your age with such a high standard of competence as yourself.)[11]

Lavinia's father was especially proud, as we see, that she had mastered humanistic cursive script, which even he had not learned.

### Laywomen as Scribes

Few laywomen would have been instructed in handwriting as intensively as was young Lavinia Guasco, and the outcomes of whatever training they received were uneven, as of course they were for men. Some women of the Medici family in the second half of the fifteenth century liked occasionally to ask men who used the pen in their own professions to copy out letters on their behalf, probably because they felt the result would be more aesthetically pleasing.[12] Another Florentine patrician, Alessandra Macinghi Strozzi (1406–1471), took an interest in the handwriting of her young son Matteo. A letter to an older son, Filippo, was dictated by her on 4 November 1448 to Matteo, then aged twelve, and she commented on his progress:

> quando iscrive adagio, e che ponga il capo a quello ha fare, iscrive bene: e così dice Antonio Strozzi, e Marco (che ho mostro loro de' fogli ch'egli scrive), che ha buona forma di lettera: ma quando iscrive ratto, diresti che

---

*Trattati di scrittura*, pp. 64–74; Franca Petrucci, 'Cresci, Giovanni Francesco', *DBI*, 30 (1984), 668–71; Stanley Morison, *Early Italian Writing-Books: Renaissance to Baroque*, ed. by Nicolas Barker (Verona: Edizioni Valdonega; London: British Library, 1990), pp. 96–111.

[11] Annibal Guasco, *Discourse to Lady Lavinia his Daughter*, ed. and trans. by Peggy Osborn (University of Chicago Press, 2003), pp. 51–52, slightly modified.

[12] Miglio, *Governare l'alfabeto*, pp. 133–62.

non fussi di suo' mano; e tal differenzia è da l'una a l'altra, quanto il bianco dal nero: e no gli posso tanto dire, che voglia iscrivere adagio.

(when he writes slowly and he concentrates on what he has to do, he writes well; and so says Antonio Strozzi [her brother], as does Marco [her son-in-law] (for I have showed them some of the sheets that he writes), and he shapes letters well; but when he writes fast, you would not recognize his hand; and the two things are as different as black and white; and whatever I say, I can't get him to write slowly.)

Much later, on 11 November 1464, when Alessandra was in her late fifties, she apologized to Filippo for her untidy writing: 'non guatare al mio bello scrivere: e s'io fussi presso a voi, non fare' queste letteracce; ché direi a bocca e fatti mia, e voi e vostri. Pazienza!' (don't look at my fine writing; and if I was with you, I wouldn't write these clumsy letters, but I'd tell you my news myself, and you'd tell me yours. Never mind!).[13]

However, if Alessandra was somewhat embarrassed about her own awkward handwriting, she clearly appreciated a good script; and there is evidence of considerable competence in handwriting among elite lay-women, sometimes used not simply to keep records or to write short documents such as letters, but also to transcribe texts to be read by others. In Chapter 1, one example of an author writing out her own works was that of Ippolita Clara, whose presentation copy of her Virgil translation is over 250 leaves long. She could have been taught to write within her household by her father, a teacher of law, or perhaps by someone else who wrote documents for professional reasons.

Even a woman from a humbler family could possess the ability to copy a long text. The Bodleian Library has a manuscript of another translation of Virgil's *Aeneid* with glosses, in 156 leaves, at the end of which the colophon, written in the form of a sonnet, tells us that the copying was concluded on the evening of 8 December 1455 by a certain Maria, daughter of a cloth-shearer:

> Era 'l sicondo di vespar sonato
> nel glorioso giorno che concepta
> fu l'umil Vergin sancta et benedecta
> per chui 'l primo peccar fu ristorato.
> A octo giorni del mese ultimato
> la faticata penna asciutta et necta
> alquanto riposai et con herecta

---

[13] *Lettere di una gentildonna fiorentina del secolo XV ai figliuoli esuli*, ed. by Cesare Guasti (Florence: Sansoni, 1877), pp. 33–34, 309.

mente l'ora vigesima uscì dallato.
Sonavan gli anni del nostro signore
cinque cinquanta quattrocento et mille
quando Maria di Matheo cimatore
finì copiare el testo et le postille
di questo clar poeta almo, et de core
che 'nfino al ciel mandò le sue faville.

Laus Deo sit semper benedictus.[14]

(The second hour of the evening had sounded on the glorious day of the conception of the humble Virgin, holy and blessed, who was free from original sin. On the eighth day of the last month I gave some rest to my weary pen, dry and clean, and the twentieth hour came forth alongside with upright mind. The year of our Lord 1455 was sounding when Maria daughter of Matteo the cloth-shearer finished copying the text and commentary of this poet, renowned and noble, and with a heart that sent its sparks as far as heaven. Praise the Lord, may He always be blessed.)

The initial on the first folio is painted by a professional artist, using gold leaf; thereafter paragraphs are marked in red or blue ink.

In the same library is another substantial manuscript, of 360 written leaves, containing the Apocalypse in translation with a vernacular commentary originating from Venice, copied in an irregular semi-gothic hand. It is decorated with a fine large coloured initial depicting St John and a floral border on the first page, professionally executed using gold leaf, and thereafter with simple coloured initials. The colophon dates the transcription with some hesitation: 'Laus Deo in nel mile e quatro çento e ~~çetotanta quatro~~ si è | fo fato questo libero per man de mi Maria in laude de Dio | e de la sua madre e del glorioxo apostolo evançelista miser | sam Çuane' (Praise be to God in 14~~74~~80 this book was made by the hand of myself, Maria, in praise of God and his mother and the glorious apostle evangelist St John).[15] Maria's language suggests she was from the Veneto, and it seems probable that she was a laywoman, since she mentions no convent.

---

[14] Oxford, Bodleian Library, MS Canon. Ital. 285, fol. 156ᵛ. On the calculation of hours starting from sunset, see Michael Talbot, 'Ore italiane: The Reckoning of the Time of Day in Pre-Napoleonic Italy', Italian Studies, 40 (1985), 51–62.

[15] MS Laud Misc. 485, fol. 366ʳ. The year was first written as 1474, then altered to 1480, and 'sie' was inserted above the line. Luisa Miglio suggests that the earlier date referred to the end of transcription, the later one to the completion of the making of the manuscript, including perhaps the decoration on fol. 1 and the binding; when 'sie', i.e. 'si è' (has been), was added, Maria did not cross out the earlier 'fo' (was): Governare l'alfabeto, pp. 200, 222–23. On Maria's possible cultural background, see Davide Tramarin, 'With Pen or Brush: Traces of Women in Fifteenth-Century Italy', in Invisible Cultures: Historical and Archaeological Perspectives, ed. by Francesco Carrer and Viola Gheller (Newcastle upon Tyne: Cambridge Scholars Publishing, 2015), pp. 97–114 (pp. 110–11).

Benedetta Niccoli, a married woman from Florence, signed two manuscript miscellanies of sacred texts written in a mercantile script. One is dated 1465 and contains texts such as sermons of St Augustine and a *sacra rappresentazione*, Feo Belcari's *Abramo e Isacco* (BRF, MS 1429). The texts in the other, which dates from 1470, include a life of St Jerome and Gospels in ottava rima (BNCF, MS II III 247). As Luisa Miglio has pointed out, Benedetta's hand in the later manuscript shows a growing self-confidence.[16]

Cultured women could well have put together manuscript collections of lyric and other verse in the sixteenth century. It has been plausibly suggested by Tobia Toscano that Onorata Tancredi used a number of manuscript sources in order to create a personal anthology for herself, now represented by MS 897 of the Biblioteca Casanatense, Rome, consisting of 205 leaves. The first part contains verse originating chiefly from Siena, where Tancredi lived until 1549: lyric poems and translations of two books of Virgil's *Aeneid*. The second part includes a substantial selection of the lyric verse of Vittoria Colonna (fols 96$^r$–152$^v$).[17]

At least one female scribe worked professionally: the daughter of Giovanni Onorio, who himself worked in Rome as a Greek calligrapher. In 1561 he was too busy to take on a commission but offered his daughter's services instead, promising to correct whatever she wrote. Together they produced a pocket-sized manuscript of Sappho and other Greek women poets that was once in the collection of Fulvio Orsini. Unfortunately, we no longer have this or any other known examples of her hand, and we do not even know her first name.[18]

---

[16] Miglio, *Governare l'alfabeto*, pp. 187–89, 202. The manuscripts are described respectively in Domenico De Robertis, 'Censimento dei manoscritti di rime di Dante: II', *Studi danteschi*, 38 (1961), 167–276 (pp. 218–19), and *Inventari dei manoscritti delle biblioteche d'Italia*, vol. X, ed. by Giuseppe Mazzatinti (Florence: Olschki, 1900), 16–18. Among other examples of laywomen who copied texts in the fifteenth century are two transcribers of religious texts, Lana Galvagni and Giovanna Martinozzi of Fano: see Miglio, *Governare l'alfabeto*, pp. 190–94. 'Filomena di Giovanni da Prato', cited as a scribe in Judith Bryce, 'Les Livres des Florentines: Reconsidering Women's Literacy in Quattrocento Florence', in *At the Margins: Minority Groups in Premodern Italy*, ed. by Stephen J. Milner (Minneapolis: University of Minnesota Press, 2005), pp. 133–61 (p. 149), is a phantom: the source (Antonio Lanza, *Lirici toscani del Quattrocento*, 2 vols (Rome: Bulzoni, 1973–75), I, 19) refers to the work *Filomena* by Giovanni da Prato.

[17] Tobia R. Toscano, *Letterati corti accademie*, pp. 72–76; Eisenbichler, *The Sword and the Pen*, pp. 224–32; Piccolomini, *Cento sonetti*, ed. by Tomasi, pp. 28–29, 33, 333.

[18] Maria Luisa Agati, *Giovanni Onorio da Maglie copista greco (1535–1563)*, suppl. 20 to *Bollettino dei classici* (Rome: Accademia Nazionale dei Lincei, 2001), pp. 60–62, 201.

*Nuns as Scribes*

It was, however, particularly within cloistered communities of nuns that Renaissance women came to be most actively involved in the production of handwritten books. This occupation could be seen to be beneficial as a spiritual exercise. The monk who composed the *Decor puellarum* believed, as we have seen, that handwriting could be turned to virtuous ends. This idea is suggested, too, by Sandro Botticelli's *Madonna del Magnificat* of about 1480, in which the Madonna has already written out two texts from the Gospel of St Luke – the Song of Zacharias and the 'Magnificat' pronounced by herself – and is holding a pen in a hand that is guided by the infant Christ.[19] Further, there was both a growing need for books within convents and a growing potential for their production because of the steady rise in the numbers of women who took vows during the Renaissance. This trend was, in part, a consequence of inflation in the cost of dowries and of resulting decisions on the part of families to devote their resources to marrying off one or two of their daughters and to send others to convents, seen as an honourable alternative. (Nuns, too, required a dowry, but it was generally smaller than that of brides.)[20] For some women, convents were far from unwished-for destinations: widows, for instance, might have preferred to take the veil rather than be forced into an unwelcome second marriage.[21] In Florence, there was a marked growth in the numbers of convents and in the numbers of women entering them between the fifteenth and sixteenth centuries. The city had 26 convents in 1415 and 47 in 1552; in the same period, the average number of nuns per convent rose from 20 to 72.7, and the proportion of religious women of all kinds rose from 2.25 per cent of the population to 13 per cent. It has been estimated that in Venice three patrician girls in five were nuns by 1581. Milanese convents saw about a fourfold increase in the number of female religious between the early sixteenth century and 1575. In one Bolognese

---

[19] Luke, 1. 46–55, 68–79. See Ronald Lightbown, *Sandro Botticelli: Life and Work*, new edn (London: Thames & Hudson, 1989), pp. 82–86, and, for a discussion of the implications of the Madonna's writing in the Quattrocento context, Susan Schibanoff, 'Botticelli's *Madonna del Magnificat*: Constructing the Woman Writer in Early Humanist Italy', *PMLA*, 109 (1994), 190–206.

[20] Gabriella Zarri, *Recinti: donne, clausura e matrimonio nella prima età moderna* (Bologna: il Mulino, 2000), pp. 55–56; Weaver, *Convent Theatre*, p. 26; Sharon T. Strocchia, *Nuns and Nunneries in Renaissance Florence* (Baltimore, MD: Johns Hopkins University Press, 2009), pp. 30–31; Massimiliano Coli, *La Cronaca del monastero domenicano di S. Giorgio di Lucca* (Pisa: ETS, 2009), pp. 148–67, 242–43. Coli gives the example of Bernardino di Stefano Bernardi of Lucca, who in 1551 bequeathed to a daughter 1,500 scudi, or 2,500 if she married, but no more than 150 if she became a nun (ibid., pp. 149–50).

[21] Baernstein, 'In Widow's Habit'; Robert L. Kendrick, *Celestial Sirens: Nuns and their Music in Early Modern Milan* (Oxford: Clarendon Press, 1996), p. 41.

convent, there was probably an eightfold increase in the population between 1508 and 1569.[22] As convents grew in number and size, so they came to play an increasingly influential role in society and in the economy. They could provide some education for young nuns and for some lay girls from well-to-do families, the *educande* or lay boarders who received instruction in practical skills as well as in spiritual and moral matters.[23] Alongside the orders living in convents, new uncloistered orders such as the Angelic Sisters of St Paul and the Company of St Ursula, both founded in northern Italy in the 1530s, were orientated towards charitable work and education in secular society.[24] The voices of individual 'living saints', whether nuns or holy laywomen, made themselves heard through writings composed by themselves or about them.[25]

In weighing up the evidence on the teaching in convents of the skills of copying texts, we need to distinguish between the instruction of lay boarders and that of nuns, while recognizing that the same nuns might have taught both sets of pupils. Sharon Strocchia has noted that, although the Augustinian nuns of the convent of Santa Maria del Fiore (known as Lapo) in Fiesole 'possessed highly developed graphic abilities' and produced books for sale, their accounts do not explicitly mention the teaching of writing to their lay pupils.[26] However, in the late sixteenth century, the convent of Santa Maria degli Angeli in Bologna had rooms, separate from the convent, for '[la] scuola della grammatica, del scrivere, del canto e della pittura' (the school of grammar, writing, singing and painting).[27] Three

[22] Richard C. Trexler, 'Le Célibat à la fin du moyen âge: les religieuses de Florence', *Annales: Économies, Sociétés, Civilisations*, 27 (1972), 1329–50 (pp. 1333, 1334, 1337); Gene Adam Brucker, 'Monasteries, Friaries, and Nunneries in Quattrocento Florence', in *Christianity and the Renaissance: Image and Religious Imagination in the Quattrocento*, ed. by Timothy Verdon and John Henderson (Syracuse, NY: Syracuse University Press, 1990), pp. 42–62; Zarri, *Recinti*, pp. 43–143; Stanley Chojnacki, *Women and Men in Renaissance Venice: Twelve Essays on Patrician Society* (Baltimore, MD: Johns Hopkins University Press, 2000), p. 39 (statistics for Florence and Venice); Weaver, *Convent Theatre*, pp. 11–20. For Milan, see Kendrick, *Celestial Sirens*, p. 38; for Bologna, Gabriella Zarri, *Le sante vive: profezie di corte e devozione femminile tra '400 e '500* (Turin: Rosenberg & Sellier, 1990), pp. 198–99.
[23] Grendler, *Schooling in Renaissance Italy*, pp. 97–100; Sharon T. Strocchia, 'Learning the Virtues: Convent Schools and Female Culture in Renaissance Florence', in *Women's Education in Early Modern Europe: A History, 1500–1800*, ed. by Barbara J. Whitehead (New York: Garland, 1999), pp. 3–46; Gabriella Zarri, 'Novizie ed educande nei monasteri italiani post-tridentini', *Via spiritus*, 18 (2011), 7–23.
[24] Grendler, *Schooling in Renaissance Italy*, pp. 392–93; Gabriella Zarri, 'From Prophecy to Discipline, 1450–1650', in *Women and Faith: Catholic Religious Life in Italy from Late Antiquity to the Present*, ed. by Lucetta Scaraffia and Gabriella Zarri (Cambridge, MA: Harvard University Press, 1999), pp. 83–112; Zarri, *Recinti*, pp. 178–84, 417–51; Baernstein, *A Convent Tale* (on the convent of San Paolo Converso of the Angelic Sisters of Milan).
[25] See especially Zarri, *Le sante vive*. [26] Strocchia, 'Learning the Virtues', p. 32.
[27] Zarri, 'Novizie ed educande', p. 16.

professed nuns were assigned to an admittedly privileged five-year-old, Maria Maddalena Cristina de' Medici, in 1615, to teach her writing ('scrivere'), needlework and 'the virtues', and also to arrange her hair.[28]

The evidence of the handwriting of nuns suggests that many novices had at least the opportunity to learn to write, if they could not already do so when they joined their convents as girls. In some cases, as we shall see, they could reach a very creditable level of technical achievement. Letters addressed to Isabella d'Este from her daughter Livia, born in 1508, who had become suor Paola in the local Clarissan convent of Corpus Domini or Santa Paola, suggest that the girl already wrote a good hand before becoming a nun but was receiving some training in handwriting. In July 1519, soon after her entry into the convent, suor Paola writes in a letter to her mother of 'questa mia mal facta lettera' (this badly formed letter of mine), which must refer to her script rather than to the contents of her epistle. Here, her hand is indeed somewhat hesitant. However, it is already more controlled and elegant in a letter written by Paola just nine months later.[29] (Isabella d'Este herself, incidentally, had been trained to write a fluent humanistic cursive hand, as seen in a letter of 1514.[30]) As Elissa Weaver has commented, the signatures of nine abbesses and prioresses of Mantua appended to a petition to the marquis, Federico Gonzaga, dated 22 April 1529, display a good set of hands of a mainly humanistic cursive nature.[31]

No doubt nuns learned calligraphic handwriting from writing-books just as laywomen did. An inventory of the books of a convent in Asti dating from around 1600 includes a copy of Giovan Francesco Cresci's *Essemplare di più sorti lettere dove si trova la vera forma del scrivere cancelleresco* (Rome: Antonio Blado for the author, 1560).[32] This copy also had an appendix on elementary penmanship, described in the inventory as a 'Prattica che con la penna al buon scrittore s'appartiene havere' (The skill that the good writer should have with the pen). This might have been a work designed for beginners such as *Il primo libro di scrivere di Iacomo Romano dove s'insegna*

[28] Weaver, *Convent Theatre*, pp. 25–26.
[29] Ibid., pp. 34–36. The letters are in ASMn, Archivio Gonzaga, busta 1895, fol. 16ʳ (24 July 1519) and busta 1897, fol. 218ʳ (17 March 1520).
[30] Reproduced in Carolyn James, 'Marriage by Correspondence: Politics and Domesticity in the Letters of Isabella d'Este and Francesco Gonzaga, 1490–1519', *Renaissance Quarterly*, 65 (2012), 321–52 (p. 345).
[31] Weaver, *Convent Theatre*, pp. 34–36. The petition is in ASMn, Archivio Gonzaga, busta 3315, no. 23.
[32] Danilo Zardin, 'Libri e biblioteche negli ambienti monastici dell'Italia del primo Seicento', in *Donne, filosofia e cultura nel Seicento*, ed. by Pina Totaro (Rome: Consiglio Nazionale delle Ricerche, 1999), pp. 347–83 (p. 368).

*la vera maniera delle cancellaresche corsive, e di tutte quelle sorti di lettere che a un buon scrittore si appartengono di sapere, et che al presente sono in uso. Con li avertimenti et regole, sopra ciascuna sorte di lettera, con le quali ogni mediocre ingegno potrà facilmente da se stesso imparare: con il modo di temperar le penne per dette sorti di lettere, et come si devono tenere in mano, per scriver bene* (Rome: Pietro Spada for the author, 1589; The first book of writing by Iacomo Romano, which teaches the true way of forming cursive chancery letters, and all those sorts of letters that a good writer should know and that are currently in use. With advice and rules on each kind of letter, with the help of which all people of normal intelligence will be able to learn easily on their own; with the method of sharpening pens for these kinds of letters, and how to hold them in order to write well).

As for the texts that nuns copied by hand, they could have several practical purposes. Nuns needed books for the liturgy, and copying them would have saved acquiring them from outside and given the community greater independence. Other texts were read aloud at mealtimes, or read silently in private reflection. Nuns recorded their own spiritual lives, sometimes at the behest of a male figure; they chronicled. life in their convents; they occasionally wrote spiritual poetry and monachization poems; and (as we have seen in the case of Beatrice Del Sera) they copied out plays that they performed to provide instructive entertainment for themselves, some of the plays already existing, some newly composed.[33] They might have official duties in writing notarial documents for their houses.[34]

Convents of all the principal orders might have at least a few nuns who were able to copy manuscripts and who sometimes specialized in this task.

---

[33] Discussions of the types of works composed in convents include Weaver, *Convent Theatre*, pp. 32–34; Gianna Pomata and Gabriella Zarri, 'Introduzione', in *I monasteri femminili come centri di cultura fra Rinascimento e Barocco: atti del convegno storico internazionale, Bologna, 8–10 dicembre 2000*, ed. by Gianna Pomata and Gabriella Zarri (Rome: Edizioni di Storia e Letteratura, 2005), pp. ix–xliv (pp. xxvii–xxxvii); Elisabetta Graziosi, 'Arcipelago sommerso: le rime delle monache tra obbedienza e trasgressione', ibid., pp. 145–73. On chronicles, see especially K. J. P. Lowe, *Nuns' Chronicles and Convent Culture in Renaissance and Counter-Reformation Italy* (Cambridge University Press, 2003). An account of the creation and copying of a mid-sixteenth-century chronicle is found in Gemma Guerrini Ferri, 'Il *Liber monialium* ed il *Libro de l'antiquità* di suor Orsola Formicini: le Clarisse e la storia del venerabile monastero romano dei Santi Cosma e Damiano in Mica Aurea detto di San Cosimato in Trastevere (Biblioteca Nazionale Centrale, Roma, mss. Varia 5 e Varia 6)', *Scrineum Rivista*, 8 (2011), 81–111, www.fupress.net/index.php/scrineum/article/view/12145 (accessed 8 November 2017). On monachization poems, see Abigail Brundin, 'On the Convent Threshold: Poetry for New Nuns in Early Modern Italy', *Renaissance Quarterly*, 65 (2012), 1125–65.

[34] For the example of Verona, see Massimo Scandola, '"Dell'officio della scrittora": fra fides e custodia. "Monache scrivane" e notai a Verona nei secoli XVII e XVIII', *Scrineum Rivista*, 10 (2013), 259–312, www.fupress.net/index.php/scrineum/article/view/13697 (accessed 8 November 2017).

A Benedictine of Florence, suor Antonia, copied out for herself some Italian translations of texts by St Augustine and others in 1424, using a semigothic hand. As she declared proudly in her colophon: 'Iste liber est sororis Antonie monialis monasterii Sancti Petri Maioris de Florentia. Manibus suis scripsit. Explevit ipsum die secundo Martii ad horam vigesimam die giovis anno millesimo quartocientesimo vigesimo tertio. Rogate Dominum pro eam' (This book belongs to Sister Antonia, nun of San Pier Maggiore of Florence. She wrote it with her own hands. She finished it on Thursday 2 March at the twentieth hour in 1424. Pray to the Lord for her).[35] Simply decorated initials were added in red and blue ink. Suor Antonia's request for readers to pray for her soul reflects scribes' desire to use writing as, among other things, a way of enhancing their hopes of salvation, and we shall see further examples of this. A nun called Sara revealed a somewhat dark sense of humour when she specified, in a colophon to a life of St Eustace, how she would punish anyone who failed to intercede for her: 'Qualunque persona leggerà questa divota leggenda prieghi Iddio per me soror Sara povera [. . .] che se voi nol farete quando sarò morta vi strangholerò' (BRF, MS 1381, fol. 134$^r$; Let whoever reads this devout life pray God for me, poor Sister Sara [. . .] and if you don't I'll strangle you when I'm dead).[36]

In Verona, suor Veronica of the Benedictine convent of Santo Spirito copied and decorated St Augustine's *De civitate Dei*, completing her task in 1472 (Genoa, Biblioteca Civica Berio, MS m.r.Cf.2.16), and in 1484 she decorated a collection of saints' lives copied by her fellow nun Scolastica (BAV, MS Ross. 941).[37] Another example of collaboration between two Benedictine sisters comes from the Florentine convent of Sant'Ambrogio: here in 1518, Agnola da Rabatta wrote out a Latin breviary, BLF, MS Conv. Soppr. 90, and Gostanza Cocchi illuminated it.[38]

---

[35] Oxford, Bodleian Library, MS Lyell 73, fol. 84$^r$. The texts are translations of Pseudo-Augustine, *Soliloquia*; extracts from Augustine, *Enarrationes in Psalmos*; and extracts from the *Maestruzzo*, the Italian version of Bartolomeo da San Concordio, *Summa de casibus conscientiae*. See Albinia de la Mare, *Catalogue of the Collection of Medieval Manuscripts Bequeathed to the Bodleian Library, Oxford, by James P. R. Lyell* (Oxford: Clarendon Press, 1971), pp. 221–23 and Plate XXVd; Miglio, *Governare l'alfabeto*, p. 224. On nuns' colophons and their terminology, see Melissa Moreton, 'Pious Voices: Nun-Scribes and the Language of Colophons in Late Medieval and Renaissance Italy', *Essays in Medieval Studies*, 29 (2013), 43–73.

[36] Teresa De Robertis and Rosella Miriello, *I manoscritti datati della Biblioteca Riccardiana di Firenze*, 3 vols (Florence: SISMEL-Edizioni del Galluzzo, 1997–2006), II, 55.

[37] Moreton, 'Pious Voices', p. 61; Tramarin, 'With Pen or Brush', pp. 108–10.

[38] Sharon Strocchia, 'Sisters in Spirit: The Nuns of Sant'Ambrogio and their Consorority in Early Sixteenth-Century Florence', *Sixteenth Century Journal*, 33 (2002), 735–67 (pp. 751–52), and Strocchia, *Nuns and Nunneries*, pp. 147–48.

Several examples of book production come from the Franciscan order of Clarissans or Poor Clares. In the mid-fifteenth century, Caterina Vigri (1413–1463), later canonized, copied parts of a breviary, decorated it with miniatures in a deliberately humble style and added about a thousand glosses. Caterina would have been well educated, since she came from a noble Bolognese family and was a member of the Ferrarese court as a child, until 1426. The breviary was written at least partly for the benefit of her religious community in Bologna: according to her early biographer, Illuminata Bembo, Caterina 'havea uno suo breviario el quale scrisse con sua grande faticha, e questo fece per potere servire a chi non n'avea, tanta era la sua karità' (had a breviary that she wrote with her own great labour, and she did this to help those who had none, such was her charity).[39]

A nun who signed herself simply 'suor Lena' copied a vernacular translation by Domenico da Montecchiello of the *Theologia mystica* attributed to the Carthusian monk Hugh of Balma in her Venetian community of Observant Clarissans. This kind of text may well have been read by herself and her fellow nuns as part of their spiritual reflection. Suor Lena's colophon tells us, with some hesitations, when she completed her task and asks us to pray for her: 'Scrita nel monasterio de le done de san françesco della crose de veniesia de l'ordene de sancta chiara de hoservançia. Nelli ani del nostro signor miser iesu cristo 1500 finito a di 3 deçembrio. s[uor]. le. bol. E tu lezitore prega dio per el scritore. Amen. de suor lena [bol. ..]. scrito de sua mano' (fol. 81ᵛ; Written in the women's monastery of San Francesco della Croce in Venice of the Observant order of St Clare. Finished on 3 December 1500. And you, reader, pray God for the writer. Amen. [The book] of suor Lena. Written in her own hand).[40]

---

[39] The manuscript is in the convent of Corpus Domini, Bologna. See Kathleen G. Arthur, 'Images of Clare & Francis in Caterina Vigri's Personal Breviary', *Franciscan Studies*, 62 (2004), 177–92; Arthur, 'Il Breviario di Santa Caterina da Bologna e "l'arte povera" clarissa', in *I monasteri femminili come centri di cultura fra Rinascimento e Barocco: atti del convegno storico internazionale, Bologna, 8–10 dicembre 2000*, ed. by Gianna Pomata and Gabriella Zarri (Rome: Edizioni di Storia e Letteratura, 2005), pp. 93–122; Irene Graziani, 'L'icona della monaca artista e le fonti storiografiche sul Breviario di Caterina Vigri', in *Pregare con le immagini: il Breviario di Caterina Vigri*, ed. by Vera Fortunati and Claudio Leonardi (Bologna: Compositori; Florence: SISMEL-Edizioni del Galluzzo, 2004), pp. 29–42 (quotation from p. 31); Rosanna Miriello, *I manoscritti del Monastero del Paradiso di Firenze* (Florence: SISMEL-Edizioni del Galluzzo, 2007), pp. 18–19. Caterina copied about 380 folios out of 510, according to Leonardi in *Pregare con le immagini*, p. 27. The 'explicit' of the breviary is dated 1452. On the autograph manuscript of Caterina's treatise and on its subsequent copying, see Caterina Vigri, *Le sette armi spirituali*, ed. by Antonella Degl'Innocenti (Florence: SISMEL-Edizioni del Galluzzo, 2000).

[40] The manuscript, now Lawrence, University of Kansas, Kenneth Spencer Research Library, MS C66, was one of two used by Bartolomeo Sorio in his edition of *La teologia mistica* (Verona: Eredi di Marco Moroni, 1852).

Like Dominican friars and together with some laywomen, nuns of the same order in Venice copied and decorated manuscripts as part of the campaign, promoted especially by fra Tommaso Caffarini in the early fifteenth century, to promote the figure of St Catherine of Siena.[41] In Florence, several manuscripts were written and decorated by some of the Dominican nuns of San Iacopo di Ripoli in via della Scala. Here Angelica Gaddi copied Domenico Cavalca's *Specchio di Croce*, a series of reflections on Christ's Passion, in 1460.[42] A nun who gives her name informally as 'Checha' (Checca, or Francesca) signed a life of St Catherine of Siena in 1468 (BRF, MS 1291) and St Catherine's *Dialogo della divina provvidenza* (BRF, MS 1391) in 1474.[43] A suor Seraphina copied the second part of Vincent Ferrer's *Trattato della vita spirituale* (BNCF, MS Pal. 75, fols 16ʳ– 38ᵛ).[44] A fine collectary (containing the collects and other prayers of the Mass) written on parchment around 1500, with musical notation, which of course required an additional skill, and decorated by two miniaturists (BNCF, MS Conv. Soppr. D VII 344), was signed: 'Ego soror Angela indigna serva domini nostri Iesu Christi scripsi manu propria hoc collectarium. Deus sit laudatus et pro me deprecatus' (I, Sister Angela, unworthy servant to our Lord Jesus Christ, wrote this collectary in my own hand. Praise God and pray to him for me).[45] This scribe, identifiable as Angela Rucellai, collaborated on a gradual (containing plainsong for masses) with a sister from another aristocratic family, Lucrezia Panciatichi, who died in 1535. The colophon reads: 'Iste liber scriptus fuit a duabus sororibus monasterii sancti Iacobi de Ripolis ad honorem domini nostri Yesu Christi. Nomina earum sunt Soror Angela et Soror Lucretia, quas Deus scribat in libro vite' (Florence, Museo di San Marco, MS 630, fol. 259ᵛ; This book was written by two sisters of the monastery of San Iacopo di Ripoli in honour of our Lord Jesus Christ. Their names are Sister Angela and Sister Lucretia. May God write them in the Book of Life). Suor Lucrezia was renowned within San Iacopo for copying choir books.[46]

[41] Fernanda Sorelli, *La santità imitabile: 'Leggenda di Maria da Venezia' di Tommaso da Siena* (Venice: Deputazione di storia patria per le Venezie, 1984), pp. 28–33.

[42] Moreton, 'Pious Voices', pp. 46, 52.    [43] Ibid.    [44] Ibid., pp. 61–62.

[45] *I manoscritti datati del fondo Conventi Soppressi della Biblioteca nazionale centrale di Firenze*, ed. by Simona Bianchi et al. (Florence: SISMEL-Edizioni del Galluzzo, 2002), p. 133; Moreton, 'Pious Voices', p. 46.

[46] Strocchia, *Nuns and Nunneries*, p. 147; Moreton, 'Pious Voices', pp. 49–50 (transcription modified); Melissa Moreton, 'Exchange and Alliance: The Sharing and Gifting of Books in Women's Houses in Late Medieval and Renaissance Florence', in *Nuns' Literacies in Medieval Europe: The Antwerp Dialogue*, ed. by Virginia Blanton, Veronica O'Mara and Patricia Stoop (Turnhout: Brepols, 2017), pp. 383–410 (p. 389).

Spiritual writings by fra Giovanni Dominici (Banchini) and others were copied between 1515 and 1518 into three manuscripts by a nun, who used a humanistic cursive script, in another Dominican convent of Florence, that of Santa Lucia in via San Gallo. She chooses to remain anonymous. In the colophon of the friar's treatise on the family, the *Regola del governo di cura familiare*, she states that her text was copied from an inaccurate source but was then emended as far as possible:

> Scripta per me Suora N. del monasterio di Sancta Lucia di via di San Gallo, compiuto a dì 28 di septembre 1515. Cavato da una copia scripta per mano d'un secolare idiota, la quale era piena di scorrectione; chi addunque leggerà la predecta operecta, si degni di perdonare agli errori che in epsa avrà trovato, massimo perché anchora io non ne entendo molto. Ma di poi capitandomi alle mani la medesima operecta dectata con molta diligentia et ben correcta, sommi ingegnata di emendare la presente el meglio che io ò potuto. Laus Deo semper.[47]

> (Written by me, Sister N., of the monastery of Santa Lucia in via San Gallo, completed on 28 September 1515. Taken from a copy written in the hand of an uneducated layman, which was full of errors. Those who read this work should therefore please forgive the errors they find in it, especially since I, too, do not understand much of it. But then, when the same work, dictated very diligently and very correct, happened to come into my hands, I endeavoured to emend it as best I could. Praise be to God always.)

This modest, and modestly anonymous, nun was writing both for her community and in order to promote her own salvation. At the end of another work in the same manuscript, she adds an entreaty that suggests that she has only recently taken her vows as a bride of Christ:

> Per carità vi priego sorelle leggitrice che oriate per me p[eccatrice] poverella e indegna io sia arsa da questo sposo novello del suo amore, e voi vegga ardere di superno calore co' suoi sancti. Compiesi le pistole del Beato Ioanni Dominici, mandate alle monache del Corpo di Cristo di Venezia. Deo gratias. Amen. Manus scriptoris salvetur omnibus horis. Explicit liber iste anno M CCCCC X6.[48]

---

[47] BNCF, MS Magl. XXXV 88, fol. 73ᵛ; Giovanni Dominici, *Lettere spirituali*, ed. by Maria Teresa Casella and Giovanni Pozzi (Freiburg: Edizioni universitarie, 1969), p. 11.

[48] BNCF, MS Magl. XXXV 88, fols 160ᵛ–61ʳ; Dominici, *Lettere spirituali*, p. 12. A similar entreaty is found on fols 186ᵛ–87ʳ of another manuscript, Magl. XXXVIII 124, written by the same nun between 1516 and 1517: Dominici, *Lettere spirituali*, p. 13. This nun copied BRF, MS 1414, dated 1518, up to fol. 120, where another female scribe took over. BRF, MS 2105 also belonged to the convent of Santa Lucia. On fol. 1ʳ a hand other than that of the main scribe dates the transcription to 1470 and attributes it to suor Lisabetta Masini and suor Ismeralda Ghiarini; however, it appears that only one hand is present in these manuscripts. See Dominici, *Lettere spirituali*, pp. 13–16;

(I beg you, sister readers, please pray for me, poor unworthy sinner, that
I may be burned by this new bridegroom with His love, and that I may see
you burn with the heavenly flame with His saints. Here end the letters of
Blessed Giovanni Dominici sent to the nuns of Corpus Christi in Venice.
Thanks be to God. Amen. May the writer's hand be saved always. Here ends
this book, 1516.)

An anonymous scribe of the early sixteenth century, who may have
belonged to one of the Dominican convents of Florence, copied extracts
from sermons given by fra Cherubino Primerani, prior of the Dominican
house of San Marco in this city (Venice, Biblioteca Nazionale Marciana,
MS It. Z. 15 (4791)). In an introductory letter, she addresses another
woman, her 'Dilettissima in Christo Ihesu sorella' (most beloved sister in
Jesus Christ), at whose request she is writing. She apologizes for her
presumption in gathering together 'alchuna cosetta delle mirabil e divine
prediche' (some little writings of the marvellous and divine sermons) of the
friar; but this is a substantial accomplishment, a volume containing nearly
100 leaves in folio written in a humanistic cursive script.[49]

Copying and decoration was carried out by nuns in two Dominican
convents founded in Lucca in the early sixteenth century by supporters of
the Savonarolan movement, those of San Giorgio and San Domenico.
According to the chronicle of San Giorgio, some of its sisters were sent to
San Domenico to acquire the necessary skills. Suor Alessandra
Guidiccioni, for instance, who became prioress of San Giorgio for seven
terms, 'fue una di quelle che ste' tre anni in sancto domenico nel qual
tempo imparò a schrivere lettera formata et solfare libri et miniarli et così
ne scrisse poi tre grandi et belli da cantare il divino offitio' (was one of those
who stayed for three years in San Domenico, and during her time there she
learned to write formal script and to write books with musical notation and
illuminate them, and thus she then wrote for us three large and fine books
for singing the divine office).[50] ('Lettera formata' signified formal large,
squarish characters, rather than a cursive script.[51]) The same skills were

Eliana Corbari, *Vernacular Theology: Dominican Sermons and Audience in Late Medieval Italy*
(Berlin: De Gruyter, 2013), pp. 83–85.

[49] Carlo Frati and A. Segarizzi, *Catalogo dei codici marciani italiani*, vol. I (Modena: G. Ferraguti,
1909), p. 16; Plebani, *Il 'genere' dei libri*, pp. 170–71.

[50] Coli, *La Cronaca del monastero domenicano*, p. 266; see also Innocenzo Taurisano, *I Domenicani in
Lucca* (Lucca: Baroni, 1914), p. 160, and Ann Roberts, *Dominican Women and Renaissance Art: The
Convent of San Domenico of Pisa* (Aldershot: Ashgate, 2008), p. 28.

[51] *Grande dizionario della lingua italiana*, ed. by Battaglia, vol. VI, s.v. *formato*, para. 9, and
Nicolas Barker, *The Glory of the 'Art of Writing': The Calligraphic Work of Francesco Alunno of
Ferrara* (Los Angeles: Cotsen Occasional Press, 2009), pp. 56, 92 and facsimile 30.

acquired by another sister of San Domenico, Eufrasia Burlamacchi, who, according to her obituary, 'Scrisse di sua mano i libbri da cantare il divino offitio di lettere grosse con le note capi versi et minii molto belli, cioè tre Antiphonali un Graduale un salmista et un collettario' (wrote in her own hand the books to sing the divine office in large letters with the notes, headings, verses and very fine illuminations, that is, three Antiphonals, a Gradual, a psalter and a collectary).[52]

The monastery of Santa Brigida al Paradiso, south-east of the centre of Florence, was a double house of Birgittine nuns and monks that produced a notable number of manuscripts from the early fifteenth century until at least 1571.[53] Rosella Miriello points out, in her catalogue of manuscripts owned and produced by the community, that the Rule set out by St Birgitta of Sweden, the *Regola del Salvatore*, instructed sisters to work with their hands when they were not praying or reading, and to have books for purposes of study.[54] Copying was particularly important for members of this order. St Birgitta appears to have been the only female saint in the period up to 1400 who is consistently depicted writing, as Lesley Smith has noted.[55] Moreover, the order was not numerous enough to make the printing of works for its members economically viable. As in other houses, the work of the convent of the Paradiso was concentrated among a small number of people. Among the nuns most active as scribes between the last quarter of the fifteenth century and the first half of the sixteenth were suor Raffaella (daughter of Arnolfo Bardi, died 1527), suor Cleofe (born Ginevra di Lorenzo di Goro Lenzi, died 1546) and suor Cecilia (daughter of the philosopher Francesco Cattani da Diacceto and still abbess in 1560 at the age of sixty-four): they wrote all or part of, respectively, at least eighteen, seventeen and ten manuscripts, some of them substantial, in semigothic

---

[52] Taurisano, *I Domenicani in Lucca*, p. 160; Roberts, *Dominican Women and Renaissance Art*, p. 28. Antiphonals (or antiphonaries) are books of plainsong for the divine office.

[53] On copying in this convent, see Miriello, *I manoscritti del Monastero del Paradiso*, and Tore Nyberg, 'Paradiso Copying Activity (15th Century Florence) and Hugh of Balma', in *The Mystical Tradition and the Carthusians* (Analecta Cartusiana, 130), vol. III, ed. by James Hogg (Salzburg: Institut für Anglistik und Amerikanistik, Universität Salzburg, 1995), pp. 87–95; Daniela Delcorno Branca, 'Il *Giardino novello*: lettere di direzione spirituale del Quattrocento trasmesse dalle monache del Paradiso', in *Da Dante a Montale: studi di filologia e critica letteraria in onore di Emilio Pasquini*, ed. by Gian Mario Anselmi et al. (Bologna: Gedit, 2005), pp. 307–22; Corbari, *Vernacular Theology*, pp. 82–83, 85, 96–99.

[54] Miriello, *I manoscritti del Monastero del Paradiso*, p. 15.

[55] Lesley Smith, '*Scriba, Femina*: Medieval Depictions of Women Writing', in *Women and the Book: Assessing the Visual Evidence*, ed. by Lesley Smith and Jane H. M. Taylor (London: British Library; University of Toronto Press, 1996), pp. 21–44 (p. 26).

hands.[56] Suor Raffaella noted at the end of the first part of one of her manuscripts that she had begun her task in 1488 and carried it out

> con assai mia faticha et disagii. Et è l'ottavo ch'io ò copiato, tutti a spirituale consolatione delle mie in Christo sorelle et non credo copiarne più eccetto la Corona de' monaci, la quale ò cominciato 'n altro volume. E sse la lettera è rusticha l'auctore e lle parole son degni, et in però sia riguardato.[57]

> (with very great toil on my part and discomforts. And it is the eighth that I have copied, all for the spiritual consolation of my sisters in Christ, and I do not expect to copy any more except the *Diadema monachorum* that I have started in another volume. And even if the script is rough, the author and the words are worthy, and thus it is to be held in respect.)

Suor Cleofe drew attention to the physical hardship of her work in similar terms in a colophon dated 10 August 1494 (Figure 2.3):

> iscritto con gran faticha e disagio la maggior parte di nocte a llume di lucerna. Prieghovi non ghuardiate alla rusticità della lettera, ma pigliate la sana e verace doctrina data dalla bocca della verità, e della sua gloriosa madre virgho Maria alla nostra madre sancta Brigida. Priegho che chi llo leggie con diligentia lo tengha, e cchi ll'acatta sì llo renda.[58]

> (Written with great toil and discomfort, mostly at night by lantern-light. I beg you not to look at the roughness of the script, but to accept the healthy and truthful doctrine given by the mouth of truth and of His glorious virgin mother Mary to our mother St Birgitta. I pray that whoever reads this diligently may keep it, and whoever borrows it may return it.)

Cleofe added a note that 'questo libro è delle suore e monache del Paradiso' (this book belongs to the sisters and nuns of the Paradiso), with her signature. Two of her other colophons, from 1485 and 1495, ask readers to pray for her soul in return for her work: 'Questo libro è delle monache et convento del Paradiso, chi llo achatta lo riguardi et rendalo in fra sei mesi l'arà tenuto, et dicha una Ave Maria per l'anima di chi s'è affatichata scrivendolo. Deo gratias' (This book belongs to the nuns and convent of the Paradiso. If you borrow it, take care of it and return it within

---

[56] Miriello, *I manoscritti del Monastero del Paradiso*, pp. 37–41. Decorations in some Paradiso manuscripts were carried out by nuns: ibid., pp. 28–29. On one instance, BNCF, MS Magl. XXXVIII 128, copied by suor Caterina Peruzzi in 1458, see ibid., pp. 138–41 and Figure 82, and Tramarin, 'With Pen or Brush', pp. 107–08.

[57] BLF, MS Acq. e doni 85, fol. 72ʳ; Miriello, *I manoscritti del Monastero del Paradiso*, p. 51. The *Diadema monachorum* is a ninth-century compilation by Smaragdus of Saint-Mihiel.

[58] BNCF, MS II_130, fol. 154ᵛ. Miriello, *I manoscritti del Monastero del Paradiso*, pp. 69–70. Cleofe repeated this theme in two other colophons: BNCF, MSS II III 270, fol. 137ᵛ, and Conv. Soppr. G II 1441, fol. 204ʳ. Miriello, *I manoscritti del Monastero del Paradiso*, pp. 73, 131.

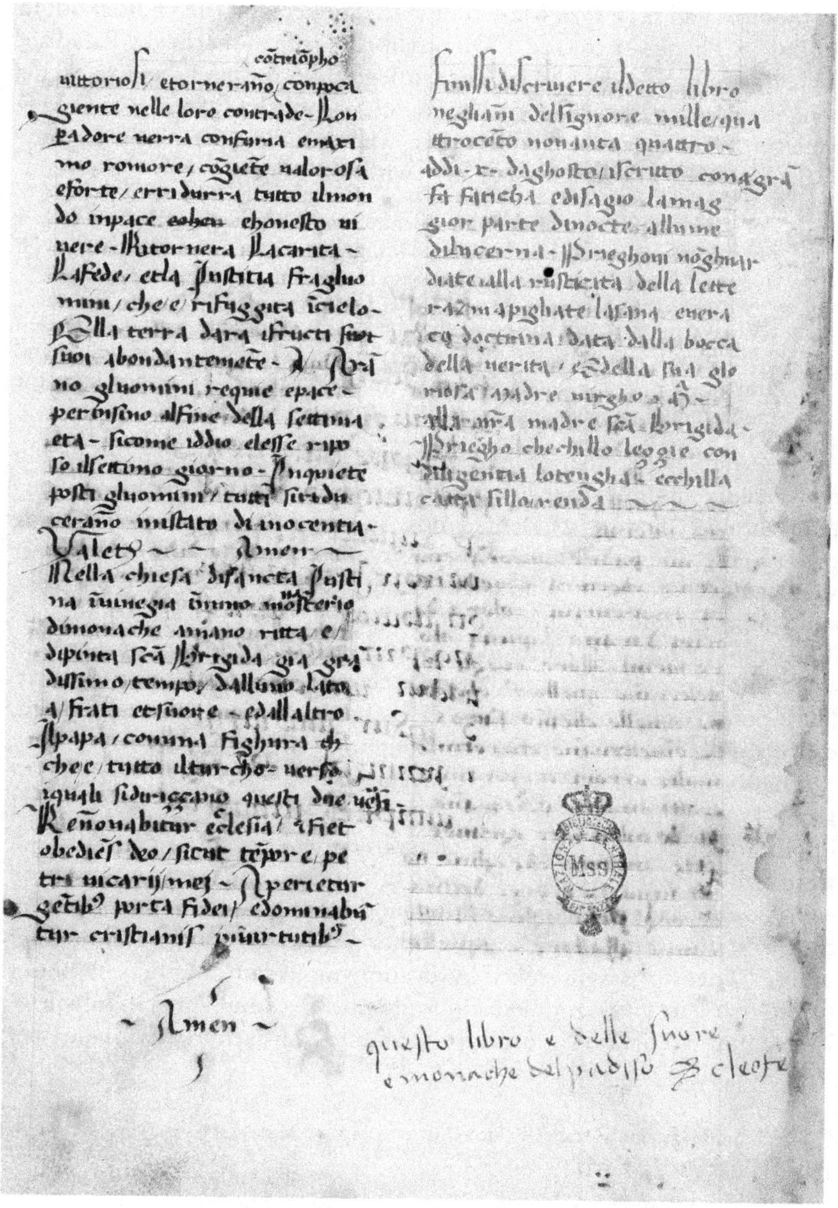

Figure 2.3 St Birgitta of Sweden, *Rivelazioni*, Books I and II, and *Ricordo di un'immagine di santa Brigida*, copied by suor Cleofe Lenzi. BNCF, MS II_130, fol. 154$^v$. Su concessione del Ministero dei Beni e delle Attività Culturali e del Turismo – Biblioteca Nazionale Centrale, Firenze. Reproduction by any means is forbidden

six months, and say a Hail Mary for the soul of her who tired herself out in writing it. Thanks be to God); 'Questo libro è delle monache del Paradiso, decte di sancta Brigida. Chi llo leggie prieghi Idio per chi l'à scricto' (This book belongs to the nuns of the Paradiso, called of St Birgitta. May whoever reads it pray God for her who wrote it).[59] Likewise, suor Raffaella ended a compilation of 1477 with the words:

> Poi ch'ài letto il libro et la visione coll'altre cose che qui sono scripte priega per me misera, peccatore. Dà il cuore a Dio intero et non diviso se gustar vuogli questo libro sancto et rendilo al monasterio del Paradiso.[60]

> (When you have read the book and the vision with the other works written here, pray for me, a wretched sinner. Give your heart to God whole and undivided if you wish to appreciate this holy book and return it to the monastery of the Paradiso.)

As these and several other colophons suggest, the manuscripts copied within the female community were intended to remain and be used there in the long term, although they could be lent to those outside. A few have notes indicating possession by individual nuns. It is possible, however, that a small number were intended for sale. One attributable to the hand of suor Raffaella, containing the life and miracles of St Birgitta, has this ownership note: 'Questo libretto si è di Bartolomeo di Leonardo di Piero di Tomaso Masi chalderaio, cipttadino fiorentino, il quale chonperò a dì XXII d'octtobre 1515' (This book belongs to Bartolomeo di Leonardo di Piero di Tomaso Masi, coppersmith, Florentine citizen, who bought [it] on 22 October 1515).[61]

The second Italian Birgittine convent was founded in Genoa around 1406. From this house, known as Scala Coeli, came the single most important piece of writing undertaken in either convent: a translation of almost all the writings of St Birgitta, in three parts. The first two contain all eight books of the *Revelations*, while the third part contains extracts from the *Revelations* and all the saint's other works except the Rule of her order.[62] The works were copied by an anonymous nun, and her colophons record that Part 1 was completed in September 1624 and Part 3 in July 1626. The paratexts of Part 1 indicate that the translation was made 'per

---

[59] BLF, MS Conv. Soppr. 466; BNCF, MSS II III 270, fol. 149ᵛ. Miriello, *I manoscritti del Monastero del Paradiso*, pp. 61, 73.

[60] Parma, Biblioteca Palatina, MS Palatino 84, fol. 144ᵛ. Miriello, *I manoscritti del Monastero del Paradiso*, pp. 180–81. The last work in the volume is a *Visione delle gioie e dei mali del mondo*.

[61] BNCF, MS Magl. XXXVIII 15, fol. 1ᵛ. Miriello, *I manoscritti del Monastero del Paradiso*, p. 136.

[62] New Haven, Yale University, Beinecke Library, MSS ZIII 0141 and ZIII 0142. See Hugh Feiss, 'The Many Lives and Languages of St. Birgitta of Sweden and Her Order', *Studia monastica*, 35 (1993), 313–29.

eccitar a maggior Divotione, tutte le Sorelle nostre, et altri, se forse la leggeranno' (fol. 4ʳ; to encourage greater devotion in all our sisters, and in others if by chance they read it); in other words, there was the possibility of circulation outside the convent walls. The scribe notes twice that she had the consent of her abbess, Paola Girolama Piccaluga (Part 1, fol. 505ᵛ, and Part 2, fol. 217ᵛ). The wording of the title page of Part 1 – *Le divine revelationi di santa Brigida Tradotte in Lingua Volgare, opera di una serva di Dio* (the work of a servant of God) – strongly suggests that the scribe was also the translator, in which case this would be the first complete translation of the *Revelations* since one made in Siena over two centuries earlier.

We saw in Chapter 1 that Beatrice Del Sera wrote out her own play in the Dominican convent of San Niccolò in Prato. Another sister of this institution, Innocenza Lelmi, combined a sense of personal devotion with a high level of technical skill when she copied and decorated a choir book in 1553. Suor Innocenza makes explicit in her colophon her investment in the manuscript and says that she presents it as a gift to the convent's singers. Although the object is beautiful, suor Innocenza apologizes for faults perceived by her:

> Io Suora Innocentia de Lelmi da Prato indegna serva di Iesù Christo à scripto notato miniato questo libro guadagnato le carte et la legatura de[l] libro tutto sopra el suo lavoro ordinario et ne fo un presente alle Cantore con pacti gli cantino una messa de morti el 7° giorno della sua sepultura et all'altre domanda per gratia una volta et 7 psalmi penitentiali mi arete excusat[a] non sta come vorrei. nel anno del Signore 1553 alli 23 di novembre.[63]

> (I, Sister Innocenza Lelmi of Prato, unworthy servant of Jesus Christ, wrote out, copied the notes and illuminated this book, paid for its paper and its binding, all in addition to her ordinary work, and I make a present of it to the singers on condition that they sing for her a requiem Mass on the seventh day after her burial, and she kindly asks the other nuns [to say] once the Seven Penitential Psalms. You will forgive me: it is not as I would wish. 23 November in the year of Our Lord 1553.)

A note in a similar vein was added by suor Eufrasia, of San Domenico in Lucca, to one of her choir books, written in 1515: in it, she asks readers to pray for her and to excuse her errors.[64]

---

[63] *S. Niccolò a Prato*, ed. by Silvestro Bardazzi and Eugenio Castellani (Prato: Edizioni del Palazzo, 1984), p. 307, Plates 274–76. I am grateful to Don Renzo Fantappiè of the Ufficio per i Beni Culturali, Diocesi di Prato, for the information that the choir book still belongs to the Conservatorio di San Niccolò di Prato.

[64] Taurisano, *I Domenicani in Lucca*, p. 161. Two of Eufrasia's illuminated initials are reproduced on pages 158 and 162.

In some convents, copying was carried out as an organized business as well as for internal use. The abbess of the Vallombrosan community of Santa Verdiana in Florence, Piera de' Medici, worked between 1445 and 1447 on a missal that had been commissioned by the abbot of Santa Maria del Ponterosso di Figline (also known as the abbey of Tagliafuni) in the Valdarno.[65] The chronicler of San Giorgio in Lucca lists the production of choir books among the tasks that, in 1527, kept the nuns occupied and provided sources of revenue:

> l'exercitio et la fatica è una gran custodia della castità et pertanto queste madre et sorelle non stanno mai ociose, sì per non perdere tempo, sì per bisogno del victo perché non hanno alchuna entrata se non di elemosine et di loro fatiche. Et per questo lavorano quanto possano et li loro lavori son questi: ordire tele di seta, incannare la seta, tessere panni lini, rachamare et cucire, (scrivere in littera grossa e libri del choro et notargli et miniargli) et simili altri exercitii iusti et honesti.[66]

> (activities and labour are good guardians of chastity, and therefore these mothers and sisters are never idle, both in order not to waste time and through need of food, for their only income comes from alms and their own labours. And for this reason they work as much as they can, and their tasks are these: to warp silk cloth, to wind silk, to weave linen, to embroider and sew, (to write the choir books in large letters and add notation and illuminate them) and similar other just and honourable tasks.)

In Florence, at least seven female convents copied and decorated liturgical manuscripts in order to supplement their income, just as they produced and sold textiles and other goods.[67] One of these was the Augustinian house of Santa Caterina al Monte, known as San Gaggio, where in the mid-fifteenth century nuns produced Books of Hours and, for the new Augustinian convent of Santa Monaca, just south of the Arno, two choir books with letters decorated in red and blue ink. One nun, Maria di Ormanno degli Albizzi, wrote out in 1453 a breviary in which she included a self-portrait (Vienna, Österreichische Nationalbibliothek, Cod. 1923).[68]

Probably the most extensive commercial scribal production within a convent was that, studied by Kate Lowe, of the Benedictines of

[65] The missal is BLF, MS Conv. Soppr. 235. See Sharon T. Strocchia, 'Abbess Piera de' Medici and Her Kin: Gender, Gifts, and Patronage in Renaissance Florence', *Renaissance Studies*, 28 (2014), 695–713 (pp. 699–701).
[66] Coli, *La Cronaca del monastero domenicano*, pp. 241–42; the words in parentheses are added in the margin. See also Taurisano, *I Domenicani in Lucca*, p. 160.
[67] Strocchia, *Nuns and Nunneries*, pp. 144–47. See, too, Weaver, *Convent Theatre*, pp. 26–29.
[68] Kathleen G. Arthur, 'New Evidence for a Scribal-Nun's Art: Maria di Ormanno degli Albizzi at San Gaggio', *Mitteilungen des Kunsthistorischen Institutes in Florenz*, 59 (2017), 271–80.

Santissima Annunziata delle Murate (literally, of women enclosed by walls, and in fact a women's prison during most of the twentieth century), near Santa Verdiana.[69] The convent had to be rebuilt, with financial support from Lorenzo de' Medici, after a fire in 1471, and the works carried out in the following years included the construction of ten small studies, described as 'scrittoini'.[70] A convent chronicle written in the late sixteenth century describes how in this period

> There were [. . .] always about eight scribes who were using formal script, in which they were very skilled, so that among all these labors, together with the gold they cut and spun carefully in the *sala grande*, they made the annual sum of at least 500 *scudi*, working to meet their needs.[71]

A second fire destroyed these ten studies in about 1498, but their reconstruction was funded by another patron, Caterina Sforza, countess of Forlì.[72] This activity was evidently very worthwhile for the nuns, and more studies were built during the sixteenth century with the help of yet another benefaction, so that there were twenty-six by the time the convent chronicle was completed in 1598.[73]

The main customers of Le Murate would have been other clerics, including nuns, as we shall see in the next chapter. This kind of commercial activity on the part of sisters enraged fra Girolamo Savonarola. He visited Le Murate in May 1495; a woodcut used on the title pages of two of the Florentine editions of his work on the Ten Commandments, addressed to the abbess, could be intended to represent this event.[74] In a sermon of 10 May 1495, Savonarola attacked the convent:

> Io fui alle Murate venerdì passato [. . .]. Io gli ho predicato del lume che bisogna avere [. . .]; che le lascino le zacchere e rete e reticelle e ulivi, che

---

[69] Kate Lowe, 'Women's Work at the Benedictine Convent of Le Murate in Florence: Suora Battista Carducci's Roman Missal of 1509', in *Women and the Book: Assessing the Visual Evidence*, ed. by Lesley Smith and Jane H. M. Taylor (London: British Library; University of Toronto Press, 1996), pp. 133–46.

[70] Giustina Niccolini, *The Chronicle of Le Murate*, ed. by Saundra Weddle (Toronto: Iter, 2011), p. 109. The chronicle is in BNCF, MS II II 509.

[71] Niccolini, *The Chronicle of Le Murate*, p. 114; translation modified to correspond more closely with the original, 'stavono sempre circa otto scrivane di lettera formata, in qual virtù heron eccellentissime', cited by Lowe, 'Women's Work', p. 145, n. 34.

[72] Niccolini, *The Chronicle of Le Murate*, pp. 141–43.    [73] Ibid., p. 179.

[74] Girolamo Savonarola, *Operetta molto divota composta da frate Hieronymo da Ferrara dell'ordine de' frati predicatori sopra e dieci comandamenti di Dio: diricta alla madonna, o vero badessa del monasterio delle Murate di Firenze: nella quale si contiene la examina de' peccati d'ogni et qualunque peccatore: che è utile et perfecta confessione* (Florence: [Bartolommeo di Libri], 1495; Giovanni Stefano di Carlo, 1508). The edition of Lorenzo Morgiani and Johannes Petri, *c.* 1495–96, has another woodcut that shows kneeling nuns receiving a book from two friars.

fanno d'oro e d'argento, e loro libriccini; secondo, se sono murate, debbono stare come hanno il nome.[75]

(I was at Le Murate last Friday [...]. I preached to them about the light we must have [...]. They should leave the knick-knacks and hairnets and [embroidered] olive branches that they make of gold and silver, and their little books. Second, if they are enclosed, they should live as their name suggests.)

The 'little books' were Books of Hours, which will also be mentioned in the following chapter. There was probably a political dimension to Savonarola's outrage, since the monastery had been patronized by Lorenzo de' Medici, to whom he had been hostile.[76] In any event, his sermon had no effect on the nuns' making of books.

The community of Le Murate used some of its books as gifts in order to thank benefactors. The nuns gave the Queen of Portugal in 1497, among other presents, what the convent's chronicle describes as 'a small book of prayers written and illuminated by their own hands in beautiful lettering'.[77] This was one of the cases in which these nuns carried out the decoration of the manuscripts that they wrote. They could also subcontract this specialized task to professionals of the book trade, working with them in a type of collaboration of which there are examples involving other convents. A case in point is a surviving manuscript that may well have been a gift. It contains the Office of the Passion and prayers by St Birgitta, written in a formal gothic rotunda hand, as was conventional for a liturgical work. The miniaturist has been tentatively identified as Tommaso di Stefano Lunetti. On the first leaf, the arms of Pope Julius II have been partially erased. The manuscript may therefore have originally been given to Julius, who donated over 2,000 scudi to the convent and supported it in other ways during his papacy.[78]

In the Bibliothèque nationale de France is a Roman missal from Le Murate, also in a gothic rotunda script (MS lat. 17323). According to its colophon (fol. 385r), copying was completed on 12 October 1509. The missal includes the text and readings for the Mass, and plainsong settings with musical notation. The scribe did not identify herself, but she is named

[75] Girolamo Savonarola, *Prediche sopra i Salmi*, ed. by Vincenzo Romano, 2 vols (Rome: Belardetti, 1969–74), I, 181–82.
[76] Niccolini, *The Chronicle of Le Murate*, pp. 12–13.      [77] Ibid., p. 137.
[78] Ibid., pp. 160, 167, 316, 321. On the former Abbey MS J.A. 6991, see J. J. G. Alexander and A. C. de la Mare, *The Italian Manuscripts in the Library of Major J. R. Abbey* (London: Faber, 1969), pp. 159–60; Lowe, 'Women's Work', p. 141 (and p. 137 for other cases of collaboration between nuns and male illuminators); *Miniatura fiorentina del Rinascimento 1440–1525: un primo censimento*, ed. by Annarosa Garzelli, 2 vols (Florence: La Nuova Italia, 1985), I, 336–37, II, Figures 1075–76.

in the convent chronicle as suor Battista Carducci. The manuscript was illuminated by the leading Florentine miniaturist, Attavante Attavanti. This is a truly magnificent volume and, whatever the original intention was when it was made in 1509, it was decided in 1516 to present it as a gift to Pope Leo X, one of the convent's Medicean benefactors, on his visit to Florence in that year. At some point after Leo's election in March 1513, the Medici arms with the papal insignia were added (fol. 13$^r$; Figure 2.4). The gift was not made in vain: the convent chronicle tells us that the pope gave the generous sum of 200 gold scudi as a sign of his gratitude.[79]

Architectural plans drawn up for the Benedictine convent of Santa Croce della Giudecca in Venice show that a more modest scribal operation was planned there early in the sixteenth century. According to this project, three studies of identical design were to be built above the courtyard. Each was to have a 'small window' and a doorway facing west, and each is labelled 'scriptoria col suo canzello', in other words, a space for writing with a gate in the doorway (Figure 2.5).[80]

The Clarissan convent of Santa Maria di Monteluce in Perugia housed about seventy nuns, several of whom came from well-to-do families. A few sisters worked as scribes, and occasionally as translators from Latin to the vernacular. Records of the convent's income and expenditure from the mid-fifteenth century note sales of breviaries, but it is not stated that these had been copied within the convent.[81] Copying at Monteluce seems in fact to have been carried out primarily or solely for the nuns' own benefit. The convent chronicle states that a suor Eufemia (born Margarita di Battista of Città di Castello), who died in 1465, was a 'donna venerabile et docta in scientia, la quale più libri haveva vulgariçati et scripti de sua mano per lo monasterio' (a venerable and learned lady, who had translated into the vernacular and copied several books for the monastery). A suor Maria di

[79] Niccolini, *The Chronicle of Le Murate*, p. 162. The story of this manuscript is examined in detail in Lowe, 'Women's Work'.

[80] Victoria Jane Primhak, 'Women in Religious Communities: The Benedictine Convents in Venice, 1400–1550' (unpublished doctoral thesis, University of London, Warburg Institute, 1991), pp. 91–92. The plan is in Venice, Archivio di Stato, Avogaria di Comun, Raspe, Santa Croce della Giudecca, busta 4.

[81] Ugolino Nicolini, 'I minori osservanti di Monteripido e lo "scriptorium" delle Clarisse di Monteluce in Perugia nei secoli XV e XVI', *Picenum seraphicum*, 8 (1971), 100–30 (pp. 108–10). For an overview of the nuns' scribal activities, see ibid., pp. 106–14, 122–24, 128–29; *Memoriale di Monteluce: cronaca del monastero delle clarisse di Perugia dal 1448 al 1838*, intro. by Ugolino Nicolini (Santa Maria degli Angeli: Edizioni Porziuncola, 1983), pp. xviii–xx, and pp. xxiii–xxvii for an inventory of books from Monteluce in the Biblioteca Comunale Augusta of Perugia; Patrizia Bertini Malgarini, Marzia Caria and Ugo Vignuzzi, 'Clarisse dell'Osservanza e scritture "di pietà" in volgare tra Foligno e Monteluce', *Bollettino storico della città di Foligno*, 31–34 (2007–11), 297–335 (pp. 310–20): Miriello, *I manoscritti del Monastero del Paradiso*, pp. 17–20.

Figure 2.4  Roman missal, copied by suor Battista Carducci. Paris, Bibliothèque nationale de France, MS lat. 17323, fol. 13ʳ

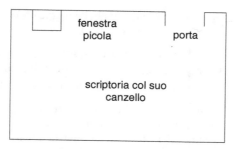

Figure 2.5  Plan of a study for writing in the convent of Santa Croce della Giudecca,
Venice

Bartolomeo da Perugia, who had entered the convent at the age of just
nine, is described on her death in 1508 as:

> docta de lectere et de scrivere; scripse uno breviario, et doi Regule vulgare,
> cioè la Regula nostra, una in carta bambagina, la quale se usa in leggere ad la
> mensa. L'altra scripse in carta pecorina, la quale ne vulghariço el sancto
> padre beato Bernardino da Feltro per nostra consolatione.[82]

> (learned in Latin and writing; she wrote a breviary, and two Rules in the
> vernacular, that is our own Rule, one on paper, which is used in reading
> during mealtimes. She wrote the other on vellum, and it was translated for
> us by the holy father Blessed Bernardino da Feltre for our consolation.)

A suor Felicita, born Eufrasia di Bretoldo of Perugia, was a prolific scribe
right up to her death in 1510:

> Scripse de sua mano lo libro delle collatione de Iohanni Cassiano, le omelie
> de sancto Gregorio, et lo suo dialogho, lo tractato de sancto Bernardo sopra
> missus est, la vita della beata Angela da Fuligno, la vita della beata Eustochia
> de Messina et più altre operecte.[83]

> (She wrote in her hand the book of the *Collationes* of John Cassian, the
> homilies of St Gregory and his *Dialogue*, the treatise of St Bernard *Super*

[82] *Memoriale di Monteluce*, pp. 28 (Eufemia), 94 (Maria).

[83] Ibid., p. 100. Several of these manuscripts are now in the Biblioteca Comunale of Perugia: MS 1019
(St Bernard's treatise on St Luke's gospel with *Le sette armi spirituali* of St Catherine of Bologna);
MS 1068, completed on 4 August 1504 (John Cassian); MS 1087, completed on 7 May 1507 (St
Gregory's sermons); MS 1105, completed on 26 May 1498 (St Gregory's dialogue); MS 1108,
completed on 25 May 1510 (Iacopa Pollichino's life of Blessed Eustochia): ibid., pp. xxiv–xxv. See
also Ignazio Baldelli, 'Codici e carte di Monteluce', appendix to Giuseppe De Luca, 'Un formulario
di cancelleria francescana e altri formulari tra il XIII e XIV secolo', *Archivio italiano per la storia della
pietà*, 1 (1951), 219–393, at pp. 387–93.

*Missus est*, the life of Blessed Angela da Foligno, the life of Blessed Eustochia of Messina and several other short works.)

Among the books copied by suor Battista (born Antonia Alfani) were two that concerned the Passion, one of them by Nicolò Cicerchia.[84] An account of her death in 1523 sums up her contribution to copying in the convent:

> Et oltra lo spiritu, era docta in sapere intendere et scrivere libri, et a consolatione delle soi figliole scripse lo libro delli sancti padri tucto de sua mano, la legenda della nostra madre sancta Chiara: la retrasse de più libri, aseptolla et compusela distinta in capitoli, come appare. La qual cosa li fo comandata dalli reverendi padri generali, che li arechavano li dicti libri, et da loro fo poi reveduta et commendata, che stava benissimo. Fece più librecti de diversi cose, et etiam questo Memoriale fo facto tucto et aseptato per sua mano per fine a qui.[85]

> (And apart from her spirit, she was learned in being able to understand and write books, and for the consolation of her daughters she wrote the book of the Holy Fathers entirely in her hand, [and] the life of our mother St Clare, which she derived from several books, put in order and drew up divided into chapters, as can be seen. She was ordered to do this by the reverend Fathers General, who brought her the said books, and it was then reviewed by them and commended as excellent. She made several little books of various writings, and also this convent record was entirely made and ordered in her hand up to here.)

This suor Battista, in other words, was working on behalf of her order, to produce books that would bring spiritual comfort to members of her community.

The sisters' work at Monteluce could also be carried out in collaboration between themselves. In about 1514, for example, the abbess Veronica Graziani ordered the transcription of a work by their confessor, the Observant friar Gabriele da Perugia, and a treatise on the Immaculate Conception, dividing the work between five sisters, all of whom used a semigothic hand. It is worth quoting in full the account of how this major operation was undertaken:

---

[84] *Memoriale di Monteluce*, pp. 107–08.

[85] Ibid., pp. 124–25 and Plates 1–5, 7; Nicolini, 'I minori osservanti di Monteripido', pp. 128–29; Bertini Malgarini, Caria and Vignuzzi, 'Clarisse dell'Osservanza', pp. 310–13. See also Maria Grazia Nico Ottaviani, *'Me son missa a scriver questa letera ... ': lettere e altre scritture femminili tra Umbria, Toscana e Marche nei secoli XV–XVI* (Naples: Liguori, 2006), pp. 138–39. The 'book of the Holy Fathers' was a translation of the *Vitae Patrum* made in the early fourteenth century by Domenico Cavalca of Pisa: see Domenico Cavalca, *Vite dei santi padri*, ed. by Carlo Delcorno, 2 vols (Florence: Edizioni del Galluzzo per la Fondazione Ezio Franceschini, 2009).

In questo tempo dello offitio della sopra dicta madre abbadessa sora
Veronicha, [...] diede ordine de fare copiare dalle sore lo devotissimo
libro intitulato Libro de vita, lo quale tracta sopra tucti li principali misteri
del nostro Signore Iesu Christo, et della sua benedecta Madre Vergine
Maria, compilato dal venerabile padre frate Gabriello da Peroscia [...]. Et
perché l'opera era grande ad ciò se havesse ad expedire più presto, essendo lo
libro in quinterni sciolto esso nostro padre li partì in quactro parti che
fussero quactro sore ad scriverlo, le quale fuorono sora Ursolina, sora
Eustochia, sora Eufrasia et sora Maria, et in ultimo lo tractato della ascen-
sione del Signore et quello dello Spiritu Sancto, et ancho quello della
Conceptione della Vergine Maria, esso padre lo fece scrivere alla nostra
madre sora Cherubina, fu incomençato ad scrivere lo dicto libro a dì xxv de
genaio, [...] et fu finito circha la uscita del mese de giugno, lo quale essendo
expedito, fu leghato in doi volume come appare. Ma el quinterno che tracta
della Inmaculatissima Conceptione della Madonna el predicto padre non
volse leghato como li altri nel libro, ma se tenesse così fermato nel libro con
qualche ponto ad ciò se potesse facilmente levare quando paresse per
qualche occasione, et questo fece esso padre a bona cautela per le varie
openione che sonno in tale opera.

Item, fu facto lo libro della vita sanctissima del nostro Signore Iesu
Christo, et della sua gloriosa Madre Vergine Maria, et lo libro delli quactro
Evangelii in vulgare, leghati in uno volume, lo quale sora Eufrasia haveva
incomençato ad scrivere prima che venisse lo sopradicto libro, et finito
quello essa sequitò e finì questo tucto de sua mano.[86]

(At this point in the term of office of the above-mentioned mother abbess
Sister Veronica, [...] she ordered the sisters to transcribe the most devout
book entitled *Book of Life*, which deals with all the major mysteries of our
Lord Jesus Christ and of his blessed mother the Virgin Mary, compiled by
the venerable father Friar Gabriello of Perugia [...]. And in order to
complete such a long work as quickly as possible, our father divided the
unbound gatherings of the book into four parts so that four sisters could
write it. They were Sister Orsolina [di Dionisio da Perugia], Sister Eustochia
[born Francesca di Severo Alfani], Sister Eufrasia [di Roberto da Gaiche]
and Sister Maria. Finally the same father had our mother Sister Cherubina
[Fabene] write out the treatise on the Ascension of the Lord and that on the
Holy Spirit, and also that on the Conception of the Virgin Mary. The
writing of the said book began on 25 January [...] and it was finished around
the end of June. Once it was completed, it was bound in two volumes as can
be seen. But the aforesaid father did not wish the gathering that deals with

[86] *Memoriale di Monteluce*, p. 107; see also p. xxv. These writings are now in Perugia, Biblioteca
Comunale Augusta, MSS 1074 (*Libro de vita*, Book I), 993 (*Libro de vita*, Book II) and 3041 (*Trattato
sull'Immacolata concezione*). See, too, Miglio, *Governare l'alfabeto*, pp. 176–77; Bertini Malgarini,
Caria and Vignuzzi, 'Clarisse dell'Osservanza', pp. 319–20. On fra Gabriele, see Dario Busolini,
'Gabriele da Perugia', *DBI*, 51 (1998), 52–53.

the Immaculate Conception of the Madonna to be bound into the book like the others; instead, it was to be kept fastened in the book with some stitches, so that it could easily be removed if desired for some occasion. This father did so as a wise precaution, because of the different opinions found in that work.

Furthermore, the book of the most holy life of our Lord Jesus Christ, and of his glorious mother the Virgin Mary, and the book of the four Gospels in the vernacular, were made and bound in one volume. Sister Eufrasia had begun to transcribe this before the above-mentioned book arrived. Once that was finished, she resumed and finished all of this one in her hand.)

In 1570 a team of three nuns of this convent undertook the copying of an account of the early Franciscan order, the *Franceschina* or *Specchio dell'Ordine Minore* by Giacomo Oddi. One sister 'prese pensiero de tutte le spese' (took charge of all expenditure), while another was responsible for the supply of paper and other materials and for correcting the text. Copying was begun by suor Virginia Randoli and completed in 1573, after Virginia's death, by suor Modesta Tezi. Decoration was commissioned from an artist outside the convent. The total cost was 30 scudi, excluding of course the work of the nuns in ruling the paper and transcribing the text, and the completed volume was estimated to be worth 60 scudi.[87] Both sisters used a formal gothic script for this manuscript, and suor Modesta's skill in this respect was noted when she died in 1577: 'spendeva il tempo in [...] inscrivere libri devoti, et cose utile, imperoché sapeva bene scrivere lettera formata' (she spent her time [...] writing devout books and useful writings, since she could write formal script well).[88]

An Observant Clarissan convent that had a close relationship with Monteluce was that of Santa Lucia in Foligno, also in Umbria. The obituary of a nun who was the daughter of a chancellor of Perugia illustrates again the practice of copying for the benefit of the whole institution:

L'ultimo dì de março [1547] morì la matre sora Catarina [Guarnieri] da Oximo. [...] Era una anima devota, pura e sempre pensava che potesse fare per utilità de questo monasterio. Epsa matre scripse el libro de sancta Melchiade e quello de Ierusalem e io, sora Antonia, ci la adiutai, e multe altre cose à scripte per consolatione de le sore, ad le quale epsa matre portava grandissima carità e amore.

(On the last day of March [1547] Mother Caterina [Guarnieri] of Osimo died. [...] She was a devout and pure soul, always thinking what she could

[87] *Memoriale di Monteluce*, pp. 206, 223.    [88] Ibid., p. 236 and Plates 10–11.

do to benefit this monastery. This mother wrote the book of St Mechthild [a translation of the *Liber spiritualis gratiae*] and that of Jerusalem [fra Francesco Suriano's treatise on the Holy Land], and I, Sister Antonia, helped her with this. She copied many other works for the consolation of the sisters, for whom this mother felt the greatest charity and love.)

Neither of the manuscripts mentioned here appears to have survived.[89]

Another instance of community building is that of the culture of creating books within the Augustinian convent of Santa Marta in Milan. This was renowned as the residence of two holy women in the late fifteenth and early sixteenth centuries: Veronica Negroni da Binasco (1445–1497) and Arcangela Panigarola (1468–1525).[90] They came from contrasting social origins but shared a reputation for divinely inspired visions, and this reputation was encouraged and used by men within the church and in the political arena, especially in order to support the authority of the French regime that seized power in Milan in 1499 and governed the state for most of the first two decades of the sixteenth century. While Veronica da Binasco's reputation endured (she was beatified in 1517), Panigarola's supporters lost faith in her mysticism around 1517–19, because her interpretation of her prophecies did not coincide with the future that they desired. Nevertheless, both women continued to be seen as important figures within the community of Santa Marta, and the work of certain nuns acting as scribes played a crucial part in this process.

The first of these copyists was Benedetta da Vimercate (1425?–1515), who entered Santa Marta in 1457. A nun who composed a chronicle of the convent in the sixteenth century, Veronica Stampa, wrote of Benedetta:

---

[89] Bertini Malgarini, Caria and Vignuzzi, 'Clarisse dell'Osservanza', pp. 300–07.

[90] On the convent and the context, see Agostino Saba, *Federico Borromeo e i Mistici del suo tempo: con la vita e la corrispondenza inedita di Caterina Vannini da Siena* (Florence: Olschki, 1933), pp. 8–15; Mario Caciagli, 'Santa Marta', in *Milano: le chiese scomparse*, ed. by Mario Caciagli, Jacqueline Ceresoli and Pantaleo Di Marzo, 3 vols (Milan: Civica Biblioteca d'Arte, 1997–99), III, 75–118; Bonora, *I conflitti della Controriforma*, pp. 31–57; Herzig, *Savonarola's Women*, pp. 155–66; John Gagné, 'Fixing Texts and Changing Regimes: Manuscript, Print, and Holy Lives in French-Occupied Milan, c. 1500–1525', in *The Saint between Manuscript and Print: Italy 1400–1600*, ed. by Alison K. Frazier (Toronto: Centre for Reformation and Renaissance Studies, 2015), pp. 379–420; *Angeliche visioni: Veronica da Binasco nella Milano del Rinascimento*, ed. by Alessandra Bartolomei Romagnoli, Emore Paoli and Pierantonio Piatti (Florence: SISMEL-Edizioni del Galluzzo, 2016). See also Massimo Firpo, 'Paola Antonia Negri, monaca angelica (1508–1555)', in *Rinascimento al femminile*, ed. by Ottavia Niccoli (Bari: Laterza, 1991), pp. 35–82 (pp. 41–42); Zarri, *Le sante vive*, pp. 95–96. For a more detailed discussion of these manuscripts, see Brian Richardson, 'Memorializing Living Saints in the Milanese Convent of Santa Marta in the Late Fifteenth and Early Sixteenth Century', in *Nuns' Literacies in Medieval Europe: The Antwerp Dialogue*, ed. by Virginia Blanton, Veronica O'Mara and Patricia Stoop (Turnhout: Brepols, 2017), pp. 209–25.

'Fu quella che scrise el libro de la beata Veronicha et molti altri libri de
oratione et tuti li libri da canto et che non sono in canto in palpere che se
adopereno al presente in Choro honia zorno' (It was she who wrote the
book of Blessed Veronica and many other prayer books, and all the singing
books and other books on paper that are now used in the choir every day).[91]
One of the prayer books that Benedetta may have written is an Office of
Santa Marta, formerly owned by the convent, which was copied in a gothic
rotunda script in black and red ink but otherwise undecorated (BAM, MS
Trotti 531). But more importantly from our point of view, suor Benedetta
composed a life of Beata Veronica and probably also made the copy of it in
BAM, MS I 179 inf., written in a semigothic hand.[92] Veronica herself,
coming from a poor family, was not very literate. In a work printed in 1518,
Isidoro Isolani, a Dominican friar from Santa Maria delle Grazie, told
a story of how Veronica, when accepted as a nun in 1463, had difficulty in
reading the divine office, but the Virgin Mary appeared to her, consoled
her and showed her three letters that symbolized all she needed to learn:
'Ne timueris filia mea, neque plurimum coneris litteras nosse. Meae nempe
voluntatis est, trium tantummodo litterarum peritiam te habere: prima
coloris alba erit, secunda nigri, tertia rubei' (Do not fear, my daughter, and
do not try very hard to know letters. Indeed, I want you to know just three:
the first will be coloured white, the second black, the third red). These
letters represented respectively purity of the heart ('cordis mundiciam'),
never being tempted by the deeds of her neighbour ('nunquam scandalum
sumas ab proximi operibus') and attentive daily meditation on at least part
of Christ's Passion ('iubeo te quottidie saltim partem passionis filii mei
quam attentissime meditari'). After this, we are told, 'litteras posthaec
Veronica haud magnipendit' (Veronica did not value literacy highly).[93]
Rather than recording her visions in writing, Veronica da Binasco

[91] BAM, MS M 19 suss., busta 1, pp. 1–37 (p. 34). The information is repeated by Filippo Argelati, *Bibliotheca scriptorum Mediolanensium*, 2 vols (Milan: in aedibus Palatinis, 1745), II, cols 1660–61: 'Artem scribendi tam optime callebat, ut ingentia volumina etiam cum musicalibus notis ad usum Chori exaraverit, aliaque scripsit' (She was so skilled in the art of writing that she even wrote out huge volumes with musical notation for the use of the choir, and wrote other things).

[92] Argelati, ibid., believed that this manuscript is in Benedetta's hand. Ownership notes on fols 1ʳ and 239ᵛ record that the book was owned at one point by suor Cecilia Visconti.

[93] Isidoro Isolani, *Inexplicabilis mysterii gesta beatae Veronicae virginis praeclarissimi monasterii Sanctae Marthae urbis Mediolani, sub observatione regulae divi Augustini* (Milan: Gottardo da Ponte, 1518), fols a2ᵛ–a3ʳ. The chronicle compiled in the seventeenth century by Giovanni Pietro Puricelli recounts the same story: 'Cruciandosi poscia lei per haver ad imparar a leggere l'Officio divino, apparsale la Beatissima Vergine, la consola; et con tre lettere le insegna ciò che deve imparare' (When she is tormented at having to learn to read the divine office, the Blessed Virgin appears to her, consoles her and with three letters teaches her what she must learn). *Chronica del monastero delle monache di Santa Martha dell'ordine di Sant'Agostino in Milano*, BAM, MS C 75 inf., fol. 9ʳ.

recounted them to another sister, Taddea Bonlei of Ferrara, who acted as her secretary from 1467 onwards.[94]

Veronica Stampa explains in her chronicle that she will deal with the life and miracles of Veronica da Binasco only briefly because of the existence of the biography compiled by Benedetta da Vimercate, 'el qual libro manifesta onia cosa' (which book reveals everything). She goes on to reveal how Benedetta's book was used. It was kept within the convent, hidden from laypeople, for some years. Then, around 1516, Isolani discussed it with Arcangela Panigarola and offered to translate it into Latin, after which his version was printed:

> essendo stato el dicto libro paregi anni nascosto da seculari et achadendo ne l'anno 1516 che uno certo frate de Santa Maria de le Gratie da Milano vene[n]do parege volte al monasterio nostro per una certa causa et parlando cum la nostra reverenda madre Archangela se exibire [*sic*] a di coregere la vita della ditta beata et transcrivere in latino, et così fece et ne fo facto uno stampo.[95]

> (After this book was hidden from laypeople for several years, it happened that in 1516 a certain friar of Santa Maria delle Grazie of Milan came several times to our monastery over a certain case and spoke to our reverend Mother Arcangela. He offered to correct the life of the said Blessed Veronica and copy it into Latin. And so he did and it was printed.)

Isolani was a supporter of the French regime, and his action was part of a campaign to promote a cult centred on the holy women of Santa Marta. When his Latin life of Veronica was printed in 1518, it was adorned with exquisite woodcuts that have been attributed to Marco d'Oggiono, an artist influenced by Leonardo da Vinci, who had painted his *Last Supper* in Santa Maria delle Grazie.[96] One woodcut shows Christ giving communion to Veronica (fols aa1$^v$ and o6$^v$). Another shows an angel directing Veronica's hand as she writes (fol. k7$^r$). We know, and the nuns of Santa Marta would have known, that other nuns held the pen on her behalf: her secretary Taddea, her biographer Benedetta. But it was important that the wider public reading this edition should think of Veronica's writings as penned directly by her under divine inspiration.

Arcangela Panigarola, a nun of the next generation who was encouraged to take on Veronica's role as a mystic during the French occupation of

---

[94] BAM, MS I 179 inf., fol. 212$^v$.

[95] Veronica Stampa's chronicle, BAM, MS M 19 suss., busta 1, pp. 36–37.

[96] On the attribution of the woodcuts, see Domenico Sedini, *Marco d'Oggiono: tradizione e rinnovamento in Lombardia tra Quattrocento e Cinquecento* (Milan: Jandi Sapi, 1989), pp. 102–03.

Milan, was of much higher social status and therefore presumably well educated. She was the daughter of Gottardo Panigarola, treasurer of the Sforza court, and was christened Margarita. She joined Santa Marta in 1483, aged about fifteen, and rose to the ranks of vicaress and then prioress of the convent.[97] Arcangela was certainly able to write herself: we have an example of her hand, serviceable rather than graceful, in a note of 1521 in which she acknowledges a donation of forty soldi from the French king, received via Giulio Cattaneo, treasurer of the president of the Milanese Senate (BAM, MS E 56 suss., fol. 68[r]). Like Veronica da Binasco, Arcangela used a secretary, suor Bonaventura Morbi, who died in 1550.[98] A possible example of Bonaventura's hand is a copy of the correspondence written in Arcangela's name, in the second decade of the century, to the French bishop Denis Briçonnet, her 'spiritual son', in BAM, MS E 56 suss., where Bonaventura is mentioned several times.[99]

In due course, as with Veronica da Binasco, an account of Arcangela's career as a mystic was committed to writing within the convent, and again a male outsider played a minor part in the process. This took several years and led ultimately to the transcription of a manuscript in two parts: a *Legenda* (or life story) and a *Libro dele revelationi* (Book of Revelations; BAM, MS O 165 sup.). The same scribe wrote both parts in an accomplished humanistic cursive hand and prefaced the revelations with an account of the story of the text, writing in her own voice and addressing 'her sister nuns' of Santa Marta (fol. 38[r–v]). She explains that in her own early years in the convent she had composed and collected writings on Arcangela's visions (some of which had probably been penned or dictated by Arcangela herself, while others were probably transcribed by her secretary Bonaventura), and she thus compiled the revelations of Arcangela up to early 1512. She then handed this section to Arcangela's confessor, the pro-French cleric Giovanni Antonio Bellotti, who translated it into Latin and continued it up to 1519. It is probable that Bellotti planned to have the Latin work printed, just as the life of Veronica da Binasco had been printed in 1518, but that the project was put aside when Arcangela's prophecy came to be seen as problematic. However, if Arcangela had lost her authority outside the walls of Santa Marta, her community continued to cherish their leading figure. A subsequent section was copied from Arcangela's own

[97] Rita Bacchiddu, 'Panigarola, Margherita (in religione Arcangela)', *DBI*, 80 (2014), 777–80.
[98] Francesco Bonardi, *Origine e progressi del venerando monastero di Santa Marta di Milano*, in BAM, MS L 56 suss., pp. 102–09.
[99] A note on the front cover indicates that this manuscript was in the possession of suor Corona Maria Madruzzi in the seventeenth century.

writings. In the late 1520s, in other words after Arcangela's death in 1525, Bellotti's Latin version was translated back into Italian by a Milanese gentleman, Princivalle da Monte, on behalf of suor Bonaventura, now vicaress of the convent.[100] Finally, the manuscript returned, as the scribe puts it,

> ale mane mie per rescriverlo in litera familiare a tute, aciò che ogni cosa se reducha al suo principio et io che haveva cominciato finisca et dia la faticha mia in tale opera ala memoria di quella che me generò in Christo e nela mia professione me promise vita eterna. (fol. 38[r])

> (to my hands to be rewritten in a hand familiar to all [the sisters], so that everything may return to its origins, and I, who had begun it, might finish and devote my efforts to such a work in memory of her who gave birth to me in Christ, and in my profession promised me eternal life.)

The scribe was writing, then, as a personal tribute to Arcangela, her spiritual mother, but also in a material form to which her sisters were accustomed.

The status of this book as an object of reverence for the nuns within Santa Marta is signalled not only by the high level of its script but also by the nature of its decoration. Initials are painted in gold and the fore-edges are gilded. The greatest care has been devoted to the image of Arcangela praying at the start of the *Libro dele revelationi* (fol. 39[r]; Figure 2.6); this must have been painted professionally, and it has been attributed to Marco d'Oggiono because of its similarity with the largest woodcut in the 1518 edition of the life of Veronica.[101] This was a case in which, for a select group of readers, the power of a single image in a manuscript would have been greater than that of the plainer image offered to the general public in a printed edition.

The suggestion that this scribe's hand was 'familiar' because she produced other documents for use by her community is supported by the existence of another manuscript in the same hand: a further copy of Benedetta da Vimercate's life of Beata Veronica (BAM, MS H 39 inf.). This manuscript is, however, relatively plain in its presentation. It seems unlikely that this scribe was a male professional working outside the

---

[100] Princivalle da Monte (or Monti) held public offices under the French regime in Milan and is mentioned as a representative of the city in a governing council in 1535: see respectively Caterina Santoro, *Gli offici del comune di Milano e del dominio visconteo sforzesco (1216–1515)* (Milan: Giuffrè, 1968), pp. 393, 416, and Vicente de Cadenas y Vicent, *La herencia imperial de Carlos V en Italia: el Milanesado* (Madrid: Hidalguia, 1978), p. 380.

[101] Sedini, *Marco d'Oggiono*, p. 109. However, Marco's date of death may have been 1524: see ibid., p. 24.

Figure 2.6  Arcangela Panigarola, *Libro dele revelationi*. BAM, MS O 165 sup., fol. 39^r. © Veneranda Biblioteca Ambrosiana

convent on behalf of the nuns, because the hand is not consistent enough; it becomes particularly irregular on the last page and even more so in the last lines.

A few other nuns copied texts within and for the convent of Santa Marta. One used her neat humanistic cursive hand to copy works including a Latin Office of Santa Marta, 'personalized' for the convent with the insertion of a rosary ('Rosarium') written by Francesco Ladino (BAM, MS Trotti 404, fols 30$^r$–37$^r$); he was elected confessor of the nuns in 1523.[102] A manuscript containing a long collection of texts addressed to the convent by Giovanni Antonio Bellotti was copied out in a more rapid, cursive script (BAM, MS P 273 sup.). It is just possible that the same person was responsible for both these manuscripts, although it is more likely that two scribes were at work. Most of the texts in the second manuscript are letters or short treatises, but one is a sermon on Christ's legacy given by Bellotti in 1521 and previously transcribed by suor Bianca Caterina da Balsamo, probably from Bellotti's text rather than from notes or from memory.[103] From another source we know that this sister held the role of 'cancelliera' or clerk of the community. She was not well educated but nevertheless composed 'cose spirituali' (spiritual writings).[104] An example of Bianca Caterina's writing, an informal version of the humanistic cursive hand, is found in a short document that she transcribed as clerk, recording a decision taken in 1525 to limit the term of office of the prioress to three years.[105]

Another scribe working within the convent has already been mentioned: the chronicler Veronica Stampa, who had become a nun in 1500. At the start of her chronicle, she tells us that she took on the office of clerk in 1517, just before Bianca Caterina: 'Essendo io suor Veronicha di Stampe l'anno del signore 1517 misa alo offitio da la canzelaria o vero thesorera del monasterio nostro' (I, Sister Veronica Stampa, in the year of Our Lord 1517 having been given the office of the chancery, or treasurer of our monastery).[106] Her hand is a version of the humanistic cursive style with some semigothic influence. At a later point in the chronicle (p. 8), a second hand adds a few words: this more orthodox cursive appears to be that of the nun who wrote out the life of Arcangela Panigarola.

---

[102] Ladino's election is recorded in Puricelli's chronicle, BAM, MS C 75 inf., fol. 65$^r$. A note in BAM, MS Trotti 404, fol. I$^{r–v}$, records that the convent offered this and other books for sale to Don Carlo Trivulzio in May 1752 but that Trivulzio sent them back, 'facendo capire a quelle monache, che erano libri da tenersi in considerazione per loro, perché trattano delle loro Beate' (pointing out to those nuns that they were books they should esteem, because they deal with their beatified sisters).

[103] 'Predica facta per el Reverendo comandatore sopra dicto nel anno 1521 el sabato sancto et poy scripta per la venerabile suora Blancha Caterina da Balsamo' (fols 31$^v$–33$^v$; Sermon given by the above-mentioned reverend *commendatore* on Easter Saturday 1521 and then written by the venerable Sister Bianca Caterina da Balsamo).

[104] Bonardi, *Origine e progressi*, in BAM, MS L 56 suss., p. 114.

[105] Inserted in BAM, MS C 75 inf., fol. 56.   [106] BAM, MS M 19 suss., busta 1, p. 1.

The cult of suor Arcangela was still strong in the convent in the mid-sixteenth century. In 1557 a certain suor Isabella da Rho gathered together a *Gierdino spirituale* (Spiritual Garden) made up of devotional writings by Arcangela and had it transcribed by another nun (BAM, MS H 258 inf.). The title page of the manuscript was decorated, probably inside the convent, with a watercolour representation of the legend according to which St Martha tamed a dragon with the help of an aspergillum or holy-water sprinkler. The colophon, dated 16 July 1557, tells us that this garden of texts was composed by Arcangela and 'racolto dalla Reverenda madre sor Isabella da Ro et rescripto in questa forma a complacenza sua' (fol. 36$^v$; collected by the Reverend Mother Isabella da Rho and copied out in this form at her pleasure).

In summary, several nuns were writing texts of one sort or another in Santa Marta between the late fifteenth and the mid-sixteenth century, and some of them were writing quite substantial books that served to promote both daily worship by the sisters and their veneration of the two renowned holy women who belonged to the convent in that period. Two nuns, Taddea Bonlei and Bonaventura Morbi, acted as secretaries of these holy women, and suor Bonaventura may have copied Arcangela Panigarola's correspondence to Denis Briçonnet (BAM, MS E 56 suss.). Benedetta da Vimercate wrote books used in liturgy and prayer (including maybe BAM, MS Trotti 531), composed a life of Veronica da Binasco and probably made the copy of it now in BAM, MS I 179 inf. An anonymous nun made a more elegant copy of this life of Veronica (BAM, MS H 39 inf.) and played the main coordinating role in transcribing the life and revelations of Panigarola (BAM, MS O 165 sup.). Other anonymous sisters wrote an Office of Santa Marta (in BAM, MS Trotti 404) and a collection of letters and treatises by Giovanni Antonio Bellotti (BAM, MS P 273 sup.). Of the nuns who acted as clerks to the convent, at least two applied their scribal skills to other tasks: Bianca Caterina da Balsamo copied out a sermon by Bellotti, and Veronica Stampa composed a convent chronicle (the first part of BAM, MS M 19 suss.). Finally, the anonymous nun working for Isabella da Rho in 1557 wrote out the anthology of writings by Arcangela Panigarola (BAM, MS H 258 inf.).

## Printing, Publishing and Bookselling

### *Laywomen and Print*

If laywomen were to become involved in making, publishing and selling printed books, they had to participate in public life as individuals. Yet this participation was restricted by a set of social conventions that were largely prejudicial to women. The chastity of women had to be guarded closely, since this was the guarantee of patrilinearity, and women were seen as frailer than men by nature.[107] They were excluded by law from all civic and public offices.[108] On the other hand, they could become owners of property and other goods through inheritance, dowries and commercial transactions, and they could make wills.[109] In Venice, the major printing centre of sixteenth-century Italy, fathers were obliged by law to provide a dowry for their daughters. These daughters then had ownership (*proprietas*) of the dowry, while their husbands had possession (*possessio*) of it and could thus make use of it. The dowry could, on request, be returned to the daughter if she was widowed, at least in part.[110] Certain states imposed limitations on the amount women could inherit (only a quarter of a husband's estate in the cases of Milan and Florence, for instance). Women might be obliged to have their commercial activities overseen by a male guardian ('mundualdo') who might be their husband or, in the case of Florence, any man; however, this obligation did not apply

[107] Ian Maclean, *The Renaissance Notion of Woman: A Study in the Fortunes of Scholasticism and Medical Science in European Intellectual Life* (Cambridge University Press, 1980), p. 78; Thomas Kuehn, 'Person and Gender in the Laws', in *Gender and Society in Renaissance Italy*, ed. by Judith C. Brown and Robert C. Davis (London and New York: Longman, 1998), pp. 87–106 (pp. 94–95). See, too, Thomas Kuehn, *Law, Family, & Women: Toward a Legal Anthropology of Renaissance Italy* (University of Chicago Press, 1991); Kuehn, 'Understanding Gender Inequality in Renaissance Florence: Personhood and Gifts of Maternal Inheritance by Women', *Journal of Women's History*, 8.2 (Summer 1996), 58–80; Julius Kirshner, 'Family and Marriage: A Socio-Legal Perspective', in *Italy in the Age of the Renaissance 1300–1550*, ed. by John M. Najemy (Oxford University Press, 2004), pp. 82–102.

[108] Maclean, *The Renaissance Notion of Woman*, p. 77; Kuehn, 'Person and Gender in the Laws', p. 91.

[109] For example, according to the will of the printer Angelo Gardane, dated 1611, his beloved daughter Diamante was to inherit, after other legacies had been paid, the rest of his books, his press and other property and use them as she wished. See Claudio Sartori, 'Una dinastia di editori musicali: documenti inediti sui Gardano e i loro congiunti Stefano Bindoni e Alessandro Raverii', *LB*, 58 (1956), 176–208 (pp. 205–07). Angelo's sister Lucieta made a will in 1579 when she was ill (p. 192), but she recovered her health. Neither of these women appear to have been involved in printing. Some further examples of women's wills can be found in Nico Ottaviani, *'Me son missa a scriver questa letera . . .'*, pp. 121–28.

[110] Anna Bellavitis, 'Women, Family, and Property in Early Modern Venice', in *Across the Religious Divide: Women, Property, and Law in the Wider Mediterranean (ca. 1300–1800)*, ed. by Jutta Gisela Sperling and Shona Kelly Wray (New York: Routledge, 2010), pp. 175–90, and Bellavitis, 'La dote a Venezia tra medioevo e prima età moderna', in *Spazi, poteri, diritti delle donne a Venezia in età moderna*, ed. by Anna Bellavitis, Nadia Maria Filippini and Tiziana Plebani (Verona: QuiEdit, 2012), pp. 5–20. On the legal background to the problem of repaying dowries, see Julius Kirshner, 'Wives' Claims against Insolvent Husbands in Late Medieval Italy', in *Marriage, Dowry, and Citizenship in Late Medieval and Renaissance Italy* (University of Toronto Press, 2015), pp. 131–60.

in Milan or Venice.[111] Women were thus able to participate in commerce, but only up to a certain point. In Venice, for example, women's commercial activities were usually of relatively low status: selling goods on the streets, selling fruit and spices, making linen, baking, shoemaking and so on.[112]

In the book trade, women could most easily become involved if they had a family connection with a male printer or bookseller, usually as his daughter, wife or widow. Their contribution might be solely or mainly that of investing their money in the enterprise. Thus, for example, in 1517 the printer Giovanni Mazzocchi drew on goods to the value of 200 lire from the dowry of his wife Elisabetta in order to help him pay off a debt of over 2,300 lire to his more powerful partner Ludovico Bonaccioli.[113] The settlement arranged for Vittoria Cuini on her marriage to the Milanese bookseller Francesco Quarantana in 1586 included an agreement that her relatives were to give Quarantana 50 scudi 'acciò possa agiutarse in lo suo negocio' (so that he can help himself in his business).[114] But when women belonged to a family who made or sold books, it was easy for them to be called on to lend unpaid help with manual tasks, since in a household of this period there was no clear separation between domestic space and workshop, or between the living quarters of members of the family and those of their employees.[115] During the lifetime of a male printer, the practical contributions of female members of the family were not likely to be recognized openly. For instance, Bernardino Benagli was a prolific producer of books and prints in Venice for sixty years from 1483 onwards, occasionally creating alliances with other male printers. He had no children

[111] Christiane Klapisch-Zuber, 'The Griselda Complex: Dowry and Marriage Gifts in the Quattrocento', in *Women, Family, and Ritual in Renaissance Italy*, trans. by Lydia G. Cochrane (University of Chicago Press, 1985), pp. 213–46 (p. 216); Kuehn, 'Person and Gender in the Laws', pp. 95, 99–101; Monica Chojnacka, *Working Women of Early Modern Venice* (Baltimore, MD: Johns Hopkins University Press, 2001), pp. 26–49. Surveys of women's economic roles and types of work in the period include, for Europe as a whole, Merry E. Wiesner-Hanks, 'Women's Economic Role', in *Women and Gender in Early Modern Europe*, 3rd edn (Cambridge University Press, 2008), pp. 101–37, and for Italy, and especially Tuscany, Samuel K. Cohn, Jr, 'Women and Work in Renaissance Italy', in *Gender and Society in Renaissance Italy*, ed. by Judith C. Brown and Robert C. Davis (London and New York: Longman, 1998), pp. 107–26.

[112] Chojnacka, *Working Women*, p. 45.

[113] Angela Nuovo, *Il commercio librario a Ferrara tra XV e XVI secolo: la bottega di Domenico Sivieri* (Florence: Olschki, 1998), pp. 98–99.

[114] Gian Ludovico Masetti Zannini, *Stampatori e librai a Roma nella seconda metà del Cinquecento: documenti inediti* (Rome: Fratelli Palombi, 1980), p. 97.

[115] Masetti Zannini, *Stampatori e librai*, pp. 61–62, and Deborah Parker, 'Women in the Book Trade in Italy, 1475–1620', *Renaissance Quarterly*, 49 (1996), 509–41 (pp. 517–19). For the situation in France, see Natalie Zemon Davis, 'Women in the Crafts in Sixteenth-Century Lyon', *Feminist Studies*, 8 (1982), 46–80.

of his own, but his wife had two nieces, Angiola and Laura Bianzago. Their help is never mentioned in Benagli's books, yet in his will of 1517 he did, at least, reward the assistance they gave him over four years. Angiola had already died by then, and so to her heirs he left 24 ducats 'de mercede et labore suo, que cum summa diligentia mihi servivit per annos quatuor continuos in pingendo figuras, ligando libros, balneando et aptando cartas ex causa stampandi' (for her wages and labour; she was of service to me with the greatest diligence for four years in painting figures, binding books, dampening and preparing the sheets for printing). To Laura he left 30 ducats 'de laboribus et vegiliis suis, quas passa est et substinuit in domo mea [...] annis quatuor similiter in pingendo figuras, ligando libros, balneando cartas et eas aptando et in regendo et gubernando quasi totum trafigum stampe figurate' (for the labours and vigils that she suffered and endured in my house [...] for four years likewise in painting figures, binding books, dampening the sheets and preparing them and in directing and managing almost the whole business of printed figures).[116] There must have been many other such cases of female labour in printing houses about which we remain ignorant. Writing on archival evidence for masculine authority in the printing houses of early modern Venice, Rosa Salzberg observes that 'The women of the family who participated in the life of the workshop, and the apprentices and journeymen who worked the presses, are all but silent in the surviving documents, but for exceptional cases.'[117]

The daughter or widow of a man in the book trade could make an attractive matrimonial prospect for someone who wished to use her experience, connections and resources in order to consolidate and expand his own business. Thus a mother and her daughter helped to hold together the syndicate that dominated printing in Venice in the late fifteenth century by means of their marriages to printers and booksellers. Paola, daughter of the renowned painter Antonello da Messina and already the widow of Bartolomeo Bonazzi of Messina, married the first man to print in

---

[116] Bartolomeo Cecchetti, 'La pittura delle stampe di Bernardino Benalio', *Archivio veneto*, 33 (1887), 538–39; Francesco Novati, 'Donne tipografe nel Cinquecento', *Il libro e la stampa*, 1 (1907), 41–49; Rosa Marisa Borraccini, 'All'ombra degli eredi: l'invisibilità femminile nelle professioni del libro. La fattispecie marchigiana', in *La donna nel Rinascimento meridionale: atti del convegno internazionale (Roma 11–13 novembre 2009)*, ed. by Marco Santoro (Pisa and Rome: Fabrizio Serra, 2010), pp. 413–28 (p. 413). Philip Gaskell explains that 'Paper had to be wetted in order to secure a good colour on the printed sheet, for there was not enough power available in the common press [...] to force the fibres of dry rag paper to take ink evenly and fully': see his *A New Introduction to Bibliography*, 2nd edn (Oxford: Clarendon Press, 1974), p. 125.

[117] Rosa Salzberg, 'Masculine Republics: Establishing Authority in the Early Modern Venetian Printshop', in *Governing Masculinities in the Early Modern Period*, ed. by Susan Broomhall and Jacqueline Van Gent (Farnham: Ashgate, 2011), pp. 47–64 (p. 49).

Venice, John of Speyer. After John's death in 1470, Paola lived in the house of the printer John Manthen of Gerresheim. Before 1474, she married another German printer, John of Cologne, and took a share in his company with Manthen. In 1477, the daughter whom Paola had had with John of Speyer, Girolama, married the bookseller Gaspar of Dinslaken, bringing with her a generous dowry, worth 3,000 ducats, provided by John of Cologne. Paola and Girolama, both represented by Gaspar, subscribed in 1480 to the formation of a publishing partnership that united the most powerful players on the Venetian printing scene, John of Cologne and Nicolas Jenson, and came to be known simply as 'la Compagnia'; the other signatories included Manthen, Girolama's brother Pietro Paolo and the merchant Peter Ugelheimer. In 1480, Paola – a veritable 'matrimonial phoenix', as Victor Scholderer described her – took her fourth husband, Reynaldus of Nijmegen, who joined the syndicate in his turn. Girolama survived Gaspar and ran the company until at least 1511, when she inherited from Gaspar books worth 660 ducats as partial restitution of her dowry.[118] After Ugelheimer's death in 1487, his widow Margarete carried on and extended his bookselling business.[119] Aldo Manuzio the Elder's Venetian publishing alliance with Andrea Torresani was strengthened by his marriage to Torresani's daughter Maria in January 1505, when he was about fifty-four years old and she was aged twenty.[120] The marriage of his grandson, Aldo Manuzio the Younger, to Francesca Lucrezia Giunti, illegitimate

---

[118] Konrad Haebler, 'Das Testament des Johann Manthen von Gerresheim', *LB*, 26 (1924), 1–9 (p. 8); Victor Scholderer, 'Printing at Venice to the End of 1481', in *Fifty Essays in Fifteenth- and Sixteenth-Century Bibliography*, ed. by Dennis E. Rhodes (Amsterdam: Hertzberger, 1966), pp. 74–89 (p. 84); Martin Lowry, *The World of Aldus Manutius: Business and Scholarship in Renaissance Venice* (Oxford: Blackwell, 1979), pp. 18–19; Mariarosa Cortesi, 'Incunaboli veneziani in Germania nel 1471', in *Vestigia: studi in onore di Giuseppe Billanovich*, ed. by Rino Avesani et al., 2 vols (Rome: Edizioni di Storia e Letteratura, 1984), I, 197–219 (pp. 200–01); Tiziana Pesenti, 'Dinslaken (Dinslach, de Islach, de Dislach, Dedislach), Gaspare (Gaspare Alemanno da Colonia)', *DBI*, 40 (1991), 167–69; Borraccini, 'All'ombra degli eredi', p. 420; Nuovo, *The Book Trade*, pp. 28–30, 129, 427.

[119] Tobias Daniels, 'Eine Geschäftsfrau im Venedig der Renaissance: Margarete Ugelheimer (geb. Molle) († ca. 1500)', in *Hinter dem Pergament: Die Welt. Der Frankfurter Kaufmann Peter Ugelheimer und die Kunst der Buchmalerei im Venedig der Renaissance*, ed. by Christoph Winterer (Munich: Hirmer, 2018), pp. 42–53.

[120] Harry George Fletcher III, *New Aldine Studies: Documentary Essays on the Life and Work of Aldus Manutius* (San Francisco: Rosenthal, 1988), p. 7; Catherine Kikuchi, 'How Did Aldus Manutius Start a Printing Dynasty?', in *Aldo Manuzio: la costruzione del mito / Aldus Manutius: The Making of the Myth*, ed. by Mario Infelise (Venice: Marsilio, 2016), pp. 25–38. For other examples of marital alliances, see Corrado Marciani, 'Editori, tipografi, librai veneti nel Regno di Napoli nel Cinquecento', *Studi veneziani*, 10 (1968), 457–554 (pp. 468–69); Parker, 'Women in the Book Trade', pp. 516–17; Marco Santoro, 'Imprenditrici o "facenti funzioni"?', in *La donna nel Rinascimento meridionale: atti del convegno internazionale (Roma 11–13 novembre 2009)*, ed. by Marco Santoro (Pisa and Rome: Fabrizio Serra, 2010), pp. 371–82 (p. 377).

daughter of Tommaso Giunti, was the means by which the Manuzio company was finally absorbed into that of the Giunti family. The couple were wed in 1572, but split up fairly soon: Francesca remained in Venice when Aldo left the city in 1576, and the marriage was later annulled. Francesca did not run the company in Venice, but probably handed her property and her stock of books over to her cousin Lucantonio Giunti the Younger.[121]

When a male printer or bookseller died, his female relatives could play a crucial part in ensuring the survival of the business while simultaneously providing for their own livelihood. In Parma in 1497, Bianca Quintrello agreed to her two sons renting a bookshop, which may have been that of her late husband, to a widow called Tedheria Cortesi. Later Bianca, who seems to have been the dominant figure, sold the contents of the shop (165 books, paper and tools) to Tedheria for the sum of 200 lire 13 soldi 7 denari.[122] In the sixteenth century, some women played crucial 'holding' roles in the operation of printing businesses at difficult transitional moments, sometimes with the support of men. Luchina Ravani appears from documentary evidence to have inherited the Venetian printing and bookselling business of her husband Pietro Ravani in early 1531 and administered it, together with her son Vettor, until at least 1540 or 1541.[123] When Melchiorre Sessa the Elder, a leading Venetian printer-publisher of the early-to-mid-sixteenth century, made his will in 1563, he judged it appropriate to make his wife Veronica Barone one of his executors, together with her two brothers. After Melchiorre's death in late 1565 or early 1566 and before their four sons came of age, Veronica carried out the complex role of running this major press. Her administrative tasks included dealing with booksellers and arranging for business to be carried out at book fairs.[124]

Writing of the world of books in sixteenth-century Rome, Gian Ludovico Masetti Zannini has commented that wives and widows of

[121] Francesca Pitacco, 'La repromissione di dote di Francesca Lucrezia Giunti e la bottega veneziana di Aldo Manuzio il Giovane', in *Intorno al Polifilo: contributi sull'opera e l'epoca di Francesco Colonna e Aldo Manuzio*, ed. by Alessandro Scarsella, Miscellanea marciana, 16 (Venice: Biblion, 2001), pp. 217–38; Nuovo, *The Book Trade*, pp. 134, 230–31.

[122] Alberto Del Prato, 'Librai e biblioteche parmensi del secolo XV', *Archivio storico per le provincie parmensi*, 2nd ser., 4 (1904), 1–56 (p. 7).

[123] Silvia Curi Nicolardi, *Una società tipografico-editoriale a Venezia nel secolo XVI: Melchiore Sessa e Pietro di Ravani (1516–1525)* (Florence: Olschki, 1984), pp. 10–12; Ascarelli and Menato, *La tipografia*, p. 358.

[124] Marciani, 'Editori, tipografi, librai veneti', pp. 468, 470, 500–06, 521–23; Ascarelli and Menato, *La tipografia*, pp. 327–28; Nuovo, *The Book Trade*, pp. 84, 85, 306, 307 n. 93.

printers and booksellers often undertook the running of the family company, even when their children had reached adulthood. Their involvement
can in some cases be explained by the contribution of their dowries, but
there is considerable evidence of what he terms a 'professional vocation' on
their part. Three generations of women of the Blado family played active
(and not merely matrimonial or maternal) roles in ensuring the survival of
printing businesses for half a century.[125] After the death of Antonio Blado
in 1567, his press was run by his heirs, his children and his widow Paola,
who was involved with the firm until her own death in 1588. Immediately
after becoming a widow, she joined the team of Roman printers put
together in 1567 by Paolo Manuzio in order to print the Roman Breviary
that had been newly revised and approved by the Council of Trent. She is
described in Manuzio's papers as 'stampatora in Campo de fiore', in other
words a female printer who was still running Antonio's printing house near
the Campo de' Fiori.[126] Other documents confirm her professional identity by naming her as 'Paola Blada stampatrice' or 'madonna Paula
stampatrice'.[127] Paola Blado was assisted in her work by the printer
Giovanni Gigliotti, who married her daughter Agnese.[128] Gigliotti's own
press passed in 1586 to his heirs, Agnese, who died in 1592, and their son
Domenico. In 1590, Agnese was living with her daughters Elisabetta and
Tarquinia, and these two may have played a part in the business. Tarquinia
is called 'stampatrix' in 1590, and in the same year the dedicatory letter of
a commentary on the Penitential Psalms by Francesco Panigarola, the
*Salmi penitentiali dichiarati da monsignor reverendissimo Panigarola*, is
addressed to the preacher's sister-in-law, Anna Visconti, and is signed
'Humili Servitrici Le Heredi di Gio. Gigliotto' (Humble servants, the
[female] heirs of Giovanni Gigliotto).[129] Another of Antonio's heirs, his
son Paolo, was supported by his wife and later widow Porzia Manni.
Paolo's brother Stefano married Livia, daughter of another woman printer
whose services Manuzio engaged for his breviary project: Lucrezia Dorico,
perhaps the widow of Luigi Dorico, who had died probably in 1559.
Manuzio calls her 'stampatrice alli Coronati', a female printer established

---

[125] Masetti Zannini, *Stampatori e librai*, pp. 61–84, from which much of the following outline is
derived (quotation from p. 62).
[126] Francesco Barberi, *Paolo Manuzio e la Stamperia del Popolo romano (1561–1570)* (Rome: Gela, 1985),
p. 75.
[127] Masetti Zannini, *Stampatori e librai*, pp. 64 and 65.
[128] Ascarelli and Menato, *La tipografia*, pp. 100–01; Marco Menato, 'Blado, Antonio e Paolo', in
Menato, *Dizionario*, 147–49.
[129] Masetti Zannini, *Stampatori e librai*, p. 69. The letter is in the edition of the *Salmi* (Rome: heirs of
Giovanni Gigliotto, 1590), fol. A2^(r–v).

near the basilica of Santi Quattro Coronati.[130] Finally, Isabella Blado, daughter of Paolo and Porzia, became the last member of the dynasty to be engaged in the book trade in Rome. In Milan, the heirs of the printer Pacifico Da Ponte, who died in 1594, were his widow Barbara Bordone and his daughter Aurelia. Editions continued to come from their press until 1636 under imprints that referred only to the late printer, such as 'Nella stampa del quondam Pacifico Ponzio', or to the family in general, 'apud Pontianos'. Other editions were produced by a company formed by Da Ponte's heirs together with Giovanni Battista Piccaglia.[131]

Other daughters and widows took on some responsibility for a print shop as heirs, or together with an heir, and were able to ensure its continuity, at least for a while. In Urbino, the married sisters Olimpia and Lorrena Commandino tried valiantly to manage the press set up in their house by their late father Federico, a mathematician, who had wished to 'far vedere al mondo molte fatiche sue' (let the world see many of his own labours). After his death in 1575, Olimpia and Lorrena inherited the press and rented it to other printers. One of these was the Roman Paolo Tartarino, to whom they let the workshop in 1585 for three years. But he produced only a few editions, and in July 1586 he was imprisoned for debts owed to the Commandino daughters and others. A legal text by Aurelio Corboli, the *Tractatus de causis*, typical of the press's specialized production, was begun by Tartarino but had to be completed in 1586 by another printer, Federico Donati, when Tartarino was sent to gaol. Eventually the sisters had to sell their press.[132] In some cases, a woman was assisted by her husband in running an inherited print shop. Livia Tesori of Orvieto took over a press from her father Pietro Matteo Tesori, who worked in Orvieto, and it was operated by her husband Luciano Pasini, who worked in Perugia and Venice in the early 1570s. Pasini then made Livia one of his own heirs, together with his nephew Giovanni Battista.[133] After Margherita Bufalini came into possession of the press of her husband Fausto Bufalini in Messina when he died in 1592, she kept the business going for a while

[130] Barberi, *Paolo Manuzio*, p. 75; Parker, 'Women in the Book Trade', pp. 522–23.

[131] Ascarelli and Menato, *La tipografia*, p. 152; Monica Galletti, 'Preliminari allo studio della presenza femminile nella proto-industria tipografica ed editoriale italiana: Milano tra il XVI e il XVII secolo', in *Itinerari del libro nella storia: per Anna Giulia Cavagna a trent'anni dalla prima lezione*, ed. by Francesca Nepori, Fiammetta Sabba and Paolo Tinti (Bologna: Pàtron, 2017), pp. 145–56 (pp. 150–51).

[132] Luigi Moranti, *L'arte tipografica in Urbino (1493–1800)* (Florence: Olschki, 1967), pp. 11–26 and 103–11; Maria Moranti, 'Commandino, Federico', in Menato, *Dizionario*, pp. 315–16 (p. 316). On Tartarino, see Ascarelli and Menato, *La tipografia*, p. 212.

[133] Ascarelli and Menato, *La tipografia*, pp. 317, 436.

under the name of 'heirs of Fausto Bufalini', and was then able to pass it on
to one of Bufalini's former employees, Pietro Brea, when she married him
in 1593.[134] In other cases, a widow or daughter was involved together with
her son. A printer-bookseller active in Rome, Giulio Bolani Accolti, who
died in 1571 or 1572, named his son Vincenzo as his heir, but Vincenzo's
mother Menica was described in a notarial deed as a 'stampatrix librorum'
(female printer of books).[135] Vincenzo was succeeded by his wife Dorotea.
She signed a contract to buy a large quantity of types in 1596, but
unfortunately she had some difficulty, at least initially, in paying the
costs of her purchase.[136] When Niccolò Bevilacqua fell ill in 1573 after
a long career as printer in Venice and then Turin, he appointed his son
Giovanni Battista as his heir; but since the latter was then aged only eight,
Niccolò gave his wife Teodosia the usufruct (that is, the right to make use)
of his possessions and the authority to 'vendere o affittare l'istrumento della
stampa' (sell or hire the instrument for printing).[137] Giovanni Battista duly
began to issue editions in 1587. Similarly, Francesca Amorosa Aspri, widow
of a printer in Camerino, Antonio Gioioso, kept the family's press in
operation from 1578, initially in company with a printer from Verona,
Girolamo Stringario, until 1585, when her son Francesco reached adulthood. The press passed in 1633 to Francesco's son-in-law, Francesco
Ghislieri.[138] When Giorgio Marescotti died intestate in 1602 after a long
career as printer, publisher and bookseller in Florence, three women helped
the family company to prolong its activities for a few years. In the course of
the lengthy litigation over the division of Marescotti's estate, his widow
Agnoletta Bati was given permission to sell the books in her possession as
profitably as she could. The couple's eldest son Cristofano took over the
press from 1604 until his death in 1611. At this point, control of the press
passed to Cristofano's widow Margherita Pugliani, together with her
daughter Caterina and her son-in-law, the printer Domenico Magliani.
Margherita managed to keep the printing house active until 1613, but

[134] Giuseppe Repici, 'Bufalini, Fausto', in Menato, *Dizionario*, pp. 215–17, and Repici, 'Brea, Pietro', ibid., pp. 195–98. On the roles of widows of Messina in later centuries, see Valentina Sestini, *Donne tipografe a Messina tra XVII e XIX secolo* (Pisa and Rome: Fabrizio Serra, 2015).
[135] Masetti Zannini, *Stampatori e librai*, pp. 41, 85–88; Claudia de Blasiis, 'Accolti, Giulio e Vincenzo', in Menato, *Dizionario*, pp. 4–5.
[136] Masetti Zannini, *Stampatori e librai*, pp. 143–44.
[137] Marina Bersano Begey and Giuseppe Dondi, *Le cinquecentine piemontesi*, 3 vols (Turin: Tipografia torinese, 1966), I, 462–73 (in which, however, the role of Teodosia is not mentioned); Ascarelli and Menato, *La tipografia*, pp. 220–22; Giovanni Dondi, 'Bevilacqua, Niccolò', in Menato, *Dizionario*, pp. 127–28.
[138] Ascarelli and Menato, *La tipografia*, pp. 199–200; Borraccini, 'All'ombra degli eredi', pp. 421–22.

archival evidence located by Deborah Parker shows that she was beset by financial problems.[139]

The engagement of female relatives with printing was thus not unusual. However, the occasions on which they are mentioned openly in the colophons of their books probably represent only a small fraction of their actual contributions. Even when their work is referred to, this is sometimes done by means of phrases referring to their late husbands or fathers. The range of possibilities is illustrated by the case of Caterina De Silvestro, widow of the German printer Sigismondo Mayr, who had been active first in Rome and then between 1503 and 1517 in Naples. De Silvestro printed at least thirteen editions between 1517 and 1523, and one can reasonably surmise that she had been involved in the family firm well before her husband's death. Three of her editions declare their origin straightfor-wardly with phrases such as 'in aedibus Catherinae de Silvestro' (in the house of Caterina De Silvestro). Five give her name but add that she was the wife of the late Sigismondo Mayr. The remaining five editions hide her name completely from sight. One of these is the volume of poems by Girolamo Britonio (1519), mentioned in the first chapter, whose colophon reads simply 'della Stampa di Maestro Sigismondo Mair Alamano'. In 1525, De Silvestro married Evangelista Presenzani, who was already working in her printing house. They produced at least one work together in 1525, the short theological tract *Monoctium: utrum haec propositio Christus in quantum homo est filius Dei naturalis sit haeretica* of Fray Gerónimo Pérez. Its colophon identifies the printers as: 'per m[agistrum] Evangelistam Papiensem et eius uxorem haeredem m[agistri] quomdam Sigismundi Mayr calcographi' (by master Evangelista of Pavia and his wife, the heir of the late master Sigismondo Mayr, printer). After that, Evangelista printed under his own name until 1526.[140]

An exceptional case of the acknowledged involvement of a printer's wife in the fifteenth century is that of the printing of Jedaiah Hapenini's short *Iggeret Behinar ha' olam* (Treatise on the Contemplation of the World) in Mantua in 1474. The colophon tells us that this edition was produced by Estellina, wife of the scribe and physician Abraham Conat, with some

[139] Ascarelli and Menato, *La tipografia*, pp. 284–85; Parker, 'Women in the Book Trade', pp. 529–32; Giampiero Guarducci, *Annali dei Marescotti tipografi editori di Firenze (1563–1613)* (Florence: Olschki, 2001), pp. xvi–xvii.

[140] Pietro Manzi, *La tipografia napoletana nel '500: annali di Sigismondo Mayr, Giovanni A. de Caneto, Antonio de Frizis, Giovanni Pasquet de Sallo (1503–1535)* (Florence: Olschki, 1971), pp. 18–21, 25, 77–105; Ascarelli and Menato, *La tipografia*, pp. 28–29; Santoro, 'Imprenditrici o "facenti funzioni"?', pp. 378–79. On the work by Pérez, see Bruce Taylor, *Structures of Reform: The Mercedarian Order in the Spanish Golden Age* (Leiden: Brill, 2000), p. 82.

assistance from another man.[141] The eighteenth-century bibliographer
Giovanni Bernardo De Rossi commented harshly on the quality of the
typography:

> In hoc enim libello Conati quidem typis, sed ab ejus uxore aut sub ejus
> nomine saltem excuso lineae ac paginae adeo sunt inaequales, modo bre-
> viores, modo longiores, ut vel artis adhuc nascentis, vel muliebris ingenii
> rem supra vires tentantis specimen debeat haberi.

> (For in this little book, which is to be sure in Conat's types, but printed by
> his wife or at least issued in her name, the lines and pages are so unequal –
> now shorter, now longer – as to suggest either the first trial of a beginner or
> the effort of a woman attempting something beyond her powers.)[142]

De Rossi goes on to translate into Latin the Hebrew colophon, which
offers a proud declaration on the part of Estellina: 'Ego Estellina uxor
domini mei, viri mei clarissimi, domini Abrahami Conati (videat is semen
ac producat dies suos amen) scripsi hanc epistolam Bechinàd olàm opitu-
lante minimo Jacobo Levi Provinciali Taraconensi, qui vivat amen' (I,
Estellina, wife of my renowned master and husband, master Abraham
Conat (may he see his offspring and prolong his days, amen), wrote this
letter *Bechinàd olàm* with help from the young Jacob Levi of the province
of Tarragona, may he live long, amen).[143]

The colophon of the *Opera della diva et serafica Catharina da Siena, in
rima, in stramotti, capituli, sonetti, epistole et sextine*, by Giovanni Pollio
Lappoli, known as Pollastra, tells us that this substantial collection of verse
was 'Impressa in Siena per donna Antonina de Maestro Enrigh da Cologna
et Andrea Piasentino, acuratissimi impressori, nel anno della nostra salute
MDV'. Heinrich of Cologne, Antonina's first husband, had been one of
the most prolific printers of the late fifteenth century, working in Brescia,
Bologna, Siena and elsewhere, with a specialization in legal texts. Andrea
Piacentino was her second husband, but perhaps played a secondary role in
printing this edition, since his name follows hers.[144]

---

[141] Vittore Colorni, 'Abraham Conat primo stampatore di opere ebraiche in Mantova e la cronologia
delle sue edizioni', *LB*, 83 (1981), 113–28; Adri K. Offenberg, 'The Chronology of Hebrew Printing at
Mantua in the Fifteenth Century: A Re-Examination', *The Library*, 6th ser., 16 (1994), 298–315.

[142] Giovanni Bernardo De Rossi, *Annales Hebraeo-typographici sec. XV* (Parma: ex Regio typographeo,
1795; repr. Amsterdam: Philo Press, 1969), pp. 110–11, cited and translated in Offenberg, 'The
Chronology of Hebrew Printing', p. 301.

[143] De Rossi, *Annales Hebraeo-typographici*, p. 111.

[144] Ascarelli and Menato, *La tipografia*, pp. 295–96. On this work by Lappoli, see Louise George Clubb
and Robert Black, *Romance and Aretine Humanism in Sienese Comedy: Pollastra's 'Parthenio' at the
Studio di Siena* (Florence: La Nuova Italia, 1993), pp. 33, 86–87, 114–17.

The name of Elisabetta Rusconi, widow of Giorgio Rusconi, appears as sole printer of several books produced between 1524 and 1527 in Venice. Some of these are substantial works, such as Ariosto's *Orlando furioso* (1524), a translation of the Bible by Nicolò Malerbi (*Biblia vulgare nova-mente impressa, corretta et hystoriata. Con le rubrice et capitulatione*, 1525) and Ovid's *Metamorphoses* with commentaries (1527). In the colophon of an edition of Iacopo Caviceo's lengthy prose romance, the *Libro del peregrino* (1526), she is identified both as printer and as co-publisher together with the Ferrarese printer-bookseller Nicolò Zoppino: 'per Helisabetta di Rusconi: ad instantia sua, et de Nicolo Zopino' (by Elisabetta Rusconi, at her instance and that of Nicolò Zoppino).[145]

By far the most prolific named woman printer was Girolama Cartolari. At some point after March 1524, she had married Baldassarre Cartolari, a member of a family of printers from Perugia, which was also her native city. The couple moved to work in Pesaro in 1529 and then to Rome in 1540. When she was widowed in 1543, Girolama took over Baldassarre's printing house in Rome and continued to run it until 1559, at first (1543–47) with the publisher Michele Tramezzino, then without him. She was evidently well trusted by authors and by the clergy. At least 111 editions are attributed to her, although the frequency of their publication declines over time. They are in both Latin and the vernacular, and they cover an extraordinarily wide range of genres and of topics, from prognostications and news reports, to documents emanating from the Vatican and the Council of Trent, and to learned works on law, medicine, theology and grammar.[146] Another woman whose activity lasted for several years, but on a much smaller scale, was Clara, wife or daughter of Giovanni Francesco Giolito, who had printed in Trino, in Piedmont, between 1560 and 1578: she signed some ten editions between 1588 and 1596. Five of these contained official ordinances and one was a slim collection of popular verse, but the others were a short Latin work on theology, two editions of a medical treatise in Latin and a substantial Latin grammar.[147] Fiorenza Zanetti,

---

[145] Baldacchini, *Alle origini dell'editoria in volgare*, pp. 194–95.

[146] Francesco Barberi, 'Annali della tipografia romana di Baldassarre jr e Girolama Cartolari (1540–1559)', *LB*, 53 (1951), 69–120; Barberi, *Tipografi romani del Cinquecento: Guillery, Ginnasio mediceo, Calvo, Dorico, Cartolari* (Florence: Olschki, 1983), pp. 147–63; Alberto Tinto, *Annali tipografici dei Tramezzino* (Venice and Rome: Istituto per la collaborazione culturale, 1968), p. xxiii; Paolo Veneziani, 'Cartolari, Baldassare', *DBI*, 20 (1977), 804–06; Ascarelli and Menato, *La tipografia*, pp. 109–10; Parker, 'Women in the Book Trade', pp. 527–29; Fabio Massimo Bertolo, 'Cartolari, Baldassarre junior e Girolama', in Menato, *Dizionario*, pp. 268–69.

[147] Bersano Begey and Dondi, *Le cinquecentine piemontesi*, III, 163–64; Ascarelli and Menato, *La tipografia*, pp. 245–46; Nuovo and Coppens, *I Giolito e la stampa*, pp. 145–46.

widow of Francesco, is named as printer in just one short work, Pomponio Brunelli's *Alphabetum Graecum, et rudimenta*, produced in Rome in 1592 at the expense of Giovanni Alfeo De Pamphilis.

In the trade of bookselling, which sometimes also involved acting as printer or publisher, it was difficult but not impossible for women to achieve success, as is shown by two contrasting stories from sixteenth-century Milan, brought to light by the researches of Kevin Stevens. Elisabetta de Barchi took over the bookshop of her husband Jacopo Corsico, 'al segno del Sole' (at the sign of the Sun), after his death at the end of 1536; she also had the care of three sons. In August 1537, Pietro Antonio Sessa agreed to manage her shop for two years and to instruct her and her eldest son 'in [. . .] arte libraria' (in the bookseller's art, that is, trading in books and binding them). The arrangement evidently did not turn out well, and in July 1538 de Barchi sold her shop to the bookseller and printer-publisher Andrea Calvo.[148] On the other hand, Calvo's own failing business was later rescued by his wife Dorotea Scoto, sister of Girolamo Scoto, a prominent printer in Venice. Calvo entered into a contract to marry Dorotea in 1528, and she brought with her a large dowry, worth 5,000 lire. She bore Andrea seven children, and was actively involved in his business from at least 1538. However, Andrea had fallen badly into debt by the early 1540s. Dorotea's dowry had, in effect, been swallowed up by his mismanaged dealings. Between 1543 and 1546, she became involved in litigation with her husband, claiming that he had spent her dowry and left her without the means to support herself and her children. Andrea died in 1547, and for nearly a decade Dorotea ran a flourishing bookshop in Milan 'al segno dell'Ancora' (at the sign of the Anchor), helped by her brother Girolamo. Among the printing companies with which she dealt was that of Gabriele Giolito in Venice. When she sold her shop and warehouse in 1556, her stock of books was double that recorded in an inventory of Calvo's stock made in 1546.[149]

A high degree of success was also achieved by Anna Zanini of Vicenza, widow of the bookseller-printer Pietro, known as Perin. From 1588 until her own death in 1596, she continued to produce and sell a very varied output of books together with her son and a daughter as 'gli heredi di Perin libraro' or 'haeredes Perini bibliopolae' (the heirs of Perin the bookseller). It may have been the profile of Anna during and after Perin's lifetime that

---

[148] Kevin M. Stevens, 'New Light on Andrea Calvo and the Book Trade in Sixteenth-Century Milan', *LB*, 103 (2001), 25–54 (pp. 35–36); Galletti, 'Preliminari allo studio', pp. 148–49.

[149] Stevens, 'New Light on Andrea Calvo', pp. 33, 47–54.

made this press, rather than the other one operating in the city, that of Agostino Dalla Noce, attractive to Maddalena Campiglia in 1588 (see Chapter 1) and that had attracted nuns of the city in 1586 and 1587 (see the next section in this chapter). Although Anna was only forty-three years old when she died, she had become wealthy enough to provide substantial dowries for her three daughters and to have a tomb built for herself, something her husband had not managed to do. In 1593 Anna and a male partner, Francesco Belloni, took over a paper mill that had fallen derelict. Her contribution to the cost of this enterprise was much greater, over 11,000 troni as opposed to Belloni's investment of just over 1,700 troni (the trono was a silver coin equivalent to the lira). Anna ensured continuity by marrying her daughter Vittoria (also known as Sabina) to the bookseller-printer Francesco Grossi with a respectable dowry of 400 ducats. She was able to leave the same sum to her two other daughters so that they could marry or become nuns. Her will of 1596 says that 'ha augumentato il negotio et facultà lasciata nel tempo della sua vita et morte per il q[uondam] suo marito' (she has increased the business and assets that her late husband left in the time of his life and death).[150]

Cecilia Tramezzino was not inclined to become closely involved in running the bookshop of her father Francesco in Via del Pellegrino (near Campo de' Fiori) in Rome when she inherited it in 1576. She had it managed first by her husband, the publisher Venturino Tramezzino, who had changed his name from Venturino Venturini. Soon after Venturino died in 1582 or 1583, she passed the business to another bookseller, Marcantonio Moretti of Perugia.[151] But Isabetta Basa, probably the daughter of the bookseller-publisher Bernardo, active in Venice and Rome, took over Bernardo's Venetian business 'all'insegna del Sole' on his death in 1599 and published four editions in 1599–1601.[152]

At the start of this chapter we looked at *Il secretario*, one of the writing-books of Marcello Scalzini. The first edition was printed in Venice in 1581 by Domenico Nicolini at the instance of the author. Nicolini printed

---

[150] Giovanni Mantese, *I mille libri che si leggevano e vendevano a Vicenza alla fine del secolo XVI* (Vicenza: Accademia Olimpica, 1968), pp. 7–19; Ascarelli and Menato, *La tipografia*, pp. 467–68; Nuovo, *The Book Trade*, pp. 380–81.
[151] Tinto, *Annali tipografici dei Tramezzino*, pp. xxvii, xxx–xxiv.
[152] Annalisa Bruni, 'Basa, Bernardo', in Menato, *Dizionario*, pp. 81–82. The editions were: Samuel ben Moses Calai, *Mishpeṭe Shemuel* (Daniele Zanetti, 1599–1600), with Basa's emblem of the Sun in the colophon; Bartolomè de Medina, *Breve instruttione de' confessori* (Daniele Zanetti for the Libraria dal Sole, 1600); Platina, *Historia delle vite dei Sommi Pontefici* (Daniele Zanetti for Isabetta di Bernardo Basa, 1600), in two parts; Christophorus Clavius, *In sphaeram Ioannis de Sacro Bosco commentarius* (Sub signo Solis, 1601).

further editions in 1585 and 1587, but now the publisher was named as
either a certain Helena Moresini (1585) or her 'commissario' (administrator, 1587). In 1581 Scalzini had been teaching in Venice and living with
Moresini, who was known also as Morosini but whose real surname was
Vegiel or Vegle. Although she had a daughter by Scalzini, he left the city
around the end of 1581, leaving her the engravings from which *Il secretario*
had been printed. The daughter was entrusted to a Franciscan friar of
French origin, Pietro Testando, who then had himself named as Moresini's
administrator. She and the friar were evidently publishing the work without the author's permission. Fearing Scalzini's return to Venice, Moresini,
no doubt encouraged by fra Pietro, accused Scalzini in 1585–86 first of
failing to keep a promise to marry her and then, before the Holy Office, of
involvement in magical practices.[153] The title page of an edition of another
of his works on handwriting, the *Regole nuove et avertimenti* printed in
Brescia in 1591, announced that the edition included an accusation against
Moresini:

> Con una narrativa, ove si scuopre, et dimostra ben chiaro di carta in carta,
> che l'opere intitolate il Secretario, stampate in Venetia del 1584, et 1585 ad
> instantia di Madonna Elena Morosina Tedesca; Et dapoi ristampate ad
> instantia del Commissario di essa, sino all'anno presente, sono tutte copie
> false, stroppiate, et difformi, che falsamente si dicono di mano, ben che
> siano sotto nome del detto Camerino Inventore.[154]

> (With an account where it is revealed and clearly shown, page by page, that
> the works entitled *Il secretario*, printed in Venice in 1584 and 1585 at the
> instance of madonna Elena Morosini, the German, and then reprinted at
> the instance of her administrator up to the present year, are all false,
> mangled and misshapen copies that falsely declare themselves to be in the
> hand, even though they are under the name, of the said Camerino their
> inventor.)

Even a woman of restricted means might become an occasional publisher, as in the case of the prostitute Margherita Maggi of Modena,
nicknamed 'la Chiappona', reputedly a woman with magical powers. She
knew by heart a version of the prayer to St Martha, a well-known genre
that, as the Holy Office rightly suspected, was used as an incantation to win
a man's affections. Margherita testified on 11 January 1594 that she had
asked Francesco Gadaldini to print the prayer, copied down from her

[153] Carlo Pasero, 'Sulla vita del calligrafo cinquecentesco Marcello Scalini (Scalzini) detto il Camerino', *Commentari dell'Ateneo di Brescia*, 133 (1934), 109–77 (pp. 118–28).
[154] Carlo Pasero, 'Marcello Scalini e la calligrafia del XVI secolo', *LB*, 35 (1933), 430–39 (pp. 437–38).

dictation, apparently in late 1592, and he had brought her back a printed copy: 'Io pregai già è un anno detto Francesco al tempo dell'uva che dovesse stampar questa oratione, et lui la pigliò in scritto come ho detto et me la portò che devono esser in circa cinque mesi' (A year ago I asked the said Francesco, at the time of the grape harvest, to print this prayer, and he took it in writing as I have said and he brought it back to me, it must be about five months ago). A copy of the printed leaf survives in the records of the Holy Office trial, held in Modena in 1597, of Gadaldini's assistant, Tomaso Zanola of Cadore, who admitted responsibility for facilitating this unusual and marginal instance of women's involvement in the making of books.[155] It begins: 'Questa oratione si dice in genochione nuove matine a digiuno con nove Pater noster, e nove Ave Maria, a laude, e reverentia di Santa Marta, che esaudisca quanto se li domanda' (Figure 2.7; This prayer is said kneeling on nine mornings while fasting with nine Our Fathers and nine Hail Marys, in praise and worship of St Martha, that she may grant what is asked of her).

## Nuns and Print

In view of the intense activity of manuscript production carried out in some convents as a means of strengthening their communities both financially and spiritually, it is not surprising that groups of nuns might also occasionally become involved in the making and publication of printed books, even though these activities demanded respectively technical skills and financial resources that would normally have been beyond their reach. The first and best-known example of a press operated within a convent comes from Florence, where in the years around 1480 the Dominican nuns of San Iacopo di Ripoli (some of whom were also scribes, as was seen earlier in this chapter) helped to produce texts in Latin and in the vernacular. The accounting daybook (*diario*) of the press survives and shows that their contributions were both indirect and direct. The nuns lent money to the

---

[155] Modena, Archivio di Stato, Tribunale dell'Inquisizione di Modena, busta 9 fasc. 6. See Mary O'Neil, 'Magical Healing, Love Magic, and the Inquisition in Late Sixteenth–Century Modena', in *Inquisition and Society in Early Modern Europe*, ed. and trans. by Stephen Haliczer (London: Croom Helm, 1987), pp. 88–114 (pp. 98–102); Maria Pia Fantini, 'La circolazione clandestina dell'orazione di Santa Marta: un episodio modenese', in *Donna, disciplina, creanza cristiana dal XV al XVII secolo: studi e testi a stampa*, ed. by Gabriella Zarri (Rome: Edizioni di Storia e Letteratura, 1996), pp. 45–65 (pp. 47–52, 63–64). On this prayer, see also Giorgio Caravale, *L'orazione proibita: censura ecclesiastica e letteratura devozionale nella prima età moderna* (Florence: Olschki, 2003), pp. 166–68; Craig Monson, *Nuns Behaving Badly: Tales of Music, Magic, Art, and Arson in the Convents of Italy* (Chicago University Press, 2010), p. 46.

Queſta oratione ſi dice in genochione nuoue matine à digiuno con noue Pater noſter , e noue Aue Marie , à laude,
e reuerentia di Santa Marta, che eſaudiſca quanto
ſe li domanda.
O Maɾta Beata , che in Chieſa ſtate , i morti guardate , i uiui
inſpi ɾate, inſpierate il cuore, e la mente, i cinque ſentimenti
i ſette ſacramenti del    ...   N.   per amor mio ſi ſon Marta
Beata, che dell'huomo è uiuo, e ſcaldo, e braſa, o Marta Beata, per amor mio andateuene à quel boſco doue bateʒò il no-
ſtro Sign, Gieſu Chriſto con i ſuoi dodici Apoſtoli, per amor
mio tagliate tre uerzele di foco di fiama, per amor mio mandatele al cuore del    ...    N non liſſe mandate, ne per porta
ne per uſcio, ne per feneſtra, mandatele, per le uene del cuore, e quelle della teſta, e quelle del polmon , e per le medole
delle oſſa, le polpe delle gambe, per amio tanto il bate, tanto
il fruſta, che per amor mio il uenga in pena, in ſuſta , tanto il
bate, tanto i f agela, che per amor mio che'l uenga in pena ,
in ſuſta, in rabia, ò Marta Beata, per amor mio ſe'l trouate ſo-
uino uoltatelo come un molino , per amor mio ſe'l trouate in
galone uoltatelo come fa un leone, per amor mio ſe'l trouate
in corpo uoltatelo come ſi fa un porco , ò Marta Beata , che
per amor mio, che'l non poſſa mai andar per uia che'l me hab
bia ſempre in fantaſia , per amor mio che'l non poſſa mai andar per ſtrada, che'l mi habbia ſempre nel cuore, e nella contra
da, ò Marta Beata, che per amor mio el non poſſa ſtar à tauo
la  pparechiata, ne in chieſa ſacrata, per amor mio in camera
ben ſpaciata , per amor mio toleteli il bere , il mangiare , il
dormire, il poſſare, ne andare, ne ſtare, ne caualcare, ne caro-
ciare, ne caminare, ne con Donna hauer à fare, per fin à tanto
che lui ſi uenga da me à contentar de tutto il mio uolere, e de
tutto quello che io li domandaɾò.

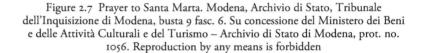

Figure 2.7  Prayer to Santa Marta. Modena, Archivio di Stato, Tribunale
dell'Inquisizione di Modena, busta 9 fasc. 6. Su concessione del Ministero dei Beni
e delle Attività Culturali e del Turismo – Archivio di Stato di Modena, prot. no.
1056. Reproduction by any means is forbidden

two friars who ran the press, Domenico da Pistoia and Piero di Salvatore da Pisa, presumably drawing on their dowries in order to do so, and also doubtless hoping for some practical benefit to their convent.[156] Some of them also acted as compositors along with male professionals. One entry for 1478 records that a substantial payment of 10 ducats made by one of the convent's stationers, a certain Bartolo, was put 'al salario delle monache nostre che componghano allo stampare alla compagnia del soprascripto Bartolo' (to the salary of our nuns who are working as compositors in partnership with the aforementioned Bartolo).[157] The daybook names an individual nun who was paid to help set type for Luigi Pulci's chivalric romance *Morgante* in 1481: 'Suor Marieta di Casa ebbe per tutto ferraio 1481 due fiorini larghi sono per parte dello aiutarci conporre al Morghante' (Sister Marietta di Casa received for all of February 1481 two broad florins for part of her helping us in composing the *Morgante*).[158]

A very different case is that of the Augustinian convent of Santa Maria Maddalena on the Giudecca in Venice, known as 'le Convertite'; in other words, its nuns were ex-prostitutes. Here a press, studied by Edoardo Barbieri, produced at least twenty-five editions on religious topics between 1557 and 1561, when there were about 300 nuns in the institution.[159] It is striking that over half of the titles are in Latin, which few if any of the nuns would have known, and that some are erudite in nature, as with the press of San Iacopo di Ripoli. The books were sold through the bookshop 'Al segno della Speranza' or 'Ad signum Spei' (At the sign of Hope) near Santa Maria Formosa, as stated on some of the title pages, and it is probable that some or all of the commissions to print came from this bookshop. The press's device shows nuns praying before the penitent Mary Magdalene. Unfortunately, the nuns were not involved in printing alone. Their confessor, a certain Zuan Piero Leoni, who may have been running the

---

[156] Melissa Conway, *The 'Diario' of the Printing Press of San Jacopo di Ripoli 1476–1484: Commentary and Transcription* (Florence: Olschki, 1999), pp. 26–27, 95, 100, 105, 106, 114, 123. On the sales of psalters and *Libri da compagnia* (Books of Hours that were intended for use for members of confraternities) as recorded in the daybook, see Cristina Dondi, *Printed Books of Hours from Fifteenth-Century Italy: The Texts, the Books, and the Survival of a Long-Lasting Genre* (Florence: Olschki, 2016), pp. 80–85.

[157] Conway, *The 'Diario'*, p. 156.

[158] Mary A. Rouse and Richard H. Rouse, *Cartolai, Illuminators and Printers in Fifteenth-Century Italy: The Evidence of the Ripoli Press* (Los Angeles: UCLA Research Library, 1988), pp. 35–36; Conway, *The 'Diario'*, pp. 43, 54, 225. The broad florin was slightly flatter and wider than its predecessor: see Richard A. Goldthwaite, *The Economy of Renaissance Florence* (Baltimore, MD: Johns Hopkins University Press, 2008), p. 52.

[159] Edoardo Barbieri, '"Per monialium poenitentium manus": la tipografia del monastero di Santa Maria Maddalena alla Giudecca, detto delle Convertite (1557–1561)', *LB*, 113 (2011), 303–53.

printing operation for his own financial benefit, had lured or forced several of them into sexual liaisons with him. This came to the notice of the Church authorities in 1561; the priest was beheaded in Piazzetta San Marco and the prioress died in prison three years later.[160] There was no more printing after their arrest. But, quite apart from the scandal that brought the initiative to an end, such an enterprise was entirely exceptional: a printing business just could not be sustained in the long term within, or even in conjunction with, a convent.

It was much easier for a convent to commission an edition. Nuns might wish to possess copies of a text primarily for their own use. An example is the Rule of St Benedict that was printed in Venice for the Cistercian convent of Santa Maria della Celestia around 1527, through or by the bookseller Andrea Rota of Lecco, working in the area of Sant'Apollinare.[161]

Nuns also commissioned books that might be intended for reading both by themselves and by others, including laywomen; their motive would have been to diffuse a spiritually improving text, but they may also have hoped to derive some income from selling copies to a bookseller. In 1513 there appeared in Siena an edition of the *Trattato della sanctissima charità* by fra Giovanni Dominici, and the colophon, set out in the form of a cross, tells us that the treatise was printed by the booksellers Simone Nardi and Giovanni Landi, who were active in the city from 1511 to 1513 (Figure 2.8):

> Impresso nella inclita citta di Siena: per Symeone di Nicolò et Giovanni di Alexandro librai: ad instantia principalmente delle venerabile et devote suore decte le mantellate del paradiso, Nella prefata Citta di Siena del terzo ordine di sancto Dominico, et di ciaschedun'altra persona: Che di questo Libro legendo pigliarà alcuna consolatione spirituale. A dì 17 del mese de octobre MCCCCCXIII.

> (Printed in the famous city of Siena by Simone di Nicolò and Giovanni di Alessandro booksellers, principally at the instance of the venerable and devout sisters called the Mantellate del Paradiso, in the aforesaid city of Siena, of the Third Order of St Dominic, and of any other person who will derive some spiritual consolation from reading this book. 17 October 1513.)

Once more, we see how a book was intended to provide women with spiritual comfort. We have information about what lay behind this

[160] Mary Laven, *Virgins of Venice: Enclosed Lives and Broken Vows in the Renaissance Convent* (London: Viking, 2002), pp. 161–65.
[161] The full title of this work is *Questa si è la regula del glorioso confessore miser Sancto Benedeto in vulgare ad instantia de le venerabile monache de la Celestia observante novamente stampata.*

✠

# Finifce

el perutiliffi/
moi Tracta/
to intitolato Amoi di Charita: cõpofto dal
Beato Souanni Dominici . Jmpieffo nella
Jnclita Citta di Siena per Symeone di Mi/
colo z Sio/
nãni di Ale/
zandro Li/
biai: ad inftã
tia principal/
mente Delle
renerabile z
deuote fuoze
decte le man
tellate del pa
radifo Mella
piefata Citta
Di Siena del
terzo ozdine
Di fancto Do
minico : z di cia
fchedun altra per/
fona: Che di quefto
Libio legendo pigliara
alcuna confolatione fpiri/
tuale . A di.17. del Mefe de Oci
**tobze. M. ccccc. xiii.**

JESUS

MARIA

Figure 2.8  Giovanni Dominici, *Trattato della sanctissima charità* (Siena: Simone
Nardi and Giovanni Landi for the Mantellate del Paradiso, 1513), fol. Y4ᵛ. © The
British Library Board. 3835.aaaa.13

colophon because the contract for printing this edition has survived.[162] The original was written on 27 February 1512/13 in the hand of Landi, who describes himself as a 'cartaio' (stationer). In summary, he agrees to have the edition printed 'a mezzo pro e danno' (sharing half the costs and profits) with the Sienese community of Third Order Dominicans, known as the Mantellate or the 'povare' (poor women) of Paradise. The print run is to be 1,000 copies, relatively large for the period. The costs of printing are estimated at about 40 ducats, and the Mantellate are to pay their half of the costs in advance, by Easter 1513. During the fourteen months after the completion of printing, Landi will use the revenue from sales to pay off first the investment made by the Mantellate and then his own: evidently the women are protecting themselves sensibly, yet Landi is confident that in due course there will be a successful outcome from his point of view as well. Once costs have been repaid, any unsold copies will be shared between the two parties. If the capital investment has not been recouped within fourteen months, they will continue to sell copies and share the revenue. It is implied that the Mantellate will play some part in retailing the copies. The contract mentions that their confessor, a certain fra Antonino of Florence, can act as their agent but is not obliged to do so, and it is clear that the community of the Mantellate, represented by their prioress, was acting absolutely independently in embarking on this venture. A comparable Sienese venture was the printing in 1535 of a religious manual for women, the *Lima spirituale* by Francesco Rappi, at the instance of suor Calidonia of the convent of Ognissanti, the nuns of San Niccolò and 'alcune altre spirituali religiose, e secolari persone desideranti di pervenire alla beatitudine di vita eterna' (some other spiritual religious and lay women who wish to achieve the beatitude of eternal life).[163] A collection dominated by a work attributed to St Bernard, *El libro de sancto Bernardo, in che modo se deve tenere munda la conscientia et le meditatione sue, et altri capituli bellissimi, et utilissimi*, was published in Bologna around 1522 by Giustiniano da Rubiera with a dedicatory letter in which suor Genevera de' Pepoli, a canoness regular of San Lorenzo, explains to suor Caterina del Gesso that she is having printed

[162] Siena, Archivio di Stato, filza S. Caterina, Oblazioni e documenti, 1494–1572, B.XXXII, v. 109 a.39. On Nardi and on this edition, see Fabio Jacometti, 'Il primo stampatore senese: Simone di Niccolò di Nardo', *La Diana*, 1 (1926), 184–202; Nicola Pallecchi, 'Una tipografia a Siena nel XVI secolo: bibliografia delle edizioni stampate da Simone di Niccolò Nardi (1502–1539)', *Bullettino senese di storia patria*, 109 (2002), 184–233 (no. 34, pp. 211–12); Mario De Gregorio, 'Landi, Giovanni', *DBI*, 63 (2004), 384–85; Dennis E. Rhodes and Michele Feo, 'Sul tipografo Simone di Niccolò Nardi da Siena', *Studi medievali e umanistici*, 3 (2005), 29–46.
[163] (Siena: Niccolò Nardi and Luca Bini, 1535.) On this work, see Zarri, *Libri di spirito*, p. 300.

a manuscript text in her possession 'a commune utilità delli servi de Christo' (fol. a2ʳ; for the common benefit of Christ's servants).

Further instances of editions promoted by nuns are found towards the end of the sixteenth century. In 1586 the reverend mother of the Dominican sisters of Vicenza commissioned two editions from a bookseller-printer mentioned in the previous section, Perin, in company with Giorgio Greco. One was a life of St Dominic with other examples of leading members of their order: *Vita, gesti, e costumi del beatissimo padre nostro s. Dominico, con alcuni altri essempi, e fioretti de padri, e frati, dell'ordine nostro, ne i principij della nostra religione*; the other was a booklet on the canonical hours, the *Trattato detto Direttorio delle hore canoniche*. An edition of the Rule of St Augustine, *Regola di S. Agostino vescovo de Hipponia*, produced by the same bookseller-printers in the following year, names as its sponsors suor Agnese Padoana, prioress, and suor Chiara Belli, nuns of Santa Maria Maddalena.[164] The title page of an edition of the *Breve trattato della preparazione del santissimo Sacramento dell'altare* by the Franciscan Ange Delpas (Rome: Guglielmo Facciotti, 1595) announces that it was printed for the Cistercian abbess and nuns of Santa Susanna in Rome.

In Bologna, the Dominican sisters of San Mattia commissioned in 1579 from a Venetian printing company, Domenico and Giovanni Battista Guerra, an edition of Leandro Alberti's *Cronichetta della gloriosa Madonna di San Luca*, an expanded version of a history first printed in 1539. A dedicatory letter to monsignor Giovanni Battista Campeggi, Bishop of Mallorca, was signed by 'la priora e suore' (the prioress and sisters) and dated 30 April 1579 (fols a1ʳ–a3ʳ). The nuns explain that the *Cronichetta* has been 'fatta da noi stampare a Venetia con quella diligenza che s'è potuta maggiore' (fol. a2ᵛ; printed in Venice at our request with the greatest possible diligence). On this occasion the nuns were using print in order to promote the rights of themselves and the sister convent of San Luca: their edition was part of a campaign to safeguard their ownership of a miraculous image of the Virgin, supposedly painted by St Luke, and thereby to safeguard the role of their communities within the city of Bologna, since the image played a prominent part in processions held annually during Holy Week.[165] It could be that the costs of the edition were met from the

[164] Brundin, Howard and Laven, *The Sacred Home*, pp. 229–30.
[165] Danielle Callegari and Shannon McHugh, '"Se fossimo tante meretrici": The Rhetoric of Resistance in Diodata Malvasia's Convent Narrative', *Italian Studies*, 66 (2011), 21–39 (pp. 34–35).

donations that the generous Bishop Campeggi made to Bolognese
convents such as theirs.

Another historical work that played a part in a local controversy was suor
Angelica Baitelli's *Annali historici dell'edificatione, erettione e dotatione del
serenissimo Monastero di S. Salvatore e S. Giulia di Brescia*. One of her
intentions in exploring her convent's archives in order to compose these
annals around 1648 was to defend the historic rights of her community
against the claims of the bishop of Brescia. Her compilation was addressed
primarily to her fellow nuns and then to the wider public; she wished, for
instance, to share her list of her convent's sacred relics with the world,
'parteciparle al mondo'.[166] On Baitelli's death in 1650 the *Annali* remained
in manuscript, but a few years later the abbess Fortunata Mondello
financed an edition in order to give the work wider publicity.[167]

---

[166] Cited from the edition of Brescia: Bendiscioli, 1794, p. 7.
[167] (Brescia: Antonio Rizzardi, 1657.) See Evangelisti, 'Angelica Baitelli', pp. 80, 82–83; Zarri, *Libri di
spirito*, pp. 219–29.

CHAPTER 3

# *Access to Texts*

Renaissance women, we have seen in the first two chapters, could have direct or indirect agency in the publication of texts and the creation of books, but the numbers of those who did so were relatively small. This chapter turns to a question that concerned a far higher proportion of women: how did they gain access to texts? As for written texts, traces of the means of acquisition of manuscript or printed copies are not abundant, but some can be found in correspondence, in inventories, in archival records of the expenditure of individuals or of the sales made by retailers, or within the books themselves. Ownership could stem from a gift, as well as occurring through a purchase from booksellers or temporarily, through borrowing, as envisaged in Robert Darnton's circuit of print publication (Figure 0.1). In the circuit of scribal publication that was proposed in the Preface (Figure 0.2), a manuscript copy would usually be acquired either from the owner of another copy – who would have it transcribed, provide it for transcription or lend it to the reader – or from a bookseller, but occasionally also from a copy displayed in public. In order to complete the picture, we shall also consider more briefly aural access to texts: women might have the opportunity to listen to them, rather than, or as well as, reading them on the page. In interpreting the evidence, we shall need to remember that it might have been difficult for women to obtain books, since their access to reading had long caused concern to men, and women who were acting independently would have felt the scrutiny of male eyes.

We shall see that all kinds of women, both religious and lay, owned books. The chapter will conclude with the well-known example of a woman of the highest social class, Isabella d'Este. But we know that books also belonged to women of much lesser status – for example, to various courtesans. Matteo Bandello, in one of his short stories, describes the home of the famous Roman courtesan Imperia (1481–1512) and writes that, on a table covered with green velvet, 'Quivi sempre era o liuto o cetra con libri di musica e altri instrumenti musici. V'erano poi parecchi libretti volgari e latini riccamente adornati' (there was always a lute or a cittern with music books and other musical instruments. There were also several small vernacular and Latin books, richly adorned).[1] Bandello, writing some time after Imperia's death, was no doubt idealizing her memory, but the inventory of the apartment of a Venetian courtesan, Julia Leoncini, known as Lombardo, who had died in 1542, included eighteen books of various kinds. Stored in a chest along with other possessions were 'Un of[ficio] della setimana santa' (An Office of Holy Week) and 'Li Trionfi del Petrarcha coverti de samito negro' (Petrarch's *Triumphi* bound in black samite). A walnut casket held 'Un oficieto coverto de veludo paonazzo, con soazze a torno d'Arzento' (A little office bound in purple velvet, with surrounding silver frames). On display in a studiolo (little study), along with numerous precious *objets d'art* and jewellery, were 'Pezze de libri n° .15. vecchi' (15 pieces of old books).[2] Another courtesan of the city, Isabella Bellocchio, had a copy of Ariosto's *Orlando furioso* on display, according to the records of a trial of 1589.[3] Not long before, in 1576, Agostino Cesareo observed that women were particularly fond of reading verse works such as this, which were also set to music: some persons 'molto si dilettono di leggere libri di poesia volgare; nella quale invaghite per loro passatempo, e ricreatione, e massime le Donne, leggono Ariosti, Petrarchi, et altri simili Auttori; e per loro dilettatione cantano di quelle rime' (take much delight in reading books of vernacular poetry, becoming enamoured of it as a pastime and recreation, especially women, read Ariostos, Petrarchs and other such authors, and sing some of those verses for their pleasure).[4]

   In looking at how all kinds of women came to possess books, we can begin with circumstances in which they received them as outright or temporary gifts, before moving on to contexts in which women played more active roles. As we shall see, the acquisition of books was not just a personal matter but was linked to women's social lives: it could derive

[1] Matteo Bandello, *Le novelle*, III. 42, in *Tutte le opere*, ed. by Francesco Flora, 2 vols (Milan: Mondadori, 1952), II, 462. On Imperia, see William F. Prizer, 'Wives and Courtesans: The Frottola in Florence', in *Music Observed: Studies in Memory of William C. Holmes*, ed. by Colleen Reardon and Susan Parisi (Warren, MI: Harmonie Park Press, 2004), pp. 401–15 (pp. 411–12). Green cloth was favoured for writing tables: Helen Smith, 'Women and the Materials of Writing', in *Material Cultures of Early Modern Women's Writing*, ed. by Patricia Pender and Rosalind Smith (Basingstoke: Palgrave Macmillan, 2014), pp. 14–35 (p. 23).

[2] Cathy Santore, 'Julia Lombardo, "somtuosa meretrize": A Portrait by Property', *Renaissance Quarterly*, 41 (1988), 44–83 (pp. 63, 71, 73).

[3] *La verità, ovvero il processo contro Isabella Bellocchio (Venezia, 12 gennaio–14 ottobre 1589)*, ed. by Marisa Milani, 2 vols (Padua: Centrostampa Palazzo Maldura, 1985), p. 150, n. 59.

[4] From Cesareo's letter to Niccolò Gaddi in BNCF, MS Magl. VII 692. Cesareo is sending a copy of his translation of the Seven Penitential Psalms. He goes on to suggest that people should instead seek pleasure in reading and singing spiritual books and poems, and that no poetry could be sweeter than singing his new version of these Psalms. I am indebted to Virginia Cox for this reference.

from, and strengthen, their bonds with other members of their family or household, with their peers and within convents.

## Gifts and Lending

Gifts of books played a part in the lives of many Renaissance women of average-to-high social status. In many cases, individual women received books as presents from members of their families or of their religious communities.

Most girls from well-to-do backgrounds would have been given a Book of Hours, containing liturgical offices, prayers and gospel readings. Manuscripts of this work were pocket-sized, and printed Book of Hours were similarly produced in small formats, usually in sixteens or in octavo. The text that lay at their heart was a short form of the daily Office of the Blessed Virgin Mary, a series of Psalms and other devotional texts in honour of the mother of Christ, to be recited communally or read in private, and the book as a whole was generally known as the Little Office of Our Lady or Hours of the Virgin.[5] This text was such a common part of a woman's possessions that the description 'libriccino di Nostra Donna' could become, through a distortion, the 'libriccino di donna' or 'da donna' (lady's little book), or simply the 'libriccino'. Christian Bec preferred not to include them in his statistical analysis of book ownership in Florence, considering them 'plus des livres-objets précieux que des livres proprements dits' (precious book-objects rather than books in the true sense).[6] The 'libriccino' was indeed highly valued and could be an object of considerable financial worth, and it was generally reproduced in Latin, a language that few girls had the opportunity to study.[7] Nevertheless, it was actively used, and women were encouraged to read its prayers in the course of their regular devotions.[8] The treatise on the upbringing of girls mentioned in Chapter 2, the *Decor puellarum*, includes a chapter (III. 3) on 'l'ordine de le devotione et exercitii de tutte le feste' (the order of devotions and exercises for all feast days), which

---

[5] Helpful overviews of medieval and Renaissance Books of Hours include Roger Wieck, *Time Sanctified: The Book of Hours in Medieval Art and Life*, with essays by Lawrence R. Poos, Virginia Reinburg and John Plummer (New York: George Braziller in association with the Walters Art Gallery, 1988), and Dondi, *Printed Books of Hours*. On women's ownership of Books of Hours, see Miglio, *Governare l'alfabeto*, pp. 225–51, and Belinda Jack, *The Woman Reader* (New Haven: Yale University Press, 2012), pp. 94–97.
[6] Christian Bec, *Les Livres des Florentins (1413–1608)* (Florence: Olschki, 1984), p. 25.
[7] Cristina Dondi's survey of Italian incunable Books of Hours lists sixty editions in Latin, eleven in Latin and Italian, and only one entirely in Italian, a translation in terza rima by Giovan Mario Filelfo printed in Venice by Bernardino de' Cori in 1488: Dondi, *Printed Books of Hours*, pp. 60–61, 337–41. Filelfo's version was printed just once in the sixteenth century (Venice: Giovanni Battista Sessa, 1502).
[8] Bryce, 'Les Livres des Florentines', pp. 141–42.

gives advice to girls on using Offices of Our Lady during the day in the intervals between attending to their housework:

> Da poi che vui haverete cenato et forniti et spaciati gli facti de casa in le vostre camere direti, se vui savereti leger, matutino de nostra donna: et se vui non savete leger dite quindece pater nostri et quindece ave marie cum le altre vostre oratione devotamente.
>
> La matina, da poi che vui haverete dispaciati tutti gli facti de casa, avanti che ve mettate a lavorar, se havete la commodità, per spacio de meza hora o più o meno, dite prima, tertia et sexta de la madonna: et chi non sa leger dica al suo altarolo cinque pater nostri et cinque ave marie per ogni hora, che seranno quindeci; et poi metterse al suo consueto lavoro.

(Once you have supped and carried out and dealt with household business, in your bedrooms you will say, if you can read, the matins of Our Lady; and if you cannot read, say fifteen Our Fathers and fifteen Hail Marys devoutly with your other prayers.

In the morning, after you have completed all household business, before starting work, if you have the possibility for about half an hour, say prime, terce and sext of Our Lady; and anyone who cannot read, say at her little altar five Our Fathers and five Hail Marys for each [canonical] hour, making fifteen in all, and then set about her usual work.)

Girls who can read should, in the course of the day, say the Offices of None, Vespers and, if they have time, Compline of Our Lady, with if possible the Seven Penitential Psalms.

The Office of Our Lady was also associated with learning to read, a process that traditionally made use of short texts in Latin. This link may be reflected in the case of the Florentine widower Virgilio d'Andrea di Berto, who recorded in 1478 that he had sent his daughter Alessandra into the care of a convent at a rate of 13 florins per year. There she would learn skills including reading well (listed last, after more obviously domestic accomplishments): 'E di poi veduto io non avere donna più né ella madre, la lasciai me la serbanssino et insengnassille tutto quello si apertiene di sapere alle fanciulle di chucire, talgliare, filare e leggere molto bene' (And then, seeing that I no longer have a wife nor she a mother, I left her in their guardianship and for them to teach her everything girls need to know about sewing, cutting, spinning and reading very well). Virgilio undertook to send Alessandra, among other items, 'uno libriccino bello e buono con tutti gl'uffici' (a fine and good little book with all the offices).[9] In the same city in 1513, Tommaso Guidetti's eleven-year-old

---

[9] Robert Black, *Education and Society in Florentine Tuscany: Teachers, Pupils and Schools, c. 1250–1500* (Leiden: Brill, 2007), pp. 666–67. A brother of Alessandra's was the humanist known as Marcello Virgilio Adriani. On the system of *serbanza*, see Grendler, *Schooling in Renaissance Italy*, pp. 96–97;

daughter Maddalena was taught by a female teacher to 'legiere i·libricino o parte d'esso' (to read the little book or part of it).[10]

These 'little books' figure regularly in the trousseau of Florentine brides, the personal items that they brought with them, called *donora* because they were gifts from the brides' families for their own use. It is probably such a book that figures in Domenico Ghirlandaio's profile portrait of Giovanna degli Albizzi Tornabuoni (*c.* 1488).[11] For her physical needs, a bride's trousseau could comprise clothing, mirrors or soap; for the care of her soul, it often included a 'libriccino di donna'. For example, the *donora* given by Giovanni Corsini to his daughter Caterina in 1419, in which the section whose value was formally estimated was worth 130 florins in total, included a pair of chests and several items of clothing, but also a rosary and a Book of Hours, each item given an individual monetary worth:

| | |
|---|---|
| 1 paio di forzieri | fiorini 24 |
| 1 ciopa bigia | fiorini 18 |
| 1 gamura, suvi once 2½ d'ariento | fiorini 10 |
| [...] | |
| 1 filza di paternostri | fiorini 4 |
| 1 libriciuolo di dona | fiorini 8[12] |
| [...] | |
| (1 pair of chests | 24 florins |
| 1 grey overdress | 18 florins |
| 1 gown, with 2½ ounces of silver on it | 10 florins |
| [...] | |
| 1 rosary | 4 florins |
| 1 Office of Our Lady | 8 florins |
| [...]) | |

In many other cases, these books would have been relatively humble copies. In 1483 the trousseau of Niccolò Machiavelli's elder sister

---

Sharon T. Strocchia, 'Taken Into Custody: Girls and Convent Guardianship in Renaissance Florence', *Renaissance Studies*, 17 (2003), 177–200.

[10] Christiane Klapisch-Zuber, 'Le chiavi fiorentine di Barbablù: l'apprendimento della lettura a Firenze nel XV secolo', *Quaderni storici*, no. 57 (Dec. 1984), 765–92 (p. 776), citing ASF, Carte strozziane, IV, 418, fol. 61ᵛ.

[11] Jacqueline Marie Musacchio, 'The Bride and Her *donora* in Renaissance Florence', in *Culture and Change: Attending to Early Modern Women*, ed. by Margaret Mikesell and Adele Seeff (Newark: University of Delaware Press, 2003), pp. 177–202 (pp. 183, 193).

[12] *Il libro di ricordanze dei Corsini (1362–1457)*, ed. by Armando Petrucci (Rome: Istituto storico italiano per il Medio Evo, 1965), pp. 109–10; Christiane Klapisch-Zuber, 'Le "zane" della sposa', *Memoria: rivista di storia delle donne*, 11–12 (1984), 12–23 (pp. 16, 17). Details of clothing can be found in Carole Collier Frick, *Dressing Renaissance Florence: Families, Fortunes, and Fine Clothing* (Baltimore, MD: Johns Hopkins University Press, 2002).

Primavera, aged eighteen, included a 'libriccino' listed among her everyday items:

> una setola lavorata
> uno spechio
> uno libriccino
> 3 borse
> uno anello da cucire d'ariento
> xvi cuffie
> [. . .]
>
> (a decorated hairbrush
> a mirror
> a little book
> 3 purses
> a silver thimble
> 16 caps
> [. . .])

This Book of Hours cannot have been of great financial worth, since it is included among the objects that her father Bernardo, who in any case was not wealthy, did not have formally valued.[13]

However, Books of Hours were often richly decorated and richly furnished status symbols that were commissioned to mark a woman's marriage or another key event in her life. A fine example is the Book of Hours made for Isabella di Chiaromonte between 1458, when she became Queen of Naples, and her death in 1465; it was decorated by an artist known as the Master of Isabella di Chiaromonte.[14] Nannina (baptized Lucrezia) de' Medici, one of the sisters of Lorenzo il Magnifico, was provided with a dowry worth over 2,500 florins when she married another Florentine patrician, Bernardo Rucellai, in 1466. The dowry included *donora* valued at 500 florins, and the catalogue of the items includes at the end, after her most elegant clothing, '1 libriccino di Nostra Donna storiato con fornimenti d'ariento' (one little book of Our Lady, illustrated, with silver

---

[13] Bernardo Machiavelli, *Libro di ricordi*, ed. by Cesare Olschki (Florence: Le Monnier, 1954), p. 182. On Primavera's trousseau, see also Catherine Atkinson, *Debts, Dowries, Donkeys: The Diary of Niccolò Machiavelli's Father, Messer Bernardo*, in *Quattrocento Florence* (Frankfurt am Main: Peter Lang, 2002), pp. 119–22, 172.

[14] Cambridge, MA, Harvard University, Houghton Library, MS Typ 463. See Tammaro De Marinis, with Denise Bloch, Charles Astruc and Jacques Monfrin, *La biblioteca napoletana dei re d'Aragona: supplemento*, 2 vols (Verona: Stamperia Valdonega, 1969), I, 275–76; Brucia Whitthoft, 'The Hours of Isabella di Chiaromonte', *Harvard Library Bulletin*, 18 (1970), 298–307; Toscano, 'Livres et lectures', pp. 297–98. The arms of Ferdinand impaled with those of Isabella, on fol. 13$^r$, show that the manuscript was made for her.

furnishings). The catalogue continues with some items that are not formally valued, and these include a Book of Hours for everyday use, 'I libriccino di Nostra Donna coperto di brochato' (one little book of Our Lady, with a brocade binding).[15]

Lorenzo himself had Books of Hours of great beauty prepared for the marriages of three of his daughters. Two of the manuscripts, now in Munich and Florence respectively, were copied in 1485 by the renowned scribe Antonio Sinibaldi, and their decoration has been attributed to Francesco Rosselli. The Munich manuscript has the Salviati coat of arms together with Medici emblems, and has therefore been linked with the marriage of Lucrezia de' Medici to Iacopo Salviati in 1488. It has a magnificent binding in gilded silver. The other manuscript copied by Sinibaldi has an empty space for the arms of the husband; it was perhaps intended as a gift for Luisa de' Medici, who unfortunately died before the wedding that was to unite her with her cousin Giovanni de' Medici. A third Book of Hours, in the Rothschild Collection, decorated by at least four artists, has the arms of the Cibo family and the peacock associated with them; it has been linked with the marriage of Maddalena de' Medici to Francesco Cibo, son of Pope Innocent VIII, in 1488.[16]

Eleonora Gonzaga, Duchess of Urbino, eldest child of Isabella d'Este and wife of Francesco Maria I della Rovere, came to own at least two Books of Hours. One is Oxford, Bodleian Library, MS Douce 29.[17] The other, British Library, MS Yates Thompson 7, written by Matteo Contugi of Volterra, had belonged to Costanzo Sforza, Lord of Pesaro, but was adapted for Eleonora: elaborate illuminations were added by Matteo da Milano around 1510–15 and prayers were altered to refer to a woman rather than a man. At the beginning of the Hours of the Virgin, the artist painted

---

[15] *Giovanni Rucellai ed il suo Zibaldone*, vol. I, '*Il Zibaldone quaresimale*', ed. by Alessandro Perosa (London: Warburg Institute, 1960), p. 33.

[16] Munich, Bayerische Staatsbibliothek, MS Clm 23639; BLF, MS Ashb. 1874; Waddesdon Manor, Rothschild Collection, MS 16. See L. M. J. Delaissé, James Marrow and John de Wit, *Illuminated Manuscripts: The James A. de Rothschild Collection at Waddesdon Manor* (Fribourg: Office du livre for the National Trust, 1977), pp. 324–47; Anna Lenzuni, 'Tre libri d'ore per le figlie di Lorenzo', in *All'ombra del lauro: documenti librari della cultura in età laurenziana*, ed. by Anna Lenzuni (Florence: Silvana Editoriale, 1992), pp. 166–68; *The Painted Page: Italian Renaissance Book Illumination 1450–1550*, ed. by Jonathan J. G. Alexander (Munich and New York: Prestel, 1994), cat. nos 31 (Ashb. 1874) and 32 (Clm 23639), pp. 92–95; Béatrice Hernad in *Aussen-Ansichten: Bucheinbände aus 1000 Jahren*, ed. by Bettina Wagner (Wiesbaden: Harrassowitz, 2006), cat. no. 45, pp. 98–99 (Clm 23639).

[17] *The Painted Page*, ed. by Alexander, cat. no. 130, p. 242; Jonathan J. G. Alexander, *The Painted Book in Renaissance Italy: 1450–1600* (New Haven: Yale University Press, 2016), p. 163.

the coat of arms of della Rovere impaling Gonzaga, with on either side the inscription 'Diva Dio[nora] Duci[ssa] Ur[bini]' (fol. 14$^r$; Figure 3.1).[18]

It has been suggested plausibly by Rowan Watson that a Book of Hours made for Eleonora de Toledo early in 1541, about eighteen months after her marriage to the Duke of Florence, Cosimo de' Medici, was intended not just as a prayer book but also as 'a manual of dynastic history', a primer in the social and political significance of the Medici. The decoration includes emblems that 'give an account of Medici history while at the same time invoking the support of imperial power'. The opening before the canonical office of sext (fols 55$^v$–56$^r$), for instance, depicts the visitation of the Magi, a subject associated with the Medici. Both pages include an emblem with the motto 'Duabus' (by two) and two crossed anchors, representing the mutual assistance given by Cosimo and Charles V. Some roundels depict the figure of Hercules, and they were presumably meant to associate Cosimo with the hero's superhuman deeds. One seems to show Hercules killing the snakes that Hera had sent to kill him at his birth, while another shows him resting on his club.[19]

A letter of Pietro Aretino thanks the bookseller Battistino da Parma for the gift of a small illustrated devotional book to his daughter Adria, born in 1537. To judge by Aretino's comments, this was a Book of Hours:

> Il libriciuolo che per la mia figlia mi mandaste è sì bello e sì ben legato, che ne saria onorevole una Reina. [. . .] Ora io vi ringrazio del dono assai, consigliandovi che ne presentiate qualch'uno ne la corte di Roma [. . .]; e così i prelati si avezzaranno a dire qualche volta l'ufficio piccolo, da che non dicono mai straccio del grande.

[18] Albinia C. de la Mare, 'New Research on Humanistic Scribes in Florence', in *Miniatura fiorentina del Rinascimento 1440–1525: un primo censimento*, ed. by Annarosa Garzelli, 2 vols (Florence: La Nuova Italia, 1985), I, 393–600 (pp. 449, n. 224, and 594); Jonathan J. G. Alexander, 'Matteo da Milano, Illuminator', *Pantheon*, 50 (1992), 32–45 (pp. 40–41); Alexander, *The Painted Book*, p. 161, n. 159.
[19] London, Victoria and Albert Museum, National Art Library, MSL/1953/1792. See Rowan Watson, 'Manual of Dynastic History or Devotional Aid? Eleanor of Toledo's Book of Hours', in *Excavating the Medieval Image: Manuscripts, Artists, Audiences. Essays in Honor of Sandra Hindman*, ed. by David S. Areford and Nina A. Rowe (Aldershot: Ashgate, 2004), pp. 179–95 (quotations from the title and pp. 183–84). The scribe signs and dates the manuscript on fol. 1$^r$: 'Aloysius scribebat Floren[tiae] Die X Februarii MDXXXX'. On Eleonora's roles within the Florentine state, see *The Cultural World of Eleonora di Toledo, Duchess of Florence and Siena*, ed. by Konrad Eisenbichler (Aldershot: Ashgate, 2004); Alessandra Contini, 'Spazi femminili e costruzione di un'identità dinastica: il caso di Leonora di Toledo duchessa di Firenze', in *La società dei principi nell'Europa moderna (secoli XVI–XVII)*, ed. by Christof Dipper and Mario Rosa (Bologna: il Mulino, 2005), pp. 295–320; Natalie Tomas, 'Eleonora di Toledo, Regency, and State Formation in Tuscany', in *Medici Women: The Making of a Dynasty in Grand Ducal Tuscany*, ed. by Giovanna Benadusi and Judith C. Brown (Toronto: Centre for Renaissance and Reformation Studies, 2015), pp. 58–89.

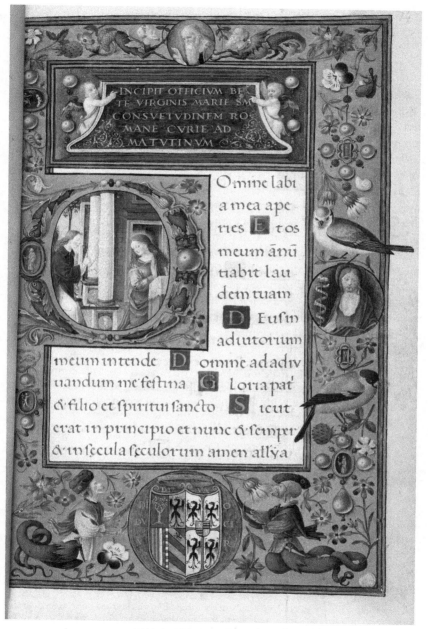

Figure 3.1 Book of Hours, Use of Rome, owned by Eleonora Gonzaga.
© The British Library Board. MS Yates Thompson 7, fol. 14ʳ

(The little book you sent me for my daughter is so beautiful and so finely
bound that it would do honour to a queen. [. . .] So now let me thank you
very warmly for this gift, and advise you to present one to all those at the
Roman Curia [. . .]; and thus the prelates will get used to reciting the little
office on occasion, since they never recite a scrap of the full office.)[20]

A trousseau was usually provided by the family of a nun when she became
a bride of Christ on entering a convent. Although the institution became the
nun's primary community, she would often retain strong ties with her natal
family. Family ties could be strengthened within the convent itself, since
novices naturally preferred to follow relatives into the same institution.[21] Cells
could be constructed by nuns' families, shared by an older and a younger
relative, and transmitted within families from generation to generation; even
nuns who did not own their cells might have to furnish them with their
families' help.[22] Claire Walker, in a study of English nuns in the seventeenth
century, comments that 'Although the monastic regimen, which was focussed
on commonality, aimed to divorce nuns from former influences, the women
rarely severed all ties with their formative communities.'[23] The furnishings of
Italian nuns' cells could include items such as books, which would have been
treasured possessions even if convents had a shared library. An example is the
trousseau of suor Isabella Tossignani, of the Benedictine convent of San Vitale
in Bologna, presented by her mother Dorotea in 1569. Among the objects
listed are these:

> Un'anchona fornita di veluto cremesino e d'oro et un'anchona fornita d'oro.
> Item uno crocifisso con due angeli dorati. Item due bambine vestite di
> ormesino azurino e verde gaio con oro e una finge Santa Margarita e l'altra
> Santa Dorothea. Item un Santo Giovanni di predacotta.
>     12 pezi di libri, 10 ligati in biancho alla romana et dui ligati di coramo
> morello con oro e li suoi signacoli.[24]

(An icon furnished with crimson velvet and gold and an icon furnished with
gold. Item, a crucifix with two gilded angels. Item, two dolls clothed in

[20] Aretino, *Lettere*, II, letter 46 (22 June 1538), pp. 50–51; Aretino, *Selected Letters*, trans. by George Bull (Harmondsworth: Penguin, 1976), letter 58, pp. 166–67, translation slightly modified.
[21] On family ties in a Florentine convent, see Francesca Medioli, 'Reti famigliari: la matrilinearità nei monasteri femminili fiorentini del Seicento. Il caso di Santa Verdiana', in *Nubili e celibi tra scelta e costrizione: secoli XVI–XX*, ed. by Margareth Lanzinger and Raffaella Sarti (Udine: Forum, 2006), pp. 11–36.
[22] Zarri, *Recinti*, pp. 82–100; Zarri, *Libri di spirito*, p. 213.
[23] Claire Walker, 'Recusants, Daughters and Sisters in Christ: English Nuns and their Communities in the Seventeenth Century', in *Women, Identities and Communities in Early Modern Europe*, ed. by Stephanie Tarbin and Susan Broomhall (Aldershot: Ashgate, 2008), pp. 61–76 (p. 61).
[24] Zarri, *Recinti*, pp. 87–88.

bright blue and green silk cloth with gold, one representing St Margaret, the other St Dorothy. Item, a St John in terracotta.

12 pieces of books, 10 bound in white in the Roman style and two bound in blackish morocco with gold and their ribbon bookmarks.)

To judge from the descriptions of the bindings, especially the last two, the books were no less highly valued than the other items.

Commenting on two inventories of books owned by a laywoman and a nun, both dating from 1600, Carmela Compare has suggested that books that are listed as older or as damaged might have been acquired as part of the women's dowries, as objects that had previously belonged to their household.[25] If this were the case, such books would have formed a link between the old and the new lives of the bride and of the novice. Federica Dallasta's studies of records of the dowries of brides and novices in Parma under the rule of the Farnese family, in the period 1545–1731, show that an 'Ufficio della Madonna' was practically the only book listed among the possessions of laywomen, but one of a small number of books, between five and eight, that were brought to the convent by new nuns, who were obliged to own certain books such as a breviary or a missal.[26] The situation in Parma changed over time: the 'Ufficio' does not appear at all in the inventories of laywomen's dowries before the 1620s, but then it is found in about 20 per cent of these inventories in the first four decades of the eighteenth century.[27] A requirement for nuns to own books essential to their devotions may be the reason for which Alessandro Vaianese, a tailor residing in Rome, received in 1539 from the abbess of Santa Chiara in Orvieto a request to bring two blankets and 'libriciolle per legerre' (little books for reading) for his sisters who were nuns in this convent.[28]

[25] Carmela Compare, 'Libri di donne e libri di monache alla fine del XVI secolo', in *Libri, biblioteche e cultura degli Ordini regolari nell'Italia moderna attraverso la documentazione della Congregazione dell'Indice: atti del convegno internazionale, Macerata, 30 maggio–1 giugno 2006*, ed. by Rosa Marisa Borraccini and Roberto Rusconi (Vatican City: Biblioteca Vaticana, 2006), pp. 583–622 (pp. 591–92). On late-sixteenth-century inventories of convent books, see also, by the same author, 'Biblioteche monastiche femminili aquilane alla fine del XVI secolo', *Rivista di storia della Chiesa in Italia*, 54 (2000), 469–516; 'I libri delle clarisse osservanti nella Provincia seraphica S. Francisci di fine '500', *Franciscana: bollettino della Società internazionale di studi francescani*, 4 (2002), 169–372; 'Inventari di biblioteche monastiche femminili alla fine del XVI secolo', *Genesis: rivista della Società Italiana delle Storiche*, 2.2 (2003), 220–32.
[26] Federica Dallasta, *Al cliente lettore: il commercio e la censura del libro a Parma nell'epoca farnesiana 1545–1731* (Milan: Franco Angeli, 2012), pp. 90–93.
[27] Federica Dallasta, *Eredità di carta: biblioteche private e circolazione libraria nella Parma farnesiana, 1545–1731* (Milan: Franco Angeli, 2010), pp. 312, 329–30.
[28] Massimo Palermo, *Il carteggio Vaianese (1537–39): un contributo allo studio della lingua d'uso nel Cinquecento* (Florence: Accademia della Crusca, 1994), pp. 32, 234.

Books were also given to nuns in other contexts. In Pisa in 1478, a nun of the convent of San Domenico received a generous donation, twenty broad florins, from a relative of one of its sisters, Niera del Lante, for the making of a breviary for her.[29] Cambridge University Library has a copy of a translation of a work ascribed to St Bonaventure, *Le devote meditatione sopra la passione del Nostro Signore*, printed around 1478, that was once presented to a nun called Alessia. She records the gift on a leaf at the end: 'Questo libro è de sor Alexia donato da suo barba frate petro mantuano ordinis predicatorum die .25. septembris. 1528' (This book belongs to Sister Alessia, given to her by her uncle, fra Pietro Mantovano OP, 25 September 1528); below this she copies a short Latin hymn about St Alexia. Suor Alessia's regular hand reflects a training that was good but conventional: she does not write completely in the humanistic style and she uses some semigothic letter shapes. The copy is soberly decorated, with a single fine miniature of the dead Christ on its opening page. Another ownership note in a relatively awkward hand shows that the book later passed to a suor Teofila Guadagna ('Questo libro sia de s[uor] teofila guadagna serva de Iesu cristo. Credo in deum', added on fol. 2$^v$).[30]

A similar kind of gift was made in 1540 by the artist Lorenzo Lotto to his nephew's daughter, suor Lucrezia d'Armano. Lotto was living in Venice with Lucrezia's father at the time, and his record of expenses includes the purchase of vernacular religious books for her:

| | |
|---|---|
| 10 decembrio, dati a Lucretia in San Bernardo un da 12 | L – s 12 |
| per comprarli, De vite de santi padri, ligata | L 3 s 2 |
| per un psalmista con la exposition vulgar ligato in carton | L 2 s 5 |
| un libro in 4° foglio, El gerson del dispretio del mondo | L – s 4 |
| | |
| (10 December, given to Lucrezia in the convent of San | L 0 s 12 |
|    Bernardo, a twelve-soldi coin | |
| to buy her a bound copy of the Lives of the Holy Fathers | L 3 s 2 |

---

[29] '1478: Item avemo più per mano di fra Lodovicho in ditto anno f. vinti larghi da Lucha dell'Ante per lo breviario di Suor Niera vagliano lire III centoundici' (1478: Item, we received in the same year through fra Lodovico twenty broad florins, worth III lire, from Luca del Lante for the breviary of suor Niera): Roberts, *Dominican Women and Renaissance Art*, p. 26.

[30] ([Venice: Nicolas Jenson?, about 1478?]), shelfmark Inc.5.B.3.2[4321]. Suor Alessia personalized this copy further by transcribing other poems, including a 'Himno de le sancte verzene' (Hymn of the Holy Virgins) on two leaves added at the front. See the entry by Abigail Brundin in *Madonnas and Miracles: The Holy Home in Renaissance Italy*, ed. by Maya Corry, Deborah Howard and Mary Laven (London: Philip Wilson, 2017), pp. 56–57 and Plate 57, and Brundin, Howard and Laven, *The Sacred Home*, pp. 153–56, Figures 5.3 and 5.4.

for a psalter with a commentary in the vernacular, bound    L 2 s 5
   in pasteboards
a book in quarto, Gerson's Contempt of the World        L – s 4)[31]

The *Lives of the Holy Fathers* would have been a version of Domenico Cavalca's translation of the *Vitae Patrum*. The copy of the Psalms may well have belonged to one of the editions translated and commented by Antonio Brucioli. The quarto copy of the *Contempt of the World* or *Imitation of Christ*, here attributed to Jean Gerson rather than to Thomas à Kempis, seems to have been an older book, chosen precisely because it was in a larger format than had become the norm for this work by 1540. There are several incunabula of the work in quarto format, but the only editions produced in this format (as opposed to octavo or smaller) in the first four decades of the sixteenth century come from Venice, Milan and Florence between 1502 and 1522. The copy given to Lucrezia may thus have been second-hand or a former family possession, which would help to explain its relatively low monetary value.

There was also the possibility of a book finding its way into a convent from a source other than relatives of nuns. A scandal broke out in Milan in 1575, in a female convent of the order of the Humiliati, Santa Maria Maddalena del Cerchio, when two risqué manuscript poems in Bergamasque dialect were found, with their musical settings, in a nun's cell. The sister in question, Paola Giustina Carpani, was a singer, and she testified that the poems had been included within an eminently respectable musical gift, 'una copia de motetti de Orlando Lasso mandatami da messer Giovan Battista mio fratello' (a copy of motets by Orlando di Lasso sent to me by my brother Giovan Battista), no doubt one of the many editions that had been printed in Venice. Her testimony mentions another gift or loan from outside the convent: 'Alle volte si è cantato li versi spirituali del thesauro della sapientia datone da messer prete Paulo' (we sometimes sang the spiritual verses of the *Thesauro della sapientia*, given to us by Father Paulo). This priest was the nuns' former confessor, and he had perhaps given them the most recent edition (Milan: Valerio and Girolamo Meda, 1568) of the *Thesauro della sapientia evangelica*, an anonymously compiled collection of sacred poetry. Suor Paola's testimony about the Lasso motets shows that it was considered normal and perfectly acceptable for nuns to receive books from relatives. However, Carlo Arese, the vicar of nuns in

---

[31] Lorenzo Lotto, *Il 'Libro di spese diverse' con aggiunta di lettere e d'altri documenti*, ed. by Pietro Zampetti (Venice: Istituto per la collaborazione culturale, 1969), p. 212; translation from Peter Humfrey, *Lorenzo Lotto* (New Haven: Yale University Press, 1997), p. 178, slightly modified.

Milan, acting on behalf of Cardinal Carlo Borromeo, decided that in this case
the story about the two Bergamasque songs having come from her brother was
a fabrication: a barber, he thought, had taken advantage of his access to the
convent for purposes of medical care and had smuggled in the songs. To make
matters worse, the barber's copy had come from the neighbouring Cistercian
monks of Sant'Ambrogio.[32] Ribald songs figure in a musical manuscript
miscellany owned by suor Elena Malvezzi of the Dominican convent of
Sant'Agnese in Bologna around 1560. It is bound with her name on the
book cover, but it is not known whether the manuscript was a gift to her or
whether she copied it from sources made available to her in the convent.[33]

Books given by relatives to laywomen did not all fall into the category of
works that were certainly or probably related to their devotions. In the
previous chapter we encountered Ippolita Sforza, daughter of a duke of
Milan. When she was betrothed in 1465, she received, as part of her dowry,
fourteen manuscripts, valued at 600 ducats in total. Three of these were
secular in content and very substantial. One was a sumptuously decorated
copy of the works of Virgil with the commentary of Servius, valued at 80
ducats, now in the Universitat de València (Biblioteca Històrica, MS 891).
The main text was copied in Milan by 'the Galeazzo Maria scribe', as
Albinia de la Mare dubbed him, since he wrote several manuscripts for
Ippolita's brother.[34] The two other non-religious manuscripts were one
decade of Livy's history of Rome, valued at 36 ducats, and Giovanni Balbi's
treatise on Latin language and usage, the *Catholicon*, valued at 80 ducats.[35]

[32] Danilo Zardin, *Donna e religiosa di rara eccellenza: Prospera Corona Bascapè, i libri e la cultura nei
monasteri milanesi del Cinque e Seicento* (Florence: Olschki, 1992), pp. 66–96; Kendrick, *Celestial
Sirens*, pp. 51–57, 65–66. On the role of barbershops in the diffusion of information and texts, see
Filippo de Vivo, *Information and Communication in Venice: Rethinking Early Modern Politics*
(Oxford University Press, 2007), pp. 98–106, 143–46.

[33] Craig Monson, 'Elena Malvezzi's Keyboard Manuscript: A New Sixteenth-Century Source', *Early
Music History*, 9 (1990), 73–128 (p. 84).

[34] Albinia C. de la Mare, 'Script and Manuscripts in Milan under the Sforzas', in *Milano nell'età di
Ludovico il Moro: atti del Convegno internazionale 28 febbraio–4 marzo 1983*, 2 vols (Milan: Archivio
storico civico e Biblioteca Trivulziana, 1983), pp. 399–408 (p. 404).

[35] Tammaro De Marinis, *La biblioteca napoletana dei re d'Aragona*, 4 vols (Milan: Hoepli,
1947–52), I, 98–99, II, 173 and Plates 266–68; Evelyn S. Welch, 'Between Milan and
Naples: Ippolita Sforza, Duchess of Calabria', in *The French Descent into Renaissance Italy,
1494–95: Antecedents and Effects*, ed. by David Abulafia (Aldershot: Variorum, 1995), pp. 123–36
(pp. 127–28); Gennaro Toscano, 'La collezione di Ippolita Sforza e la biblioteca di Alfonso
duca di Calabria', in *La Biblioteca reale di Napoli al tempo della dinastia aragonese: Napoli,
Castel Nuovo, 30 settembre–15 dicembre 1998*, ed. by Gennaro Toscano (Valencia: Generalitat
Valenciana, 1998), pp. 251–67; Toscano, 'Livres et lectures', pp. 299–307; Bryce, '"Fa finire
uno bello studio"'; Concetta Bianca, 'Le biblioteche delle principesse nel regno aragonese', in
*La donna nel Rinascimento meridionale: atti del convegno internazionale (Roma 11–13 novembre
2009)*, ed. by Marco Santoro (Pisa and Rome: Fabrizio Serra, 2010), pp. 403–12 (pp. 406–08).

(As we have seen, Ippolita studied Latin.) For one of the daughters of
Renée de France mentioned in the first chapter, Lucrezia d'Este, a printed
copy of Ariosto's *Orlando furioso* was especially illuminated by the bookseller Niccolò Garanta in 1556, as a gift from her brother Luigi.[36]

As in the case of the Cambridge copy of *Le devote meditatione* attributed
to St Bonaventure that came into the ownership of suor Teofila Guadagna,
books could pass from one nun to another within convents.[37] We do not
know how Teofila received her book, perhaps as the result of a gift or of
a legacy from suor Alessia. The same uncertainty applies to a copy of
Bonaventure's *Opuscula* (Brescia: Bernardino Misinta for Angelo
Britannico, 1497), now in the British Library.[38] A sixteenth-century note,
written in a neat humanistic cursive hand on fol. a3ʳ, indicates that the
book was 'Ad Usum sor[or]is Marie d[e] Albano Et sor[or]is Ma[ri]e
Cleophe d[e] solario' (For the use of sisters Maria di Albano and Maria
Cleofe di Solario) of the convent of Santa Chiara in Sassari. This note was
later cancelled and below it is given the name of another owner: 'Al uso di
suor Hortensia Maria Alberici Del Santiss[i]mo Sacram[en]to'.

Ownership notes may reveal that a book was a gift from one nun to
another. For example, a copy of an Italian translation of the sermons on the
Song of Songs by St Bernard of Clairvaux (Milan: Ulrich Scinzenzeler, 1494),
in the Biblioteca Nazionale Centrale Vittorio Emanuele II of Rome (shelfmark 70.6.D.37), has at the top of the first leaf a handwritten note that states
that 'Questo libro è delle s[uor]e di S. Giorgio dell'ordine di san Franc[esc]o
a uso di s[uor]a Vangelista de' Doti concesso allei dalla ministra' (This book
belongs to the sisters of San Giorgio of the order of St Francis, for the use of
Sister Evangelista Doti, with the permission of the [female] minister). Over
this note is pasted another, which shows that the book was later given to a nun
in another convent because of a family link: 'Questo libro donò s[uor]a
Appollonia del monastero di San Giorgio [. . .] a s[uor]a Cicilia di Ridolphi
monaca del monastero di san Niccolò di [. . .] per che gl'era di s[uor]a
Diamante zia di s[uora] Cicilia' (Sister Apollonia of the monastery of San
Giorgio gave this book to Cecilia Ridolfi, nun of the monastery of San
Niccolò of [. . .] because it belonged to Sister Diamante, Sister Cecilia's
aunt). A fifteenth-century collection of spiritual letters, now BAV, MS
Barb. Lat. 3932, has an ownership note of the Franciscan convent of
Sant'Onofrio in Florence, followed by another note: 'Questo libro è di

---

[36] Giuseppe Campori, *Notizie dei miniatori dei principi estensi* (Modena: Vincenzi, 1872), p. 20.
[37] On gifts of devotional texts between nuns, especially from older to younger ones, see Moreton,
'Exchange and Alliance', pp. 390–402.
[38] Shelfmark IA. 31263; described in *Catalogue of Books*, VII, 992.

suora Annalena che gnene decte suora Beatrice' (This book belongs to Sister
Annalena, who was given it by Sister Beatrice).[39] Suor Prospera Bascapè, a nun
of a patrician family who was involved in the scandal of suor Paola Carpani in
1575, just mentioned, left her books, including a catechism, to a prioress of her
convent, Ippolita Besozzi.[40] Suor Raffaella Bardi, who, as was seen in Chapter
2, was one of the scribes working in the double house of Santa Brigida al
Paradiso in Florence, noted on a manuscript collection of three spiritual texts
in the vernacular: 'ebbi questo libro da frate Lucha vechio perché gliele chiesi'
(I received this book from old fra Luca because I asked him for it).
A subsequent note, 'Delle suore et convento del Paradiso' ([Property] of the
nuns and convent of the Paradiso), similar to the note in Figure 2.3, indicates
that this gift to an individual was then shared by all.[41]

   There were, however, perceived dangers inherent in granting personal
favours to another member of the clergy. In order to combat possible
abuses, Pope Clement VIII decreed in 1594 that no member of the regular
clergy, male or female, could make 'doni, et presenti di qualunque sorte'
(gifts and presents of any kind) to another, on the grounds that these
could be the cause of 'gravi incommodi, et mali ancora, sotto specie di
bene' (serious troubles and even evils, in the guise of good), such as
seeking favour in order to obtain 'gradi, et Dignità' (ranks and dignities).
There were some exceptions that would have allowed gifts of inexpensive
religious books for the use of a whole religious house: 'Eccettuando però
alcuni leggieri, et piccioli doni da mangiare, o da bere, overo spettanti
a devotione, o Religione, i quali però [. . .] si doveranno solamente dare
sempre in nome commune del Monasterio, et mai in nome particolare'
(Excepting, though, some insignificant and small gifts of food or drink,
or concerning devotion or religion, which, however, [. . .] must only and
always be given in the common name of the monastery, and never in the
name of an individual).[42] Very wide and coordinated publicity was given
to this ruling by means of editions printed throughout Italy, and the
pope's letter stipulated that vernacular translations of the decree were to
be made for the use of nuns.[43] Copies of this prohibition were to be

[39] Delcorno Branca, 'Il *Giardino novello*', p. 312.
[40] Zardin, *Donna e religiosa*, pp. 58, n. 4, 65, 261.
[41] BLF, MS Conv. Soppr. 289, fol. 39ᵛ; Miriello, *I manoscritti del Monastero del Paradiso*, p. 55.
[42] *Constitutione della santità di nostro sig. papa Clemente ottavo, con la quale prohibisce a tutti li regolari dell'uno, et l'altro sesso il poter dar, o mandar presenti ad alcuno* (Vicenza: heirs of Perin libraro, 1594), fols A2ᵛ, A3ᵛ and A4ʳ.
[43] Other editions, all of 1594, include: *Sanctissimi in Christo patris et d. n. d. Clementis divina providentia pp. 8 Constitutio de largitione munerum utriusque sexus regularibus interdicta* (Milan: heirs of Pacifico Da Ponte); *Constitutione per la qual si vieta a tutti i regolari dell'uno et l'altro sesso, che non possano fare*

affixed in public places and distributed in full or in summary form to religious houses. A copy of an undated vernacular edition printed in Florence is bound into a manuscript originating from the Monastero del Paradiso in that city.[44]

Gifts could reach women from beyond the grave in the form of bequests. In a legacy of 1374, the wife of a Florentine, Niccolò Monachi, left prayer books including 'uno suo libricciuolo di donna' to female relatives, as well as an Office of the Virgin to her son.[45] An Augustinian friar preferred to leave his books to his married sister in Rome in 1435, rather than bequeathing them to his own convent.[46] In a somewhat complex bequest set out in a will of 1474, Grazioso Graziosi Berardelli of Perugia left all his books to two monasteries of his city, which then had to give four of them to Clarissan nuns: 'et dent et dare teneantur duos libros vulgari sermoni monialibus Sancte Agnetis, vid[elicet] librum *Vite sanctorum patrum* et librum *Patientie* et duos alios monialibus Sancti Antonii de Padue pariter in vulgari, vid[elicet] librum *Legendarum sanctorum* et *Speculum crucis*' (and let them give and be obliged to give two books in the vernacular to the nuns of Sant'Agnese, namely the book of Lives of the Holy Fathers and the book of Patience, and two others to the nuns of Sant'Antonio di Padova, also in the vernacular, namely the book of Lives of the Saints and the

---

*qual si voglia dono* (Brescia: Vincenzo Sabbio); *Sommario della constitutione per la quale si prohibisce alli religiosi regolari il fare donativi* (Reggio: Ercoliano Bartoli); *Sanctissimi in Christo patris, et D. N. Clementis divina providentia PP. 8. Constitutio de largitione munerum utriusque sexus Regularibus interdicta* (Ferrara: Giovanni Battista Bellagamba); *Sommario della Constitutione di N. S. papa Clemente 8: per la quale si prohibisce alli religiosi regolari dell'uno, et l'altro sesso il fare donativi, overo presenti. Tradotta in volgare, et in guisa di compendio eraccolta, per maggiore intelligenza di ciascuno: e particolarmente per rispetto delle monache, conforme all'ordine di sua santità* (Bologna: Vittorio Benacci); *Bolla della Santità di nostro sign. Papa Clemente ottavo, che proibisce a tutti i frati, et alle monache di qualsivoglia religione, che non possino donare, nè far presenti a persona* (Florence: Sermartelli); *Constitutione del santissimo signor nostro papa Clemente ottavo, nella quale si proibisce a Regulari dell'uno, et dell'altro sesso di dare presenti* (Perugia: heirs of Andrea Bresciano); *S[anctissi]mi in Christo patris et D. N. D. Clementis divina providentia papae octavi Constitutio de largitione munerum utriusque sexus regularibus interdicta* (Rome: Stamperia Camerale); *Ordinatione della santità di n. s. Clemente per divina providenza papa VIII dove espressamente si prohibisce a tutti li regolari dell'uno et l'altro sesso, a non poter far presenti per l'avenire* (Rome: Stamperia Camerale); *Constitutione del santiss. in Christo Padre, e sig. n. il sig. Clemente per divina providenza papa VIII, sopra la liberalità dei doni vietati a i regolari dell'uno, e dell'altro sesso: volgarizzata in Napoli* (Naples: Orazio Salviani for Giovanni Iacomo Carlino and Antonio Pace).
[44] BRF, MS 2878; Miriello, *I manoscritti del Monastero del Paradiso*, p. 170.
[45] Klapisch-Zuber, 'Le chiavi fiorentine di Barbablù', p. 789, n. 72.
[46] Katherine Gill, 'Open Monasteries for Women in Late Medieval and Early Modern Italy', in *The Crannied Wall: Women, Religion, and the Arts in Early Modern Europe*, ed. by Craig A. Monson (Ann Arbor: University of Michigan Press, 1992), pp. 15–47 (p. 32). For other examples of books inherited by women, ranging from a Bible to a dialogue by Pietro Aretino, see Tippelskirch, *Sotto controllo*, pp. 50–51, 55 and n. 52.

Mirror of the Cross).[47] The *Legendae sanctorum* by Giovanni da Varazze (Jacobus de Voragine) is now better known as the *Legenda aurea*. The three other works were by Domenico Cavalca: his translation of the *Vitae Patrum* and two of his spiritual treatises, the *Medicina del cuore ovvero trattato della Pazienza* and the *Specchio di Croce*.

The humanist Giovanni Pontano, who died in 1503, left his scholarly library of about fifty volumes to his daughter Eugenia, his eldest surviving child (his son Lucio Francesco had died in a tragic accident in 1498). In 1505 Eugenia formally donated all the books to the church of San Domenico Maggiore in Naples, with her husband's agreement.[48] Records of inheritances in northern Italy provide similar evidence for a later period. Moderata Fonte appears to have inherited her father's library in Venice, albeit in a somewhat irregular way, since the books should probably have passed to her brother, Leonardo.[49] In Pavia, the property passed on to a certain Silvia Pietra by her father in 1578 included not only precious objects such as jewels but also printed literary works such as Ariosto's *Orlando furioso*, *La dilettevole historia del valorosissimo Parsaforesto re della gran Brettagna* translated from French and Giraldi's lyric collection *Le fiamme*. In 1644, Antonia Alciati received, as part of a large bequest from her father, some 'libri con le sue casse' (books with their chests) worth 1,300 lire.[50] By the second half of the sixteenth century, care had to be taken that an inheritance of books did not land someone in trouble because of their content. A Venetian doctor, Nicolò Massa, left all his books, Latin and vernacular, to his daughter in 1569, with the proviso that any that had been prohibited by the Council of Trent were to be burned.[51] On the other hand, a bequest of books might have a purely monetary worth. Orazio Diola, mentioned in Chapter 1 as a translator of a work on the Franciscan order, wished to augment the value of the dowry of his niece Prudenzia and thus, in the will that he drew up in 1589, he left to her either 130 printed copies of his translation, which were currently in Rome in the possession of

---

[47] Costanzo Tabarelli, *Documentazione notarile perugina sul Convento di Monteripido nei secoli XIV e XV* (Perugia: Deputazione di storia patria per l'Umbria, 1977), p. 100. These instructions were repeated in a document of 1482: see ibid., p. 128.

[48] Erasmo Percopo, *Vita di Giovanni Pontano*, ed. by Michele Manfredi (Naples: ITEA, 1938), pp. 313–14.

[49] Ross, *The Birth of Feminism*, p. 199.

[50] Chiara Porqueddu, *Il patriziato pavese in età spagnola: ruoli familiari, stile di vita, economia* (Milan: Unicopli, 2012), pp. 400, 405.

[51] Anna Bellavitis and Isabelle Chabot, 'People and Property in Florence and Venice', in *At Home in Renaissance Italy*, ed. by Marta Ajmar-Wollheim and Flora Dennis (London: V & A Publications, 2006), pp. 76–85 (p. 81).

the printer-bookseller Girolamo Franzini, no doubt with the intention that she could have them sold, or the sum at which they were valued, fifty gold scudi.[52]

Books could sometimes be gifted to women from outside the family or the convent. Isotta Nogarola thanked the Veronese nobleman Giorgio Bevilacqua in 1436 or 1437 for sending to her and her sister Ginevra a work on the death of St Jerome, perhaps the letter attributed to Eusebius of Cremona.[53] Elite women might receive books from authors, or from those in the circles of authors, as part of the processes by which new works were circulated socially. Women would, of course, be given a copy of works from authors who had chosen them as dedicatees or hoped to do so. Lucrezia Marinella became anxious in 1595 when Margherita Gonzaga d'Este did not acknowledge that she had received a manuscript of the *Colomba sacra*, sent from Venice to Ferrara through an intermediary.[54] At the end of a collection of *Prose antiche* edited by him in 1547 (fol. K4[r]), Anton Francesco Doni included a letter in which he asked a secretary of the Medici, Giovanni Conti, to present the work to his dedicatee Eleonora de Toledo, whose coat of arms is displayed on the title page. This request suggests that Eleonora was seen as a potential patron in her own right, rather than as an intermediary or broker in Doni's relationship with her husband Duke Cosimo.

Some authors presented their works in other contexts. The British Library has a copy of the first edition of Iacopo Sannazaro's poem *De partu Virginis* (Naples: Antonio Frezza, 1526, shelfmark G.10031), printed on vellum, with Vittoria Colonna's initials and the emblem of a column surmounted by a crown on fol. A4[r]: this must have been a gift from the author. Colonna's correspondence mentions other manuscript and printed works presented to her, such as a manuscript of Lodovico Martelli's tragedy *Tullia* sent by Claudio Tolomei, Tolomei's *Oratione de la pace* sent by a mutual friend, Giacomo Beldandi, and sonnets from Lodovico Dolce. The religious reformer Pier Paolo Vergerio intended to send her an account of conversations with Marguerite de Navarre in a fair copy.[55] It is probable that Pietro Aretino sent printed copies of his paraphrase of the Seven

[52] Dallasta, 'Orazio Diola traduttore', pp. 587, 589.   [53] Nogarola, *Complete Writings*, pp. 36–37.
[54] Lalli, 'Scrivere per le Gonzaga', pp. 407–10.
[55] Colonna, *Carteggio*, letters XLIII (7 April 1531), pp. 67–68, and LVII (7 May 1533), pp. 86–87 (Tolomei); LXXIV (15 December 1536), pp. 124–26 (Dolce); CXVI (1540), pp. 194–97 (Vergerio). Vergerio would also have sent her 'quattro discorsi sulle materie di Germania' (four discourses on the subjects of Germany) in June 1540 but did not do so then, 'perché io non ho via secura' (letter CXV, pp. 191–93; because I do not have a safe means). For gifts of books to Colonna from Giuseppe Betussi and Pietro Aretino, see Ranieri, 'Vittoria Colonna', pp. 264–67.

Penitential Psalms to Colonna and to Veronica Gambara, since he imagines them as among the future readers of the work in his dedicatory letter,
addressed to Antonio de Leyva: 'godo nel vedere la sacra VITTORIA
Colonna fervidamente considerare insieme col mirabile ALFONSO
Davolos le sante parole di questa mia dovuta fatica: la quale sarà continua
oratione de la spiritale Veronica Gambara' (I rejoice to see the holy Vittoria
Colonna fervently contemplating, together with the wonderful Alfonso
d'Avalos, the holy words of this fitting labour of mine, which will be the
continuous prayer of the spiritual Veronica Gambara).[56]

Wives of rulers similarly received, from men of letters or publishers, books
that were both solicited and unsolicited. Among these women were two of
the female dedicatees mentioned in Chapter 1. Several of the books given by
authors to Renée de France chimed with her spiritual interests. Among them
was Heinrich Bullinger's commentary on St Matthew's Gospel, freshly
printed in Switzerland, in 1542. A letter, or a draft of a letter, datable to
1537 shows that John Calvin intended to send her two short works, one of
which may have been in manuscript, the other printed. In some cases, Renée
rewarded the donor with a gift of money.[57] Joanna of Austria was seeking in
early 1575 a copy of Lodovico Castelvetro's translation of, and commentary
on, Aristotle's *Poetics*, which had been printed in Vienna in 1570: Maffio
Venier in Rome reported to her that he had been unable to locate a copy, but
instead she received one from Antonio Avogadro in Siena.[58] The printer
Gabriele Giolito presented the Grand Duchess with Lodovico Dolce's
biography of her father Ferdinand of Habsburg, freshly printed by him in
Venice in 1566. It was to be read by her, he wrote, and then passed to her
father-in-law, Grand Duke Cosimo: although the gift made to Joanna came
first in time, it was evidently considered less important than the subsequent
presentation of the book to her husband. Giolito also sent a copy to another
of Ferdinand's daughters who had married into a noble Italian family,
Eleonora of Austria, the devout wife of Duke Guglielmo Gonzaga of
Mantua. Pier Filippo Asirelli offered poems on religious subjects to Joanna
in 1577. A certain Francesco Carbonati sent to her in 1578 a prayer ('orazione') that invited the archangels to protect the Medici family during her

[56] Cited from *I sette salmi de la penitentia di David* (Venice: Francesco Marcolini, 1539), fol. A3ʳ. See also Colonna, *Carteggio*, letter LXXXIX (9 January 1538), pp. 151–53.
[57] Franceschini, "Literarum studia nobis communia"', pp. 215–16. On Calvin's letter, see John Calvin, *Ioannis Calvini Scripta didactica et polemica*, IV, *Epistulae duae (1537); Deux discours (Oct. 1536)*, ed. by Alexander De Boer and Frans Pieter Van Stam (Geneva: Droz, 2009), pp. xviii–xx.
[58] ASF, Mediceo del Principato, vol. 5923, fol. 148 (1 February 1575, Avogadro); vol. 5925, fol. 530 (24 February 1575, Venier).

pregnancy; he also hoped he would be able to send her part of St Ambrose's garment before the birth. Unfortunately, in spite of Carbonati's invocations, Joanna died in childbirth two months later, aged just thirty-one.[59] A book given to Lucrezia Gonzaga of Gazzuolo by the author, a fra Francesco Ferrarese, between 1546 and 1552, may have been a copy of Francesco Visdomini's *Homelie dello Spirito Santo*, printed in Venice by Andrea Arrivabene in 1551 and 1552.[60]

Akin to gift-giving, and sometimes difficult to distinguish clearly from it, was lending. Women, like men, could have passing ownership of books in this way. Antonino Pierozzi, archbishop of Florence from 1446 to 1459, acting as spiritual advisor to the Florentine Dada degli Adimari, offered to lend her 'the *Morali*' (possibly St Gregory's commentary on the Book of Job) or a similar vernacular book.[61] In Cortona, suor Marzia of the Ospedale di Santa Maria della Misericordia wrote on 26 July 1465 to Pantasilea, the widow of Pandolfo Baglioni of Perugia, to return a book that had been lent to her during a visit from Pantasilea. Suor Marzia had apparently shared the book with her community, since she comments that 'n'abiamo aùto grande consolatione' (we got much consolation from it).[62] Nearly a century later, a laywoman of a noble Venetian family, Giulia Da Ponte, thanked Giorgio Gradenigo in an undated letter for books that were shared and welcomed by her family in Spilimbergo: 'I due libri mandati alle mie figliuole, le quali confesso, come scrivete voi, esser due altre a me stessa, e di più che non dite, io due lor medesime, sono stati grati a tutta questa unità' (The two books sent to my daughters – who I admit are, as you write, twin living images of myself, and moreover I am a living image of them – were most welcome to this whole household).[63] These daughters, Emilia and Irene di Spilimbergo, were voracious readers within their household, as their grandfather testified in 1559.[64] Within convents, nuns

---

[59] ASF, Mediceo del Principato, vol. 5094, fol. 90 (27 March 1566, Giolito and Duchess Joanna); vol. 5927, fols 238 (18 March 1577) and 251 (1 April 1577, Asirelli); vol. 5927, fol. 131 (4 February 1578, Carbonati); ASMn, Archivio Gonzaga, busta 1498 (Giolito and Duchess Eleonora). For the gifts to the duchesses Joanna and Eleonora, see Nuovo and Coppens, *I Giolito e la stampa*, p. 254.

[60] Brundin, Howard and Laven, *The Sacred Home*, pp. 149–51. On Visdomini, see Emily Michelson, 'An Italian Explains the English Reformation (with God's Help)', in *A Linking of Heaven and Earth: Studies in Religious and Cultural History in Honor of Carlos M. N. Eire*, ed. by Emily Michelson, Scott K. Taylor and Mary Noll Venables (Farnham: Ashgate, 2012), pp. 33–48.

[61] Judith Bryce, 'Dada degli Adimari's Letters from Sant'Antonino: Identity, Maternity, and Spirituality', *I Tatti Studies: Essays in the Renaissance*, 12 (2009), 11–53 (p. 35).

[62] Nico Ottaviani, *'Me son missa a scriver questa letera . . . '*, pp. 140–41, 155–56.

[63] Bernardino Pino, *Della nuova scielta di lettere di diversi nobilissimi huomini [. . .] libro secondo* (Venice: Giovanni Antonio Rampazetto, 1582), fols ll8ᵛ–mm1ʳ.

[64] Richardson, *Printing, Writers and Readers*, p. 150.

lent books to one another, especially those books that were not used for their everyday devotions but were recreational or of wider cultural interest.[65] Texts of plays were borrowed between religious women, sometimes as part of an exchange. Maria Maddalena de' Pazzi, a tertiary Dominican of Santa Maria degli Angeli in via della Colonna, Florence, writes in 1592 to thank a nun in another convent for the loan of a play that she has copied and is returning: 'Vi rimando con la presente la rapresentazione del figliol prodigo. Scusatemi se l'ho tenuta più che non era l'intento mio; peroché non l'abbiàn potuta copiar prima' (I am sending back with this letter the Play of the Prodigal Son. Forgive me if I kept it longer than I intended, because we could not copy it earlier). The wording of her letter also suggests a collaboration between the nuns of Santa Maria in transcribing plays.[66]

A notarial document of 1453 enabled the loan of a precious breviary from the convent of Sant'Antonio di Padova in Perugia to a tertiary sister of St Francis who was becoming a nun in the neighbouring convent of Monteluce. This included a safeguard to prevent the convent of Monteluce from appropriating the book after the nun's death:

> Sorores tertii ordinis Sancti Francisci, comorantes in locho Sancti Antonii de Padua sito in porta Sancti Angeli, creaverunt in eorum procuratorem ser Bartolomeum ser Roberti ad concedendum monasterio Sancte Marie Montis Lucidi usum unius breviarii ipsius monasterii sub assidibus ligati foderatis coreo rubeo cum pictorillis de argento, miniato, deaurato, in vita sor[oris] Eugenie olim conmorantis in dicto locho Sancti Antonii de Padua et nunc in dicto monesterio Sancte Marie Montis Lucidi et quousque ipsa sor[oris] Eugenia vixerit, dummodo dictum monasterium Sancte Marie Montis Lucidi promictat et se obliget ad restitutionem dicti breviarii post mortem dicte d[ominae] Eugenie.[67]

> (The sisters of the Third Order of St Francis, dwelling in the place of Sant'Antonio di Padova at Porta Sant'Angelo, nominated as their procurator ser Bartolomeo son of ser Roberto in order to grant to the monastery of Santa Maria di Monteluce the use of a breviary of that monastery, bound in boards covered with red morocco with silver clasps, illuminated, gilded, for the lifetime of Sister Eugenia formerly dwelling in the said place of Sant'Antonio di Padova and now in the said monastery of Santa Maria di

[65] Zardin, 'Mercato librario', pp. 213–15.

[66] Weaver, *Convent Theatre*, pp. 71–73 (quotation from p. 72). On a manuscript of entertainments for Florentine nuns that passed into the ownership of Margherita Gonzaga d'Este in the late sixteenth century, see Laurie Stras, 'The *Ricreationi per monache* of suor Annalena Aldobrandini', *Renaissance Studies*, 26 (2012), 34–59.

[67] Tabarelli, *Documentazione notarile perugina*, pp. 59–60.

Monteluce and for as long as Sister Eugenia shall live, provided that the said monastery of Santa Maria di Monteluce promises and makes itself liable to return the said breviary after the death of the said lady Eugenia.)

## Commissioning Manuscripts

Both lay and religious women were sometimes able to pay for the production and decoration of manuscript books for their own use. An intriguing record in the accounts, studied by Evelyn Welch, of Paola Malatesta Gonzaga, who became the first marchioness of Mantua in the early fifteenth century, suggests that her female companions in the court could play some role in manuscript production: a 'domicella' or lady-in-waiting of hers was paid 12 soldi in 1417 'pro faciendo impaginari unum librum'. The sense of *impaginare* here is uncertain: probably, it simply means writing the book out, but more technically it may refer to the ruling of pages ready for copying, or to the division of the text between pages. In any case, it was evidently a fairly responsible task, since 12 soldi was worth over half the monthly sum of 1 lira that the marchioness paid her ladies-in-waiting in addition to their board and lodging.[68] More normally, court ladies would subcontract specialized scribal work to outsiders. For instance, in 1418 Paola Malatesta bought a missal for a considerable sum from Giacomo Galopini, a priest who was also an illuminator and bookbinder, and then paid Galopini for its decoration and binding and for writing additions to it: 'Item pro himiniando unum Missale et faciendo unum Calendarium ante ipsum Missale, empto hei antea ducatis xviii, et in parte posteriori aliquas orationes, pro ligando et copiando cum azolis et clavis, die viiii marci lire viiii s. x.' (Item, for illuminating a missal and making a calendar before the said missal, previously bought from [Galopini] for 18 ducats, and some prayers at the end, for binding and copying with clasps and bosses, on 9 March, 9 lire 10 soldi). This sum was roughly equivalent to 2.5 ducats.[69]

In 1420, Paola Malatesta had another missal created. This involved the initial purchase of 24 gatherings of vellum, at 4 soldi each, together with

[68] Evelyn Welch, 'The Art of Expenditure: The Court of Paola Malatesta Gonzaga in Fifteenth-Century Mantua', *Renaissance Studies*, 16 (2002), 306–17 (p. 313). Payments to two professionals for *impaginare* are mentioned in Attilio Portioli, 'Giacomo Galopini prete e miniatore mantovano del secolo XV', *Archivio storico lombardo*, 3rd ser., 11 (1899), 330–47 (p. 337).
[69] Portioli, 'Giacomo Galopini', p. 332; Welch, 'The Art of Expenditure', p. 314, n. 40. For the value of the Mantuan lira against the florin in this period, see Peter Spufford, *Handbook of Medieval Exchange* (London: Royal Historical Society, 1986), p. 94.

the paint and glue used for the illumination. There was also a sum for a thoughtful gesture: 'et magistro domino scriptori pro portata vini lib. XI, IIII' (and to the master scribe for provision of wine, 11 lire 4 soldi). It proved necessary to buy twenty-five more gatherings of vellum, now costing 5 soldi each. The written sheets were then taken for decoration by Galopini. Another payment was made to a goldsmith: 'pro uncia una et granis duo argenti de liga, aurato, in uno fulcimento unius Missaleto pro magnifica Domina nostra. L. VI' (for one ounce and two grains of silver alloy, gilded, in a bookrest of a missal for our magnificent lady, 6 lire).[70] To have fine books such as these made to order was expensive: the cost of this new missal came to over 65 lire. This was a small amount in terms of the marchioness's annual income, which in 1420 was over 22,000 lire, but it was more than, for instance, the annual salary of the highest-paid male members of her household such as her estate manager, which was 60 lire.[71] These commissions would have been initiated in a spirit of piety and for the pleasure of possessing beautiful objects, but doubtless also with a sense that ownership of such books was socially prestigious, since they evidenced the marchioness's wealth and good taste. The ornate bookrest may well have been intended not simply to be of practical help when the marchioness read her missal, but also to display it to members of her family and her close circle. Paola acquired books in other ways. Later, in 1429, she purchased a manuscript containing the letters of Seneca. A finely decorated manuscript of Nicholas of Lyra's commentary on the Bible (*Postilla litteralis super totam Bibliam*), now Manchester, John Rylands Library, MSS Lat. 29–31, was copied by a Franciscan, Ugolino Marini Gibertuzzi of Sarnano, on the orders of Pandolfo Malatesta, Archbishop of Patras, and was completed by fra Ugolino in Pesaro in 1402; as Ubaldo Meroni has suggested, it may then have come to the Marchioness Paola through inheritance from Pandolfo, who was her brother.[72]

A particularly lavish double commission was planned by Isabella di Chiaromonte in 1463. She paid 48 ducats, about what a skilled worker would have hoped to earn in a year, just for eighty gatherings (*quinterni*) of royal-format vellum that were to be used to make a Bible for Bianca

[70] Portioli, 'Giacomo Galopini', pp. 335–37.    [71] Welch, 'The Art of Expenditure', pp. 310, 313.

[72] Montague Rhodes James, *A Descriptive Catalogue of the Latin Manuscripts in the John Rylands Library at Manchester*, 2 vols (Manchester University Press, 1921), I, 81–87; Ubaldo Meroni, *Mostra dei codici gonzagheschi: la biblioteca dei Gonzaga da Luigi I ad Isabella. Biblioteca Comunale 18 settembre–10 ottobre* (Mantua: [n. pub.], 1966), p. 51; Paolo Pellegrini, 'Vecchie e nuove schede sull'umanesimo mantovano', *Res publica litterarum*, 35 (2012), 80–121 (p. 97).

Maria Visconti, Duchess of Milan, and a missal for herself. The Bible was perhaps intended as a gift in connection with the forthcoming marriage of Isabella's son Alfonso to Bianca Maria's daughter, Ippolita Sforza.[73]

In Florence, Tommasa Gianfigliazzi commissioned Bartolomeo d'Antonio Varnucci to illuminate her own breviary in 1470 and a small breviary for two of her daughters, who were Benedictine nuns, in 1470–71. The receipt for payment for the second commission states that 'quello [Bartolomeo] lavorò in miniare uno breviario camereccio overo portatile fecie fare detta Monna Tommasa per suora Marietta e Perpetua sue figliole monache nelle Murate [. . .] pagò contanti per noi [. . .]' (he [Bartolomeo] worked at illuminating a breviary for a bedroom, i.e. portable, that the said Monna Tommasa had made for her daughters Marietta and Perpetua, nuns in Le Murate; she paid us cash).[74] Another commission that was intended for both a mother and her daughters came from a Florentine widow, also of the fifteenth century, Costanza Cicciaporci. The colophon of a manuscript miscellany of mainly religious works, including extracts from the *Fior di virtù* (a treatise on virtues and vices) and lives of saints by Domenico Cavalca, but also the first section of Petrarch's *Triumphus Cupidinis* (Triumph of Love), declares: 'Questo libro à ffatto scrivere mona Ghostantia donna fu di Benedetto Cicciaporci el quale alibro à ffatto fare per consolatione dell'anima sua e secondariamente a chonsolazione delle sue figliuole' (Costanza, wife of the late Benedetto Cicciaporci, had this book written. She had it made for the consolation of her soul and secondly for the consolation of her daughters). The manuscript passed, in fact, into the possession of one of her daughters, Lucrezia.[75]

Within convents, manuscript books could be made to order for individual nuns who did not wish to create their own books, did not

[73] De Marinis, *La Biblioteca napoletana*, II, 245, doc. 190; Toscano, 'Livres et lectures', p. 296; Toscano, 'I manoscritti miniati'; Bianca, 'Le biblioteche', p. 405.

[74] Mirella Levi d'Ancona, *Miniatura e miniatori a Firenze dal XIV al XVI secolo: documenti per la storia della miniatura* (Florence: Olschki, 1962), pp. 31, 35. On a Book of Hours illuminated by this artist, see Maria Grazia Ciardi Duprè Dal Poggetto, 'Un offiziolo "camereccio" e altre cose di Bartolomeo Varnucci', *Antichità viva*, 10.5 (1971), 39–48. On books owned by Florentine women, see Bryce, 'Les Livres des Florentines'.

[75] BNCF, MS II II 89, fol. 144[r]; see Carlo Delcorno, 'Per l'edizione delle *Vite dei Santi Padri* del Cavalca', *Lettere italiane*, 30 (1978), 47–87 (pp. 55–57). Costanza's husband may have been the 'B. Ciciaporci' listed as the author of a canzone da ballo in the *Croniche fiorentine* of Benedetto Dei, who died in 1492: Francesco Luisi, 'Minima fiorentina: sonetti a mente, canzoni a ballo e cantimpanca nel Quattrocento', in *Musica franca: Essays in Honor of Frank A. D'Accone*, ed. by Irene Alm, Alyson McLamore and Colleen Reardon (Stuyvesant, NY: Pendragon Press, 1996), pp. 79–95 (p. 89).

have the time or the ability to do so or wanted a product of professional standard. An example that illustrates how, in this context, too, such commissions could be linked to family bonds comes from fifteenth-century Siena. Here the Augustinian nuns of Santa Marta wrote to the Gesuate nuns of Sant'Abundio requesting payment for an office and a psalter that they had copied. A separate invoice for illumination was to follow; perhaps this task had been subcontracted to a male professional. The nuns also requested another payment for a third book, a larger psalter:

> Mandiamvi questo exemplo del comuno, che ci avete mandato a chiedare, lo quale è fornito. [...] Et vorremo che mandaste el resto de' denari di questa scriptura di questo psalterio piccolo, del quale havete già dato lire xxiiii et restate a dare lire sei per resto de la scriptura, cioè per questo comuno che abiamo scripto hora. De la miniatura non ve ne parlo hora: faremo poi di per sé un'altra volta: et di questo vi preghiamo, che n'aviamo bisogno per la festa nostra di sancta Martha: et dire a quella di quello altro psalterio maggiore, che ci mandi e' danari per conto di quinterni tredici. Non ci arricordiamo di patto, se non che alla nostra stima verrebbe vincti soldi el quinterno e non ne vorremo mancho.

> (We send you this sample of the office that you sent to request from us, and is completed. [...] We would like you to send the rest of the money for writing this small psalter, for which you have already given 24 lire and you owe 6 lire for the rest of the writing, that is, for this office that we have written now. About the illumination I will not speak to you now; we will do this separately another time. And we ask you for this because we need it for our feast of St Martha [29 July]. And ask [that nun] about that other bigger psalter, to send us the money for thirteen gatherings. We cannot recall an agreement, except that in our estimate it would come to 20 soldi the gathering and we would not wish less.)

The Augustinians had another, more practical, request to make. They lived just within the city walls, but they had heard that the nuns of Sant'Abundio, whose convent lay a little way outside the city, kept geese, and so their letter, becoming touchingly informal, took the opportunity to ask for a gift of quills. A sister also sent her greetings to her aunt in Sant'Abundio and asked for quills for her personal use:

> Vorremo in grande servitio ci serviste di qualche penna buona da scrivare che c'è stato decto che tenete dell'oche. Salutate suor Cornelia da parte della sua nipote suor Orsola de' Sozzini: et dice ancora lei s'ella li potesse mandare due o tre penne, che impara a scrivare, et dice che se la à fare scrivare psalterio, ho nulla altra cosa, che 'l mandi a posta alliei, che come l'arà imparato che glielo

scrivarà, sì che s'ella ci manda mai nulla facci richiedare suor Orsola di Francesco Sozzini partitamente, et dare nelle sue mani.[76]

(We would like you as a great favour to provide us with some good quills for writing, because we have been told that you keep geese. Greet Sister Cornelia on behalf of her niece Sister Orsola Sozzini. And [Orsola], too, asks if [Cornelia] could send two or three quills, because she is learning to write, and [Orsola] says that if [Cornelia] has to have a psalter or something else written, she will send it expressly to her, for as soon as she has learned she will write it for her; so that if [Cornelia] ever sends anything, have Sister Orsola di Francesco Sozzini asked for separately, and have it delivered to her hands.)

Another case in which one convent ordered a high-quality manuscript from another concerns Florence and the Benedictine nuns of Le Murate, whose commercial scribal activities were mentioned in Chapter 2. In 1511 the nuns of another Benedictine convent in the city, Sant'Ambrogio, needed a diurnal (containing the text of the monastic services held between dawn and nightfall). They ordered it from their neighbours in Le Murate and made further payments for decoration by Attavante Attavanti and for binding. The priest (and later bishop) Giovanni Battista Bonciani acted as go-between, as is shown by the records of the transaction, the first of which is dated 23 September:

E a dì 23 detto lire ventotto paghate a madonna delle Murate per la schrittura d'uno libriccino detto diurnaluzo per le monache portò messer Giovanbatista Bonciani chonto a uscita segnato J, c. 235 – lire 28.

E insino a dì 9 detto lire otto paghate a Vante miniatore per la miniatura del sopra detto diurnaluzo, portò messer Giovanbatista detto a uscita segnato J, c. 285 – lire 8.

E a dì 24 detto lire due soldi due paghati a Raffaello chartolaio per la leghatura di detto diurnaluzo portò e[l] detto chontanti a uscita segnato J, c. 285 – lire 2 soldi 2.[77]

---

[76] Scipione Borghesi and Luciano Banchi, *Nuovi documenti per la storia dell'arte senese* (Siena: Torrini, 1898), pp. 361–62. The source is given as Siena, Archivio di Stato, Carte del Monastero di S. Abundio. The papers of the monastery are now in Siena, Biblioteca Comunale degli Intronati, MS B. X. 7. Another partial translation is found in Mary Rogers and Paola Tinagli, *Women in Italy, 1350–1650: Ideals and Realities. A Sourcebook* (Manchester University Press, 2005), p. 219. On Santa Marta, see Diana Norman, 'An Abbess and a Painter: Emilia Pannocchieschi d'Elci and a Fresco from the Circle of Simone Martini', *Renaissance Studies*, 14 (2000), 273–300. On Sant'Abundio as a convent of Gesuate, see Colleen Reardon, '*Veni sponsa Christi*: Investiture, Profession and Consecration Ceremonies in Sienese Convents', *Musica Disciplina*, 50 (1996), 271–97 (p. 285).

[77] ASF, Conv. Soppr. 79, filza 60, fol. 253, cited in Eve Borsook, 'Cults and Imagery at Sant'Ambrogio in Florence', *Mitteilungen des Kunsthistorischen Institutes in Florenz*, 25 (1981), 147–202 (pp. 184, 202); see also Innocenzo Cervelli, 'Bonciani, Giovanni Battista', *DBI*, 11 (1969), 676, and Lowe, 'Women's Work', pp. 141–42.

(And on the said 23rd day twenty-eight lire paid to the abbess of Le Murate for writing a little book called little diurnal for the nuns, Giovambatista Bonciani took the money, expenditure account J, fol. 235 – 28 lire.

And until the said 9th day eight lire paid to Attavante miniaturist for the illumination of the above-mentioned little diurnal, the said Giovambatista took it, expenditure account J, fol. 285 – 8 lire.

And on the said 24th day two lire two soldi paid to Raffaello stationer for the binding of the said little diurnal, the said man took it cash, expenditure account J, fol. 285 – 2 lire 2 soldi.)

Nuns could receive a personal income from the investment of their dowries,[78] and in the collections of the British Library are examples of manuscripts that were commissioned by nuns with their own resources. A splendid missal on vellum was made for Sandra Cianchini, abbess of a convent near Pontassieve in Tuscany. The script and decorations are evidently the work of professionals. The opening (fol. 7$^r$) has fine illuminated margins and initials. The colophon tells us about the commission:

Anno domini Millesimo cccc°lvij tempore quo sanctissimus in Christo pater et dominus Calixtus papa tertius Rome residebat. Domina Sandra Iohannis Cianchini de Gavignano abbatissa monasterij sancte Marie de Rosano ordinis sancti Benedicti diocessis Fesulane civis tunc presul erat dominus Leonardus de Pescia Istud singulare missale fecit fieri ad honorem Dei et beate Marie virginis. Amen. In quo vel pro quo missali ipsa predicta domina Sandra abbatissa dicti monasterij spendidit et exposuit quinquagi[n]ta florenos sermone vulgari di sogiello. Hec scripta.[79] (fol. 292$^r$)

(In the year of our Lord 1457, when the most holy father in Christ and lord Pope Calixtus III was residing in Rome [1455–58], lady Sandra di Giovanni Cianchini of Gavignano, abbess of the monastery of Santa Maria at Rosano, of the order of St Benedict, in the diocese of Fiesole, whose bishop was then lord Leonardo [Salutati] of Pescia, had this singular missal made in honour of God and the Blessed Virgin Mary. Amen. In which or for which missal the aforesaid lady Sandra abbess of

---

[78] Weaver, *Convent Theatre*, pp. 28–29. Suor Angelica Baitelli would have received 100 lire annually through a bequest from her aristocratic father: Evangelisti, 'Angelica Baitelli', p. 72.

[79] MS Add. 14802; see Watson, *Catalogue of Dated and Datable Manuscripts*, I, no. III. Fiorini di suggello or sealed florins (coins kept in sealed bags) were worth slightly less than gold florins: see Goldthwaite, *The Economy of Renaissance Florence*, pp. 52–54. Below the colophon has been added a list of donations made to the convent by the abbess's brother Piero in 1457 and 1459, including three farms, two glass windows in the church and a small house in the country ('un casolare'). The notes suggest that Sandra died in 1457.

the said monastery spent and offered fifty florins known in the vernacular as sealed. These things were written.)

A decorated breviary was made for a Piedmontese novice on her entry into the convent of Scala Coeli in Genoa, and a rubric preceding the psalter records her motivation:

> MCCCCLXX die dominico xviii Februarii, eodem die pro septuagesima currente, ego soror Margarita filia Alexii Salucii ingressa sum monasterium sacre observantie sanctarum Marie virginis et Brigide de Ianua nuncupatum. Et ad honorem Dei et salutem anime mee hunc breviarium secundum ordinem nostrum pro meo usu scribi volui. Qui liber inceptus est die XV Martii eiusdem anni. (fol. 16$^r$; Figure 3.2)[80]

> (On Septuagesima Sunday 18 February 1470, I, Sister Margarita, daughter of Alessio of Saluzzo, entered the monastery called of the holy observance of Saints Mary the Virgin and Birgitta in Genoa. And for the honour of God and the salvation of my soul I wished this breviary according to our order to be written for my use. Which book was begun on 25 March of the same year.)

A much humbler manuscript, undecorated, contains an investiture ceremony for novice Clarissans (*Ordo quando aliqua de novo ingreditur monasterium*).[81] Its colophon, which is in the vernacular, indicates the sister who commissioned copying and presumably intended it for use in her institution: 'Questo libro à facto scrivere la veneranda suora Agata di Nicolò d'Andrea Nicoli. Pregate Dio per lei. A dì venti d'octobre 1518' (fol. 24$^r$; The venerable Sister Agata di Nicolò d'Andrea Nicoli had this book written. Pray to God for her. 20 October 1518). The hand is somewhat uncertain, perhaps that of another nun of the convent.

Taken together, these commissions by laywomen and nuns suggest that, unlike men, women had manuscripts made to order chiefly when they needed a book that would accompany their everyday devotions or that would provide spiritual 'consolation'.[82] Women could be motivated by their desire for personal salvation, and we saw in the previous chapter that this was also the case with the manuscripts that they copied themselves. They could order copying as individuals or as a group, in the case of convents. Within these institutions, the community-building function of the commissions is evident, but the commissions of individual laywomen

---

[80]  MS Add. 38604; see Watson, *Catalogue of Dated and Datable Manuscripts*, I, no. 389.

[81]  MS Harl. 2920; see Watson, *Catalogue of Dated and Datable Manuscripts*, I, no. 714. The order can be identified from the mentions of Sts Francis and Clare on fols 10$^v$, 16$^r$ and 27$^r$.

[82]  On the spiritual and even curative functions of women's reading in the period after the Council of Trent, see Tippelskirch, *Sotto controllo*, pp. 69–78.

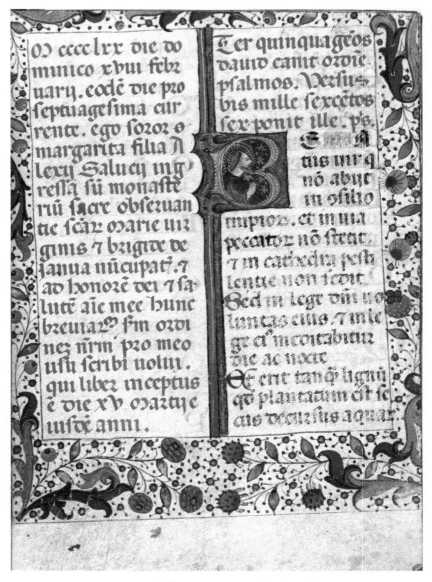

Figure 3.2 Breviary made for suor Margarita of Scala Coeli, Genoa, 1470.
© The British Library Board. MS Add. 38604, fol. 16ʳ

and clerics, too, could serve to enhance their prestige in the eyes of their peer group or to strengthen bonds between female members of a family.

## Purchasing Books

While only well-to-do women could afford to have a manuscript written for themselves, a wider range of women could purchase books ready-made from booksellers or from another person, even if they did so less frequently than men.[83]

Fine manuscripts were sought out by some laywomen from wealthy families. Isotta Nogarola implied in a letter to an uncle that she needed his financial help to buy a manuscript of the historian Livy that was in her hands but would cost her fifty gold coins.[84] Ippolita Sforza could afford to spend more freely. As she travelled southwards from Milan in 1465 to marry the future king of Naples, she stayed with the Medici family in Florence and took the opportunity to purchase a manuscript of a work of Ptolemy, maybe the *Geographia*, and maybe in a copy similar to that now in the New York Public Library (MS MA 97), which was made in Florence in the 1460s or 1470s.[85] At the end of the following year, Ippolita's secretary in Naples, Baldo Martorelli, informed her mother in a letter that the young princess was incurring considerable expenses in her new married life, including a large sum spent on an unspecified book. Rather than being concerned by this, he was proud that she had made this purchase at her own initiative: 'uno libro XL ducati, né l'ha comprato de mio recordo, anze de sua propria volontà, come fece el Tolomeo a Fiorenza' (a book for 40 ducats, nor did she buy it at my suggestion, but rather of her own will, as she did with the Ptolemy in Florence).[86]

The printing business that operated in the Dominican convent of San Iacopo di Ripoli in Florence in the years around 1480, mentioned in the last section of Chapter 2, produced books that were much more affordable, and it sold some of them both to and through women. Printing of a vernacular version of the life of St Catherine of Siena by fra Raimondo Della Vigna (Raimundus De Vineis), the *Legenda della mirabile vergine Beata Caterina da Siena*, was completed on 24 March 1477. Notes in a copy in the

---

[83] In Pavia, for example, booksellers recorded no sales of books to women: Porqueddu, *Il patriziato pavese*, p. 226.
[84] Nogarola, *Opera*, I, 44; Nogarola, *Complete Writings*, p. 39.
[85] Jonathan J. G. Alexander, James H. Marrow and Lucy Freeman Sandler, *The Splendor of the Word: Medieval and Renaissance Manuscripts at the New York Public Library* (London and Turnhout: New York Public Library and Harvey Miller, 2005), cat. no. 77, pp. 340–42.
[86] Letter to Eleonora d'Aragona, 29 December 1466, in De Marinis, *La Biblioteca napoletana*, I, facsimile between pages 98 and 99; Sforza, *Lettere*, p. lxxix.

Biblioteca Riccardiana, Florence, record two early owners as a woman of
Picchena, near San Gimignano, and then another woman who was probably her daughter: 'Questo libro è di monna Dianora di Lamberto da
Picchena. Questo libro è di monna Lisabetta di Jacopo da Picchena'.[87] The
wife of a certain Lenzone bought a copy of the work in October 1477,
although the record of the transaction is somewhat unclear:

> A dì 25 la moglie di Lenzone … ebbe una legenda di sancta Katerina sciolta
> portolla uno suo figlulo e ser Stefano prete maestro che insegnia legere ai
> suoi figliuoli àcci a dà e danari riportolla. […] El dì di sancto Symone e Juda
> la soprascripta donna di Lenzone ebbe una legenda come di sopra cioè
> istampiamola. A dì 9 di dicembre ricevo soldi 40 per la soprascripta legenda –
> lire 2.[88]

> (On the 25th the wife of Lenzone … had a *Legenda* of St Catherine,
> unbound. One of her sons took it, and ser Stefano, the priest and school-
> master who is teaching her sons to read, owes us the money; he brought [the
> *Legenda*] back. […] On the feast of Sts Simon and Jude [28 October] the
> above-mentioned wife of Lenzone had a *Legenda* as above, i.e. we are
> printing it. On 9 December I receive 40 soldi for the above-mentioned
> *Legenda* – 2 lire.)

In May 1477, a monna Lorenza received a copy of the *Legenda* that she
returned in June; in July 1481, fra Barnaba of San Marco took a bound and
decorated copy to show to a woman who wanted to buy it, but later
returned it. A nun in the convent purchased a school textbook for a male
relative in July 1477: 'Entrata a dì 29 di ditto da suor Betta per uno
Donatello pel cugniato – soldi 6' (Paid on the 29th of the said month,
from Sister Betta for a Donatello [elementary Latin grammar] for her
brother-in-law). Monna Marietta, widow of Bernardo della Tosa, paid
30 soldi for a *Confessionale* in February 1477/8.[89]

The *Legenda* of St Catherine was the first substantial volume issued by the
Ripoli press, and a fairly costly one. Fra Domenico da Pistoia, the director of
the press, records in the daybook the distribution and sale of copies for
between 2 and 3 lire, equivalent to around three or four days' wages for
a skilled labourer. One of the marketing techniques he used at an early stage
was to give copies not only to men, but also to prioresses of other Dominican
houses and to a laywoman, so that they could try to sell them on the press's

---

[87] Conway, *The 'Diario'*, p. 70, n. 22.
[88] Ibid., p. 135. 'Àcci a dà', i.e. 'a dare', is conjectural; Conway transcribes 'acciada'. Compare 'accia
dare', p. 145, and 'aveva a dare annoi', p. 148.
[89] Ibid., pp. 119 (Lorenza), 209 (fra Barnaba), 110 (suor Betta), 152 (Marietta).

behalf. The success of these women was mixed. The prioress of San Vincenzo d'Annalena, in the Oltrarno, managed to sell only one of the two *Legende* placed with her. The prioress of Santa Lucia returned her copy, and fra Domenico had no better luck when he passed it on to the prioress of San Giuliano. A copy was sold, however, through a certain monna Gianna, and in July some unspecified nuns, presumably those of San Iacopo, sold a *Legenda* for 3 lire.[90] This evidence suggests at least the possibility that other presses, too, used networks of women as informal agents for the sale of certain kinds of books to other women.

In Chapter 1 and earlier in the present chapter, we saw how the pious reputation of Renée de France, Duchess of Ferrara, encouraged some male authors to dedicate editions of their works to her or to give her copies of them. Both Renée's piety and her close interest in the reform of the Church were supported by her acquisition of a substantial number of books for herself and for her household, which had over 160 members.[91] She took responsibility for the education of her three daughters, born between 1531 and 1537, of her male and female servants and even of several of their children, and naturally she wanted to encourage their reading and discussion of Scripture. For this purpose as well as for her own edification, Renée bought, and had copied out, various kinds of texts, as her records of expenditure show.[92] Most favoured were French and Italian translations

[90] Especially on fols 13–18 of the daybook. The friar's notes include: 'A dì 28 di ditto detti alla priora di Sancto Vincentio dell'ordine nostro due legende di sancta Katerina perché ce le vendessi. Ànne vendute una e datomi e denari cioè l'à vendute lire tre – lire tre. [. . .] A dì detto detti alla priora di Sancta Lucia dell'ordine nostro una delle legende di sancta Katerina per che ce la vendessi. La detta legenda riavemola a dì 9 d'aprile e portamola alla priora di Sancto Giuliano. Rendeccela. [. . .] A dì 9 d'aprile una legenda a mona Giana vendella a dì 14 di magio. [. . .] A dì 9 di luglio portai alla priora di Sancto Vincentio dell'ordine nostro due legende di sancta Katerina perché ce le vendessi rendute. [. . .] A dì 24 di luglio le monache venderono una legenda lire tre.' Conway, *The 'Diario'*, pp. 115, 120, 121. ('On the 28th of the said month [March 1477], I gave the prioress of San Vincenzo of our order two *Legende* of St Catherine so that she could sell them for us. She has sold one and given me the money, i.e. she has sold it for 3 lire. [. . .] On the said day I gave the prioress of Santa Lucia of our order one of the *Legende* of St Catherine so that she could sell it for us. We had the said *Legenda* back on 9 April and took it to the prioress of San Giuliano. She gave it back to us. [. . .] On 9 April, a *Legenda* to monna Gianna; she sold it on 14 May. [. . .] On 9 July, I took to the prioress of San Vincenzo of our order two *Legende* of St Catherine so that she could sell them for us; returned. [. . .] On 24 July, the nuns sold a *Legenda* for 3 lire.) See also Rouse and Rouse, *Cartolai, Illuminators and Printers*, pp. 44–45. Three copies were sold in May 1477 for 2 lire 10 soldi, and another in December for 2 lire (Conway, *The 'Diario'*, pp. 119, 143). The press might also lend a book: on 28 February 1481/2, for instance, fra Lorenzo 'nostro' ('our' friar Lorenzo) borrowed two confessionals, a bound *Defecerunt* and an unbound *Omnis mortalium cura*, in order to lend them to the widow of Donato Acciaiuoli (ibid., p. 224).
[91] On the problems caused by the duchess's large 'famiglia', see Gino Benzoni, 'Ercole II d'Este', *DBI*, 43 (1993), 107–26 (p. 111).
[92] Franceschini, '"Literarum studia nobis communia"', pp. 207–32 (pp. 211–16; the quotations that follow are from p. 212). The accounts are in the registers of Turin, Archivio di Stato, Camera dei

of all or parts of the Bible, especially the Psalms. Perhaps these were also
used by those learning to read, in place of Latin texts. Thus in 1535 two
psalters were purchased for Renée's four-year-old daughter Anna. One was
a commissioned manuscript, a payment of 10 lire and 8 bolognini being
made 'pour escripture d'un petit livre en parchemin contenant Les Sept
Pseaulmes pour servir a madame la princesse' (for writing a small book on
vellum containing the Seven Psalms, for the use of my lady the princess);
the other was 'ung Psautier de l'impression de Venise' (a psalter printed in
Venice), probably one of the editions of Brucioli's version printed in 1531
and 1534, which was mentioned earlier as one of the gifts made by Lorenzo
Lotto. Other purchases included works on Latin and Greek grammar and
literary works by authors such as Plautus, Terence and Homer in the
original Latin or Greek. The books were normally bought by male court
officials on Renée's behalf. Until 1544 they were ordered from Venice and
occasionally from Bologna; thereafter most were purchased from, or bound
by, the Ferrarese bookseller Paride della Mella. Brucioli and others must
have known of this programme of reading when making the dedications to
Renée's daughters that were mentioned in the first chapter. At least one of
Renée's own volumes was bound for her in white calfskin by a binder based
in Bologna: a book of games based on cultural knowledge, *Cento giuochi
liberali et d'ingegno* (Bologna: Anselmo Giaccarelli at the author's expense,
1551), written by Innocenzio Ringhieri and dedicated by him to the French
queen, Catherine de' Medici. The personal nature of its binding suggests it
was commissioned by Renée herself: the front cover has the motto 'Di real
sangue nata' (Born of royal blood), while the back has the punning motto
'In Christo sol Renata' (Renata/Reborn in Christ alone). This copy, now in
the Fondazione Giorgio Cini in Venice, may be the only book to survive
from Renée's library; many volumes of hers were burned in 1600 because of
the suspicions surrounding her heterodoxy.[93]

The account book of an upper-class Florentine widow, Maria Ridolfi
Strozzi, shows that she bought '6 canzonieri de imparar musica' (6 song-
books for learning music) for her son Filippo in 1553. It is likely that women
also purchased such books for use in their own social entertainments. At

conti di Piemonte, Conti e ricapiti delle Case de' signori duca di Genevois, Nemours, Aumale,
Chartres e Gisors dal 1397 al 1686.

[93] Tammaro De Marinis, 'Legatura artistica fatta per Renata di Francia Duchessa di Ferrara',
*Gutenberg-Jahrbuch* (1964), 373–74; Piccarda Quilici, 'Legature di corte italiane', in *Il libro a corte*,
ed. by Amedeo Quondam (Rome: Bulzoni, 1994), pp. 239–72 (p. 257); Belligni, *Renata di Francia*,
pp. 286, 320–21. On this work, see James Haar, 'On Musical Games in the 16th Century', *Journal of
the American Musicological Society*, 15 (1962), 22–34; Lina Bolzoni, *La stanza della memoria: modelli
letterari e iconografici nell'età della stampa* (Turin: Einaudi, 1995), pp. 120–26.

the start of this chapter, it was noted that the courtesan Imperia was said to have music books on display. The title page of Andrea Antico's *Frottole intabulate da sonare organi* (Rome: Andrea Antico, 1517) has a woodcut image of a woman at the keyboard and another woman singing (with a monkey playing the lute),[94] while Leandro Bassano's portrayal of a family's music-making in *The Concert* (1592; Florence, Galleria degli Uffizi) depicts an old woman playing from a music book in the foreground, surrounded by males and other women who are using other music books.

Although, as we saw in Chapter 2, nuns might produce their own books in order to support their devotions, some convents, even those that numbered scribes and miniaturists among their members, would need to acquire books from outside their walls. A basic necessity was a missal, and in the early sixteenth century the Dominicans of San Giorgio in Lucca were given 'un messale et altri fornimenti per dir la messa' (a missal and other necessary items to say mass) by fra Nicolao Michelozzi of the Dominicans of San Romano.[95] More often, nuns would have to purchase books for services. Chiara Gambacorta, founder of the convent of San Domenico in Pisa in the late fourteenth century, wrote to a book dealer to say that her community was glad of all books, but had special need of a lectionary (containing Bible readings) or a Bible.[96] The accounts of the convent of Monteluce in Perugia record that two expensive manuscript breviaries were bought in 1460–61 by the abbess Lucia di Pietro da Foligno, in one case from a friar for 28 florins, in the other from a monk for 18 florins.[97] The same house paid for two books in 1535: 'fo comprato un messale in forma de lectera grossa; et uno libero dicto deli Sancti padri pure in forma per lo coro' (we bought a printed missal in large print, and a book entitled of the Holy Fathers [Cavalca's translation of the *Vitae Patrum*], also printed, for the choir).[98] There is also a record of one sister of Monteluce selling a book to another in the early sixteenth century, with the money going to the convent: 'li dicte dinare receve del breviario che sora Christina ha venduto a sora Tecla' ([the convent] receives the said money for the breviary that suor Cristina has sold to suor Tecla).[99] In 1462, the nuns of Santa Brigida al Paradiso in Florence bought a manuscript of sermons by St Bernard for 30

[94] Flora Dennis, 'Music', in *At Home in Renaissance Italy*, ed. by Ajmar-Wollheim and Dennis, pp. 228–43 (p. 232). The significance of the image is discussed in Kate van Orden, *Music, Authorship, and the Book in the First Century of Print* (Berkeley: University of California Press, 2014), pp. 34–35.
[95] Coli, *La Cronaca del monastero domenicano*, p. 245.
[96] Roberts, *Dominican Women and Renaissance Art*, p. 26.
[97] Nicolini, 'I minori osservanti di Monteripido', p. 109.    [98] *Memoriale di Monteluce*, p. 140.
[99] Baldelli, 'Codici e carte di Monteluce', p. 387.

lire, using as intermediary a frate Egidio, who was a member and occasional scribe of their convent.[100] Sisters of the convent of San Domenico in Pisa paid, through their confessor, for the illumination of a lectionary in Florence in 1519–20.[101] The Milanese convent of Santa Maria Maddalena del Cerchio, mentioned earlier in this chapter, made purchases of missals and other unspecified 'libri spirituali'.[102]

Detailed evidence for purchases made by nuns around the end of the sixteenth century comes from the credit ledger of a small-scale Florentine bookseller, Piero di Giuliano Morosi, whose commercial activities, carried out in a shop near the Bargello between 1589 and 1608, have been studied by Tim Carter, Paul Gehl and others.[103] Of course, sales made on credit to trusted clients would have been different in nature from cash sales made to passing customers, but records of them can still shed light both on the extent to which some women made purchases from bookshops and on the ways in which they shopped. Morosi specialized in selling printed liturgical books, prayer books and other devotional literature to religious institutions and to private citizens. To judge from his credit business, laywomen and nuns formed a minority, but a fairly substantial minority, of the customers of bookshops in general. Morosi's ledger lists in total 3,073 sales to 459 customers, of whom 98 (some 21 per cent) were women. Just 14 of these were laywomen. The high proportion of female clergy in comparison with laywomen, around 86 per cent, is to be expected in view of the nature of Morosi's stock, but it is higher than that of male clergy to laymen, about 40 per cent. The nuns, who came from twenty Florentine convents including Le Murate, bought mainly breviaries and diurnals in octavo, and offices of individual saints. One of the bestsellers among the convent clientele was a breviary annotated in the ledger as 'calice', referring to the woodcut of a chalice on its title page (Venice: Lucantonio Giunti the

---

[100] BNCF, MS Conv. Soppr. E I 1321; Miriello, *I manoscritti del Monastero del Paradiso*, pp. 15, 43, 116–17.

[101] Roberts, *Dominican Women and Renaissance Art*, p. 26.

[102] Zardin, *Donna e religiosa*, pp. 206–07.

[103] Tim Carter, 'Music-Selling in Late Sixteenth-Century Florence: The Bookshop of Piero di Giuliano Morosi', *Music and Letters*, 70 (1989), 483–504; Paul F. Gehl, 'Libri per donne: le monache clienti del libraio fiorentino Piero Morosi (1588–1607)', in *Donna, disciplina, creanza cristiana dal XV al XVII secolo: studi e testi a stampa*, ed. by Gabriella Zarri (Rome: Edizioni di Storia e Letteratura, 1996), pp. 67–82; Gehl, 'Credit Sales Strategies in the Late Cinquecento Book Trade', in *Libri, tipografi, biblioteche: ricerche storiche dedicate a Luigi Balsamo*, ed. by Istituto di Biblioteconomia e Paleografia, Università degli Studi, Parma, 2 vols (Florence: Olschki, 1997), I, 193–206 (pp. 195–97, 203–04). I follow here the figures given in the last of these essays, pp. 193, 197, 198.

Younger, 1572). Among devotional works, a leading title was the *Giardino spirituale* of the Milanese cleric Paolo Morigia.

Morosi got to know the nuns who were his customers personally. When he cannot recall the name of one of them, he describes her as 'quella guercia piccina' (that little cross-eyed one).[104] Two records show that he could have met them either in his shop or in their convents. Suor Brigida, the purchasing agent for the Franciscan convent of Sant'Orsola, was a regular customer of Morosi's for four years, during which she purchased seventy-one items over twenty-nine occasions. On 13 October 1590, he recorded sales to her of books including a tiny office whose binding was decorated with gold tooling, and noted that she was to collect them: 'Suora Brigida in Sant'Orsola de' dare per li a pie, leva lei ... uno Officio 64, con oro, L2' (Sister Brigida in the St Orsola convent owes for the items below, to be taken away by her ... 1 office, 64mo, with gold, at Lire 2).[105] Suor Fiammetta, a customer from another Franciscan convent, Santi Girolamo e Francesco, placed an order in 1589 worth 11 lire for two printed books, a small-format diurnal and an Office of the Virgin. Both were finely bound, with 'carte smaltate, cordovano nero pien d'oro, arabeschi, lettere, serami milanesi' (glazed edges, black cordovan full gilt, gilt arabesques, gilt initials, Milanese-style clasps). Morosi himself took these books to the convent, south of the Arno, and received his cash 'alle grate', in other words through the gratings that separated the nuns from the outside world.[106]

Morosi had books bound for his customers, in-house or by outside craftsmen. The entry for suor Brigida just cited mentions some extra binding work carried out for her on two Books of Hours and on another book: 'per avere messo i serami a dua libricini con le fette di quoio, tutte indorate, milanese, s13.d4; per legatura di uno diurno ... d'accordo' (for attaching clasps to two little books with leather ties, full gilt, Milanese-style, soldi 13 denari 4; for the binding of a diurnal, as agreed).[107]

While nuns made purchases from Morosi on behalf of their convent as a whole, they also appear to have bought at least some books for their personal use, using their own financial resources or those of their families. Significantly, the bindings commissioned by them could reflect their continuing attachment to their families of origin. Two copies of a monastic breviary of 1592 now in the Biblioteca Nazionale of Florence were bound with the nuns' religious name picked out in gold on the front

[104] Gehl, 'Libri per donne', p. 69.

[105] Paul F. Gehl, 'Describing (and Selling) Bindings in Sixteenth-Century Florence', *Italian Studies*, 53 (1998), 38–51 (p. 41).

[106] Ibid., p. 48.     [107] Ibid., p. 42.

cover and the name of their patrician families on the back cover: in one case, the owner is suor Maura Bacci (Magl. 15.7.738); in the other, it is suor Prudenza Baldovinetti (B.10_33).[108] These breviaries thus display simultaneous allegiances to two communities, one social, the other spiritual.

Several of Morosi's sales were made to men who were acting on behalf of women, and his records thus also illustrate the practice of having books bought by agents.[109] Respectable Italian laywomen would normally not have shopped for themselves but would have made purchases through male intermediaries or relatives. In this way they could avoid appearing in public places and being seen as personally involved in negotiation, since prices of books, like those of other goods, fluctuated and some bartering might be involved.[110] Moreover, women could extend their range of choice by comparing the offers made to those acting on their behalf.[111]

However, as Filippo de Vivo has written of early modern Venice, 'women's possibilities for frequenting public spaces were inversely proportional to their social status'.[112] Women of lower rank would thus have had the opportunity to buy the books offered by pedlars such as the 'Libraro' (bookseller) and seller of 'belle historie' (fine stories) depicted in Ambrogio Brambilla's print of Roman street sellers and their cries, *Ritratto de quelli che vanno vendendo et lavorando per Roma* (Portrait of those who go around Rome selling and working), of 1582.[113] There was a long-standing tradition of itinerant tradesmen selling cheap texts and images, especially on feast days, along with services or items such as remedies or perfumes.[114]

Among the cheap items that pedlars sold mainly to or for women were flag-shaped fans consisting of a sheet of paper folded in two, with the two halves then glued together and attached to a wooden handle. These fans

---

[108]  Gehl, 'Libri per donne', pp. 77 and 82, Figures 2 and 3.        [109]  Ibid., p. 69.

[110]  Carter, 'Music-Selling in Late Sixteenth-Century Florence', p. 496; Evelyn S. Welch, *Shopping in the Renaissance: Consumer Cultures in Italy 1400–1600* (New Haven: Yale University Press, 2005), pp. 85–92.

[111]  Welch, 'The Art of Expenditure', p. 312; Welch, *Shopping in the Renaissance*, pp. 218–25; Gentilcore, *Medical Charlatanism*, p. 248.

[112]  De Vivo, *Information and Communication*, p. 113.

[113]  On depictions of street sellers in Rome, see Jean Delumeau, *Vie économique et sociale de Rome dans la seconde moitié du XVIᵉ siècle*, 2 vols (Paris: De Boccard, 1957–59), I, 29–30 and Figure 1, between pages 112 and 113; Masetti Zannini, *Stampatori e librai*, pp. 10–13. Brambilla's print is reproduced in Cesare D'Onofrio, *Roma nel Seicento* (Florence: Vallecchi, 1969), and in Brice Gruet, *La Rue à Rome, miroir de la ville: entre l'émotion et la norme* (Paris: Presses de l'Université Paris Sorbonne, 2006), pp. 196–200 (Figure 96).

[114]  Rosa Salzberg, '"In the Mouths of Charlatans": Street Performers and the Dissemination of Pamphlets in Renaissance Italy', *Renaissance Studies*, 24 (2010), 638–53; Salzberg, '"Selling Stories and Many Other Things in and Through the City": Peddling Print in Sixteenth-Century Florence and Venice', *Sixteenth Century Journal*, 42 (2011), 737–59 (pp. 737, 738, n. 4, 743, 749–50).

could have more than a practical function since, as well as being patterned (as depicted for example in Paolo Veronese's *Venus and Adonis* of *c*. 1580 in the Museo del Prado, Madrid), the paper was often printed with the texts of poems or woodcut images.[115] An example of a text intended self-referentially for use as a fan is a single leaf containing Giulio Cesare Croce's *Capitolo in lode delle ventarole* (Capitolo in praise of fans), which survives in a single copy, printed after 1575.[116] Cardinal Carlo Borromeo in Milan prohibited in 1578 sales of 'ventaline di cartone' (card fans) on which were printed 'storie, canzoni, sonetti, madrigali di tono lascivo' (stories, songs, sonnets, madrigals lewd in tone), after discovering that they were bought mainly by 'meretrici e ragazze da marito' (prostitutes and marriageable girls). Indeed, although one of Cesare Vecellio's images of noblewomen, specifically a contemporary Venetian noblewoman at a public festivity, shows her holding a fan, so does his image of a 'public prostitute'. Borromeo decreed that fans with texts had to be replaced by ones bearing the arms of the pope and the emperor.[117] Nevertheless, this kind of text was still produced with the Church's approval in Bologna up to the eighteenth century. A poem by Croce about the boys who sell fans was printed in the city in 1639 (*Barceletta piacevolissima, sopra i fanciulli, che vanno vendendo le ventarole per la città*) and again in 1725 (*Barceletta sopra i fanciulli, che vendono ventarole*) 'con licenza de' superiori' (with the licence of the superiors). The poem urges women to buy fans both painted and printed:

> Alle belle Ventarole,
> chi ne compra, e chi ne vole
> col suo manico garbato
> a piacer, e a buon mercato.
>
> Sù sù Donne, sù Donzelle,
> ecco qua come son belle,
> nobilmente lavorate,
> ben dipinte, e ben stampate.

(Come to the fine fans, some buy them and others want them, with their elegant handle, as you fancy them and cheap. Come on ladies, come on girls,

---

[115] Alberto Milano, 'Prints for Fans', *Print Quarterly*, 4 (1987), 2–19; Dennis, 'Music', pp. 240–41.

[116] This copy, and copies of the two editions mentioned below, is reproduced at https://bub.unibo.it /it/collezioni-e-cataloghi/giulio-cesare-croce/ (accessed 22 May 2019).

[117] Zardin, *Donna e religiosa*, p. 71. See Cesare Vecellio, *De gli habiti antichi et moderni di diverse parti del mondo* (Venice: Damiano Zenaro, 1590), fol. R3[r], illustrating 'Gentildonne a feste publiche', on which Vecellio writes: 'in mano portano bellissimi ventagli intessuti, che hanno il manico d'oro' (fol. R4[r]; they hold very beautiful woven fans with gold handles), and fol. T2[r], illustrating 'Meretrici publiche'.

look how beautiful they are, nobly wrought, finely painted and finely printed.)

One stanza describes the types of texts printed on the fans:

> Qua vedrete bei Sonetti,
> stanze, rime, e dotti detti,
> madrigali, e vilanelle,
> e capricci, e cose belle.

(Here you'll see fine sonnets, stanzas, rhymes, learned sayings, madrigals, villanellas, fancies and fine compositions.)

## Listening

A means of gaining access to texts that was perhaps more important for women than for men was through their voicing in speech or song, especially in the contexts of recreation or devotion. A performance might have just one or two listeners, but listening was also a collective activity, sometimes taking place in public. The selling of cheap books, just mentioned, could be linked with performances, by itinerant singers or 'charlatans', of the texts that they contained.[118] The audiences present at open-air entertainments were without doubt predominantly male, but there is some evidence that women could be present. A fifteenth-century *Cantare dei tre preti* refers to a public of 'damigelli e mercatanti, | uomini e ddonne' (fine young men and merchants, men and women), and the cantare of *Guiscardo e Gismonda* opens with an address to 'Done ligiadre e voi gioveni amanti, | che qui conduce voluntà d'udire' (Fair ladies and you, young lovers, brought to this place by a desire to hear).[119] The professional poet-performer Serafino Aquilano (1466–1500) found audiences among members of all social classes and among women, according to his contemporary biographer, Vincenzo Calmeta: 'Nel recitare de' soi poemi era tanto ardente e con tanto giudizio le parole con la musica consertava che l'animo de li ascoltanti, o dotti o mediocri o plebei o donne, equalmente commoveva' (In performing his verse, he was so passionate and he blended words and music so judiciously that he moved the spirit of listeners equally, whether they were learned or of middling status or lower-class

---

[118] Salzberg, "'Selling Stories and Many Other Things'", pp. 742, 749.
[119] *Cantari novellistici dal Tre al Cinquecento*, ed. by Elisabetta Benucci, Roberta Manetti and Franco Zabagli, 2 vols (Rome: Salerno Editrice, 2002), I, 272 (the textual variants noted here all refer to women) and II, 652.

or women).[120] Luca Degl'Innocenti has drawn attention to a woodcut of a performance by a singer – shown holding his *lira da braccio* – at which women are present, included in an edition of Luigi Pulci's chivalric romance *Morgante*, printed in Venice in 1521.[121] In an edition of the previous year, this image was intended to depict the poet Horace, and the setting was the countryside, but for the readers of the Pulci edition it would have corresponded with a familiar scene, a *cantastorie* performing before a mixed urban audience. And, as Degl'Innocenti has pointed out, the Florentine *cantastorie* Cristofano, known as l'Altissimo, twice refers to the 'muses' who were among his audience in Piazza San Martino in Florence in the early sixteenth century, which strongly suggests that women were present.[122] Giacomo Franco's engraving of the 'Intartenimento che dano ogni giorno li Ciarlatani in Piazza di S. Marco al Populo, d'ogni natione che mattina e sera ordinariamente vi concore' (Entertainment given daily by the charlatans in Piazza San Marco to the people of every nation who normally flock there morning and evening) shows one performer holding out a book, maybe for sale, and there is a woman – admittedly the only one – standing in a group further away in the square.[123]

Within the household, women might hear texts sung during social entertainments, as mentioned in the previous section, or read aloud for the purposes of recreation, information or devotion. Around 1490, Giovanni Sabadino degli Arienti of Bologna wrote that his late wife Francesca '[h]avea piacere assai in audire legere li versi de Virgilio' (took great pleasure in hearing Virgil's poetry read aloud), and that a widow of his city 'lege, ode et intende voluntiera cum atentione cose gentile' (reads, hears and understands noble things with pleasure and attentively).[124] The *Domenicale e santuario* of the devout Ferrarese humanist Lodovico Pittorio,

---

[120] Vincenzo Calmeta, 'Vita del facondo poeta vulgare Serafino Aquilano', in *Prose e lettere edite e inedite*, ed. by Cecil Grayson (Bologna: Commissione per i testi di lingua, 1959), pp. 60–77 (pp. 75–76).

[121] Luigi Pulci, *Morgante magiore* (Venice: Guglielmo da Fontaneto, 1521), fol. AA8ᵛ. See Luca Degl'Innocenti, 'Il poeta, la viola e l'incanto: per l'iconografia del canterino nel primo Cinquecento', in *'Al suon di questa cetra': ricerche sulla poesia orale del Rinascimento* (Florence: Società editrice fiorentina, 2016), pp. 65–77.

[122] Luca Degl'Innocenti, *I 'Reali' dell'Altissimo: un ciclo di cantari fra oralità e scrittura* (Florence: Società editrice fiorentina, 2008), p. 192, n. 28. The relevant passages in *Il primo libro de' Reali* (Venice: Giovanni Antonio Nicolini da Sabbio, 1534) are: 'Uditor degni, muse pellegrine' (XXIII. 12. 1; Worthy listeners, refined muses) and 'Uditor grati, muse e semidei' (XXV. 12. 1; Welcome listeners, muses and demigods).

[123] Giacomo Franco, *Habiti d'huomeni et donne venetiane* (Venice: Giacomo Franchi, 1609), unnumbered fol., reproduced for instance in Gentilcore, *Medical Charlatanism*, Figure 11.

[124] Giovanni Sabadino degli Arienti, *Gynevera delle clare donne*, ed. by Corrado Ricci and Alberto Bacchi della Lega (Bologna: Romagnoli, 1888), pp. 365, 376.

also known as Bigus (Modena: Domenico Rococciola, [*c.* 1498–1504?], and several sixteenth-century editions) was intended in part for reading aloud in the home: the full title claims that all families that included someone who could read should own the work, and whoever read or heard it would be consoled. The same author's collection of homilies for Lent, *Omiliario quadragisimale* (Modena: Domenico Rococciola, 1506), are dedicated to suor Beatrice d'Este, abbess of the convent of Sant'Antonio in Polesine, with the aim of providing 'lettione da far leggere alla mensa' (reading to be read aloud during mealtimes) for her and all the nuns. Pittorio explains that the length of his homilies is calculated to fit the time available: 'ho avvertito di far questo che le lettioni delle ferie siano sì longhe che ciascuna sia bastante per il legere di tutto il desinare e quelle delle domeniche per il desinare e per la cena insieme' (I have taken care to make the readings on weekdays long enough in each case for the midday meal and those on Sundays for the midday meal and supper together).[125] The trial of a certain Franceschina by the Holy Office in Venice in 1548 reveals that she had the apprentice of her husband, a silk-weaver, read to the couple from the Bible.[126] The practice of excerpting and compiling choice passages in miscellanies such as that of Costanza Cicciaporci, mentioned earlier in this chapter, also lent itself well to sociable reading. The author of the *Decor puellarum* was alert to the dangers that reading aloud might present to young women, and he writes of:

> lo udir, da lo quale l'anima de le donzelle lievemente rimane atoxichata et morta; et per tanto ve priego, fugite le fabule et historie, cancione, libri, et parole, che contegna materia de luxuria, de gola, et amor carnali, ni de noze ni de simel vani et sensuali parlari. (IV. 6)

> (hearing, by which the soul of young girls can easily be poisoned and killed; and I therefore beseech you, avoid fables and stories, songs, books and words that deal with lust, gluttony and carnal love, or weddings or similar vain and sensual talk.)

Two examples of women's access to texts within the household through the ear, as well as, or rather than, through the eye, can be related to the practices of dedication and gift-giving, discussed respectively in Chapter 1

---

[125] Anna Maria Fioravanti Baraldi, 'Testo e immagini: le edizioni cinquecentesche dell'*Omiliario quadragesimale* di Ludovico Pittorio', in *Girolamo Savonarola da Ferrara all'Europa*, ed. by Gigliola Fragnito and Mario Miegge (Florence: SISMEL-Edizioni del Galluzzo, 2001), pp. 139–54 (pp. 146–48); Boillet, 'Vernacular Sermons on the Psalms', pp. 201–02.

[126] John Martin, *Venice's Hidden Enemies: Italian Heretics in a Renaissance City* (Berkeley: University of California Press, 1993), p. 83.

and earlier in this chapter. In 1525, the Florentine author Agnolo Firenzuola sent to his patron, the noblewoman Caterina Cibo, Duchess of Camerino, a manuscript of his dialogues entitled the *Ragionamenti*, and gave her this invitation in his dedicatory letter: 'quando talore farete tregua con le vostre più importanti faccende, [. . .] alle vostre tavole leggeteli, o gli ascoltate mentre che altri gli legge' (when on occasion you seek repose from your more important business, read them at your table or listen to them while someone else reads them).[127] The circumstances of one of the dedications made to Christine of Lorraine show how it arose out of the habit of listening to texts read aloud. Scipione Ammirato, a salaried historian of the Medici court, dedicated to her in October 1594 a political work, his discourses on Tacitus. This was not the kind of text normally associated with female readers; yet Ammirato claimed that, just as Grand Duke Cosimo de' Medici had listened to the *Istorie fiorentine* that he had commissioned from him, so Christine had spent some time listening to many of these discourses:

> Dopo haver io havuto il savio Principe Gran Duca Cosimo per ascoltatore di dieci libri della mia Istoria suocero vostro, [. . .] a grandissima grazia mi ho reputato, che l'Altezza Vostra di propria volontà si sia compiaciuta per più sere parimente ancor ella d'essere stata ascoltatrice di molti de' miei discorsi. Et quel che molto più ho a recarmi a ventura a capo d'alcun anno passato si è l'haver ella voluto copia d'alcuno di essi.

> (After I had had the wise prince Grand Duke Cosimo, your father-in-law, as a listener to the ten books of my History, [. . .] I have considered it a very great favour that Your Highness, too, has been pleased of your own will, for several evenings, to be a listener to many of my discourses. And what I must put down to an even greater fortune after some years is your having desired a copy of some of them.)

When the Grand Duchess wrote to thank the author for his dedication on 13 December 1594, she showed awareness of its meaning in terms of the wider reception of the work: she believed it would be read and received 'con universale approbazione sotto il nome nostro' (with universal approbation under our name). We also know that Christine intended to listen to Ammirato's printed text in the first instance: she assures him that 'ben presto comincieremo a farcelo leggere' (we shall very soon begin to have it read to us).[128]

---

[127] Agnolo Firenzuola, *Le novelle*, ed. by Eugenio Ragni (Rome: Salerno Editrice, 1971), p. 12.

[128] Scipione Ammirato, *Discorsi sopra Cornelio Tacito* (Florence: Filippo Giunti the Younger, 1594), fol. +2$^{r-v}$; Christine's letter is in Scipione Ammirato, *Opuscoli*, 3 vols (Florence: Amadore Massi and Lorenzo Landi, 1637–42), II, 433. Grand Duke Ferdinand also expected to listen to readings from

Perhaps because of Christine's interest in Tacitus, one of her daughters, Caterina, received in 1628, through her confessor, Fulgenzio Gemma, a letter from the priest Angelo Maria Adimari, accompanying the gift of a book on politics written by his brother Alessandro. This was no doubt a sequence of fifty sonnets based on maxims of Tacitus, printed that year in Florence. Angelo Maria's otherwise very conventional letter is significant here because it refers to two ways in which Caterina might study the text:

> Mons[igno]re Gemma presenterà a V[ostra] A[ltezza] S[erenissi]ma con questa mia un'opera Politica che mio fratello ha dato in luce, quale se bene non sarà degna d'essere onorata da V[ostra] A[ltezza] con l'ascoltarla, o mirarla, spero tuttavia che per sua innata gentilezza si compiacerà favorirla, e le servirà per vagheggiare in essa se stessa, essendo, potrò dire, un ritratto del suo valore.[129]

> (Monsignor Gemma will present to Your most serene Highness, with this letter of mine, a political work that my brother has published. Even if it is unworthy of being honoured by Your Highness by listening to it or looking at it, I nevertheless hope that, through your innate kindness, you will deign to favour it and it will allow you to contemplate yourself in it, since I may say that it portrays your worth.)

'Listening' or 'looking at', rather than just 'reading': these alternatives suggest that for Caterina, as for her mother, access to texts could depend a great deal on what was read aloud to her as well as what she read silently.[130] Women doubtless read to others as well: Sabadino degli Arienti wrote in his biography of Ippolita Sforza that she '[l]egea egregiamente cum suavi accenti et resonantia' (read very finely with sweet tones and resonance).[131]

For women as for men in the early modern period, we therefore need to envisage a third communications circuit that includes listening. It needs to take account of the most common kind of performance, in which a written text was spoken or sung to one or more listeners; but it should also

the book, as his letter to Ammirato of the same date shows: 'l'habbiamo ricevuto volentierissimo per farcelo leggere nell'hore che potremo rubare dalle continue occupazioni del governo nostro' (ibid., p. 434; we have been most pleased to receive [the book] to have it read to us in the hours we can steal from the continual business of our government). See also Elisabetta Stumpo, 'Rapporti familiari e modelli educativi: il caso di Cristina di Lorena', in *Le donne Medici nel sistema europeo delle corti XVI–XVIII secolo: atti del convegno internazionale, Firenze, San Domenico di Fiesole, 6–8 ottobre 2005*, ed. by Giulia Calvi and Riccardo Spinelli, 2 vols (Florence: Polistampa, 2008), I, 257–68 (p. 260).

[129] ASF, Mediceo del Principato, vol. 6113, fol. 569 (21 March 1628). The first edition, *La Polinnia, ovvero cinquanta sonetti d'Alessandro Adimari fondati su sentenze di G. Cor. Tacito con argom[enti] a ciascuno d'essi, ch'uniti insieme formano un breve discorso polit[ico] e morale* (Florence: Pietro Cecconcelli, 1628), is reproduced in the edition of Bruno Giancarlo (Terni: Thyrus, 2007).

[130] For further examples, see Richardson, *Manuscript Culture in Renaissance Italy*, pp. 228–29.

[131] Arienti, *Gynevera*, p. 339.

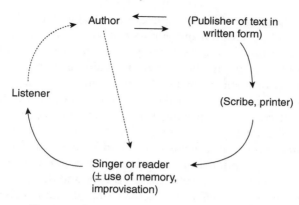

Figure 3.3 A communications circuit for oral culture

incorporate the practices of memorization and of improvisation, allowing for the possibility of the text passing orally from the author to a performer, who might be the author (Figure 3.3). Improvisers in the Renaissance were mostly male, but there is at least one account of a performance by a woman. According to Francesco Sansovino, Cassandra Fedele (*c.* 1465–1558) extemporized in song during the entertainments that followed one of the four banquets given annually by the Venetian doge for other patricians:

> Si legge che in uno de' predetti conviti in tempo del Doge Agostino Barbarigo, Cassandra Fedele, giovanetta assai bella, et illustre per molte scienze, cantò su la lira versi latini all'improvisa, con tanta maraviglia de i circonstanti, che ne acquistò gloria per tutta Italia.[132]

> (One reads that in one of these banquets, while Agostino Barbarigo was doge [1486–1501], Cassandra Fedele, a young lady most beautiful and famed for her wide learning, sang Latin verses extempore to the lira. The audience was so full of wonder that she won glory throughout Italy.)

## The Case of Isabella d'Este

The cultural activities of and around Isabella d'Este as Marchioness of Mantua exemplify, on a grand scale, several of the practices examined in

---

[132] *Venetia città nobilissima et singolare* (Venice: Giacomo Sansovino, 1581), Book XI, fol. Bbb2$^r$. See also Brian Richardson, 'Improvising Lyric Verse in the Renaissance: Contexts, Sources and Imitation', in *Cultural Reception, Translation and Transformation from Medieval to Modern Italy: Essays in Honour of Martin McLaughlin*, ed. by Guido Bonsaver, Brian Richardson and Giuseppe Stellardi (Cambridge: Legenda, 2017), pp. 97–116.

this chapter: the giving of books, sometimes linked with the dedication of the text; the lending, creation and purchase of books; and the performance of texts. Her case also illustrates some ways in which a woman could help to fashion her identity within her social and cultural circles through her ownership both of books as material objects and of the texts they contained. Isabella had a single-minded passion, especially in the earlier part of her life, for collecting and displaying works of literature together with other rare and valuable objects: works of art and antiquities, stone vases, marble or bronze statues, engraved gems, coins and medallions. She took full advantage of her exceptional opportunities to pursue these enthusiasms. As a daughter of a duke of Ferrara, Ercole I d'Este, and the wife, from 1490 when she was not yet sixteen, of Francesco Gonzaga, she was able to wield very strong influence over others. She commanded financial resources of which most women could only dream. Her dowry was worth about 30,000 ducats, and it included items such as jewels and silverware that could be used as security for loans. Revenues from taxes and lands provided an annual income that she managed to increase from 6,000 ducats to about 8,000.[133] There were, of course, serious constraints on how much she could spend on her personal pursuits, as opposed to maintaining her large household and supporting her spouse and her son Federico Gonzaga, born in 1500; but, as Evelyn Welch writes, the marchioness 'did not need to ask the marquis's permission before spending substantial sums of money'.[134]

Isabella adapted rooms, within her suite of apartments or 'camerini' in the Gonzaga palace complex in Mantua, in order to house and display her collections, and one of these rooms came to be called the studiolo. Her creation of such a space had important precedents among her female relatives. Ippolita Sforza, whose brother Ludovico Maria Sforza married Isabella's sister Beatrice and who herself married Alfonso II d'Aragona, Duke of Calabria, brother of Isabella's mother Eleonora d'Aragona, created a study for herself in the Castel Capuano of Naples. Her secretary Baldo Martorelli wrote on 29 December 1466 to inform Ippolita's mother, Bianca Maria Visconti, that 'Sua S. fa al presente finire uno bello studio et dice volere studiare' (Her Ladyship is currently completing a beautiful study

[133] William F. Prizer, 'Isabella d'Este and Lucrezia Borgia as Patrons of Music: The Frottola at Mantua and Ferrara', *Journal of the American Musicological Society*, 38 (1985), 1–33 (p. 14); Stephen Campbell, *The Cabinet of Eros: Renaissance Mythological Painting and the 'Studiolo' of Isabella d'Este* (New Haven: Yale University Press, 2004), pp. 55–57; Welch, *Shopping in the Renaissance*, pp. 253–58.
[134] Welch, *Shopping in the Renaissance*, p. 258.

and says she wishes to study). A letter of 6 January 1466/7 from Ippolita to her mother refers to the room as completed:

> Havendo facto finire uno mio studio per leggere et scrivere alcuna volta, prego V[ostra] Ill[ustrissi]ma S[ignoria], sicome altre volte glie ho scritto, glie piaccia farme retrare al naturale la Ex[cellen]tia del S[ignor] mio patre et V[ostra] et tutti li mei Ill[ustrissimi] fratelli et sorelle.[135]

> (Having completed a study for myself to read and write from time to time, I ask Your most illustrious Ladyship, as I have written to you on other occasions, to be kind enough to have a portrait made from life of His Excellency my father and yourself and all my illustrious brothers and sisters.)

Eleonora d'Aragona had two sets of rooms in Ferrara that Isabella would have known well, one in the Castel Vecchio and another in an adjoining space known as the 'zardino de Madama' (my lady's garden). The former, at least, contained a study and the latter, although more private, was occasionally used to receive distinguished visitors.[136] Isabella's own rooms in Mantua were initially in the Castello di San Giorgio, part of the Palazzo ducale. From an early point, by 1491, she started to have decorative work done on the studiolo. By 1508 she had also brought into use the room underneath the studiolo, known as the grotta. She thus now had two rooms in which to display the paintings that from 1496 onwards she commissioned from Andrea Mantegna and other leading artists, and the many other objects that she collected. Between 1519 and 1522, Isabella moved to a more comfortable suite of rooms on the ground floor of the adjoining Corte Vecchia. Here again she created a studiolo and a grotta, this time next to each other.

As is suggested by portraits of men sitting alone in their studies, these rooms were places for private reading and writing ('per leggere et scrivere', as Ippolita Sforza put it) and for thought. However, they were also spaces to be seen by select members of the public, and they could be used for conversation.[137] Judith Bryce has argued that Ippolita Sforza's project to

---

[135] Sforza, *Lettere*, p. 24, and Sforza, *Duchess and Hostage in Renaissance Naples*, p. 82. On books owned by Ippolita Sforza, see earlier in this chapter.

[136] Thomas Tuohy, *Herculean Ferrara: Ercole d'Este (1471–1505) and the Invention of a Ducal Capital* (Cambridge University Press, 1996), pp. 98–114, 209; Dora Thornton, *The Scholar in his Study: Ownership and Experience in Renaissance Italy* (New Haven: Yale University Press, 1997), pp. 91–92; Campbell, *The Cabinet of Eros*, pp. 59–62; Marco Folin, 'Studioli, vie coperte, gallerie: genealogia di uno spazio del potere', in *Il camerino di alabastro: Antonio Lombardo e la scultura all'antica*, ed. by Matteo Ceriana (Milan: Silvana, 2004), pp. 97–101 (pp. 100, 102); Folin, 'Bastardi e principesse nelle corti del Rinascimento: spunti di ricerca', *Schifanoia*, 28–29 (2005), 167–74 (pp. 171–72).

[137] See Thornton, *The Scholar in his Study*, pp. 116–20 and 175, on conversation and sociability in the study.

create her study in Naples included 'an element of image-management
[. . .], a deliberate intention to create a public persona in alien territory, to
attract respect and approbation'.[138] Isabella's rooms and the cabinets within
them were kept locked, yet she ensured that approved persons had access to
them even while she was away from Mantua. When a party of visitors,
including the English ambassador, wished to visit in late 1514 during her
absence in Rome, she gave instructions on 10 November to a trusted
member of her household, Maddalena Tagliapietra: 'Circa la chiave di la
Grotta, dicemo che quando ce sono qualche gentilhomini che la voliano
vedere debiati pur dare la chiave a Zoan Jacomo castellano, facendovila poi
restituire' (About the key of the grotta, we say that, when there are some
gentlemen who may wish to see it, you must give the key to Gian Giacomo
the castellan and have it returned to you afterwards).[139] Some of those who
were allowed to tour Isabella's apartments left admiring accounts.[140] The
Vicentine nobleman Gian Giorgio Trissino used either the reputation of
the apartments or his memory of a personal visit to them in the encomiastic
description of the fruits of Isabella's generous spending in his dialogue
*I ritratti*. Trissino put into the mouth of Bembo, the main speaker, the
rhetorical question:

> Chi meglio, e più volentieri di costei sa spendere ne le cose lodevoli,
> e spandere dove il bisogno conosce; e questa sua liberalità si può chiaramente
> comprendere da le splendide sue vestimenta, da i paramenti di casa magni-
> fici, e da le fabriche belle, dilettevoli, e quasi divine, con alcuni dolcissimi
> camerini pieni di rarissimi libri, di picture bellissime, di antique sculture
> meravigliose, e di moderne, che si avicinano a quelle, di Camei, di tagli, di
> Medaglie, e di gemme elettissime. Et insomma di tante altre cose pretiose,
> e rare abondevoli sono, che ad un tempo diletto grandissimo, e non piccola
> meraviglia porgono a i riguardanti.[141]

---

[138] Bryce, '"Fa finire uno bello studio"', p. 58; see, too, p. 62 on the '"public", or "quasi-public",
dimension' of the books included in Ippolita's dowry.

[139] C. Malcolm Brown, '"Lo insaciabile desiderio nostro de cose antique": New Documents on Isabella
d'Este's Collection of Antiquities', in *Cultural Aspects of the Italian Renaissance: Essays in Honour of
Paul Oskar Kristeller*, ed. by Cecil H. Clough (Manchester University Press, 1976), pp. 324–53 (p.
330, n. 37). In a letter of 25 July 1514, Gian Giacomo Calandra was ordered by Isabella to ask
Maddalena for the key to the grotta when she wanted her copy of the *Carcer d'amore* sent to Milan:
Roberta Iotti, 'Phenice unica, virtuosa e pia: la corrispondenza culturale di Isabella', in *Isabella
d'Este: la primadonna del Rinascimento*, ed. by Daniele Bini, Quaderno di *Civiltà Mantovana*, 2nd
edn (Mantua: Il Bulino, 2006), pp. 167–83 (p. 171).

[140] See Clifford M. Brown, with Anna Maria Lorenzoni and Sally Hickson, *Per dare qualche splendore
a la gloriosa città di Mantua: Documents for the Antiquarian Collection of Isabella d'Este* (Rome:
Bulzoni, 2002), pp. 23–34, on accounts of visits from 1512 onwards.

[141] *I ritratti* (Rome: Ludovico degli Arrighi and Lautizio Perugino, 1524), fol. D2^(r–v), spelling partly
modernized.

(Who knows better and more willingly than she does how to spend money in worthy objects, and to extend largesse where there is a need? This generosity of hers can be seen clearly in her splendid clothing, her magnificent household adornments, her beautiful, delightful and almost divine apartments, with some very pleasant little rooms full of the rarest books, the most beautiful paintings, marvellous ancient sculptures and modern ones nearby, cameos, intaglios, medals and the most exquisite gems. In short, they abound in so many other precious and rare objects that they provide onlookers with the greatest delight together with no little wonder.)

Trissino's description anticipates, on a smaller scale, Castiglione's account at the start of *Il libro del cortegiano* of the library treasures of the ducal palace in Urbino, where Duke Federico da Montefeltro 'con grandissima spesa adunò un gran numero di eccellentissimi e rarissimi libri greci, latini ed ebraici, quali tutti ornò d'oro e d'argento, estimando che questa fusse la suprema eccellenzia del suo magno palazzo' (at great cost [. . .] collected a large number of the finest and rarest books, in Greek, Latin and Hebrew, all of which he adorned with gold and silver, believing that they were the crowning glory of his great palace).[142] It is also notable that Ariosto's first reference to Isabella in his *Orlando furioso*, in Melissa's prophecy to Bradamante, draws attention equally to her patronage of arts and of letters before going on to praise her other qualities:

> De la tua chiara stirpe uscirà quella
> d'opere illustri e di bei studii amica,
> ch'io non so ben se più leggiadra e bella
> mi debba dire, o più saggia e pudica,
> liberale e magnanima Isabella.

(Your illustrious house shall give birth to that friend of glorious deeds and fair studies, liberal, great-hearted Isabel; I know not which to put first, her beauty and grace, or her sagacity and virtue.)[143]

Allusions such as these show how effective Isabella's collections were in the making of her social identity. Her prudent liberality, her possession of rarities housed in a resplendent décor, her generous sharing of private space with a distinguished public: these were the keynotes of the image that she

---

[142] Castiglione, *Il libro del cortegiano*, I. 2, pp. 82–83; Castiglione, *The Book of the Courtier*, p. 41. The wording of the earlier redaction of 1520–21 is similar: Castiglione, *La seconda redazione del Cortegiano di Baldassarre Castiglione*, ed. by Ghino Ghinassi (Florence: Sansoni, 1968), pp. 5–6.

[143] Ludovico Ariosto, *Orlando furioso secondo l'edizione del 1532 con le varianti delle edizioni del 1516 e del 1521*, ed. by Santorre Debenedetti and Cesare Segre (Bologna: Commissione per i testi di lingua, 1960), XI. 59 in the 1516 and 1521 editions, XIII. 59 in the 1532 edition; Ariosto, *Orlando furioso*, trans. by Guido Waldman (Oxford University Press, 1998), p. 134.

wished to create of a woman unique among her contemporaries. And through accounts such as Trissino's, others, too, could become virtual visitors to her 'camerini'.

It is to be expected that Trissino, as an author, should list 'rarissimi libri' before even Isabella's paintings, among the delights of her 'camerini', but four kinds of evidence suggest that books did indeed form a significant part of her collections: references to them in her correspondence; the existence of works that were dedicated or presented to her and that we can therefore assume she owned; surviving manuscripts and printed books with her coat of arms; and at least one post-mortem inventory, which is headed 'Inventario delli libri lassati per la q[uondam] felice memoria della Ill[ustrissima] S[ignora] Isabella d'Este marchesana di Manta' (Inventory of the books left by the late lamented most illustrious lady Isabella d'Este Marchioness of Mantua), and lists 133 books.[144] This document may not be an exact record of the state of Isabella's book collection on her death in 1539, and it does not include all the works that other evidence indicates she must have possessed at some point. Like other such lists, it gives only basic information about the contents of books, and it does not always identify their authors, but it does usually note how a book was bound, its format, whether it was handwritten and whether it had vellum rather than paper as its support. At least sixty-six of her books were manuscript, and that proportion, of around 50 per cent, is unusually high for the period.[145]

One would expect Isabella's collection of books to have been substantial, since her paternal and maternal families, the Este and the d'Aragona, and her husband's family, the Gonzaga, all collected books. Her collection bears comparison with those of two of her husband's uncles, Cardinal Francesco Gonzaga and Gianfrancesco Gonzaga.[146] The inventory of her books has some similarities with those of the collection of Barbara Hohenzollern of Brandenburg, who died in 1481 and was the wife of Ludovico Gonzaga, grandfather of Isabella's husband: her library contained seventy-one books, almost all of them manuscripts, in both Latin

[144] ASMn, Archivio Gonzaga, busta 400, fols 184ʳ–87ᵛ; published in Luzio and Renier, *La coltura*, pp. 273–77, and in Giancarlo Malacarne, 'Collezionismo e querelle librarie: l'inventario dei libri "lassati" dalla "quondam" Isabella d'Este', *Civiltà mantovana*, 3rd ser., 40, no. 119 (March 2005), 121–31.

[145] For comparative examples, see Richardson, *Manuscript Culture in Renaissance Italy*, p. 9.

[146] Their book collections are discussed in D. S. Chambers, *A Renaissance Cardinal and His Worldly Goods: The Will and Inventory of Francesco Gonzaga (1444–1483)* (London: Warburg Institute, 1992), and Chambers, 'A Condottiere and His Books: Gianfrancesco Gonzaga (1446–96)', *Journal of the Warburg and Courtauld Institutes*, 70 (2007), 33–97 (pp. 79–97).

and the vernacular. Among them was a collection of sacred plays and poetry sent to the marchioness by their Florentine author, Feo Belcari.[147]

Yet Isabella's collection must have been different in size and nature from those of most elite women of the late Quattrocento and early Cinquecento. Only a small proportion of the volumes in her inventory consists of devotional or spiritually improving reading, the sort of texts that women were urged to read by men. Many items were contemporary secular works newly acquired, rather than older works or inherited books. The collection presents a marked contrast with, for instance, two libraries of her female relatives from the previous generation. The inventory of the small collection of Margherita of Bavaria, Isabella's mother-in-law, was drawn up on her death in 1479; of its nineteen books, only one, a herbal in German ('liber herbarum in theotonico'), is definitely not devotional nor spiritual in content.[148] Of the seventy-four books listed in the post-mortem inventory of Eleonora d'Aragona, of 1493, not many more than a dozen were secular: a printed translation of Pliny's *Natural History*, a manuscript of Fazio degli Uberti (the *Dittamondo* with Guglielmo Capello's commentary), a *Commentary* by Julius Caesar, Bartolomeo Gogio's *De laudibus mulierum*, a 'libreto in versi latini, de le laude de madama' (little book in Latin verse, in praise of my lady) in manuscript, and so on. The rest were religious texts such as breviaries, missals, Bible extracts, lives of saints, Epistles and Gospels, Offices of Our Lady and printed sermons.[149] None of them apparently figure in the inventory of Isabella's books, and this suggests that few, if any, were inherited by her. On the volumes owned by Antonia del Balzo, wife of Gianfrancesco Gonzaga, D. S. Chambers observes that the 1496 inventory of her main residence, the castle of Bozzolo,

> does not record many books kept in Antonia's own apartments there: there are just eighteen titles [. . .], four of them printed editions, in her *studio*. About half of these are religious, including an illuminated Psalter and a copy of the Gospels, but she also had works by Boccaccio, Dante and Petrarch,

[147] Andrea Canova, 'Le biblioteche dei Gonzaga nella seconda metà del Quattrocento', in *Principi e signori: le biblioteche nella seconda metà del Quattrocento. Atti del Convegno di Urbino, 5–6 giugno 2008*, ed. by Guido Arbizzoni, Concetta Bianca and Marcella Peruzzi (Urbino: Accademia Raffaello, 2010), pp. 39–66 (pp. 43–47).

[148] Meroni, *Mostra dei codici gonzagheschi*, pp. 62–63.

[149] On Eleonora's books, see the inventory in Giulio Bertoni, *La Biblioteca Estense e la coltura ferrarese ai tempi del Duca Ercole I (1471–1505)* (Turin: Loescher, 1903), pp. 229–33, and Federica Toniolo, 'Livres et images de femmes à la cour des Este à Ferrare', in *Livres et lectures de femmes en Europe entre Moyen Âge et Renaissance*, ed. by Anne-Marie Legaré (Turnhout: Brepols, 2007), pp. 311–24 (pp. 317–18).

various collections of stories (*novelle*), and 'a book of the decades of Livy'. Additionally, in a leather-covered case in her *camera*, she had five Books of Hours [. . .], three of them illuminated. It is noted that she had brought these three from her [father's] home, and the last of the five was one she used daily.[150]

In the early sixteenth century, no other courtly woman seems to have had a collection similar to that of Isabella. A list of books owned in 1502–03 by a rival consort, her sister-in-law Lucrezia Borgia, includes just seventeen items, of which eight are of a religious nature; two are specified as manuscript books, six as printed.[151] We have seen that, from the 1530s to the 1550s, Renée de France bought, or had copied out, various kinds of texts – scriptural, grammatical, rhetorical, historical, literary – and had them bound, but many of these books were intended for the cultural and spiritual education of her three daughters and of the children of members of her household in the Ferrarese court. Eleonora de Toledo, wife of Duke Cosimo I of Florence, had her own writing-room or 'scrittoio' within her suite of rooms in the Palazzo della Signoria. However, this was a small space intended primarily to store financial records.[152] Isabella's collection was closer in size to those of some elite men. To take just three of several possible examples, the Milanese courtier and poet Gasparo Visconti had a library of 147 volumes on his death in 1499; in the same year, 81 books are found in the inventory of Cristoforo Castiglione in Mantua; and there were 145 books (including only about 21 manuscripts) in the list of books owned in 1524 by his son Baldassarre.[153]

Isabella acquired her collection of works of art through a few commissions, through much shopping on the open market, often carried out on her behalf by courtiers or elite artisans, and through gift-giving. Where her

[150]  Chambers, 'A Condottiere and his Books', p. 83.
[151]  Gregorovius, *Lucrezia Borgia*, Appendix 65, pp. 370–71. For further examples of women's libraries from this period, see Richardson, *Printing, Writers and Readers*, pp. 148–49.
[152]  Bruce L. Edelstein, 'The Camera Verde: A Public Center for the Duchess of Florence in the Palazzo Vecchio', *Mélanges de l'École Française de Rome: Italie et Méditerranée*, 115 (2003), 51–87; Edelstein, 'La fecundissima Signora Duchessa: The Courtly Persona of Eleonora di Toledo and the Iconography of Abundance', in *The Cultural World of Eleonora di Toledo, Duchess of Florence and Siena*, ed. by Konrad Eisenbichler (Aldershot: Ashgate, 2004), pp. 71–97; Ilaria Hoppe, 'A Duchess' Place at Court: The Quartiere di Eleonora in the Palazzo della Signoria in Florence', ibid., pp. 98–118; Robert W. Gaston, 'Eleonora di Toledo's Chapel: Lineage, Salvation and the War against the Turks', ibid., pp. 157–80.
[153]  Bortolo Martinelli, 'La biblioteca (e i beni) di un petrarchista: Gasparo Visconti', in *Veronica Gambara e la poesia del suo tempo nell'Italia settentrionale: atti del Convegno (Brescia-Correggio, 17–19 ottobre 1985)*, ed. by Cesare Bozzetti, Pietro Gibellini and Ennio Sandal (Florence: Olschki, 1989), pp. 213–61 (pp. 224–26); Guido Rebecchini, *Private Collectors in Mantua, 1500–1630* (Rome: Edizioni di Storia e Letteratura, 2002), pp. 110–19, 312–17.

books were concerned, all of these sources came into play, but the first two only to a limited extent, and she also acquired texts through borrowing and copying. As regards commissioning texts, Isabella, like most patrons, appears to have arranged for the composition of new works of literature rarely if at all. She may have promoted two works by Mario Equicola that had propagandistic value: his oration in praise of the late Dominican tertiary Osanna Andreasi, *In conservatione[m] divae Osanne Andreasiae Mantuanae oratio ad d[ominam] Isabella Estensem Mantuae principem* ([Mantua: Francesco Bruschi], not before 1518) and his account of the marchioness's pilgrimage to the Dominican shrine of St Mary Magdalene at La Sainte-Baume in Provence, *D[ominae] Isabellae Estensis Mantue principis iter in Nerbonensem Galliam* ([Mantua: Francesco Bruschi], not after 1520).[154] Isabella devoted a limited amount of her resources to the production of books. She occasionally employed scribes to copy manuscripts or illuminators to adorn them.[155] A project to decorate a manuscript of Pliny's *Natural History* was left unfinished when its illuminator, Pietro Guindaleri of Cremona, died in 1506. This is probably now Turin, Biblioteca Nazionale, MS J.I.22–23, copied by Matteo Contugi in 1463–68.[156] Isabella commissioned a breviary from a scribe and illuminator based in Ferrara, Cesare dalle Vieze, who was working on it in 1511 and sent it to her in 1514.[157]

Another such project demonstrates Isabella's desire to possess fashionable novelties. In 1516, she commissioned Cesare dalle Vieze to copy out Petrarch's Italian poetry for her, and gave detailed instructions in a letter of 8 January 1516 to an intermediary in Ferrara, the nobleman Alfonso Trotti. With this she enclosed a printed copy that Cesare was to imitate closely, an octavo Giunti edition in italic type rather than one of the Aldine editions of 1501 and 1514. She wanted the copy made on vellum, of course, and in order to control its quality she sent twelve ruled quires of it to Ferrara:

[154] Stephen Kolsky, *Mario Equicola: The Real Courtier* (Geneva: Droz, 1991), pp. 150–52, 161–64; Alessandra Villa, *Istruire e rappresentare Isabella d'Este: il 'Libro de natura de amore' di Mario Equicola* (Lucca: Maria Pacini Fazzi, 2006), p. 147.

[155] Meroni, *Mostra dei codici gonzagheschi*, pp. 67–68.

[156] Luzio and Renier, *La coltura*, pp. 11, 61, n. 86; Meroni, *Mostra dei codici gonzagheschi*, pp. 67, 80–81; Giordana Mariani Canova in *Andrea Mantegna e i Gonzaga: Rinascimento nel Castello di San Giorgio. Catalogo della mostra*, ed. by Filippo Trevisani (Milan: Electa, 2006), cat. no. III.15, pp. 234–43; Stefano L'Occaso in *Mantegna 1431–1506*, ed. by Giovanni Agosti and Dominique Thiébaut (Paris: Hazan and Musée du Louvre, 2008), cat. nos. 110–11, pp. 278–81; Canova, 'Le biblioteche dei Gonzaga', pp. 55–56. A 'Plinio scritto a mano in carta pergamena in foglio desligato' (Pliny, manuscript, on vellum, folio, unbound) is item 107 in the post-mortem inventory.

[157] Campori, *Notizie dei miniatori*, pp. 18–19.

Mandiamovi lo alligato Petrarcha di stampa fiorentina, qual è molto corretto. Volemo che advertati M[aest]ro Cesare a scriverlo a parola per parola,
et littera per littera come sta questo: facendo conto di dipingere et non di
scrivere: perché sapemo che esso non scrive molto corretto, dicendoli che
'l comincia alli sonetti: scrivendo quelli et le canzoni cossì successive come
sta in questo che vi mandiamo, lassando stare per hora li capituli, quali
vorremo poi che scrivi separatamente. Advertetelo anche l'habbi mente a far
capire uno sonetto per faciata, et a questa posta le havemo fatto rigare de
XIV righe l'una. La forma de la littera volemo che sii de la sorte che è questa
mostra alligata, quale lui fece quando era qui.

(We are sending you with this the Petrarch printed in Florence, which is
very correct. We wish you to instruct master Cesare to copy it out word for
word and letter for letter as it stands, as if he were painting rather than
copying, for we know that he does not copy very correctly. Tell him to start
with the sonnets, copying them and the canzoni one after another as they are
in this [book] we are sending, leaving out for the time being the capitoli [i.e.
the *Triumphi*], which we would like him then to copy separately. Instruct
him, too, to take care to make one sonnet fit into each page, and with this in
mind we have had each page ruled with fourteen lines. We want the shape of
the script to be as in the attached sample, which he made when he was here.)

Cesare, however, asked for sheets that would allow wider margins, and
Isabella had to send him another batch.[158] She was thus meticulously
concerned with the content and appearance of her new copy: rather than
seeking out a fourteenth- or fifteenth-century manuscript of Petrarch such
as those owned by Cardinal Francesco Gonzaga,[159] she wished to invest her
money in a fine manuscript copy of a recent edition that she considered
philologically correct (perhaps on the advice of a courtier such as
Equicola), thus combining uniqueness with up-to-dateness.

There is some evidence of Isabella's shopping for books, but for printed
ones more often than for manuscripts, and always through an agent of
some kind, as was typical of women of high social status.[160] Soon after her
marriage, she acquired an illuminated Bible sent to her on approval by the

[158] Luzio and Renier, *La coltura*, pp. 20–21. If Cesare went on to copy Petrarch's *Triumphi*, this could
be item 54 in the inventory, 'Sonetti e Trionfi del Petrarca scritti a mano in carta pergamena in
ottavo coperti di coramo giallo indorato fornito d'argento eccetto una parte' (Petrarch's *Sonnets* and
*Triumphs* written by hand on vellum, in octavo, bound in yellow morocco, gilded, with silver
furnishings except for one part); item 53 contains the *Triumphi* alone. On the Florentine Petrarchs
of 1504, 1510 and 1515, edited by Francesco Alfieri for Filippo Giunti, see Carlo Dionisotti,
*Machiavellerie* (Turin: Einaudi, 1980), pp. 338–40.
[159] Cardinal Francesco had at least two fine Quattrocento manuscripts of Petrarch, one copied by
Bartolomeo Sanvito: see *Splendours of the Gonzaga: Catalogue*, ed. by David Chambers and
Jane Martineau (London: Victoria & Albert Museum, 1981), pp. 114–15.
[160] Welch, *Shopping in the Renaissance*, pp. 216, 218–19, 221–25.

Mantuan representative in Venice, Giorgio Brognolo; it is not clear whether this was manuscript or printed.[161] The young Isabella also had a burning interest in tales such as chivalric romances, which were highly prized in the Estense court, and on 17 September 1491 she nonchalantly asked Brognolo to make a note of those to be found, most probably in print, in all the bookshops of Venice:

> Vorressimo che uno dì mandasti uno di vostri per tutte le appoteche de libri da vendere sono in Venetia et facesti fare notta de tutti li libri che lì sono in vulgare, tanto in rima quanto in prosa, che contengano batalie, historie et fabule, cossì de moderni como de antiqui et maxime de li paladini de Franza, et ogni altro che se trovarà et mandarceli quanto più presto potereti.

> (We would like you one day to send one of your men around all the bookshops in Venice and get him to make a note of all the books that are there in the vernacular, both in verse and in prose, containing battles, histories and tales, of both modern and ancient times and especially of the paladins of France, and any others that can be found, and send them to us as quickly as you can.)

Brognolo duly sent her a list from which she selected nine books: Justin's abridgement of the history of Pompeius Trogus (of which there are two copies in the inventory, items 39 and 111, the latter a manuscript); the Epistles of Phalaris; Boccaccio's *Comedia delle ninfe fiorentine* or *Ameto*; four chivalric narratives (*Merlino, Falconetto, Fierabraccia, Dama Rovenza*); a life of Julius Caesar; and a work on the condottiere Jacopo Piccinino.[162] On 25 July 1514, when she was in Milan, Isabella wrote that she had had all the bookshops of the city searched in vain for a copy of the *Carcer d'amore*.[163] Another intermediary who was used for Isabella's purchases was her husband's secretary, Iacopo D'Atri. On 13 January 1510, she asked him to obtain in France the chivalric romance *Tirant lo Blanch* by Joanot Martorell in Catalan, presumably one of the two editions printed in Spain, and 'un vocabulista de lingua francese, quale intendemo se vende in Franza impresso' (a French dictionary, which we understand is on sale in France in print), intended perhaps to help her to read chivalric romances or works

---

[161] Brown, *Per dare qualche splendore*, p. 92.

[162] Luzio and Renier, *La coltura*, pp. 7–8; Antonia Tissoni Benvenuti, 'Il mondo cavalleresco e la corte estense', in *I libri di 'Orlando innamorato'* (Modena: Panini, 1987), pp. 13–33 (p. 24 and Plate 25); Iotti, 'Phenice unica', p. 170.

[163] Luzio and Renier, *La coltura*, pp. 9, 135; Iotti, 'Phenice unica', p. 171. Manfredi's translation of this work, on which see Kolsky, 'Lelio Manfredi traduttore cortigiano', was first printed in Venice on 1 July 1514, but in the letter of the 25th Isabella was probably referring to a search for a printed Spanish text, of which a copy is listed in the inventory, item 43.

such as her 'libro di canzone francese' (book of French songs), item 80 in the inventory.[164]

The marchioness developed a taste, too, for collecting the octavo editions that Aldo Manuzio began to print in Venice in 1501, but only as long as she could obtain especially fine copies chosen from the few printed on 'carta bona' (vellum). Around three months after the first edition, a Virgil, had appeared in April 1501, Isabella ordered vellum copies of this text and of a Petrarch and an Ovid that she knew were imminent. She wrote to an agent of hers in Venice, the instrument-maker Lorenzo da Pavia, on 8 July 1501:

> Sono stati portati in questa terra ad vendere alcuni Virgilii stampati in forma picola, de littera minuta et quasi cancelleresca che multo ne piaceno et intendemo che 'l se comencia ad stampare de li Petrarchi. Desideramo havere uno volume de l'una e l'altra opera, cioè uno Virgilio et uno Petrarca de la medesima forma et stampa, ma voresimo che fussino in cartha bona; [. . .] et lo medesimo fareti de le opere de Ovidio, che ne fareti piacere assai.[165]

> (Some Virgils have been brought to this city for sale, printed in small format, in tiny and almost italic types, which please us greatly. We understand that some Petrarchs are starting to be printed. We wish to have a copy of each work, that is, a Virgil and a Petrarch of the same format and printing, but we should like them to be on vellum; [. . .] and you will do the same for the works of Ovid, thus giving us great pleasure.)

Isabella ordered a second vellum Petrarch, together with a Dante, on 22 November 1502. The bindings to be created for these volumes were also of importance. On 3 August 1501, Lorenzo sent the first Petrarch unbound, in case Isabella wished to have it bound and covered 'de qualque bela cosa con le saraie de arezento' (with some fine material with silver clasps). He added that he could have it bound in Venice 'dal melio mastro che sia' (by the best master there is), if she wished, but he also knew of an exceptionally good binder in Flanders. Isabella said she wanted this volume bound in Mantua, 'ad uno bono maestro' (by a good master). In 1503, Lorenzo sent her two Petrarchs that had been bound in Flanders at a cost of

---

[164] Luzio and Renier, *La coltura*, pp. 9, 245. The romance by Joanot Martorell is item 5 in the inventory: 'uno libro de Tirante lonblanch in spagnolo in foglio coperto di corame rosso' (a book of *Tirant lo Blanch* in Spanish in folio bound in red morocco). Later Isabella owned a volume of works in French by Clément Marot, item 119 in the inventory. On her lack of knowledge of French, see Prizer, 'Isabella d'Este and Lucrezia Borgia as Patrons of Music', p. 18.

[165] Clifford M. Brown, *Isabella d'Este and Lorenzo da Pavia: Documents for the History of Art and Culture in Renaissance Mantua* (Geneva: Droz, 1982), pp. 55–56.

5.5 ducats. The British Library has an Aldine Petrarch of 1501, printed on vellum, with the Este arms impaled with those of the Gonzaga on fol. A2$^r$, and this is probably the copy sent by Lorenzo that Isabella wanted to have bound locally: the simple illumination was probably carried out in Mantua rather than in Venice.[166] This could be the Petrarch listed as item 115 in the inventory, but its present binding is not original. The inventory describes a Petrarch 'coperto de coramo negro indorato con li fornimenti d'argento' (bound in black morocco, gilded, with silver furnishings). The London volume, which came from the Cracherode Collection, is now bound in black goatskin with gilded decoration and traces of two clasps, and has patterned gilded fore-edges; however, Anthony Hobson has shown that this binding must originally have belonged to another book.[167]

Only about fifteen Petrarchs were printed on vellum, and moreover Aldo promised Lorenzo da Pavia that he himself would select the best sheets to make up the marchioness's copy. Of course, they were expensive. The Petrarch and the Virgil cost three ducats each, Lorenzo informed Isabella, whereas a Petrarch on paper cost 4 marcelli unbound, equivalent to about one-third of a ducat. In 1505 the marchioness decided to create a volume composed of all the Latin texts that Aldo had printed so far in octavo. She wrote to him on 16 May to order 'desligati tutti quelli che ne ritroviati haver che siano raretti dal Virgilio in fora, qual habiamo' (unbound, all those you can find that are rather rare, except for the Virgil, which we have), and asked him to be sure to provide her with well-produced vellum copies of his future printings. When she accepted the Latin volumes that he offered, Aldo sent her on 9 June five authors unbound and three 'ligati insemi, et meniati' (bound together and illuminated). He suggested a total payment of between twelve and sixteen ducats if she wished to keep them, almost inviting negotiation, and Isabella, keeping an eye on her expenditure, naturally haggled with Aldo over his prices.[168]

---

[166] Shelfmark C.20.b.29. See Helena K. Szépe, 'Bordon, Dürer and Modes of Illuminating Aldines', in *Aldus Manutius and Renaissance Culture: Essays in Memory of Franklin D. Murphy*, ed. by David S. Zeidberg (Florence: Olschki, 1998), pp. 185–200 (p. 188).

[167] Anthony Hobson, 'Some Deceptive Bookbindings', in *The Medieval Book: Glosses from Friends and Colleagues of Christopher de Hamel*, ed. by James H. Marrow, Richard A. Linenthal and William Noel ('t Goy-Houten: Hes & De Graaf, 2010), pp. 250–57 (pp. 250–52). I am very grateful to the late Anthony Hobson for information on this binding.

[168] For an overview, see Luzio and Renier, *La coltura*, pp. 12–15; for the texts of the letters, see Brown, *Isabella d'Este and Lorenzo da Pavia*, pp. 55–59 (8 July–27 August 1501), 72 (22 November 1502), 74–75 (17 June 1503), 207–08 (summary of the correspondence); Iotti, 'Phenice unica', pp. 178–79 (16 May–30 June 1505). On the Petrarch edition of 1501, see Giuseppe Frasso, 'Appunti sul

Isabella's shopping for books thus combined financial expenditure with considerable use of her personal contacts and influence in order to secure copies that were not normally on sale in Mantua or were special in nature. However, purchases in any case played a relatively small role in the building up of her collection: much more important were acquisitions that depended entirely on her social position. On the one hand, her excellent connections enabled her to borrow texts that would not have been available on the open market and that could then be copied for her. On the other hand, authors could send their texts to her as gifts, often dedicating them to her.

Requesting loans or gifts of texts, whether manuscript or printed, was a common and necessary practice in Isabella's age, but in this activity she had the advantage of high rank. In August 1491, just before she asked Brognolo to search the Venetian bookshops for adventure stories and histories, she wrote imperiously to two men, Lodovico de Brugiis and Francesco Donati, to ask them to send her post-haste their copies of two romances, respectively the *Innamoramento di Carlo Magno e dei suoi paladini* (probably printed) and the *Drusiano dal Leone* (probably manuscript). Their eagerness to be of service, when they answered, reflects the marchioness's power. Lodovico, for instance, replied that he did not in fact own the *Innamoramento*, but 'desideroso de servir V[ostra] Ex[cellentia], ho mandato a comprarne uno a Vinegia et dopoi lo ho facto ligare et aminiare, et mandolo a presentare a V[ostra] Cel[situdine]' (wishing to serve Your Excellency, I sent to buy one in Venice and then I had it bound and illuminated, and I am sending it to be presented to Your Highness).[169]

When Isabella wanted a copy of a work by a contemporary, she sometimes contacted the author directly. She wrote in August 1491 to Matteo Maria Boiardo, count of Scandiano, to point out, somewhat testily, that she had not yet received a response to her recent request for a manuscript copy of the newly composed section of his chivalric romance:

> Ve scrivessemo l'altro dì pregandove che ne volesti mandare quella parte del *Innamoramento de Orlando* che novamente haveti composto, ma non habiamo recevuto resposta alcuna; per il che di novo ve pregamo vogliate mandarcela, che trascorsa una volta che l'haveremo, subito ve la remetteremo.

"Petrarca" aldino del 1501', in *Studi in onore di Giuseppe Billanovich*, ed. by Rino Avesani et al. (Rome: Edizioni di Storia e Letteratura, 1984), pp. 315–35.

[169] Luzio and Renier, *La coltura*, pp. 8–9; Tissoni Benvenuti, 'Il mondo cavalleresco e la corte estense', pp. 23–24. The *Innamoramento* had been printed in Venice in 1481 and already twice in 1491, in Bologna (February) and again in Venice (July).

(We wrote to you the other day asking you to send us that part of the *Innamoramento de Orlando* that you have composed recently, but we have received no reply; we therefore ask you again to send it to us. Once we have looked through it, we will send it back to you straight away.)

Boiardo replied that he had nothing new for her, but he generously offered to have his original manuscript of Book III, as yet unprinted, copied for her. Isabella accepted with pleasure.[170]

The marchioness also approached writers indirectly, through an intermediary of high status; in this way, she lessened the risk of losing face if the author declined to help. In January 1491 or shortly before, she had written directly to Antonio Tebaldeo to request some of his works, but he explained that he did not provide copies himself; if she wanted something of his, she would have to approach her husband's uncle Ludovico Gonzaga, Bishop of Mantua. In December of the same year, she tried again, but this time requested the Ferrarese nobleman Giovanni Maria Trotti to ask Tebaldeo on her behalf for specific forms of verse – 'vinti o vinticinque de li più belli sonetti che lui ha composto, et cussì dui o tre capituli' (twenty or twenty-five of the finest sonnets he has written, and similarly two or three capitoli) – and to remind the poet Niccolò da Correggio, a relative of hers, to send something he had promised her.[171] In the following year she asked Giorgio Brognolo in Venice to obtain poems from Antonio Vinciguerra for 'un recolecto de capitoli et sonetti morali' (a collection of capitoli and moral sonnets) that she was putting together.[172] On 10 July 1501, as part of an ambitious project to form a complete collection of contemporary literature for her study, she tried to secure possession of the manuscript works of a recently deceased Paduan poet, Niccolò Lelio Cosmico, by writing thus to Alfonso Trotti in Ferrara:

> Per ornare el nostro studio tenemo cura de havere le opere de tutti li auctori moderni, sì latini come volgari, fra' quali intendemo essere deli primi el q[uondam] M[esser] Cosmico, et persuademone che per esser stato vui suo charo discipulo et herede, habiate tutte o la magiore parte delle opere sue presso vui, aut sapiati dove siano. Mandiamo lì per questo effetto Bernardino Mazono. Pregamovi che vogliati consignarli tutto quello che

[170] Neil Harris, *Bibliografia dell'"Orlando Innamorato"*, 2 vols (Modena: Panini, 1988–91), II, 41–43; Tissoni Benvenuti, 'Il mondo cavalleresco e la corte estense', p. 29.

[171] Luzio and Renier, *La coltura*, pp. 104–05; Iotti, 'Phenice unica', p. 170. In 1504 Tebaldeo, in straitened circumstances, asked Isabella for a gift of four shirts and said he could pay her only in verses: Iotti, 'Phenice unica', pp. 170–71.

[172] Luzio and Renier, *La coltura*, pp. 185–86. On Vinciguerra's moral verse, see Bruno Beffa, *Antonio Vinciguerra Cronico, segretario della Serenissima e letterato* (Bern: Peter Lang, 1975), and Dionisotti, *Machiavellerie*, pp. 94–98.

haveti del suo et informarlo se alcuno ha altro, mettendolo suso la via de haverlo [. . .]. Li faremo exemplare subito et remetteremoveli.

(In order to adorn our study, we are determined to have the works of all modern authors, both Latin and vernacular. Among these, we understand that one of the foremost is the late Cosmico. We are certain that, since you were his dear disciple and heir, you have all or most of his works with you, or you know where they are. We are sending Bernardino Mazzone there for this purpose. We ask you to give him all you have of Cosmico's and to inform him if anyone has anything else, pointing him in the right direction to get it. We shall have them copied straight away and send them back to you.)

It was no coincidence that her messenger, Mazzone, was a professional scribe: no doubt he had instructions to take the manuscripts away and do the copying on Isabella's behalf.[173] In her attempts to obtain much-prized new verse by Iacopo Sannazaro, Isabella used the agency of Iacopo D'Atri in 1503 and 1507, and then that of another nobleman, Andrea Matteo Acquaviva, Marquis of Bitonto, in 1514–15.[174] Isabella could also ask others to provide copies of manuscript texts owned by them. As we have just seen in the case of Vinciguerra, early in her married life she was keen to create collections of works of a particular genre, and in 1493 she was compiling 'uno libretto de Aegloge de diversi auctori' (a little book of eclogues by different authors). A plea went from her to Ludovico Pio in Carpi for any appropriate compositions he had, for example by Gualtiero Sanvitale; they arrived by messenger a few days later.[175]

Texts were sent to Isabella spontaneously by many authors. These works ranged in size and significance from an extensive masterpiece, Ariosto's *Orlando furioso*, to the brief and occasional.[176] Compositions such as a sonnet or strambotto would have been copied, in the first instance, on single sheets or leaves of paper and were not included in the inventory of the marchioness's books, but collectively they formed a significant element in her collection. In one case, the works came to form a group, a series of laments on the death in 1511 of her dog Aura. This heroic creature, a canine Lucretia, had thrown herself from a balcony in order to preserve her virginity when a male dog was harassing her.[177] In another case, a single

[173] Luzio and Renier, *La coltura*, p. 122. On Mazzone, see Meroni, *Mostra dei codici gonzagheschi*, p. 67.
[174] Luzio and Renier, *La coltura*, pp. 251–57; Iotti, 'Phenice unica', p. 179.
[175] Luzio and Renier, *La coltura*, pp. 204–05.
[176] For the presentation of copies of the *Furioso* of 1516 and 1532, see Luzio and Renier, *La coltura*, pp. 125–26; Conor Fahy, L *"Orlando furioso' del 1532: profilo di una edizione* (Milan: Vita e Pensiero, 1989), pp. 98, 168; Iotti, 'Phenice unica', p. 182.
[177] Luzio and Renier, *La coltura*, pp. 30–32.

short work was the forerunner of a planned collection. In November 1512, the marchioness received from Nicolò Liburnio in Venice a manuscript of one of his *Selvette*, a substantial collection of writings in prose and verse. This particular *Selvetta* contained a eulogy of her, her retinue of ladies-in-waiting and the garden of her suburban villa of Porto Mantovano, in which she was currently having hundreds of trees planted. Liburnio wanted to see if she approved of this sample of his work; if she did, he would have it printed. She replied with great alacrity the next day to indicate her approval and to say that she looked forward to receiving the whole work. As was seen in Chapter 1, Liburnio prefaced the printed edition of the *Selvette* that appeared in 1513 with a dedication to Isabella, in which the wider reading public could learn of her study of poetry and other liberal disciplines. Two copies are listed in the inventory, items 85 and 87, both of them on vellum, perhaps a presentation copy each for herself and the marquis.[178]

Other members of Isabella's circles who were aware of her passion for new verse provided manuscript copies of works in their possession. In 1502 Eleonora del Balzo, Marchioness of Crotone, sent her from Naples poems by Ioan Francesco Caracciolo and Cariteo (Benet Gareth).[179] Iacopo D'Atri passed on to her in 1506 a capitolo by Vincenzo Calmeta on the poet's undeserved separation from his beloved.[180] Emilia Pio, companion of the Duchess of Urbino, enclosed two sonnets by the late Cardinal Galeotto Franciotti della Rovere, nephew of Julius II, with a letter of 1508.[181] Here, as in many other cases, Isabella's acquisition of texts was both a result and a demonstration of her social leverage.

What roles did these texts, and the provision of these texts, play in the lives of Isabella d'Este and those in her circle? She will certainly have derived aesthetic pleasure from her books and their bindings, as a connoisseur of exquisitely produced objects. She must have obtained

[178] Ibid., pp. 172–75. On Liburnio, see Carlo Dionisotti, 'Nicolò Liburnio e la letteratura cortigiana', in *Appunti su arti e lettere* (Milan: Jaca Book, 1995), pp. 81–109. On the villa, see Clifford M. Brown, '"Al suo amenissimo Palazzo di Porto": Biagio Rossetti and Isabella d'Este', *Atti e memorie dell'Accademia Nazionale Virgiliana*, n.s., 58 (1990), 33–56.

[179] Luzio and Renier, *La coltura*, p. 261, n. 54; Marco Santagata, *La lirica aragonese: studi sulla poesia napoletana del secondo Quattrocento* (Padua: Antenore, 1979), p. 71; Anna Maria Lorenzoni, 'Tra francesi e spagnoli: le fortunose vicende di Eleonora Orsini del Balzo, marchesa di Crotone, attraverso carteggi inediti dell'Archivio Gonzaga', in *Per Mantova una vita: studi in memoria di Rita Castagna*, ed. by Anna Maria Lorenzoni and Roberto Navarrini (Mantua: Publi-Paolini, 1991), pp. 113–44.

[180] Alessandro Luzio and Rodolfo Renier, *Mantova e Urbino: Isabella d'Este ed Elisabetta Gonzaga nelle relazioni famigliari e nelle vicende politiche* (Turin and Rome: Roux, 1893), p. 99, n. 1; Luzio and Renier, *La coltura*, p. 244; Calmeta, *Prose e lettere*, ed. by Grayson, p. xlii.

[181] Vittorio Cian, 'Pietro Bembo e Isabella d'Este Gonzaga', *GSLI*, 9 (1887), 81–136 (pp. 114–15).

personal satisfaction from reading at least some of them, especially romances such as the chivalric works that she requested or the *Carcer d'amore*, which she said she wanted to read 'per nostro spasso' (for our enjoyment),[182] and works with which she had a personal connection or in which she was praised, such as Liburnio's *Selvette* or Trissino's *I ritratti*. In her correspondence, she mentions the pleasure and benefit she receives from works when she writes to thank authors for sending them, although she does not discuss her reading in any detail.[183] What her correspondence and other evidence can tell us much more about is the part that texts and their ownership also played in the formation of her relationships with others and of her cultural prestige. We can look at four aspects of this: her association with living authors; her participation in the lending of texts; her displaying of books; and the use of some of her texts for musical performance.

An important factor contributing to the status of elite women was the public praise given to them by male writers, since women's own voices were relatively muted. The key proof of a writer's allegiance was his or her dedication of a text. The terminology of tribute and obligation that was, or should have been, typical of an author's depiction of a dedicatee is typified by the letter to Isabella, dated 22 March 1502, in which Galeotto Del Carretto sets out the subject matter of his verse tragedy *La Sophonisba* and then explains why he was sending a copy to her:

> considerando poi l'antiquo obligo et innata servitù et osservanza in verso di vostra altezza, quale è stata di sì efficace sorte, che come da' miei giovenili anni me gli ha dedicato, et come suo suddito inchinato in assenza mia a visitarla col tributo di qualche mia rima, così mi sospinge a perseverare insino che lo spirito mio reggerà queste ossa, non mi sciogliendo mai dal volontario e spontaneo mio antico obbligo, et come per qualche impedimento e mal disposte conditioni de tempi, ho pur fatto qualche intervallo in non havergli mandato de le mie rime il dovuto tributo, che oro et argento non è in me di potergli mandare, nè quella ne ha di bisogno, nè manco lo ricerca, mi è parso, per non cadere in contumacia, di mandargli questa opera mia continuata.[184]

> (I consider then my long-standing obligation and innate devotion and obedience towards Your Highness. [This obedience] has been so effective in nature that, just as since my youth it has made me dedicated to you and has inclined me, as your subject, to visit you in my absence with the tribute

---

[182] Luzio and Renier, *La coltura*, p. 9; Iotti, 'Phenice unica', p. 171.

[183] For the examples of Calmeta (1504) and Trissino (1514), see Iotti, 'Phenice unica', pp. 172–73.

[184] Galeotto Del Carretto, *La Sophonisba tragedia* (Venice: Gabriele Giolito, 1546), fol. A5$^{r-v}$.

of some lyric verses of mine, so it drives me to persevere for as long as my
spirit supports these bones, without ever freeing me from my voluntary and
spontaneous long-standing obligation. As it has been some time, because of
various obstacles and adverse times, since I sent you the due tribute of my
verses – for I do not have the means to send you gold and silver, nor do you
need or even seek it – it seemed right to me, in order not to be guilty of
disobedience, to send you this continuous work of mine.)

However, two well-known poets who had apparently promised to dedicate their collected verse to Isabella died before finalizing a presentation
manuscript. A crucial moment in her claiming sole possession of their works
thus came just after the authors' deaths. The first case was that of the poet
Antonio Pistoia. With a letter of 18 June 1499, he had sent Isabella
a manuscript copy of a tragedy in terza rima that he had dedicated to her
father Duke Ercole d'Este, *Philostrato e Pamphila doi amanti*, with a promise
to send her shortly a collection of his verse:

Ill[ustrissi]ma mia Madonna, mando questo libretto della Tragedia nomi-
nata *Pamphila*, la quale presentai la Quaresima passata, se non per far noto
a quella la mia servitù per uno nuntio delli *Sonetti faceti* ch'io in breve
settimane li donerò, a quella sola tale opera solazevole intitolata.[185]

(Most illustrious lady, I am sending this little book of the tragedy entitled
*Pamphila*, which I presented during Lent just past. I do this simply to let you
know of my devotion, as a forerunner of the humorous sonnets that I shall
give you in a few weeks' time, an amusing work dedicated to you alone.)

However, by the time that Pistoia died on 29 April 1502, he had failed to
send Isabella his dedicated manuscript of verse. She wrote about six weeks
later to Niccolò da Correggio, who (she had heard) had determined to put
together a manuscript of Pistoia's complete works. She reminded
Correggio that she had the right to the dedication:

Quando viveva, il Pistoia se offerse e promise molte volte mettere insieme in
una opera tutte le cose per lui composte, et intitularne a nui; ma per non averli
servito il tempo, non ha potuto esequirlo. Intendemo che la Signoria Vostra
ha preso cura di ritrovarle et farne uno codice: che molto ne piace et
laudemola di questo piissimo officio; ma gli ricordamo che La non voglia
privarne di quella rasone che, per dispositione et legato del poeta, gli havemo.

(During his lifetime, Pistoia offered and repeatedly promised to put two
confessionals, together in one work all the writings he had composed and to

[185] Luzio and Renier, *La coltura*, pp. 208–09; Carla Rossi, *Il Pistoia: spirito bizzarro del Quattrocento*
(Alessandria: Edizioni dell'Orso, 2008), pp. 64–65.

dedicate them to us; but, since he did not have the time, he was unable to carry this out. We understand that you have undertaken to find them and make a manuscript of them. We welcome and applaud this most dutiful task; but we remind you not to deprive us of that legal title that we have to them, through the poet's disposition and bequest.)

Isabella would have been concerned that the collection made by Correggio would circulate, whether in manuscript or print, without formal acknowledgement of her ownership. An ornate manuscript copy of Pistoia's sonnets, dedicated to her, was eventually copied by Giovanni Francesco Gianninello, another of the executors of Pistoia's estate, and presented to her in late 1511.[186]

Six years later, Isabella's desire for exclusiveness and her domineering nature were seen again in her unseemly haste to gain possession of another manuscript of verse by a recently deceased poet. This time the author was Correggio himself, and Isabella seems to have been both demanding a specific book and asserting her inherited rights to the texts contained within it. The justification for her claim, made in letters from her to Correggio's son Gian Galeazzo and to Correggio's widow written just sixteen days after the poet's death in February 1508, was far from straightforward. A collection of Correggio's verse had certainly at one stage been dedicated to Isabella. But her highhanded tone in a letter to Gian Galeazzo appears to conceal a fear that his father had subsequently withdrawn the dedication and, to make matters worse, had addressed the collection instead to Lucrezia Borgia:

> Per il mandato nostro intendemo la scusa che fa la S[ignoria] V[ostra] de non potersi per adesso resolvere circa la richiesta nostra del libro de le opere del seg[no]re vostro padre de fe[lice] me[moria] intitulato ad noi per rispecto de le occupationi vi accadeno per il recente caso suo, et per voler prima far rivedere et corregere tutte le cose sue, de le quale fareti parte che ni piacerà. Replicamo che per hora volemo havervi per iscuso, bastandoni in questa visitatione nostra havere advertita la S[ignoria] V[ostra] de le ragioni che havemo in lo libro alligato de l'opere del seg[no]re vostro patre, anchora che non fossi fora di tempo nè ad noi il dimandarlo, nè ad vui senza altra exceptione darcelo de presenti, essendo nui cussì vera herede de dicto libro, como vui seti de l'altre cose et facultà sua; nè accade metterlo altramente in compromesso, perché

[186] Luzio and Renier, *La coltura*, pp. 210–11; Rossi, *Il Pistoia*, pp. 82–86 (quotation from p. 82). On this case, see also Antonio Cammelli, *I sonetti faceti secondo l'autografo ambrosiano*, ed. by Erasmo Pèrcopo (Naples: Jovene, 1908), pp. xi–xiii, and Luzio and Renier, *La coltura*, pp. 208–11. On Gianninello or Zaninello, see Sally Hickson, '"To See Ourselves as Others See Us": Giovanni Francesco Zaninello of Ferrara and the Portrait of Isabella d'Este by Francesco Francia', *Renaissance Studies*, 23 (2009), 288–310. On the problem of writers defecting from one woman patron to another, see Lisa K. Regan, 'Ariosto's Threshold Patron: Isabella d'Este in the *Orlando furioso*', *Modern Language Notes*, 120 (2005), 50–69 (pp. 64, 66).

havendolo apresso, como confessati, et non intesa contraria dispositione de l'auctore, potevati vedere il libro, se non l'haveti visto, cum la intitulatione nostra et mandarlo ad chi n'è patrona, maxime promittendovi nui di non darlo fori senza vostra participatione, avenga che di ragione lo potessimo fare.

(From our envoy we learn of Your Lordship's excuse that you are unable to decide for the moment about our request for the book of your late father's works dedicated to us, because you are occupied with this recent event and because you wish first to have revisions and corrections made to all his writings, which, we are pleased to say, you will communicate. We reply that for now we wish to excuse you, since it is enough in this visitation of ours to have informed you of the legal titles we have to the above-mentioned book of your father's works, even though it would not be before time either for us to ask for it or for you to give it to us immediately without further objection, since we are the true heir of the said book just as you are the heir of his other writings and possessions. Nor does this mean putting it otherwise in danger because, since you have it with you, as you admit, and no disposition to the contrary on the author's part has been heard, you could see the book, if you have not done so already, with the dedication to us and send it to whom it belongs, especially since we promise you not to publish it without your involvement, even though we would be entitled to do so.)

Continuing the dispute over ownership in the same legal tone, Gian Galeazzo argued that his father had not given the book to her during his lifetime, and so he was heir to it as he was to the rest of Niccolò's property. Isabella countered that, while the poet might not have intended to give her the specific copy she had seen, he had wanted to have a copy transcribed and given to her. Gian Galeazzo was right to want to have Niccolò's works corrected, she argued, but she wanted them to be published with a dedication to her: 'Sì che, quanto più corrette et approbate serranno, tanto più ni serranno grate, pur che usiscano col titulo nostro quelle che già ni erano intitulate' (So that, the more correct and approved they are, the more welcome they will be to us, as long as those that were already dedicated to us are published with the dedication to us). The promise that Gian Galeazzo made in return was highly ambiguous: he would ensure that any 'intitulatione' (dedication) followed what he considered to be his father's wish. It was reported in August that Lucrezia herself was setting out for the town of Correggio, south of Mantua, in order to obtain the poet's works, and this seemed only to confirm that the poet Correggio was one that got away from Isabella: he had indeed transferred his allegiance and removed his original dedication.[187]

[187] Alessandro Luzio and Rodolfo Renier, 'Niccolò da Correggio', *GSLI*, 21 (1893), 205–64, and 22 (1894), 65–119 (quotations from vol. 22, 76–77 and 80–81). See, too, Luzio and Renier, *La coltura*,

Another intervention of Isabella's suggests that, in this period, a dedicatee was seen as owning a work. In 1519, Vida sent her, probably through Castiglione, a manuscript of his poem *De bombyce*. Isabella liked the work very much and, as was mentioned in Chapter 1, made rather half-hearted attempts to have it printed. Was Isabella doing this for the benefit of Vida, of the reading public or of herself? Certainly, her image would have benefited from the praises of her and of her son Francesco that are embedded in the poem (Book I. 6–9, where Vida invokes her support, and Book II. 1–25). As for Vida, she was certainly not putting his wishes first. He wrote to Mario Equicola that he was not keen on printing this work on its own; he preferred to wait a few months and have it printed in Venice as part of a collection of his verse. But he had to recognize that Isabella had a right to have his poem printed since it now belonged to her: 'La Excell[enti]a S[ua] può fare come gli piace perché è sua cosa' (Her Excellency can do as she wishes, since it is her property).[188]

The formation of Isabella's collection thus provided valuable opportunities for writers and others to give or lend new texts to her and to be admitted figuratively within the walls of her apartments in the Palazzo ducale. The practices of making dedications and of presenting gift copies allowed writers to consolidate relationships of clientage with patrons or to establish new ones, and to fashion their identities as clients in the eyes of others. This prospect would have been especially attractive to someone such as Liburnio, who was not of high social status. Some authors would doubtless have conceived of Isabella as a 'threshold patron', to use Lisa Regan's term,[189] in the hope of then becoming a client of the more powerful marquis Francesco, but Isabella's own sphere of influence as a patron was considerable. Liburnio asked to be numbered 'inter clientulos tuos, quos innumeros habes' (among your insignificant clients, whose number is endless).[190] A certain rivalry between authors seeking Isabella's favour may lie behind the explanation that Equicola, always and only

p. 129; Claudio Gallico, 'Un libro di poesia di musica dell'epoca d'Isabella d'Este', *Bollettino storico mantovano*, Quaderno 4 (Mantua, 1961), pp. 46–48; Enrico Fenzi, 'Tra Isabella e Lucrezia: Niccolò da Correggio', in *Lucrezia Borgia: storia e mito*, ed. by Michele Bordin and Paolo Trovato (Florence: Olschki, 2006), pp. 43–74 (pp. 54–60). Carlo Dionisotti, 'Nuove rime di Niccolò da Correggio', *Studi di filologia italiana*, 17 (1959), 135–88, shows that MS Harl. 3406 of the British Library, containing over 400 poems by Correggio, was not the copy that Isabella had seen but was probably a transcription prepared by a secretary with a view to a printed edition. There are references to her as dedicatee, but the compiler must have been concerned to exclude the dedication of the collection or to leave it vague (pp. 142–43).

[188] Luzio and Renier, *La coltura*, pp. 152–56 (quotations from pp. 154 and 155). The copy sent to Isabella may be British Library, MS Harl. 3933, written on vellum, but not decorated.

[189] Regan, 'Ariosto's Threshold Patron', p. 65.    [190] Luzio and Renier, *La coltura*, p. 173.

a prose writer, inserted into the proem to Book I of his *De natura de amore* (dedicated to Isabella), about why he preferred to omit the exaggerated sighs and laments of certain lyric poets from his treatise: 'Pretermettemo alcuni che de amorosi effecti hanno scritto [. . .]. Volemo che alcuni scrittori in solingo et denso bosco, non in nostro libro, querelando se crucieno' (We pass over some who have written about the effects of love [. . .]. We wish some writers to torment themselves plaintively in a lonely and dense wood, not in our book).[191]

At the same time, it is evident how important the relationship with authors could also be for a dedicatee such as Isabella: she needed to be seen as the object of homage from writers as diverse as Pistoia and Vida. A passage towards the end of the *Orlando furioso* depicts through ekphrasis how the voices of authors could be seen as necessary to the public renown of elite women. The knight Rinaldo comes across a fountain covered by a vault that is supported by a series of eight statues of female contemporaries of Ariosto, and the women are resting their feet on the shoulders of male authors who hold in their hands copious writings and whose open mouths are singing the women's praises. The two men supporting Isabella are the Mantuan poets Gian Giacomo Calandra and Gian Giacomo Bardellone:

> I duo che mostran disïosi affetti
> che la gloria di lei sempre risuone,
> Gian Iacobi ugualmente erano detti,
> l'uno Calandra, e l'altro Bardelone.

(The two who evinced a fervent desire to give a perpetual resonance to her glory were both named Gian Jacobi, one Calandra, the other Bardelone.)[192]

Isabella's sister-in-law Elisabetta Gonzaga would have seemed especially fortunate, since she is praised by two scholar-writers whose renown was already great in 1516 when the first edition of the *Furioso* was printed, Iacopo Sadoleto and Bembo.

---

[191] Mario Equicola, *De natura de amore* (Venice: Lorenzo Lorio, 1525), fol. a2ʳ. On this passage, see Stefano Cracolici, '"Remedia amoris sive elegiae": appunti sul dialogo antierotico del Quattrocento', in *Il sapere delle parole: studi sul dialogo latino e italiano del Rinascimento*, ed. by Walter Geerts, Annick Paternoster and Franco Pignatti (Rome: Bulzoni, 2001), pp. 23–35 (pp. 24–25). I am grateful to Stefano Cracolici for this suggestion.

[192] Ariosto, *Orlando furioso*, XXXVIII. 82 (1516 edition), XXXVIII. 85 (1521), XLII. 85 (1532); Ariosto, *Orlando furioso*, trans. by Waldman, p. 506. On these two poets and Isabella, see Luzio and Renier, *La coltura*, pp. 73–76. Calandra is depicted as praising Isabella in Equicola's *Nec spe nec metu* of 1513: Campbell, *The Cabinet of Eros*, p. 199.

The example of Cosmico has shown how Isabella sought to borrow
rare texts in order to have them copied for her collection. If she wanted to
borrow texts, she needed to reciprocate by lending, in an economy of
exchange that bound her to others and others to her. A Venetian patrician
who had a strong interest in both short stories and linguistic usage,
Giovan Francesco Valerio (or Valier), wrote to Isabella in 1511 to request,
for a few days, 'dui testi delle cento novelle antichi' (two old texts of the
hundred short stories), that is, Boccaccio's *Decameron*; 'l'uno ne vidd'io
nella grotta, l'altro, che è il migliore, nel camerino di m[esser] Zuan
Jacomo Calandra, in carta bona' (one of them I saw in the grotta, the
other, which is the better one, in the little room of Gian Giacomo
Calandra, on vellum).[193] We know that Isabella did lend her texts, at
least from time to time and within her extended family. For instance, she
provided her copy of Demetrios Moschos's translation of Philostratus's
*Imagines* for her brother Alfonso d'Este and tried to retrieve it in 1515–16.
She lent her manuscript of Pistoia to Francesco Berni in 1531 and to
Alessandro Bentivoglio in 1532.[194] Her ownership of rare or unique copies
of poems newly composed by Serafino Aquilano put her in a position of
power: anyone who wanted a copy had to turn to her. Thus on
25 April 1498 her brother Cardinal Ippolito d'Este wrote to her from
Pavia to say: 'Essendo desideroso d'haver qualche cosa bona de Seraphino
prego V[ostra] Ill[ustrissim]a S[ignoria] che me voglia far copiare alcuni
soi strambotti et qualche altra cosa zentile chel habbia composto nova-
mente et mandarmeli qua' (Since I wish to have some good compositions
by Serafino, I ask Your illustrious Ladyship to be good enough to have
copied some of his strambotti and some other nice poems that he has
composed recently, and send them to me here).[195] Yet, just as Isabella
craved ownership of manuscript texts that were unique, so she could be
reluctant to let what she possessed be shared by too many others. When
she allowed Gonzaga relatives to have capitoli by Serafino Aquilano, she
took great care to ensure that the copies would go no further. A group of
his poems sent by her to Cardinal Ippolito d'Este in 1497 contained some
new matter and, she was assured on behalf of Ippolito, 'altro che Dio e lui

[193] Luzio and Renier, *La coltura*, pp. 165–66. Valerio was chosen by the Aldine press to revise the language
of Castiglione's *Libro del cortegiano* for the first edition of 1528: Ghino Ghinassi, 'L'ultimo revisore del
"Cortigiano"', in *Dal Belcalzer al Castiglione: studi sull'antico volgare di Mantova e sul 'Cortegiano'*, ed. by
Paolo Bongrani (Florence: Olschki, 2006), pp. 161–206; Fabio Massimo Bertolo, 'Nuovi documenti
sull'edizione principe del "Cortegiano"', *Schifanoia*, 13–14 (1992), 133–44 (p. 137).
[194] Luzio and Renier, *La coltura*, pp. 15–16 (Philostratus), 211 (Pistoia); Koortbojian and Webb,
'Isabella d'Este's Philostratos', p. 260.
[195] Bertolotti, 'Varietà archivistiche e bibliografiche'; Luzio and Renier, *Mantova e Urbino*, p. 93.

non la vederà' (no one other than God and he will see it).[196] She laid down strict conditions when she lent her husband's copy of the medieval Greek writer Eustathius to Cesare d'Aragona in 1518: 'Suplico V[ostra] S[ignoria] voglia farlo tenere con deligentia et fare che non capiti in mano di troppe persone, perché essendo cosa rara, è da tener caro né lassarlo vedere a molti, per non diminuirli la reputatione' (I beg you to have it kept carefully and ensure it does not fall into the hands of too many people. Since it is rare, it must be held dear and it must not be allowed to be seen by many, so as not to lessen its reputation).[197] As a guardian of rare or unique texts, Isabella had power that she was very reluctant to dissipate.

Another example illustrates both the practice of lending and borrowing texts within the family circle and that of reading aloud, discussed in the previous section. In 1500, Isabella wrote to Antonia del Balzo, by now the widow of Gianfrancesco Gonzaga, one of Isabella's husband's uncles, to ask for a copy of the romance *Tirant lo Blanch* (perhaps unsuccessfully, since we have seen that she later asked Iacopo D'Atri to obtain this work).[198] In 1510, Antonia was unwell and on 5 March she wrote to Isabella to request, in turn, the loan of some chivalric romances from the collection of Isabella's husband, so that they could be read aloud to her:

> Non possendo per la mia indisposizione andar molto atorno, volontieri per passar tempo una parte del giorno sento legere et tanto più piacere ho quanto che intenda qualche cosa ch'io mai non habbia intesa, onde per questo supplico la Ex[cellentia] V[ostra] voglia essere contenta compiacermi de alcuni libri de quelli de lo ill[ustrissi]mo Sig[no]r suo consorte, cioè li dui de la *Tavola retonda*, la *Historia del Re Artus* et quella de *Gottifredo de Boione*.

> (Being unable because of my indisposition to get around much, in order to pass the time, I like to listen to reading for part of the day, and I take all the more pleasure when I hear some work I have never heard. So I beg Your Excellency to be kind enough to please me with some of the books of your most illustrious husband, namely the two of the *Round Table*, the *Story of King Arthur* and that of *Godfrey of Bouillon*.)

Two days later, Antonia wrote to report to Isabella: 'ho havuto li libri franzesi [...] et cussì lavorando me li facio legere per spassare il tempo' (I have received the French books [...] and thus I have them read to me while I work, to pass the time).[199]

---

[196] Luzio and Renier, *Mantova e Urbino*, p. 92. For a similar example, see Richardson, *Manuscript Culture in Renaissance Italy*, p. 268.

[197] Luzio and Renier, *La coltura*, p. 17.     [198] Ibid., p. 9.

[199] Ibid., pp. 9–10; Peyronel Rambaldi, *Una gentildonna irrequieta*, pp. 47–49 (see also pp. 25–30).

While Isabella was sometimes cautious about lending rare texts, visitors to her rooms in the Palazzo ducale, such as Valerio, could certainly see her collection of books. As was noted earlier, Trissino listed these among the objects on show in her apartments, and Isabella wanted books 'per ornare el nostro studio', as we saw she wrote in 1501 to Alfonso Trotti. 'Ornare' here seems to have two senses. Through their subject matter, the books endowed her apartments with splendour, revealing her intellectual tastes and cultural refinement, just as the mythological paintings and antiquities did. But the books also provided visual adornment, as part of a culture of magnificent display. We know that Isabella attached great importance to the garb worn by texts. When she received Gianninello's copy of Pistoia's verse, now unfortunately lost, she commented particularly on the binding as well as on the dedication: 'Zo. Francesco Gianinello mi ha mandato a donare un libro de li Sonecti del Pistoia meglio ligato, sì di nova inventione come di li ornamenti, che vedessimo mai, a nui intitolato: il quale ni è stato summamente grato' (Giovanni Francesco Gianninello has sent me as a gift a book of the sonnets of Pistoia, the best bound, both for its novel design and for its ornaments, that we have ever seen, dedicated to us; it was extremely welcome to us).[200] The postmortem inventory shows that the great majority of her volumes, including romances, had fine bindings, while several were written or printed on vellum. All of the first half-dozen entries, for example, specify elegant bindings:

> Primo un libro di musicha francesa in carta pergamina coperto di veluto turchino co li fornimenti d'argento
> Item uno libro chiamato Cornucopia in foglio coperto di coramo negro indorato
> Item Aristide greco scritto a mano in foglio nostrano coperto di foglio ros[s]o con li fornimenti di ottone usato
> Item Amadis de Gaula coperto di coramo rosso
> Item uno libro de Tirante lonblanch in spagnolo in foglio coperto di coramo rosso
> Item la musica di Franchino scritta a mano in foglio coperto di rosso

> (First, a book of French music on vellum bound in blue velvet with silver furnishings
> Item, a book called *Cornucopia* [by Niccolò Perotti], in folio, bound in black morocco, gilded
> Item, [Aelius] Aristides in Greek, manuscript, in Mantuan folio, bound in red with brass furnishings, used

---

[200] Luzio and Renier, *La coltura*, p. 210.

Item, *Amadis de Gaula* bound in red morocco
Item, *Tirant lo Blanch* in Spanish, in folio, bound in red morocco
Item, the music of Franchino [Gaffurio], manuscript, in folio, bound in red)

Other colours that are specified for the morocco of the bindings are blackish ('morello'), greyish ('bretino'), dark tan ('taneto'), pinkish ('incarnato'), crimson ('cremisino'), yellow, white and green. There does not appear to be any link between the colour of bindings and the content of books. Eleonora d'Aragona's books (see note 149 in this chapter) similarly had fine bindings, with colours including red, crimson, green, white, black, 'morello' and grey ('biretino').

In which room or rooms did the marchioness keep her books? The studiolo is clearly the strongest possibility, as suggested by the word 'studio' in her letter to Trotti, by contemporary paintings of studies with books displayed on shelves or lecterns of various kinds, and by examples such as that of Baldassarre Castiglione, some of whose books were kept 'fora in el studio' (outside in the study).[201] At least some books may have been kept in the grotta: as mentioned above, Valerio saw a *Decameron* there, and Equicola's dedicatory letter of the translation of Philostratus refers to 'le Icone [...] digne della tua aurea grotta' (the Images [...] worthy of your golden grotta).[202] However, it has been suggested that the term 'grotta' was used for the suite of rooms as a whole as well as for one of the rooms.[203] A letter of 1516 reports that the door of the 'camerino della libraria' (the little room of the library) had been found unlocked and books removed from 'li so armari' (its cupboards).[204] Perhaps, as the book collection had grown, it had now been moved to a dedicated space within the first set of apartments. This report of 1516 also shows that some books at least were stored in cupboards, maybe laid flat but visible through grilles, as in the trompe-l'œil marquetry panels in the studiolo of the ducal palace of Urbino. Others might have been on shelves with their spines outwards, and one or two might have been open on lecterns, showing the script and any decorations. Carpaccio's *The Vision of St Augustine* in the Scuola di San Giorgio degli Schiavoni, Venice (c. 1505) depicts both these practices. In

---

[201] Rebecchini, *Private Collectors in Mantua*, p. 314.

[202] Foligno, 'Di alcuni codici', p. 71; Koortbojian and Webb, 'Isabella d'Este's Philostratos', Plate 43b.

[203] Giuseppe Gerola, 'Trasmigrazioni e vicende dei Camerini di Isabella d'Este', *Atti e memorie dell'Accademia virgiliana di Mantova*, n.s., 21 (1929), 253–90 (p. 254); Brown, '"Lo insaciabile desiderio nostro de cose antique"', p. 324.

[204] Luzio and Renier, *La coltura*, p. 5, n. 14; Clifford M. Brown, *Isabella d'Este in the Ducal Palace in Mantua: An Overview of her Rooms in the Castello di San Giorgio and the Corte Vecchia* (Rome: Bulzoni, 2005), p. 38.

view of the attention paid to bindings, it seems likely in any case that Isabella's books were intended to provide a colourful display.

The texts acquired by the marchioness did not only contribute to the material culture on show in her apartments: some of them were also linked with musical performances, by herself – since she could play several instruments and accompanied herself while she sang – and by others. She employed musicians such as Bartolomeo Tromboncino to set new verse for her to sing, and another well-known composer, Marchetto Cara, was employed by her husband Francesco. Poets regularly sent her manuscript copies of their lyric compositions to be set to music.[205] Members of Isabella's courtly community would thus often have had their first access to some verse through the singing voice rather than through the written word. Music was represented in various ways in the decorations of the studioli and the grotte: for instance, Apollo plays the lyre as the Muses dance in Mantegna's *Parnassus*, and the device of musical symbols relevant to her contralto voice (the 'impresa delle pause') appeared on the ceiling of the first grotta and elsewhere. The first studiolo and grotta would have been too cramped for music-making; Campbell estimates that the original study, 'monastic and cell-like', 'could comfortably accommodate perhaps two or three persons in addition to its owner'.[206] But the second studiolo and grotta in the Corte Vecchia were more spacious. In any case, there can be no doubt that performances linked to some of the texts owned by Isabella (probably among those on loose sheets of paper) took place within the suite of apartments where the texts were held.[207]

At present only a few manuscript and printed books once owned by Isabella d'Este can be identified more or less securely as items in libraries in Italy and elsewhere, such as the Turin manuscript of Pliny and the British Library's Aldine Petrarch of 1501 mentioned above. Ubaldo Meroni has suggested links between other manuscripts and Isabella, but in only two cases with any certainty: Sannazaro's *Arcadia*, formerly Turin, Biblioteca

[205] See, for example, Prizer, 'Isabella d'Este and Lucrezia Borgia as Patrons of Music'; Prizer, 'Una "virtù molto conveniente a madonne": Isabella d'Este as a Musician', *Journal of Musicology*, 17 (1999), 10–49; Richardson, *Manuscript Culture in Renaissance Italy*, pp. 244, 248–49.

[206] Campbell, *The Cabinet of Eros*, p. 62; see, too, pp. 87–113.

[207] Iain Fenlon, *Music and Patronage in Sixteenth-Century Mantua*, 2 vols (Cambridge University Press, 1980), I, 15–22; Fenlon, 'The Gonzaga and Music', in *Splendours of the Gonzaga: Catalogue*, ed. by David Chambers and Jane Martineau (London: Victoria & Albert Museum, 1981), pp. 87–94; Fenlon, 'Music and Learning in Isabella d'Este's Studioli', in *La corte di Mantova nell'età di Andrea Mantegna*, ed. by Cesare Mozzarelli, Robert Oresko and Leandro Ventura (Rome: Bulzoni, 1997), pp. 353–67; Thornton, *The Scholar in his Study*, pp. 122–23.

Nazionale, MS N.V.53, destroyed in the fire of 1904 (item 68 in the inventory, 'in foglio coperta di coramo negro fornita d'argento'; in folio, bound in black morocco with silver furnishings), and Bernardo Tasso's *Epithalamio nelle nozze del Signor Federico Gonzaga Duca di Mantova et di Madonna Margherita Paleologa*, Gotha, Forschungsbibliothek, Memb. II 107 (item 72, 'in carta pergamena in quarto coperto di coramo negro indorato'; on vellum, in quarto, bound in black morocco, gilded).[208] Among other books in the inventory, the 'libro di musicha francesa' (item 1) has been identified tentatively with a collection of 123 pieces for wind players composed by Josquin Desprez and others, now Rome, Biblioteca Casanatense, MS 2856. In the coat of arms on fol. 3[v], the Este arms are impaled with those of the Gonzaga, but on the dexter side (to the viewer's left) rather than the sinister, which would be normal for the bride. The dating and circumstances of commissioning of this manuscript have thus been disputed: it has been variously proposed that it was copied in the Este court to mark Isabella's betrothal in 1480 or to mark her wedding in 1490, or that it originally had nothing to do with the Gonzaga but Isabella had had a different coat of arms overpainted with that of her husband's family.[209] A manuscript work entitled *Timon comedia* in the inventory, item 13, is not attributed to an author, but this must be the copy of Galeotto Del Carretto's *Comedia de Timon greco* sent to her by the author on 2 January 1498, now Modena, Biblioteca Estense Universitaria, MS Campori Appendice 311 = γ.S.2.27. On 14 January, Del Carretto wrote again to say that the copy had been made for him by 'uno novo scriptore' (a new scribe) who had made an error, and he asked for it to be corrected.[210]

It is possible to suggest, with varying degrees of confidence, identifications of some books owned by the marchioness that are not listed in the

[208] *Beiträge zur ältern Litteratur; oder, Merkwürdigkeiten der Herzogl. öffentlichen Bibliothek zu Gotha*, ed. by Friedrich Jacobs and Friedrich August Ukert, 3 vols (Leipzig: Dyk, 1835–43), I, 185–86; Rodolfo Renier, 'Codici dell'Arcadia', *GSLI*, 11 (1888), 299–301; Meroni, *Mostra dei codici gonzagheschi*, pp. 66, 69. Cornelia Hopf of the Forschungsbibliothek Gotha kindly informs me that the Tasso manuscript now has a light-brown morocco binding.
[209] José M. Llorens, 'El codice Casanatense 2856 identificado como el Cancionero de Isabella d'Este (Ferrara) esposa de Francesco Gonzaga (Mantua)', *Anuario musical*, 20 (1967), 161–78; Fenlon, 'Music and Learning in Isabella d'Este's Studioli', pp. 363–64; *A Ferrarese Chansonnier: Roma, Biblioteca Casanatense 2856. 'Canzoniere di Isabella d'Este'*, ed. by Lewis Lockwood (Lucca: Libreria musicale italiana, 2002), pp. xi–xxxii; Joshua Rifkin, 'Munich, Milan, and a Marian Motet: Dating Josquin's "Ave Maria . . . virgo serena"', *Journal of the American Musicological Society*, 56 (2003), 239–350 (pp. 314–22); Anna Alberati in *Andrea Mantegna e i Gonzaga*, ed. by Trevisani, cat. no. III.25, pp. 264–65.
[210] Turba, 'Galeotto Del Carretto', pp. 107–09; Marzia Minutelli, 'Poesia e teatro di Galeotto Dal Carretto: riflessioni in margine al carteggio con Isabella d'Este', *Nuova rivista di letteratura italiana*, 7 (2004), 123–78 (pp. 153–54).

inventory. A Book of Hours that has the Gonzaga arms only, sold by Sotheby's in Munich in 1979, could have belonged to her, it has been proposed; it may have been commissioned while she was still young, before being illuminated in 1490 by the brothers Gherardo and Monte di Giovanni.[211] A manuscript copied by Bartolomeo Sanvito, now Harvard University, Houghton Library, MS Typ 213, was very probably in Isabella's possession. The earlier part, fols 13$^r$–68$^v$, containing the Office of the Virgin, may have been written in the late 1480s and presented to Isabella as a gift on her marriage. The sections formed by fols 1$^r$–12$^v$ and 70$^r$–149$^v$ were probably written and added shortly afterwards, in the early 1490s. They consist respectively of a Mantuan calendar and prayers: the Penitential Psalms and the Offices of the Dead, of the Cross and of the Holy Spirit. In a few places, these prayers are personalized in order to be said by a lady named 'Ysabella'; fol. 142$^v$, for instance, has a petition to Christ, 'obsecro te per sanctam crucem tuam adiuvare digneris me famulam tuam Ysabellam' (I beseech you by your holy cross to deign to help me, your servant Isabella).[212] Two manuscripts of the Biblioteca Teresiana of Mantua that have the arms of Gonzaga impaling Este are Lodovico Andreasi's *Elegiarum libri duo*, MS 1354 (I.VI.27) and Antonio de' Conti's *Triumphale opus*, MS 1355 (I.VI.28). But it is uncertain whether they belonged to Isabella or to her husband. Since the first book of Andreasi's elegies is dedicated to her and the second to the marquis, the former manuscript may well have been presented to them both on the occasion of their marriage; and although Conti dedicated his work to Isabella, he presented a copy to Francesco in 1493.[213] The presentation copy of Correggio's *Fabula Psiches et Cupidinis*, dedicated to Isabella, now BAV, MS Reg. Lat. 1601, was probably not item 52 in the inventory, 'Romanci del S.r Nicolò da Coreggio scritti a mano in carta pergamena in ottavo coperti di veluto bretino' (Romances of Niccolò da Correggio, manuscript, on vellum, in octavo, bound in grey velvet), since this book

---

[211] Meroni, *Mostra dei codici gonzagheschi*, p. 69, Plate 134; *Miniatura fiorentina*, ed. by Garzelli, I, 328–29; II, Plate 991–93.

[212] Albinia C. de la Mare and Laura Nuvoloni, *Bartolomeo Sanvito: The Life and Work of a Renaissance Scribe*, ed. by Anthony R. A. Hobson and Christopher de Hamel (Paris: Association internationale de bibliophilie, 2009), pp. 35, 49–50, 290–91, 426–27.

[213] Luzio and Renier, *La coltura*, p. 177 (Conti); Meroni, *Mostra dei codici gonzagheschi*, p. 84, Plates 130 and 131; Raffaella Perini, 'Manoscritti gonzagheschi conservati presso la Biblioteca Comunale di Mantova', *Civiltà mantovana*, 105 (November 1997), 45–55 (pp. 53–55). MS 1354 was once attributed to Sanvito but its hand has now been judged reminiscent of that of an imitator of his, Guido Bonatti: de la Mare and Nuvoloni, *Bartolomeo Sanvito*, p. 334.

presumably included at least one other work, perhaps the *Fabula di Cefalo*.[214]

While only a few of Isabella d'Este's books can now be identified with any certainty, we still have enough evidence to reach some general conclusions about the functions of her collection. Ownership of books was for her, of course, primarily a source of personal pleasure and information; but it was also, as for other members of the elite, though to a greater extent than it would have been for most women, one of the factors that helped to establish social and cultural status and to communicate it to others. In her case, this process happened in a set of interrelated ways, some of which were consequences of the nature of her collection and of the means by which she put it together, others of which were used consciously. Isabella's books were on show in apartments that were semi-private but that she left open to select visitors whose oral or written accounts could then make the collection and its setting famous. Most of the books were beautifully made. They would also have impressed others because they did not contain the kind of texts one would conventionally expect to find in a woman's collection. Among other things, the library included an unusually high proportion of secular works or translations by contemporary writers, and an unusually high proportion of manuscripts; and of course these two features were linked, because the marchioness liked to be the exclusive or near-exclusive owner of texts. Ownership of texts acquired mainly not through her purchasing power but in an economy of exchange and of gift-giving could demonstrate the ability to draw on the resources of an elite cultural community and to make careful use of intermediaries, and in turn this ownership conferred power when other members of that community desired to borrow her texts. The vellum Aldine octavos, although acquired in a market economy, reflected privileged relationships with the man who was fast establishing himself as Italy's most fashionable and scholarly printer. Her acquisition of books could reflect her close association with living authors, her patronage of them, and their allegiance and admiration; and these aspects must have been particularly important for women, since far fewer authorial dedications were made to them. In certain cases, moreover, the possession of rare or unique texts could lead to exclusive musical performances or recitations for the benefit of honoured guests.

In her apartments, Isabella was able to display to members of her cultural community, and indirectly to a wider public, certain qualities:

---

[214] Dionisotti, 'Nuove rime di Niccolò da Correggio', p. 149; Niccolò da Correggio, *Opere*, ed. by Antonia Tissoni Benvenuti (Bari: Laterza, 1969), pp. 499–500, 512–13.

traditional virtues such as magnificence and shrewd liberality, together with a new and unique combination of cultural interests and accomplishments, fostered by her exceptional contacts with leading writers, artists and musicians. These were the qualities that helped to set her apart from and above others – above many men and especially above other women. In her affirmation of these attributes, Isabella's books, no less than the rest of her collections, played an integral part.

# Conclusion: Women's Agency and the Social Circulation of Texts

Arjun Appadurai has written perceptively on the added significance with which commodities can become freighted as they are circulated. An understanding of 'the concrete, historical circulation of things', Appadurai suggests, does not depend simply on 'the view that things have no meanings apart from those that human transactions, attributions, and motivations endow them with'. It is also necessary, he writes,

> to follow the things themselves, for their meanings are inscribed in their forms, their uses, their trajectories. It is only through the analysis of these trajectories that we can interpret the human transactions and calculations that enliven things. Thus [...] it is the things-in-motion that illuminate their human and social context.[1]

The same can be said of texts-in-motion and the contexts in which women created, promoted and benefited from them in Renaissance Italy. For women of all states and all walks of life – a bride, a mother, a widow, a cloistered nun, a courtesan, a marchioness and so on – texts could become endowed with new meanings and values as they followed their trajectories of transmission around the written or oral communication circuits.

The evidence considered in the first chapter suggested several ways in which women's agency in the author–publisher nexus was related to their social, cultural and spiritual identities and to the communities to which they belonged. The circulation of texts offered women some degree of cultural sociability. Authors such as Ippolita Clara and Vittoria Colonna in the early part of the sixteenth century, and then Laura Terracina, Laura Battiferri and Arcangela Tarabotti, used manuscript or print to address individuals or groups of people with whom they had ties. As women gained greater agency within print culture, they reached out to a wide readership

[1] Arjun Appadurai, 'Introduction: Commodities and the Politics of Value', in *The Social Life of Things: Commodities in Cultural Perspective*, ed. by Arjun Appadurai (Cambridge University Press, 1986), pp. 3–63 (p. 5).

that would have seen their use of the new medium as pioneering. When women participated actively in the scribal or print publication of works composed by others, their contributions could help to strengthen the identity of religious communities, as in the cases of Ludovica Torelli and Giulia Gonzaga. Women could be chosen as dedicatees of texts for reasons that went beyond the mere desire, on the part of the author or whoever else was publishing the works, to seek their favour. Involving them with the circulation of a text in this way seems to have had two deeper purposes. The first was to ennoble the work in the eyes of readers by associating it with the female dedicatee's perceived personal stature within her own circles. The second aim, although this remained unspoken, was, we can surmise, to create in other readers a sense of affinity with the ideal reader represented by this dedicatee.

Women's involvement in making and selling books as amateurs or professionals, studied in Chapter 2, very often arose from the familial or religious communities in which they lived, and it could in turn serve to foster those groups. Scribal work flourished within some female convents. Here it not only achieved a highly respectable level of technical accomplishment, but was one of the elements that served to fashion the collective identity of these communities, in which, as Stephanie Tarbin and Susan Broomhall put it, 'women identified with other women, or were so perceived by others'.[2] The production by nuns of handwritten books, even of complex choir books, was largely independent of men, and it was here that women had the greatest freedom of agency: only occasionally did they call on male illuminators to decorate manuscripts for them, and transcription could be organized and executed independently of men. Copying could provide income or could prompt gifts that helped to ensure the financial stability of a convent, as it did for Le Murate in Florence. Perhaps more importantly, it could help to provide a sense of cohesion and mutual support between individual members of the institution. For instance, the anonymous Augustinian who copied the *Libro dele revelationi* of Arcangela Panigarola in Santa Marta in Milan was explicitly writing for the benefit of her sisters. For the nuns of this house, writing manuscripts helped to keep alive memories of the two holy women through whom the renown of their convent had spread. By no means all convents encouraged writing, but cases such as those of Santa Marta and of Monteluce in

---

[2] Stephanie Tarbin and Susan Broomhall, 'Introduction', in *Women, Identities and Communities in Early Modern Europe*, ed. by Stephanie Tarbin and Susan Broomhall (Aldershot: Ashgate, 2008), pp. 1–9 (p. 1).

Perugia were not regarded as exceptional. They indicate, rather, that the creation of manuscripts was an aspect of book production to which women religious made a distinctive contribution during the Italian Renaissance, and that it affected the daily lives, worship and meditation of many members of their orders. In the context of print, laywomen who were connected with printing houses or bookshops by marriage or by descent could assist in their operations and thus promote the economic well-being of their households. In a few cases, women of religious orders made use of print publication, very occasionally even helping to run printing presses, in order to stimulate devotion or to advance the interests of their convents.

Books were often acquired by women within the context of social relationships, as the third chapter demonstrated. Newly-weds such as Primavera Machiavelli or novices such as Isabella Tossignani received books as gifts from their natal households. Giving, lending and sharing books could provide comfort and enjoyment, 'consolatione' and 'spasso', for other women, thus strengthening bonds of blood and friendship. Sharing texts directly through the medium of the reading or singing voice added a further degree of sociability. Possession of finely written and decorated books, such as a Book of Hours, a missal, a breviary or a collection of verse, helped to mark women's social and cultural status in the eyes of others. Isabella d'Este's acquisition, display and lending of certain works would have demonstrated her privileged relationships with authors, composers, scribes, printers and her own peer group. For elite women such as her, possession could mean not simply ownership of a copy of a text but also the right to have the work dedicated to her and published under her name.

Women's agency in textual culture in Renaissance Italy had a great deal in common with that of women elsewhere in Europe, as can be seen from some examples of recent research. Helen Smith has shed light on the presences of women throughout the circuit of book production in early modern England, for instance as translators, patrons, dedicatees and participants in printing and bookselling businesses before and after their husbands' deaths.[3] Women in Renaissance France, Susan Broomhall has shown, received and gave books as gifts, worked as scribes, illuminators, printers and booksellers, and ventured into print publication as authors.[4] Annie Parent, Beatrice Beech, Roméo Arbour and others have documented

[3] Helen Smith, *'Grossly Material Things': Women and Book Production in Early Modern England* (Oxford University Press, 2012).

[4] Susan Broomhall, *Women and the Book Trade in Sixteenth-Century France* (Aldershot: Ashgate, 2002).

the contributions of women, in collaboration with men, to running businesses within the Parisian book trade, as in the cases of Charlotte Guillard, Yolande Bonhomme and Jeanne Cassot, and the crucial roles of wives in creating alliances between printers.[5] The importance of inheritance and gifts in the acquisition of books by Frenchwomen is borne out by an essay of Brigitte Buettner.[6] Sandra Establés Susán has surveyed the growing involvement of women in family-based printing and bookselling companies in Spain and Latin America; examples include Brígida Maldonado, who for several years managed the press of her husband Juan Cromberger after his death in 1540, and Jerónima Gutiérrez, who helped her husband Juan Pablos (Giovanni Paoli) to set up a press in Mexico City in the same period.[7] Women working in the book trade in Germany and elsewhere have been studied by Albrecht Classen.[8] There are many similarities between the motives for which nuns made use of their scribal skills in Italy and in other countries. Cynthia Cyrus has described how sisters in Germany could produce manuscripts in collaboration, could copy them for sale or for the consolation ('trost') of other sisters and, as individuals, could use their colophons to ask readers to pray for their salvation.[9] A German nun's scribal activity could be seen as reinforcing the devotional qualities of her life, as was the case in Italian houses.[10] In the

[5] Annie Parent, *Les Métiers du livre à Paris au XVIe siècle (1535–1560)* (Geneva: Droz, 1974), pp. 137–38 (Guillard), 193–94 (alliances), 206–08 (Cassot); Beatrice Hibbard Beech, 'Charlotte Guillard: A Sixteenth-Century Business Woman', *Renaissance Quarterly*, 36 (1983), 345–67; Beech, 'Yolande Bonhomme: A Renaissance Printer', *Medieval Prosopography*, 6.2 (Autumn 1985), 79–100; Beech, 'Women Printers in Paris in the Sixteenth Century', *Medieval Prosopography*, 10.1 (Spring 1989), 75–93; Roméo Arbour, *Les Femmes et les métiers du livre en France (1600–1650)* (Chicago and Paris: Garamond Press and Didier Érudition, 1998); Annie Parent-Charon, 'À propos des femmes et des métiers du livre dans le Paris de la Renaissance', in *Des femmes et des livres: France et Espagne, XIVe–XVIIe siècle*, ed. by Dominique de Courcelles and Carmen Val Julián (Paris: École des Chartes, 1999), pp. 137–48; Rémi Jimenes, *Charlotte Guillard: une femme imprimeur à la Renaissance* (Tours: Presses Universitaires François-Rabelais; Presses Universitaires de Rennes, 2017).
[6] Brigitte Buettner, 'Women and the Circulation of Books', in *Women and Book Culture in Late Medieval and Early Modern France*, ed. by Martha W. Driver with Cynthia J. Brown, special issue of the *Journal of the Early Book Society*, 4 (2001), 9–31.
[7] Sandra Establés Susán, 'La actividad femenina en los negocios de producción, edición y venta de libros impresos en España e Hispanoamérica (siglos XVI–XVIII)', in *Doce siglos de materialidad del libro: estudios sobre manuscritos e impresos entre los siglos VIII y XIX*, dir. by Manuel José Pedraza Gracia, ed. by Helena Carvajal González and Camino Sánchez Oliveira (Prensas de la Universidad de Zaragoza, 2017), pp. 355–63.
[8] Albrecht Classen, 'Frauen als Buchdruckerinnen im deutschen Sprachraum des 16. und 17. Jahrhunderts', *Gutenberg-Jahrbuch* (2000), 181–95, and Classen, 'Frauen im Buchdruckergewerbe des 17. Jahrhunderts', *Gutenberg-Jahrbuch* (2001), 220–36.
[9] Cynthia J. Cyrus, *The Scribes for Women's Convents in Late Medieval Germany* (University of Toronto Press, 2009), pp. 77–89, 180–81, 193–202.
[10] Ibid., pp. 206–10.

Birgittines' mother house in Sweden, sisters copied manuscripts in the vernacular and in Latin for their institution and for external patrons.[11] Nuns in and around Brussels were active in copying works, including sermons that they had heard preached.[12] The practices of sociable reading and listening from which Italian laywomen could benefit also had parallels in other cultures. Marguerite de Navarre sometimes listened to a reading from a historian, a poet or another 'useful' author while doing her needlework.[13] Margaret Hoby and Anne Clifford were just two of the Englishwomen who stitched while someone read to them.[14] In the England of the eighteenth century, reading aloud was still a 'soundtrack to other domestic activities', as Abigail Williams puts it in her study of 'the orality in the history of the book'.[15]

The Preface of this book recalled Don McKenzie's conception of bibliography as encompassing 'not only the technical but the social processes' of the transmission of texts, 'the human motives and interactions' that are involved in their production, transmission and consumption. This broadly based approach is essential if we are to understand fully the roles that women in Renaissance Italy played in this sphere, in which technical and social processes were closely interwoven. The ways in which some laywomen and nuns succeeded in contributing to the practical aspects of transmission were shaped by the particular conditions that governed women's lives. At the same time, textual culture could have a special human value for the women who participated at some point in the communications circuits: it enabled them to nurture and to express their individual enthusiasms and talents, it strengthened their connectedness with others, especially with other women, and it enriched the lives of their social and spiritual communities.

---

[11] Ingela Hedström, 'Vadstena Abbey and Female Literacy in Late Medieval Sweden', in *Nuns' Literacies in Medieval Europe: The Hull Dialogue*, ed. by Virginia Blanton, Veronica O'Mara and Patricia Stoop (Turnhout: Brepols, 2013), pp. 253–72.

[12] Patricia Stoop, 'Nuns' Literacy in Sixteenth-Century Convent Sermons from the Cistercian Abbey of Ter Kameren', in *Nuns' Literacies in Medieval Europe: The Hull Dialogue*, ed. by Virginia Blanton, Veronica O'Mara and Patricia Stoop (Turnhout: Brepols, 2013), pp. 293–312, and Stoop, 'From Reading to Writing: The Multiple Levels of Literacy of the Sister Scribes in the Brussels Convent of Jericho', in *Nuns' Literacies in Medieval Europe: The Kansas City Dialogue*, ed. by Virginia Blanton, Veronica O'Mara and Patricia Stoop (Turnhout: Brepols, 2015), pp. 47–66.

[13] Broomhall, *Women and the Book Trade*, p. 20.

[14] Smith, *'Grossly Material Things'*, pp. 199, 201.

[15] Abigail Williams, *The Social Life of Books: Reading Together in the Eighteenth-Century Home* (New Haven: Yale University Press, 2017), pp. 43, 3.

# Bibliography of Works Published since 1700

Adams, Thomas R. and Nicolas Barker, 'A New Model for the Study of the Book', in *A Potencie of Life: Books in Society*, ed. by Nicolas Barker (London: British Library, 1994), pp. 5–43

Adimari, Alessandro, *La Polinnia*, ed. by Bruno Giancarlo (Terni: Thyrus, 2007)

Adorni Braccesi, Simonetta, '"Telifilo Filogenio [Girolamo Borro] sopra la perfectione delle donne": un libro, un editore e il controllo sopra la stampa nella Lucca del Cinquecento', in *La fede degli Italiani: per Adriano Prosperi*, vol. I, ed. by Guido dall'Olio, Adelisa Malena and Pierroberto Scaramella (Pisa: Edizioni della Normale, 2011), 223–35

   *'Una città infetta': la repubblica di Lucca nella crisi religiosa del Cinquecento* (Florence: Olschki, 1994)

Agati, Maria Luisa, *Giovanni Onorio da Maglie copista greco (1535–1563)*, suppl. 20 to *Bollettino dei classici* (Rome: Accademia Nazionale dei Lincei, 2001)

Agosti, Giovanni and Dominique Thiébaut, eds, *Mantegna 1431–1506* (Paris: Hazan and Musée du Louvre, 2008)

Albareda, Anselmo M., 'Intorno alla scuola di orazione metodica stabilita a Monserrato dall'abate Garsias Jiménez de Cisneros (1493–1510)', *Archivum historicum Societatis Iesu*, 25 (1956), 254–316

Albonico, Simone, 'Ippolita Clara e le sue rime', in *Ordine e numero: studi sul libro di poesia e le raccolte poetiche nel Cinquecento* (Alessandria: Edizioni dell'Orso, 2006), pp. 95–122

Alexander, J. J. G. and A. C. de la Mare, *The Italian Manuscripts in the Library of Major J. R. Abbey* (London: Faber, 1969)

Alexander, Jonathan J. G., 'Matteo da Milano, Illuminator', *Pantheon*, 50 (1992), 32–45

   *The Painted Book in Renaissance Italy: 1450–1600* (New Haven: Yale University Press, 2016)

   ed., *The Painted Page: Italian Renaissance Book Illumination 1450–1550* (Munich and New York: Prestel, 1994)

Alexander, Jonathan J. G., James H. Marrow and Lucy Freeman Sandler, *The Splendor of the Word: Medieval and Renaissance Manuscripts at the New York Public Library* (London and Turnhout: New York Public Library and Harvey Miller, 2005)

Allonge, Guillaume, 'Le scrittrici nella prima età moderna', in *Atlante della letteratura italiana*, ed. by Sergio Luzzatto and Gabriele Pedullà, 3 vols (Turin: Einaudi, 2010–12), II, 119–26

Alston, Robin C., *Books with Manuscript* (London: British Library, 1994)

Anderson, Jaynie, 'Rewriting the History of Art Patronage', *Renaissance Studies*, 10 (1996), 129–38

Andretta, Stefano, *La venerabile superbia: ortodossia e trasgressione nella vita di suor Francesca Farnese (1593–1651)* (Turin: Rosenberg & Sellier, 1994)

Appadurai, Arjun, ed., *The Social Life of Things: Commodities in Cultural Perspective* (Cambridge University Press, 1986)

Arbour, Roméo, *Les Femmes et les métiers du livre en France (1600–1650)* (Chicago and Paris: Garamond Press and Didier Érudition, 1998)

Aretino, Pietro, *Lettere*, ed. by Paolo Procaccioli, 6 vols (Rome: Salerno Editrice, 1997–2002)

   *Selected Letters*, trans. by George Bull (Harmondsworth: Penguin, 1976)

   *Teatro*, II, ed. by Giovanna Rabitti, Carmine Boccia and Enrico Garavelli (Rome: Salerno Editrice, 2010)

Argelati, Filippo, *Bibliotheca scriptorum Mediolanensium*, 2 vols (Milan: in aedibus Palatinis, 1745)

Arienti, Giovanni Sabadino degli, *Gynevera delle clare donne*, ed. by Corrado Ricci and Alberto Bacchi della Lega (Bologna: Romagnoli, 1888)

Ariosto, Ludovico, *Orlando furioso*, trans. by Guido Waldman (Oxford University Press, 1998)

   *Orlando furioso secondo l'edizione del 1532 con le varianti delle edizioni del 1516 e del 1521*, ed. by Santorre Debenedetti and Cesare Segre (Bologna: Commissione per i testi di lingua, 1960)

Armstrong, Nancy and Leonard Tennenhouse, eds, *The Ideology of Conduct: Essays on Literature and the History of Sexuality* (New York: Methuen, 1987)

Arthur, Kathleen G., 'Il Breviario di Santa Caterina da Bologna e "l'arte povera" clarissa', in *I monasteri femminili come centri di cultura fra Rinascimento e Barocco: atti del convegno storico internazionale, Bologna, 8–10 dicembre 2000*, ed. by Gianna Pomata and Gabriella Zarri (Rome: Edizioni di Storia e Letteratura, 2005), pp. 93–122

   'Images of Clare & Francis in Caterina Vigri's Personal Breviary', *Franciscan Studies*, 62 (2004), 177–92

   'New Evidence for a Scribal-Nun's Art: Maria di Ormanno degli Albizzi at San Gaggio', *Mitteilungen des Kunsthistorischen Institutes in Florenz*, 59 (2017), 271–80

Atkinson, Catherine, *Debts, Dowries, Donkeys: The Diary of Niccolò Machiavelli's Father, Messer Bernardo, in Quattrocento Florence* (Frankfurt am Main: Peter Lang, 2002)

Bacchiddu, Rita, 'Panigarola, Margherita (in religione Arcangela)', *DBI*, 80 (2014), 777–80

Baernstein, P. Renée, *A Convent Tale: A Century of Sisterhood in Spanish Milan* (New York: Routledge, 2002)

'In Widow's Habit: Women between Convent and Family in Sixteenth-Century Milan', *Sixteenth Century Journal*, 25 (1994), 787–807

Baldacchini, Lorenzo, *Alle origini dell'editoria in volgare: Niccolò Zoppino da Ferrara a Venezia. Annali (1503–1544)* (Manziana: Vecchiarelli, 2011)

Baldelli, Ignazio, 'Codici e carte di Monteluce', appendix to Giuseppe De Luca, 'Un formulario di cancelleria francescana e altri formulari tra il XIII e XIV secolo', *Archivio italiano per la storia della pietà*, 1 (1951), 219–393, at pp. 387–93

Bandello, Matteo, *Tutte le opere*, ed. by Francesco Flora, 2 vols (Milan: Mondadori, 1952)

Barberi, Francesco, 'Annali della tipografia romana di Baldassarre jr e Girolama Cartolari (1540–1559)', *LB*, 53 (1951), 69–120

    *Paolo Manuzio e la Stamperia del Popolo romano (1561–1570)* (Rome: Gela, 1985)

    *Tipografi romani del Cinquecento: Guillery, Ginnasio mediceo, Calvo, Dorico, Cartolari* (Florence: Olschki, 1983)

Barbieri, Edoardo, *Le bibbie italiane del Quattrocento e del Cinquecento*, 2 vols (Milan: Editrice Bibliografica, 1992)

    'Di certi usi della Sacra Scrittura condannati: "Il Salmista secondo la Bibbia"', *LB*, 120 (2018), 75–109

    '"Per monialium poenitentium manus": la tipografia del monastero di Santa Maria Maddalena alla Giudecca, detto delle Convertite (1557–1561)', *LB*, 113 (2011), 303–53

Bardazzi, Silvestro and Eugenio Castellani, eds, *S. Niccolò a Prato* (Prato: Edizioni del Palazzo, 1984)

Barker, Nicolas, *The Glory of the 'Art of Writing': The Calligraphic Work of Francesco Alunno of Ferrara* (Los Angeles: Cotsen Occasional Press, 2009)

    ed., *A Potencie of Life: Books in Society* (London: British Library, 1994)

Bartolomei Romagnoli, Alessandra, Emore Paoli and Pierantonio Piatti, eds, *Angeliche visioni: Veronica da Binasco nella Milano del Rinascimento* (Florence: SISMEL-Edizioni del Galluzzo, 2016)

Battaglia, Salvatore, ed., *Grande dizionario della lingua italiana*, 21 vols (Turin: UTET, 1961–2002)

Battiferra degli Ammannati, Laura, *Laura Battiferra and Her Literary Circle: An Anthology*, ed. and trans. by Victoria Kirkham (University of Chicago Press, 2006)

Battiferri degli Ammannati, Laura, *I sette salmi penitenziali di David con alcuni sonetti spirituali*, ed. by Enrico Maria Guidi (Urbino: Accademia Raffaello, 2005)

Bausi, Francesco, 'Le rime di e per Tullia d'Aragona', in *Les Femmes écrivains en Italie au Moyen Age et à la Renaissance: actes du colloque international, Aix-en-Provence, 12, 13, 14 novembre 1992* (Aix-en-Provence: Université de Provence, 1994), pp. 275–92

Beal, Peter, *In Praise of Scribes: Manuscripts and Their Makers in Seventeenth-Century England* (Oxford: Clarendon Press, 1998)

Bec, Christian, *Les Livres des Florentins (1413–1608)* (Florence: Olschki, 1984)

Beech, Beatrice Hibbard, 'Charlotte Guillard: A Sixteenth-Century Business Woman', *Renaissance Quarterly*, 36 (1983), 345–67

'Women Printers in Paris in the Sixteenth Century', *Medieval Prosopography*, 10.1 (Spring 1989), 75–93

'Yolande Bonhomme: A Renaissance Printer', *Medieval Prosopography*, 6.2 (Autumn 1985), 79–100

Beffa, Bruno, *Antonio Vinciguerra Cronico, segretario della Serenissima e letterato* (Bern: Peter Lang, 1975)

Bellavitis, Anna, 'La dote a Venezia tra medioevo e prima età moderna', in *Spazi, poteri, diritti delle donne a Venezia in età moderna*, ed. by Anna Bellavitis, Nadia Maria Filippini and Tiziana Plebani (Verona: QuiEdit, 2012), pp. 5–20

'Women, Family, and Property in Early Modern Venice', in *Across the Religious Divide: Women, Property, and Law in the Wider Mediterranean (ca. 1300–1800)*, ed. by Jutta Gisela Sperling and Shona Kelly Wray (New York: Routledge, 2010), pp. 175–90

Bellavitis, Anna and Isabelle Chabot, 'People and Property in Florence and Venice', in *At Home in Renaissance Italy*, ed. by Marta Ajmar-Wollheim and Flora Dennis (London: V & A Publications, 2006), pp. 76–85

Belligni, Eleonora, *Renata di Francia (1510–1575): un'eresia di corte* (Turin: UTET, 2011)

Bembo, Pietro, *Le rime*, ed. by Andrea Donnini, 2 vols (Rome: Salerno Editrice, 2008)

Benini Clementi, Enrica, *Riforma religiosa e poesia popolare a Venezia nel Cinquecento: Alessandro Caravia* (Florence: Olschki, 2000)

Benucci, Elisabetta, Roberta Manetti and Franco Zabagli, eds, *Cantari novellistici dal Tre al Cinquecento*, 2 vols (Rome: Salerno Editrice, 2002)

Benzoni, Gino, 'Ercole II d'Este', *DBI*, 43 (1993), 107–26

Bercusson, Sarah, 'Giovanna d'Austria and the Art of Appearances: Textiles and Dress at the Florentine Court', *Renaissance Studies*, 29 (2015), 683–700

'Joanna of Austria and the Negotiation of Power and Identity at the Florentine Court', in *Medici Women: The Making of a Dynasty in Grand Ducal Tuscany*, ed. by Giovanna Benadusi and Judith C. Brown (Toronto: Centre for Renaissance and Reformation Studies, 2015), pp. 128–53

Bersano Begey, Marina and Giuseppe Dondi, *Le cinquecentine piemontesi*, 3 vols (Turin: Tipografia torinese, 1966)

Bertini Malgarini, Patrizia, Marzia Caria and Ugo Vignuzzi, 'Clarisse dell'Osservanza e scritture "di pietà" in volgare tra Foligno e Monteluce', *Bollettino storico della città di Foligno*, 31–34 (2007–11), 297–335

Bertolo, Fabio Massimo, 'Nuovi documenti sull'edizione principe del "Cortegiano"', *Schifanoia*, 13–14 (1992), 133–44

Bertolotti, Antonino, 'Varietà archivistiche e bibliografiche', *Il bibliofilo*, 7 (1880), 26–27

Bertoni, Giulio, *La Biblioteca Estense e la coltura ferrarese ai tempi del Duca Ercole I (1471–1505)* (Turin: Loescher, 1903)

Biagioli, Mario, *Galileo, Courtier: The Practice of Science in the Culture of Absolutism* (University of Chicago Press, 1993)

Bianca, Concetta, 'Le biblioteche delle principesse nel regno aragonese', in *La donna nel Rinascimento meridionale: atti del convegno internazionale (Roma 11–13 novembre 2009)*, ed. by Marco Santoro (Pisa and Rome: Fabrizio Serra, 2010), pp. 403–12

Bianchi, Simona, Adriana Di Domenico, Rosaria Di Loreto, Giovanna Lazzi, Marco Palma, Palmira Panedigrano, Susanna Pelle, Carla Pinzauti, Paola Pirolo, Anna Maria Russo, Micaela Sambucco Hammoud, Piero Scapecchi, Isabella Truci and Stefano Zamponi, eds, *I manoscritti datati del fondo Conventi Soppressi della Biblioteca nazionale centrale di Firenze* (Florence: SISMEL-Edizioni del Galluzzo, 2002)

Bianco, Monica and Vittoria Romani, 'Vittoria Colonna e Michelangelo', in *Vittoria Colonna e Michelangelo*, ed. by Pina Ragionieri (Florence: Mandragora, 2005), pp. 145–64

Biffi, Marco and Raffaella Setti, 'Varchi consulente linguistico', in *Benedetto Varchi, 1503–1565: atti del convegno, Firenze, 16–17 dicembre 2003*, ed. by Vanni Bramanti (Rome: Edizioni di Storia e Letteratura, 2007), pp. 25–67

Black, Robert, *Education and Society in Florentine Tuscany: Teachers, Pupils and Schools, c. 1250–1500* (Leiden: Brill, 2007)

Blackburn, Bonnie J., 'Fortunato Martinengo and His Musical Tour around Lake Garda: The Place of Music and Poetry in Silvan Cattaneo's *Dodici giornate*', in *Fortunato Martinengo: un gentiluomo del Rinascimento fra arti, lettere e musica*, ed. by Marco Bizzarini and Elisabetta Selmi (Brescia: Morcelliana, 2018), pp. 179–209

Boccaccio, Giovanni, *Comedia delle ninfe fiorentine (Ameto)*, ed. by Antonio Enzo Quaglio (Florence: Sansoni, 1963)

Boillet, Élise, 'L'Arétin et l'actualité des années 1538–1539: les attentes du "Fléau des princes"', in *L'Actualité et sa mise en écriture dans l'Italie des XVᵉ–XVIIᵉ siècles*, ed. by Danielle Boillet and Corinne Lucas (Paris: Université Paris III Sorbonne Nouvelle, 2005), pp. 103–17

'Vernacular Sermons on the Psalms Printed in Sixteenth-Century Italy: An Interface between Oral and Written Cultures', in *Voices and Texts in Early Modern Italian Society*, ed. by Stefano Dall'Aglio, Brian Richardson and Massimo Rospocher (London: Routledge, 2017), pp. 200–11

Bolzoni, Lina, *La stanza della memoria: modelli letterari e iconografici nell'età della stampa* (Turin: Einaudi, 1995)

Bongi, Salvatore, *Annali di Gabriel Giolito de' Ferrari da Trino di Monferrato stampatore in Venezia*, 2 vols (Rome: Ministero della Pubblica Istruzione, 1890–97)

'Le Rime dell'Ariosto', *Archivio storico italiano*, 5th ser., 2 (1888), 267–76

Bonora, Elena, *I conflitti della Controriforma: santità e obbedienza nell'esperienza religiosa dei primi barnabiti* (Florence: Le Lettere, 1998)

Boorman, Stanley, *Ottaviano Petrucci: Catalogue Raisonné* (New York: Oxford University Press, 2006)

Borghesi, Scipione and Luciano Banchi, *Nuovi documenti per la storia dell'arte senese* (Siena: Torrini, 1898)

Borraccini, Rosa Marisa, 'All'ombra degli eredi: l'invisibilità femminile nelle professioni del libro. La fattispecie marchigiana', in *La donna nel Rinascimento meridionale: atti del convegno internazionale (Roma 11–13 novembre 2009)*, ed. by Marco Santoro (Pisa and Rome: Fabrizio Serra, 2010), pp. 413–28

Borsetto, Luciana, *L'"Eneida" tradotta: riscritture poetiche del testo di Virgilio nel XVI secolo* (Milan: Unicopli, 1989)

Borsook, Eve, 'Cults and Imagery at Sant'Ambrogio in Florence', *Mitteilungen des Kunsthistorischen Institutes in Florenz*, 25 (1981), 147–202

Borzelli, Angelo, *Marcantonio Passero: librario nel 500 napolitano* (Naples: Aldo Lubrano, 1941)

Bourdieu, Pierre, 'The Forms of Capital', trans. by Richard Nice, in *Handbook of Theory and Research for the Sociology of Education*, ed. by John G. Richardson (New York: Greenwood, 1986), pp. 241–58

Brandoli, Caterina, 'Nigrisoli, Antonio Maria', *DBI*, 78 (2013), 565–66

Brognoligo, Gioachino, 'Il poemetto di Clizia veronese', in *Studi di storia letteraria* (Rome and Milan: Società editrice Dante Alighieri, 1904), pp. 135–53

Broomhall, Susan, *Women and the Book Trade in Sixteenth-Century France* (Aldershot: Ashgate, 2002)

Brown, Clifford M., '"Al suo amenissimo Palazzo di Porto": Biagio Rossetti and Isabella d'Este', *Atti e memorie dell'Accademia Nazionale Virgiliana*, n.s., 58 (1990), 33–56

—— *Isabella d'Este and Lorenzo da Pavia: Documents for the History of Art and Culture in Renaissance Mantua* (Geneva: Droz, 1982)

—— *Isabella d'Este in the Ducal Palace in Mantua: An Overview of Her Rooms in the Castello di San Giorgio and the Corte Vecchia* (Rome: Bulzoni, 2005)

Brown, Clifford M., with Anna Maria Lorenzoni and Sally Hickson, *Per dare qualche splendore a la gloriosa città di Mantua: Documents for the Antiquarian Collection of Isabella d'Este* (Rome: Bulzoni, 2002)

Brown, C. Malcolm, '"Lo insaciabile desiderio nostro de cose antique": New Documents on Isabella d'Este's Collection of Antiquities', in *Cultural Aspects of the Italian Renaissance: Essays in Honour of Paul Oskar Kristeller*, ed. by Cecil H. Clough (Manchester University Press, 1976), pp. 324–53

Brown, Horatio F., *The Venetian Printing Press 1469–1800* (London: Nimmo, 1891)

Brucker, Gene Adam, 'Monasteries, Friaries, and Nunneries in Quattrocento Florence', in *Christianity and the Renaissance: Image and Religious Imagination in the Quattrocento*, ed. by Timothy Verdon and John Henderson (Syracuse, NY: Syracuse University Press, 1990), pp. 42–62

Brundin, Abigail, 'On the Convent Threshold: Poetry for New Nuns in Early Modern Italy', *Renaissance Quarterly*, 65 (2012), 1125–65

—— *Vittoria Colonna and the Spiritual Poetics of the Italian Reformation* (Aldershot: Ashgate, 2008)

'Vittoria Colonna in Manuscript', in *A Companion to Vittoria Colonna*, ed. by Abigail Brundin, Tatiana Crivelli and Maria Serena Sapegno (Leiden: Brill, 2016), pp. 39–68

Brundin, Abigail, Deborah Howard and Mary Laven, *The Sacred Home in Renaissance Italy* (Oxford University Press, 2018)

Bryce, Judith, 'Dada degli Adimari's Letters from Sant'Antonino: Identity, Maternity, and Spirituality', *I Tatti Studies: Essays in the Renaissance*, 12 (2009), 11–53

'"Fa finire uno bello studio et dice volere studiare": Ippolita Sforza and Her Books', *Bibliothèque d'Humanisme et Renaissance*, 64 (2002), 55–69

'Les Livres des Florentines: Reconsidering Women's Literacy in Quattrocento Florence', in *At the Margins: Minority Groups in Premodern Italy*, ed. by Stephen J. Milner (Minneapolis: University of Minnesota Press, 2005), pp. 133–61

Buettner, Brigitte, 'Women and the Circulation of Books', in *Women and Book Culture in Late Medieval and Early Modern France*, ed. by Martha W. Driver with Cynthia J. Brown, special issue of the *Journal of the Early Book Society*, 4 (2001), 9–31

Bugatti, Vera, 'Orizzonti spirituali nella trattatistica dedicata alla Paleologa', *Civiltà mantovana*, 41, no. 121 (2006), 6–21

Bujanda, J. M. de, *Index de Rome: 1557, 1559, 1564. Les Premiers Index romains et l'Index du Concile de Trente* (Sherbrooke: Centre d'études de la Renaissance, 1990)

*Index de Venise, 1549; Venise et Milan, 1554* (Sherbrooke: Centre d'études de la Renaissance, 1987)

Busetto, Giorgio, 'Coppa, Iacopo, detto Iacopo Modenese', *DBI*, 28 (1983), 584–86

Busolini, Dario, 'Gabriele da Perugia', *DBI*, 51 (1998), 52–53

Caciagli, Mario, 'Santa Marta', in *Milano: le chiese scomparse*, ed. by Mario Caciagli, Jacqueline Ceresoli and Pantaleo Di Marzo, 3 vols (Milan: Civica Biblioteca d'Arte, 1997–99), III, 75–118

Cadenas y Vicent, Vicente de, *La herencia imperial de Carlos V en Italia: el Milanesado* (Madrid: Hidalguia, 1978)

Calabritto, Monica, 'Women's *imprese* in Girolamo Ruscelli's *Le imprese illustri* (1566)', in *The Italian Emblem: A Collection of Essays*, ed. by Donato Mansueto in collaboration with Elena Laura Calogero (Glasgow: Glasgow Emblem Studies, 2007), pp. 65–91

Callegari, Danielle and Shannon McHugh, '"Se fossimo tante meretrici": The Rhetoric of Resistance in Diodata Malvasia's Convent Narrative', *Italian Studies*, 66 (2011), 21–39

Calmeta, Vincenzo, *Prose e lettere edite e inedite*, ed. by Cecil Grayson (Bologna: Commissione per i testi di lingua, 1959)

Calvin, John, *Ioannis Calvini Scripta didactica et polemica*, IV, *Epistulae duae (1537); Deux discours (Oct. 1536)*, ed. by Alexander De Boer and Frans Pieter Van Stam (Geneva: Droz, 2009)

Camerini, Paolo, *Annali dei Giunti*, vol. I, 2 parts (Florence: Sansoni, 1962–63)

Cammelli, Antonio, *I sonetti faceti secondo l'autografo ambrosiano*, ed. by Erasmo Pèrcopo (Naples: Jovene, 1908)

Campbell, Stephen, *The Cabinet of Eros: Renaissance Mythological Painting and the 'Studiolo' of Isabella d'Este* (New Haven: Yale University Press, 2004)

Campiglia, Maddalena, *Flori: A Pastoral Drama*, ed. by Virginia Cox and Lisa Sampson, trans. by Virginia Cox (University of Chicago Press, 2004)

Campori, Giuseppe, *Notizie dei miniatori dei principi estensi* (Modena: Vincenzi, 1872)

Canova, Andrea, 'Le biblioteche dei Gonzaga nella seconda metà del Quattrocento', in *Principi e signori: le biblioteche nella seconda metà del Quattrocento. Atti del Convegno di Urbino, 5–6 giugno 2008*, ed. by Guido Arbizzoni, Concetta Bianca and Marcella Peruzzi (Urbino: Accademia Raffaello, 2010), pp. 39–66

Caponetto, Salvatore, 'Renata di Francia e il calvinismo a Ferrara e Faenza', in *La riforma protestante nell'Italia del Cinquecento* (Turin: Claudiana, 1992), pp. 279–90

Caravale, Giorgio, *L'orazione proibita: censura ecclesiastica e letteratura devozionale nella prima età moderna* (Florence: Olschki, 2003)

Carter, Tim, 'Music-Selling in Late Sixteenth-Century Florence: The Bookshop of Piero di Giuliano Morosi', *Music and Letters*, 70 (1989), 483–504

Carusi, Enrico, 'Un codice sconosciuto delle "Rime spirituali" di Vittoria Colonna, appartenuto forse a Michelangelo Buonarroti', in *Atti del IV Congresso nazionale di studi romani*, ed. by Carlo Galassi Paluzzi, 5 vols (Rome: Istituto di studi romani, 1938), IV, 231–41

Casadei, Alberto, 'Sulle prime edizioni a stampa delle "Rime" ariostesche', *LB*, 94 (1992), 187–95

Casamassima, Emanuele, 'Ludovico degli Arrighi detto Vicentino copista dell'Itinerario del Varthema (cod. Landau Finaly 9, Biblioteca Nazionale Centrale di Firenze)', *LB*, 64 (1962), 117–62

*Trattati di scrittura del Cinquecento italiano* (Milan: Il Polifilo, 1966)

Castiglione, Baldesar, *The Book of the Courtier*, trans. by George Bull (Harmondsworth: Penguin, 1976)

*Il libro del cortegiano con una scelta delle opere minori*, ed. by Bruno Maier, 2nd edn (Turin: UTET, 1964)

*La seconda redazione del Cortegiano di Baldassarre Castiglione*, ed. by Ghino Ghinassi (Florence: Sansoni, 1968)

Castillo Gómez, Antonio, *Dalle carte ai muri: scrittura e società nella Spagna della prima Età moderna*, trans. by Laura Carnelos (Rome: Carocci, 2016)

'Writings on the Streets: Ephemeral Texts and Public Space in the Early Modern Hispanic World', in *Approaches to the History of Written Culture: A World Inscribed*, ed. by Martyn Lyons and Rita Marquilhas (Basingstoke: Palgrave Macmillan, 2017), pp. 73–96

*Catalogue of Books Printed in the XVth Century Now in the British Museum*, 9 vols (London: British Museum, 1909–49)

Cavalca, Domenico, *Vite dei santi padri*, ed. by Carlo Delcorno, 2 vols (Florence: Edizioni del Galluzzo per la Fondazione Ezio Franceschini, 2009)

Cecchetti, Bartolomeo, 'La pittura delle stampe di Bernardino Benalio', *Archivio veneto*, 33 (1887), 538–39

Cereta, Laura, *Collected Letters of a Renaissance Feminist*, ed. and trans. by Diana Robin (University of Chicago Press, 1997)

*Epistolae*, ed. by Jacopo Filippo Tomasini (Padua: Sardi, 1640)

Cervelli, Innocenzo, 'Bonciani, Giovanni Battista', *DBI*, 11 (1969), 676

Chambers, D. S., 'A Condottiere and His Books: Gianfrancesco Gonzaga (1446–96)', *Journal of the Warburg and Courtauld Institutes*, 70 (2007), 33–97

*A Renaissance Cardinal and His Worldly Goods: The Will and Inventory of Francesco Gonzaga (1444–1483)* (London: Warburg Institute, 1992)

Chambers, David and Jane Martineau, eds, *Splendours of the Gonzaga: Catalogue* (London: Victoria & Albert Museum, 1981)

Chartier, Roger, *Forms and Meanings: Texts, Performances, and Audiences from Codex to Computer* (Philadelphia: University of Pennsylvania Press, 1995)

Chojnacka, Monica, *Working Women of Early Modern Venice* (Baltimore, MD: Johns Hopkins University Press, 2001)

Chojnacki, Stanley, *Women and Men in Renaissance Venice: Twelve Essays on Patrician Society* (Baltimore, MD: Johns Hopkins University Press, 2000)

Cian, Vittorio, 'Pietro Bembo e Isabella d'Este Gonzaga', *GSLI*, 9 (1887), 81–136

Ciardi Duprè Dal Poggetto, Maria Grazia, 'Un offiziolo "camereccio" e altre cose di Bartolomeo Varnucci', *Antichità viva*, 10.5 (1971), 39–48

Classen, Albrecht, 'Frauen als Buchdruckerinnen im deutschen Sprachraum des 16. und 17. Jahrhunderts', *Gutenberg-Jahrbuch* (2000), 181–95

'Frauen im Buchdruckergewerbe des 17. Jahrhunderts', *Gutenberg-Jahrbuch* (2001), 220–36

Clubb, Louise George and Robert Black, *Romance and Aretine Humanism in Sienese Comedy: Pollastra's 'Parthenio' at the Studio di Siena* (Florence: La Nuova Italia, 1993)

Cohn, Samuel K., Jr, 'Women and Work in Renaissance Italy', in *Gender and Society in Renaissance Italy*, ed. by Judith C. Brown and Robert C. Davis (London and New York: Longman, 1998), pp. 107–26

Coli, Massimiliano, *La Cronaca del monastero domenicano di S. Giorgio di Lucca* (Pisa: ETS, 2009)

Collett, Barry, *A Long and Troubled Pilgrimage: The Correspondence of Marguerite d'Angoulême and Vittoria Colonna, 1540–1545* (Princeton: Princeton Theological Seminary, 2000)

Collier Frick, Carole, *Dressing Renaissance Florence: Families, Fortunes, and Fine Clothing* (Baltimore, MD: Johns Hopkins University Press, 2002)

Collina, Beatrice, 'Women in the Gutenberg Galaxy', in *Arcangela Tarabotti: A Literary Nun in Baroque Venice*, ed. by Elissa B. Weaver (Ravenna: Longo, 2006), pp. 91–105

Colonna, Vittoria, *Carteggio di Vittoria Colonna marchesa di Pescara*, ed. by Ermanno Ferrero and Giuseppe Müller (Turin: Loescher, 1889)

*Sonnets for Michelangelo*, ed. and trans. by Abigail Brundin (University of Chicago Press, 2005)

Colorni, Vittore, 'Abraham Conat primo stampatore di opere ebraiche in Mantova e la cronologia delle sue edizioni', *LB*, 83 (1981), 113–28

Compare, Carmela, 'Biblioteche monastiche femminili aquilane alla fine del XVI secolo', *Rivista di storia della Chiesa in Italia*, 54 (2000), 469–516

'Inventari di biblioteche monastiche femminili alla fine del XVI secolo', *Genesis: rivista della Società Italiana delle Storiche*, 2.2 (2003), 220–32

'I libri delle clarisse osservanti nella Provincia seraphica S. Francisci di fine '500', *Franciscana: bollettino della Società internazionale di studi francescani*, 4 (2002), 169–372

'Libri di donne e libri di monache alla fine del XVI secolo', in *Libri, biblioteche e cultura degli Ordini regolari nell'Italia moderna attraverso la documentazione della Congregazione dell'Indice: atti del convegno internazionale, Macerata, 30 maggio–1 giugno 2006*, ed. by Rosa Marisa Borraccini and Roberto Rusconi (Vatican City: Biblioteca Vaticana, 2006), pp. 583–622

Contini, Alessandra, 'Spazi femminili e costruzione di un'identità dinastica: il caso di Leonora di Toledo duchessa di Firenze', in *La società dei principi nell'Europa moderna (secoli XVI–XVII)*, ed. by Christof Dipper and Mario Rosa (Bologna: il Mulino, 2005), pp. 295–320

Conway, Melissa, *The 'Diario' of the Printing Press of San Jacopo di Ripoli 1476–1484: Commentary and Transcription* (Florence: Olschki, 1999)

Corbari, Eliana, *Vernacular Theology: Dominican Sermons and Audience in Late Medieval Italy* (Berlin: De Gruyter, 2013)

Correggio, Niccolò da, *Opere*, ed. by Antonia Tissoni Benvenuti (Bari: Laterza, 1969)

Corry, Maya, Deborah Howard and Mary Laven, eds, *Madonnas and Miracles: The Holy Home in Renaissance Italy* (London: Philip Wilson, 2017)

Corsaro, Antonio, 'Manuscript Collections of Spiritual Poetry in Sixteenth-Century Italy', in *Forms of Faith in Sixteenth-Century Italy*, ed. by Abigail Brundin and Matthew Treherne (Aldershot: Ashgate, 2009), pp. 33–56

Cortesi, Mariarosa, 'Incunaboli veneziani in Germania nel 1471', in *Vestigia: studi in onore di Giuseppe Billanovich*, ed. by Rino Avesani, Mirella Ferrari, Tino Foffano, Giuseppe Frasso and Agostini Sottili, 2 vols (Rome: Edizioni di Storia e Letteratura, 1984), I, 197–219

Cotugno, Alessio and David A. Lines, eds, *Venezia e Aristotele (ca. 1450–ca. 1600): greco, latino e italiano* (Venice: Marcianum Press, 2016)

Cox, Virginia, 'Members, Muses, Mascots: Women and Italian Academies', in *The Italian Academies 1525–1700: Networks of Culture, Innovation and Dissent*, ed. by Jane E. Everson, Denis V. Reidy and Lisa Sampson (Cambridge: Legenda, 2016), pp. 132–69

*The Prodigious Muse: Women's Writing in Counter-Reformation Italy* (Baltimore, MD: Johns Hopkins University Press, 2011)

*A Short History of the Italian Renaissance* (London: I. B. Tauris, 2016)

*Women's Writing in Italy, 1400–1650* (Baltimore, MD: Johns Hopkins University Press, 2008)

ed., *Lyric Poetry by Women of the Italian Renaissance* (Baltimore, MD: Johns Hopkins University Press, 2013)

Cracolici, Stefano, '"Remedia amoris sive elegiae": appunti sul dialogo antierotico del Quattrocento', in *Il sapere delle parole: studî sul dialogo latino e italiano del Rinascimento*, ed. by Walter Geerts, Annick Paternoster and Franco Pignatti (Rome: Bulzoni, 2001), pp. 23–35

Crivelli, Tatiana, 'The Print Tradition of Vittoria Colonna's *Rime*', in *A Companion to Vittoria Colonna*, ed. by Abigail Brundin, Tatiana Crivelli and Maria Serena Sapegno (Leiden: Brill, 2016), pp. 69–139

Croce, Benedetto, 'Un sonetto dell'Aretino e un ritratto di Maria d'Aragona, marchesana del Vasto', in *Aneddoti di varia letteratura*, I (Bari: Laterza, 1953), 359–65

Curi Nicolardi, Silvia, *Una società tipografico-editoriale a Venezia nel secolo XVI: Melchiore Sessa e Pietro di Ravani (1516–1525)* (Florence: Olschki, 1984)

Cursi, Elena, '"Per certo donna Fiammetta veggio voi non havere letto gli *Asolani* del Bembo": lettere di dedica e postille nelle edizioni del primo Cinquecento dell'*Elegia di Madonna Fiammetta*', *Studi sul Boccaccio*, 36 (2008), 39–61

Cyrus, Cynthia J., *The Scribes for Women's Convents in Late Medieval Germany* (University of Toronto Press, 2009)

Daenens, Francine, 'Superiore perché inferiore: il paradosso della superiorità della donna in alcuni trattati italiani del Cinquecento', in *Trasgressione tragica e norma domestica: esemplari di tipologie femminili della letteratura europea*, ed. by Vanna Gentili (Rome: Edizioni di Storia e Letteratura, 1983), pp. 11–50

Dallasta, Federica, *Al cliente lettore: il commercio e la censura del libro a Parma nell'epoca farnesiana 1545–1731* (Milan: Franco Angeli, 2012)

*Eredità di carta: biblioteche private e circolazione libraria nella Parma farnesiana, 1545–1731* (Milan: Franco Angeli, 2010)

'Orazio Diola traduttore delle "Croniche de gli ordini instituiti da padre San Francesco" di Marcos de Lisboa (1581–1591) e la sua biblioteca', *Collectanea Franciscana*, 85 (2015), 523–93

Dalmas, Davide, 'Antonio Brucioli editore e commentatore di Petrarca', in *Antonio Brucioli: humanisme et évangélisme entre Réforme et Contre-Réforme. Actes du colloque de Tours, 20–21 mai 2005*, ed. by Élise Boillet (Paris: Champion, 2008), pp. 131–45

D'Ancona, Alessandro, *La poesia popolare italiana*, 2nd edn (Livorno: Giusti, 1906)

Daniels, Tobias, 'Eine Geschäftsfrau im Venedig der Renaissance: Margarete Ugelheimer (geb. Molle) († ca. 1500)', in *Hinter dem Pergament: Die Welt. Der Frankfurter Kaufmann Peter Ugelheimer und die Kunst der Buchmalerei im Venedig der Renaissance*, ed. by Christoph Winterer (Munich: Hirmer, 2018), pp. 42–53

Darnton, Robert, 'What Is the History of Books?', in *The Kiss of Lamourette: Reflections in Cultural History* (London and Boston: Faber and Faber, 1990), pp. 107–35

'"What Is the History of Books?" Revisited', *Modern Intellectual History*, 4 (2007), 495–508

Davis, Natalie Zemon, 'Beyond the Market: Books as Gifts in Sixteenth-Century France', *Transactions of the Royal Historical Society*, 5th ser., 33 (1983), 69–88

'Women in the Crafts in Sixteenth-Century Lyon', *Feminist Studies*, 8 (1982), 46–80

Degl'Innocenti, Luca, *'Al suon di questa cetra': ricerche sulla poesia orale del Rinascimento* (Florence: Società editrice fiorentina, 2016)

I *'Reali' dell'Altissimo: un ciclo di cantari fra oralità e scrittura* (Florence: Società editrice fiorentina, 2008)

De Gregorio, Mario, 'Landi, Giovanni', *DBI*, 63 (2004), 384–85

Delaissé, L. M. J., James Marrow and John de Wit, *Illuminated Manuscripts: The James A. de Rothschild Collection at Waddesdon Manor* (Fribourg: Office du livre for the National Trust, 1977)

de la Mare, Albinia C., *Catalogue of the Collection of Medieval Manuscripts Bequeathed to the Bodleian Library, Oxford, by James P. R. Lyell* (Oxford: Clarendon Press, 1971)

'New Research on Humanistic Scribes in Florence', in *Miniatura fiorentina del Rinascimento 1440–1525: un primo censimento*, ed. by Annarosa Garzelli, 2 vols (Florence: La Nuova Italia, 1985), I, 393–600

'Script and Manuscripts in Milan under the Sforzas', in *Milano nell'età di Ludovico il Moro: atti del Convegno internazionale 28 febbraio–4 marzo 1983*, 2 vols (Milan: Archivio storico civico e Biblioteca Trivulziana, 1983), pp. 399–408

de la Mare, Albinia C. and Laura Nuvoloni, *Bartolomeo Sanvito: The Life and Work of a Renaissance Scribe*, ed. by Anthony R. A. Hobson and Christopher de Hamel (Paris: Association internationale de bibliophilie, 2009)

Delcorno, Carlo, 'Per l'edizione delle *Vite dei Santi Padri* del Cavalca', *Lettere italiane*, 30 (1978), 47–87

Delcorno Branca, Daniela, 'Il *Giardino novello*: lettere di direzione spirituale del Quattrocento trasmesse dalle monache del Paradiso', in *Da Dante a Montale: studi di filologia e critica letteraria in onore di Emilio Pasquini*, ed. by Gian Mario Anselmi, Bruno Bentivogli, Alfredo Cottignoli, Fabio Marri, Vittorio Roda, Gino Ruozzi and Paola Vecchi Galli (Bologna: Gedit, 2005), pp. 307–22

Del Prato, Alberto, 'Librai e biblioteche parmensi del secolo XV', *Archivio storico per le provincie parmensi*, 2nd ser., 4 (1904), 1–56

Del Sera, Beatrice, *Amor di virtù: commedia in cinque atti, 1548*, ed. by Elissa Weaver (Ravenna: Longo, 1990)

Delumeau, Jean, *Vie économique et sociale de Rome dans la seconde moitié du XVI^e siècle*, 2 vols (Paris: De Boccard, 1957–59)

De Maio, Romeo, 'Belprato, Giovanni Vincenzo', *DBI*, 8 (1966), 49

De Marinis, Tammaro, *La biblioteca napoletana dei re d'Aragona*, 4 vols (Milan: Hoepli, 1947–52)

'Legatura artistica fatta per Renata di Francia Duchessa di Ferrara', *Gutenberg-Jahrbuch*, 1964, 373–74

De Marinis, Tammaro, with Denise Bloch, Charles Astruc and Jacques Monfrin, *La biblioteca napoletana dei re d'Aragona: supplemento*, 2 vols (Verona: Stamperia Valdonega, 1969)

Dennis, Flora, 'Music', in *At Home in Renaissance Italy*, ed. by Marta Ajmar-Wollheim and Flora Dennis (London: V & A Publications, 2006), pp. 228–43

De Robertis, Domenico, 'Censimento dei manoscritti di rime di Dante: II', *Studi danteschi*, 38 (1961), 167–276

De Robertis, Teresa and Rosella Miriello, *I manoscritti datati della Biblioteca Riccardiana di Firenze*, 3 vols (Florence: SISMEL-Edizioni del Galluzzo, 1997–2006)

De Rossi, Giovanni Bernardo, *Annales Hebraeo-typographici sec. XV* (Parma: ex Regio typographeo, 1795; repr. Amsterdam: Philo Press, 1969)

de Vivo, Filippo, *Information and Communication in Venice: Rethinking Early Modern Politics* (Oxford University Press, 2007)

Dialeti, Androniki, 'The Publisher Gabriel Giolito de' Ferrari, Female Readers, and the Debate about Women in Sixteenth-Century Italy', *Renaissance and Reformation*, 28 (2004), 5–32

Dionisotti, Carlo, *Machiavellerie* (Turin: Einaudi, 1980)

    'Nicolò Liburnio e la letteratura cortigiana', in *Appunti su arti e lettere* (Milan: Jaca Book, 1995), pp. 81–109

    'Nuove rime di Niccolò da Correggio', *Studi di filologia italiana*, 17 (1959), 135–88

Dominici, Giovanni, *Lettere spirituali*, ed. by Maria Teresa Casella and Giovanni Pozzi (Freiburg: Edizioni universitarie, 1969)

Dondi, Cristina, *Printed Books of Hours from Fifteenth-Century Italy: The Texts, the Books, and the Survival of a Long-Lasting Genre* (Florence: Olschki, 2016)

D'Onghia, Luca, 'Due paragrafi sulla fortuna dialettale del "Furioso"', in *'Tra mille carte vive ancora': ricezione del 'Furioso' tra immagini e parole*, ed. by Lina Bolzoni, Serena Pezzini and Giovanna Rizzarelli (Lucca: Pacini Fazzi, 2010), pp. 281–98

D'Onofrio, Cesare, *Roma nel Seicento* (Florence: Vallecchi, 1969)

Edelstein, Bruce L., 'The Camera Verde: A Public Center for the Duchess of Florence in the Palazzo Vecchio', *Mélanges de l'École Française de Rome: Italie et Méditerranée*, 115 (2003), 51–87

    'La fecundissima Signora Duchessa: The Courtly Persona of Eleonora di Toledo and the Iconography of Abundance', in *The Cultural World of Eleonora di Toledo, Duchess of Florence and Siena*, ed. by Konrad Eisenbichler (Aldershot: Ashgate, 2004), pp. 71–97

Eisenbichler, Konrad, *The Sword and the Pen: Women, Politics, and Poetry in Sixteenth-Century Siena* (University of Toronto Press, 2012)

    ed., *The Cultural World of Eleonora di Toledo, Duchess of Florence and Siena* (Aldershot: Ashgate, 2004)

Establés Susán, Sandra, 'La actividad femenina en los negocios de producción, edición y venta de libros impresos en España e Hispanoamérica (siglos XVI–XVIII)', in *Doce siglos de materialidad del libro: estudios sobre manuscritos e impresos entre los siglos VIII y XIX*, dir. by Manuel José Pedraza Gracia, ed. by Helena Carvajal González and Camino Sánchez Oliveira (Prensas de la Universidad de Zaragoza, 2017), pp. 355–63

Evangelisti, Silvia, 'Angelica Baitelli, la storica', in *Barocco al femminile*, ed. by Giulia Calvi (Rome and Bari: Laterza, 1992), pp. 71–95

Ezell, Margaret J. M., *Social Authorship and the Advent of Print* (Baltimore, MD: Johns Hopkins University Press, 1999)

Faggioli, Sarah Christopher, 'Di un'edizione del 1532 della "Dichiaratione" di Rinaldo Corso alle Rime spirituali di Vittoria Colonna', *GSLI*, 191 (2014), 200–10

Fahy, Conor, *L'"Orlando furioso' del 1532: profilo di una edizione* (Milan: Vita e Pensiero, 1989)

'The Venetian Ptolemy of 1548', in *The Italian Book, 1465–1800: Studies Presented to Dennis E. Rhodes on his 70th Birthday*, ed. by Denis Reidy (London: British Library, 1993), pp. 89–115

Fanara, Rosangela, 'Sulla struttura del *Canzoniere* di J. Sannazaro: posizione e funzione della dedica a Cassandra Marchese', *Critica letteraria*, 35 (2007), 267–76

Fantini, Maria Pia, 'La circolazione clandestina dell'orazione di Santa Marta: un episodio modenese', in *Donna, disciplina, creanza cristiana dal XV al XVII secolo: studi e testi a stampa*, ed. by Gabriella Zarri (Rome: Edizioni di Storia e Letteratura, 1996), pp. 45–65

Feiss, Hugh, 'The Many Lives and Languages of St. Birgitta of Sweden and Her Order', *Studia monastica*, 35 (1993), 313–29

Fenlon, Iain, 'The Gonzaga and Music', in *Splendours of the Gonzaga: Catalogue*, ed. by David Chambers and Jane Martineau (London: Victoria & Albert Museum, 1981), pp. 87–94

'Music and Learning in Isabella d'Este's Studioli', in *La corte di Mantova nell'età di Andrea Mantegna*, ed. by Cesare Mozzarelli, Robert Oresko and Leandro Ventura (Rome: Bulzoni, 1997), pp. 353–67

*Music and Patronage in Sixteenth-Century Mantua*, 2 vols (Cambridge University Press, 1980)

Fenzi, Enrico, 'Tra Isabella e Lucrezia: Niccolò da Correggio', in *Lucrezia Borgia: storia e mito*, ed. by Michele Bordin and Paolo Trovato (Florence: Olschki, 2006), pp. 43–74

Ferente, Serena, 'La duchessa ha qualcosa di dire', in *Atlante della letteratura italiana*, ed. by Sergio Luzzatto and Gabriele Pedullà, 3 vols (Turin: Einaudi, 2010–12), I, 421–26

Ferino-Pagden, Sylvia, ed., *Vittoria Colonna: Dichterin und Muse Michelangelos* (Vienna: Skira, 1997)

Fioravanti Baraldi, Anna Maria, 'Testo e immagini: le edizioni cinquecentesche dell'*Omiliario quadragesimale* di Ludovico Pittorio', in *Girolamo Savonarola da Ferrara all'Europa*, ed. by Gigliola Fragnito and Mario Miegge (Florence: SISMEL-Edizioni del Galluzzo, 2001), pp. 139–54

Firenzuola, Agnolo, *Le novelle*, ed. by Eugenio Ragni (Rome: Salerno Editrice, 1971)

Firpo, Massimo, 'Paola Antonia Negri, monaca angelica (1508–1555)', in *Rinascimento al femminile*, ed. by Ottavia Niccoli (Bari: Laterza, 1991), pp. 35–82

——— 'Pietro Carnesecchi, Caterina de' Medici e Juan Valdés: di una sconosciuta traduzione francese dell'*Alphabeto christiano*', in *Dal Sacco di Roma all'Inquisizione: studi su Juan de Valdés e la Riforma italiana* (Alessandria: Edizioni dell'Orso, 1998), pp. 147–60

Firpo, Massimo and Dario Marcatto, eds, *I processi inquisitoriali di Pietro Carnesecchi (1557–1567)*, 2 vols (Vatican City: Archivio segreto vaticano, 1998–2000)

Flaminio, Marcantonio, *Apologia del 'Beneficio di Christo' e altri scritti inediti*, ed. by Dario Marcatto (Florence: Olschki, 1996)

Fletcher, Harry George, III, *New Aldine Studies: Documentary Essays on the Life and Work of Aldus Manutius* (San Francisco: Rosenthal, 1988)

Foligno, Cesare, 'Di alcuni codici gonzagheschi ed estensi appartenuti all'abate Canonici', *Il libro e la stampa*, n.s., I, fasc. 3 (1907), 69–75

Folin, Marco, 'Bastardi e principesse nelle corti del Rinascimento: spunti di ricerca', *Schifanoia*, 28–29 (2005), 167–74

——— 'Studioli, vie coperte, gallerie: genealogia di uno spazio del potere', in *Il camerino di alabastro: Antonio Lombardo e la scultura all'antica*, ed. by Matteo Ceriana (Milan: Silvana, 2004), pp. 97–101

Franceschini, Chiara, '"Literarum studia nobis communia": Olimpia Morata e la corte di Renata di Francia', *Schifanoia*, 28–29 (2005), 207–32

Frasso, Giuseppe, 'Appunti sul "Petrarca" aldino del 1501', in *Studi in onore di Giuseppe Billanovich*, ed. by Rino Avesani, Mirella Ferrari, Tino Foffano, Giuseppe Frasso and Agostino Sottili (Rome: Edizioni di Storia e Letteratura, 1984), pp. 315–35

Frati, Carlo and A. Segarizzi, *Catalogo dei codici marciani italiani*, vol. I (Modena: G. Ferraguti, 1909)

Fubini Leuzzi, Maria, 'Un'Asburgo a Firenze fra etichetta e impegno politico: Giovanna d'Austria', in *Le donne Medici nel sistema europeo delle corti XVI– XVIII secolo: atti del convegno internazionale, Firenze, San Domenico di Fiesole, 6–8 ottobre 2005*, ed. by Giulia Calvi and Riccardo Spinelli, 2 vols (Florence: Polistampa, 2008), I, 233–56

Gagné, John, 'Fixing Texts and Changing Regimes: Manuscript, Print, and Holy Lives in French-Occupied Milan, c. 1500–1525', in *The Saint between Manuscript and Print: Italy 1400–1600*, ed. by Alison K. Frazier (Toronto: Centre for Reformation and Renaissance Studies, 2015), pp. 379–420

Galilei, Galileo, *Le opere*, ed. by Antonio Favaro, 20 vols (Florence: Barbèra, 1890– 1909)

Galletti, Monica, 'Preliminari allo studio della presenza femminile nella proto-industria tipografica ed editoriale italiana: Milano tra il XVI e il XVII secolo', in *Itinerari del libro nella storia: per Anna Giulia Cavagna a trent'anni dalla prima lezione*, ed. by Francesca Nepori, Fiammetta Sabba and Paolo Tinti (Bologna: Pàtron, 2017), pp. 145–56

Gallico, Claudio, 'Un libro di poesia di musica dell'epoca d'Isabella d'Este', *Bollettino storico mantovano*, Quaderno 4 (Mantua, 1961), pp. 46–48

Garavelli, Enrico, ed., 'Lodovico Domenichi', www.nuovorinascimento.org/cinquecento/domenichi.pdf

Garzelli, Annarosa, ed., *Miniatura fiorentina del Rinascimento 1440–1525: un primo censimento*, 2 vols (Florence: La Nuova Italia, 1985)

Gaskell, Philip, *A New Introduction to Bibliography*, 2nd edn (Oxford: Clarendon Press, 1974)

Gaston, Robert W., 'Eleonora di Toledo's Chapel: Lineage, Salvation and the War against the Turks', in *The Cultural World of Eleonora di Toledo, Duchess of Florence and Siena*, ed. by Konrad Eisenbichler (Aldershot: Ashgate, 2004), pp. 157–80

Gehl, Paul F., 'Credit Sales Strategies in the Late Cinquecento Book Trade', in *Libri, tipografi, biblioteche: ricerche storiche dedicate a Luigi Balsamo*, ed. by Istituto di Biblioteconomia e Paleografia, Università degli Studi, Parma, 2 vols (Florence: Olschki, 1997), I, 193–206

— 'Describing (and Selling) Bindings in Sixteenth-Century Florence', *Italian Studies*, 53 (1998), 38–51

— 'Libri per donne: le monache clienti del libraio fiorentino Piero Morosi (1588–1607)', in *Donna, disciplina, creanza cristiana dal XV al XVII secolo: studi e testi a stampa*, ed. by Gabriella Zarri (Rome: Edizioni di Storia e Letteratura, 1996), pp. 67–82

— 'The "maiuschule moderne" of Giovambaptista Verini: From Music Texts to Calligraphic Musicality', in *Writing Relations: American Scholars in Italian Archives. Essays for Franca Petrucci Nardelli and Armando Petrucci*, ed. by Deanna Shemek and Michael Wyatt (Florence: Olschki, 2008), pp. 41–70

— 'Writing Manuals', *Humanism for Sale*, www.humanismforsale.org/text/archives/335

Gentilcore, David, *Medical Charlatanism in Early Modern Italy* (Oxford University Press, 2006)

Gerola, Giuseppe, 'Trasmigrazioni e vicende dei Camerini di Isabella d'Este', *Atti e memorie dell'Accademia virgiliana di Mantova*, n.s., 21 (1929), 253–90

Ghinassi, Ghino, 'L'ultimo revisore del "Cortigiano"', in *Dal Belcalzer al Castiglione: studi sull'antico volgare di Mantova e sul 'Cortegiano'*, ed. by Paolo Bongrani (Florence: Olschki, 2006), pp. 161–206

Ghirlanda, Daniele, 'La raccolta Farnese: un piccolo canzoniere di Pietro Bembo', in *Il Petrarchismo: un modello di poesia per l'Europa*, 2 vols (Rome: Bulzoni, 2006), II, ed. by Floriana Calitti and Roberto Gigliucci, 117–31

Gill, Katherine, 'Open Monasteries for Women in Late Medieval and Early Modern Italy', in *The Crannied Wall: Women, Religion, and the Arts in*

*Early Modern Europe*, ed. by Craig A. Monson (Ann Arbor: University of Michigan Press, 1992), pp. 15–47

Girardi, Raffaele, 'La scrittura cantabile', in *Modelli e maniere: esperienze poetiche del Cinquecento meridionale* (Bari: Palomar, 1999), pp. 27–78

Gnocchi, Alessandro, 'Un manoscritto delle rime di Pietro Bembo', *Studi di filologia italiana*, 60 (2002), 217–36

Goldthwaite, Richard A., *The Economy of Renaissance Florence* (Baltimore, MD: Johns Hopkins University Press, 2008)

Graziani, Irene, 'L'icona della monaca artista e le fonti storiografiche sul Breviario di Caterina Vigri', in *Pregare con le immagini: il Breviario di Caterina Vigri*, ed. by Vera Fortunati and Claudio Leonardi (Bologna: Compositori; Florence: SISMEL-Edizioni del Galluzzo, 2004), pp. 29–42

Graziosi, Elisabetta, 'Arcipelago sommerso: le rime delle monache tra obbedienza e trasgressione', in *I monasteri femminili come centri di cultura fra Rinascimento e Barocco: atti del convegno storico internazionale, Bologna, 8–10 dicembre 2000*, ed. by Gianna Pomata and Gabriella Zarri (Rome: Edizioni di Storia e Letteratura, 2005), pp. 145–73

Gregorovius, Ferdinand, *Lucrezia Borgia nach Urkunden und Korrespondenzen ihrer eigenen Zeit*, 5th edn (Stuttgart and Berlin: Cotta, 1911)

Grendler, Paul F., *The Roman Inquisition and the Venetian Press, 1540–1605* (Princeton University Press, 1977)

*Schooling in Renaissance Italy: Literacy and Learning, 1300–1600* (Baltimore, MD: Johns Hopkins University Press, 1989)

Gruet, Brice, *La Rue à Rome, miroir de la ville: entre l'émotion et la norme* (Paris: Presses de l'Université Paris Sorbonne, 2006)

Guarducci, Giampiero, *Annali dei Marescotti tipografi editori di Firenze (1563–1613)* (Florence: Olschki, 2001)

Guasco, Annibal, *Discourse to Lady Lavinia His Daughter*, ed. and trans. by Peggy Osborn (University of Chicago Press, 2003)

*Ragionamento a donna Lavinia sua figliuola, della maniera del governarsi ella in corte; andando per dama alla serenissima infante donna Caterina, duchessa di Savoia*, ed. by Helena L. Sanson, *Letteratura italiana antica*, 11 (2010), 61–139

Guasti, Cesare, ed., *Lettere di una gentildonna fiorentina del secolo XV ai figliuoli esuli* (Florence: Sansoni, 1877)

Guerrini Ferri, Gemma, 'Il *Liber monialium* ed il *Libro de l'antiquità* di suor Orsola Formicini: le Clarisse e la storia del venerabile monastero romano dei Santi Cosma e Damiano in Mica Aurea detto di San Cosimato in Trastevere (Biblioteca Nazionale Centrale, Roma, mss. Varia 5 e Varia 6)', *Scrineum Rivista*, 8 (2011), 81–111, www.fupress.net/index.php/scrineum/article/view/12145

Haar, James, 'On Musical Games in the 16th Century', *Journal of the American Musicological Society*, 15 (1962), 22–34

Haebler, Konrad, 'Das Testament des Johann Manthen von Gerresheim', *LB*, 26 (1924), 1–9

Hand, Joni M., *Women, Manuscripts and Identity in Northern Europe, 1350–1550* (Farnham: Ashgate, 2013)

Harris, Neil, *Bibliografia dell"Orlando Innamorato'*, 2 vols (Modena: Panini, 1988–91)

Hauvette, Henri, *Un exilé florentin à la cour de France au XVI<sup>e</sup> siècle: Luigi Alamanni (1495–1556). Sa vie et son œuvre* (Paris: Hachette, 1903)

Hedström, Ingela, 'Vadstena Abbey and Female Literacy in Late Medieval Sweden', in *Nuns' Literacies in Medieval Europe: The Hull Dialogue*, ed. by Virginia Blanton, Veronica O'Mara and Patricia Stoop (Turnhout: Brepols, 2013), pp. 253–72

Herzig, Tamar, *Christ Transformed into a Virgin Woman: Lucia Brocadelli, Heinrich Institoris, and the Defense of the Faith* (Rome: Edizioni di Storia e Letteratura, 2013)

——— 'The Rise and Fall of a Savonarolan Visionary: Lucia Brocadelli's Contribution to the Piagnone Movement', *Archiv für Reformationsgeschichte*, 95 (2004), 34–60

——— *Savonarola's Women: Visions and Reform in Renaissance Italy* (University of Chicago Press, 2008)

Hickson, Sally, '"To See Ourselves as Others See Us": Giovanni Francesco Zaninello of Ferrara and the Portrait of Isabella d'Este by Francesco Francia', *Renaissance Studies*, 23 (2009), 288–310

Hobson, Anthony, *Renaissance Book Collecting: Jean Grolier and Diego Hurtado de Mendoza, Their Books and Bindings* (Cambridge University Press, 1999)

——— 'Some Deceptive Bookbindings', in *The Medieval Book: Glosses from Friends and Colleagues of Christopher de Hamel*, ed. by James H. Marrow, Richard A. Linenthal and William Noel ('t Goy-Houten: Hes & De Graaf, 2010), pp. 250–57

Hoppe, Ilaria, 'A Duchess' Place at Court: The Quartiere di Eleonora in the Palazzo della Signoria in Florence', in *The Cultural World of Eleonora di Toledo, Duchess of Florence and Siena*, ed. by Konrad Eisenbichler (Aldershot: Ashgate, 2004), pp. 98–118

Humfrey, Peter, *Lorenzo Lotto* (New Haven: Yale University Press, 1997)

Iotti, Roberta, 'Phenice unica, virtuosa e pia: la corrispondenza culturale di Isabella', in *Isabella d'Este: la primadonna del Rinascimento*, ed. by Daniele Bini, Quaderno di Civiltà Mantovana, 2nd edn (Mantua: Il Bulino, 2006), pp. 167–83

Jack, Belinda, *The Woman Reader* (New Haven: Yale University Press, 2012)

Jacobs, Friedrich and Friedrich August Ukert, eds, *Beiträge zur ältern Litteratur; oder, Merkwürdigkeiten der Herzogl. Öffentlichen Bibliothek zu Gotha*, 3 vols (Leipzig: Dyk, 1835–43)

Jacobson Schutte, Anne, 'The *Lettere volgari* and the Crisis of Evangelism in Italy', *Renaissance Quarterly*, 28 (1975), 639–88

Jacometti, Fabio, 'Il primo stampatore senese: Simone di Niccolò di Nardo', *La Diana*, 1 (1926), 184–202

James, Carolyn, 'Marriage by Correspondence: Politics and Domesticity in the Letters of Isabella d'Este and Francesco Gonzaga, 1490–1519', *Renaissance Quarterly*, 65 (2012), 321–52

James, Montague Rhodes, *A Descriptive Catalogue of the Latin Manuscripts in the John Rylands Library at Manchester*, 2 vols (Manchester University Press, 1921)

Jimenes, Rémi, *Charlotte Guillard: une femme imprimeur à la Renaissance* (Tours: Presses Universitaires François-Rabelais; Presses Universitaires de Rennes, 2017)

Kaborycha, Lisa, 'Expressing a Habsburg Sensibility in the Medici Court: The Grand Duchess Giovanna d'Austria's Patronage and Public Image in Florence', in *Medici Women as Cultural Mediators, 1533–1743*, ed. by Christina Strunck (Milan: Silvana, 2011), pp. 89–109

Kelly, Joan, 'Did Women Have a Renaissance?', in *Women, History, and Theory: The Essays of Joan Kelly* (University of Chicago Press, 1984), pp. 19–50

Kendrick, Robert L., *Celestial Sirens: Nuns and Their Music in Early Modern Milan* (Oxford: Clarendon Press, 1996)

Kennedy, William J., *Authorizing Petrarch* (Ithaca, NY: Cornell University Press, 1994)

Kikuchi, Catherine, 'How Did Aldus Manutius Start a Printing Dynasty?', in *Aldo Manuzio: la costruzione del mito / Aldus Manutius: The Making of the Myth*, ed. by Mario Infelise (Venice: Marsilio, 2016), pp. 25–38

King, Catherine, *Renaissance Women Patrons: Wives and Widows in Italy, c. 1300–c. 1550* (Manchester University Press, 1998)

Kirkham, Victoria, 'Laura Battiferra degli Ammannati's *First Book* of Poetry: A Renaissance Holograph Comes Out of Hiding', *Rinascimento*, 2nd ser., 36 (1996), 351–91

Kirshner, Julius, 'Family and Marriage: A Socio-Legal Perspective', in *Italy in the Age of the Renaissance 1300–1550*, ed. by John M. Najemy (Oxford University Press, 2004), pp. 82–102

—— 'Wives' Claims against Insolvent Husbands in Late Medieval Italy', in *Marriage, Dowry, and Citizenship in Late Medieval and Renaissance Italy* (University of Toronto Press, 2015), pp. 131–60

Klapisch-Zuber, Christiane, 'Le chiavi fiorentine di Barbablù: l'apprendimento della lettura a Firenze nel XV secolo', *Quaderni storici*, no. 57 (Dec. 1984), 765–92

—— 'The Griselda Complex: Dowry and Marriage Gifts in the Quattrocento', in *Women, Family, and Ritual in Renaissance Italy*, trans. by Lydia G. Cochrane (University of Chicago Press, 1985), pp. 213–46

—— 'Le "zane" della sposa', *Memoria: rivista di storia delle donne*, 11–12 (1984), 12–23

Kolsky, Stephen, 'Lelio Manfredi traduttore cortigiano: intorno al "Carcer d'Amore" e al "Tirante il Bianco"', *Civiltà mantovana*, 3rd ser., 29, no. 10 (1994), 45–69

—— *Mario Equicola: The Real Courtier* (Geneva: Droz, 1991)

—— 'Moderata Fonte, Lucrezia Marinella, Giuseppe Passi: An Early Seventeenth-Century Feminist Controversy', *Modern Language Review*, 96 (2001), 973–89

Koortbojian, Michael and Ruth Webb, 'Isabella d'Este's Philostratos', *Journal of the Warburg and Courtauld Institutes*, 56 (1993), 260–67

Kuehn, Thomas, *Law, Family, & Women: Toward a Legal Anthropology of Renaissance Italy* (University of Chicago Press, 1991)

'Person and Gender in the Laws', in *Gender and Society in Renaissance Italy*, ed. by Judith C. Brown and Robert C. Davis (London and New York: Longman, 1998), pp. 87–106

'Understanding Gender Inequality in Renaissance Florence: Personhood and Gifts of Maternal Inheritance by Women', *Journal of Women's History*, 8.2 (Summer 1996), 58–80

Lalli, Rossella, 'Scrivere per le Gonzaga: Lucrezia Marinella e la promozione a corte delle sue opere (1595–1618)', in *Donne Gonzaga a corte: reti istituzionali, pratiche culturali e affari di governo*, ed. by Chiara Continisio and Raffaele Tamalio (Rome: Bulzoni, 2018), pp. 405–16

Laven, Mary, *Virgins of Venice: Enclosed Lives and Broken Vows in the Renaissance Convent* (London: Viking, 2002)

Lenzuni, Anna, 'Tre libri d'ore per le figlie di Lorenzo', in *All'ombra del lauro: documenti librari della cultura in età laurenziana*, ed. by Anna Lenzuni (Florence: Silvana Editoriale, 1992)

Levi d'Ancona, Mirella, *Miniatura e miniatori a Firenze dal XIV al XVI secolo: documenti per la storia della miniatura* (Florence: Olschki, 1962)

Librandi, Rita, *La letteratura religiosa* (Bologna: il Mulino, 2012), pp. 47–69

Lightbown, Ronald, *Sandro Botticelli: Life and Work*, new edn (London: Thames & Hudson, 1989)

Llorens, José M., 'El codice Casanatense 2856 identificado como el Cancionero de Isabella d'Este (Ferrara) esposa de Francesco Gonzaga (Mantua)', *Anuario musical*, 20 (1967), 161–78

Lockwood, Lewis, ed., *A Ferrarese Chansonnier: Roma, Biblioteca Casanatense 2856. 'Canzoniere di Isabella d'Este'* (Lucca: Libreria musicale italiana, 2002)

Lorenzoni, Anna Maria, 'Tra francesi e spagnoli: le fortunose vicende di Eleonora Orsini del Balzo, marchesa di Crotone, attraverso carteggi inediti dell'Archivio Gonzaga', in *Per Mantova una vita: studi in memoria di Rita Castagna*, ed. by Anna Maria Lorenzoni and Roberto Navarrini (Mantua: Publi-Paolini, 1991), pp. 113–44

Lotto, Lorenzo, *Il 'Libro di spese diverse' con aggiunta di lettere e d'altri documenti*, ed. by Pietro Zampetti (Venice: Istituto per la collaborazione culturale, 1969)

Love, Harold, *Scribal Publication in Seventeenth-Century England* (Oxford: Clarendon Press, 1993)

Lowe, Kate, 'Women's Work at the Benedictine Convent of Le Murate in Florence: Suora Battista Carducci's Roman Missal of 1509', in *Women and the Book: Assessing the Visual Evidence*, ed. by Lesley Smith and Jane H. M. Taylor (London: British Library; University of Toronto Press, 1996), pp. 133–46

Lowe, K. J. P., *Nuns' Chronicles and Convent Culture in Renaissance and Counter-Reformation Italy* (Cambridge University Press, 2003)

Lowry, Martin, *Nicholas Jenson and the Rise of Venetian Publishing* (Oxford: Blackwell, 1991)

    *The World of Aldus Manutius: Business and Scholarship in Renaissance Venice* (Oxford: Blackwell, 1979)

Lucioli, Francesco, review of Laura Terracina, *Discorsi sopra le prime stanze de' canti d'Orlando furioso*, ed. by Rotraud von Kulessa and Daria Perocco (2017), *Archiv für das Studium der neueren Sprachen und Literaturen*, 255 (2018), 468–83

Luisi, Francesco, 'Minima fiorentina: sonetti a mente, canzoni a ballo e cantimpanca nel Quattrocento', in *Musica franca: Essays in Honor of Frank A. D'Accone*, ed. by Irene Alm, Alyson McLamore and Colleen Reardon (Stuyvesant, NY: Pendragon Press, 1996), pp. 79–95

Luzio, Alessandro and Rodolfo Renier, *La coltura e le relazioni letterarie di Isabella d'Este Gonzaga*, ed. by Simone Albonico (Milan: Bonnard, 2005)

    *Mantova e Urbino: Isabella d'Este ed Elisabetta Gonzaga nelle relazioni famigliari e nelle vicende politiche* (Turin and Rome: Roux, 1893)

    'Niccolò da Correggio', *GSLI*, 21 (1893), 205–64, and 22 (1894), 65–119

Machiavelli, Bernardo, *Libro di ricordi*, ed. by Cesare Olschki (Florence: Le Monnier, 1954)

Maclean, Ian, *The Renaissance Notion of Woman: A Study in the Fortunes of Scholasticism and Medical Science in European Intellectual Life* (Cambridge University Press, 1980)

McIver, Katherine A., *Women, Art, and Architecture in Northern Italy, 1520–1580: Negotiating Power* (Farnham: Ashgate, 2006)

    ed., *Wives, Widows, Mistresses, and Nuns in Early Modern Italy: Making the Invisible Visible through Art and Patronage* (Farnham: Ashgate, 2012)

McKenzie, D. F., *Bibliography and the Sociology of Texts* (Cambridge University Press, 1999)

Malacarne, Giancarlo, 'Collezionismo e querelle librarie: l'inventario dei libri "lassati" dalla "quondam" Isabella d'Este', *Civiltà mantovana*, 3rd ser., 40, no. 119 (March 2005), 121–31

Mantegna, Giovanni Alfonso, *Le rime*, ed. by Maria Rosaria Bifolco (Salerno: Edisud, 2001)

Mantese, Giovanni, *I mille libri che si leggevano e vendevano a Vicenza alla fine del secolo XVI* (Vicenza: Accademia Olimpica, 1968)

Manutius, Aldus, *Humanism and the Latin Classics*, ed. and trans. by John N. Grant (Cambridge, MA: Harvard University Press, 2017)

Manzi, Pietro, *La tipografia napoletana nel '500: annali di Sigismondo Mayr, Giovanni A. de Caneto, Antonio de Frizis, Giovanni Pasquet de Sallo (1503–1535)* (Florence: Olschki, 1971)

Marciani, Corrado, 'Editori, tipografi, librai veneti nel Regno di Napoli nel Cinquecento', *Studi veneziani*, 10 (1968), 457–554

Marcolini, Francesco, *Scritti: lettere, dediche, avvisi ai lettori*, ed. by Paolo Procaccioli (Manziana: Vecchiarelli, 2013)

Marotti, Arthur F., *Manuscript, Print, and the English Renaissance Lyric* (Ithaca, NY: Cornell University Press, 1995)

Martin, John, *Venice's Hidden Enemies: Italian Heretics in a Renaissance City* (Berkeley: University of California Press, 1993)

Martinelli, Bortolo, 'La biblioteca (e i beni) di un petrarchista: Gasparo Visconti', in *Veronica Gambara e la poesia del suo tempo nell'Italia settentrionale: atti del Convegno (Brescia-Correggio, 17–19 ottobre 1985)*, ed. by Cesare Bozzetti, Pietro Gibellini and Ennio Sandal (Florence: Olschki, 1989), pp. 213–61

Masetti Zannini, Gian Ludovico, *Stampatori e librai a Roma nella seconda metà del Cinquecento: documenti inediti* (Rome: Fratelli Palombi, 1980)

Matraini, Chiara, *Rime e Lettere*, ed. by Giovanni Rabitti (Bologna: Commissione per i testi di lingua, 1989)

— *Selected Poetry and Prose*, intro. by Giovanna Rabitti, ed. and trans. by Elaine Maclachlan (University of Chicago Press, 2007)

Matter, E. Ann, Armando Maggi and Maiju Lehmijoki-Gardner, '*Le rivelazioni* of Lucia Brocadelli da Narni', *Archivum fratrum praedicatorum*, 71 (2001), 311–44

Mazzatinti, Giuseppe, ed., *Inventari dei manoscritti delle biblioteche d'Italia*, vol. X (Florence: Olschki, 1900)

Medioli, Francesca, 'Reti famigliari: la matrilinearità nei monasteri femminili fiorentini del Seicento. Il caso di Santa Verdiana', in *Nubili e celibi tra scelta e costrizione: secoli XVI–XX*, ed. by Margareth Lanzinger and Raffaella Sarti (Udine: Forum, 2006), pp. 11–36

*Memoriale di Monteluce: cronaca del monastero delle clarisse di Perugia dal 1448 al 1838*, intro. by Ugolino Nicolini (Santa Maria degli Angeli: Edizioni Porziuncola, 1983)

Meroni, Ubaldo, *Mostra dei codici gonzagheschi: la biblioteca dei Gonzaga da Luigi I ad Isabella. Biblioteca Comunale 18 settembre–10 ottobre* (Mantua: [n. pub.], 1966)

Michelson, Emily, 'An Italian Explains the English Reformation (with God's Help)', in *A Linking of Heaven and Earth: Studies in Religious and Cultural History in Honor of Carlos M. N. Eire*, ed. by Emily Michelson, Scott K. Taylor and Mary Noll Venables (Farnham: Ashgate, 2012), pp. 33–48

Miglio, Luisa, *Governare l'alfabeto: donne, scrittura e libri nel medioevo* (Rome: Viella, 2008)

Milani, Marisa, ed., *La verità, ovvero il processo contro Isabella Bellocchio (Venezia, 12 gennaio–14 ottobre 1589)*, 2 vols (Padua: Centrostampa Palazzo Maldura, 1985)

Milano, Alberto, 'Prints for Fans', *Print Quarterly*, 4 (1987), 2–19

Minutelli, Marzia, 'Poesia e teatro di Galeotto Dal Carretto: riflessioni in margine al carteggio con Isabella d'Este', *Nuova rivista di letteratura italiana*, 7 (2004), 123–78

Minutolo, Ceccarella, *Lettere*, ed. by Raffaele Morabito (Naples: Edizioni Scientifiche Italiane, 1999)

Miriello, Rosanna, *I manoscritti del Monastero del Paradiso di Firenze* (Florence: SISMEL-Edizioni del Galluzzo, 2007)

Monson, Craig, 'Elena Malvezzi's Keyboard Manuscript: A New Sixteenth-Century Source', *Early Music History*, 9 (1990), 73–128

*Nuns Behaving Badly: Tales of Music, Magic, Art, and Arson in the Convents of Italy* (Chicago University Press, 2010)

Montaigne, Michel de, *Journal de voyage*, ed. by François Rigolot (Paris: Presses Universitaires de France, 1992)

Montella, Luigi, *Una poetessa del Rinascimento: Laura Terracina. Con un'antologia delle None rime inedite* (Salerno: Edisud, 2001)

Moranti, Luigi, *L'arte tipografica in Urbino (1493–1800)* (Florence: Olschki, 1967)

Moreton, Melissa, 'Exchange and Alliance: The Sharing and Gifting of Books in Women's Houses in Late Medieval and Renaissance Florence', in *Nuns' Literacies in Medieval Europe: The Antwerp Dialogue*, ed. by Virginia Blanton, Veronica O'Mara and Patricia Stoop (Turnhout: Brepols, 2017), pp. 383–410

'Pious Voices: Nun-Scribes and the Language of Colophons in Late Medieval and Renaissance Italy', *Essays in Medieval Studies*, 29 (2013), 43–73

Mori, Elisabetta, 'Isabella de' Medici: Unraveling the Legend', in *Medici Women: The Making of a Dynasty in Grand Ducal Tuscany*, ed. by Giovanna Benadusi and Judith C. Brown (Toronto: Centre for Renaissance and Reformation Studies, 2015), pp. 91–127

Morison, Stanley, *Early Italian Writing-Books: Renaissance to Baroque*, ed. by Nicolas Barker (Verona: Edizioni Valdonega; London: British Library, 1990)

Mortimer, Ruth, 'The Author's Image: Italian Sixteenth-Century Printed Portraits', *Harvard Library Bulletin*, n.s., 7, no. 2 (summer 1996)

Musacchio, Jacqueline Marie, 'The Bride and Her *donora* in Renaissance Florence', in *Culture and Change: Attending to Early Modern Women*, ed. by Margaret Mikesell and Adele Seeff (Newark, DE: University of Delaware Press, 2003), pp. 177–202

Mutini, Claudio, 'Bacio Terracina, Laura', *DBI*, 5 (1963), 61–63

Nagel, Alexander, 'Gifts of Michelangelo and Vittoria Colonna', *Art Bulletin*, 79 (1997), 647–68

Newbigin, Nerida, 'Antonia Pulci and the First Anthology of *Sacre Rappresentazioni* (1483?)', *LB*, 118 (2016), 337–61

Niccolini, Giustina, *The Chronicle of Le Murate*, ed. by Saundra Weddle (Toronto: Iter, 2011)

Nico Ottaviani, Maria Grazia, *'Me son missa a scriver questa letera . . . ': lettere e altre scritture femminili tra Umbria, Toscana e Marche nei secoli XV–XVI* (Naples: Liguori, 2006)

Nicolini, Benedetto, *Ideali e passioni nell'Italia religiosa del Cinquecento* (Bologna: Libreria antiquaria Palmaverde, 1962)

Nicolini, Ugolino, 'I minori osservanti di Monteripido e lo "scriptorium" delle Clarisse di Monteluce in Perugia nei secoli XV e XVI', *Picenum seraphicum*, 8 (1971), 100–30

Nifo, Agostino, *De Pulchro et Amore*, ed. and trans. by Laurence Boulègue, 2 vols (Paris: Les Belles Lettres, 2003–11)

Nogarola, Isotta, *Complete Writings: Letterbook, Dialogue on Adam and Eve, Orations*, ed. and trans. by Margaret L. King and Diana Robin (University of Chicago Press, 2004)

—— *Opera quae supersunt omnia*, ed. by Jenő Ábel, 2 vols (Vienna: Gerold, 1886)

Norman, Diana, 'An Abbess and a Painter: Emilia Pannocchieschi d'Elci and a Fresco from the Circle of Simone Martini', *Renaissance Studies*, 14 (2000), 273–300

Novati, Francesco, 'Donne tipografe nel Cinquecento', *Il libro e la stampa*, 1 (1907), 41–49

Nuovo, Angela, *The Book Trade in the Italian Renaissance*, trans. by Lydia G. Cochrane (Leiden: Brill, 2013)

—— *Il commercio librario a Ferrara tra XV e XVI secolo: la bottega di Domenico Sivieri* (Florence: Olschki, 1998)

Nuovo, Angela and Christian Coppens, *I Giolito e la stampa nell'Italia del XVI secolo* (Geneva: Droz, 2005)

Nyberg, Tore, 'Paradiso Copying Activity (15th Century Florence) and Hugh of Balma', in *The Mystical Tradition and the Carthusians* (Analecta Cartusiana, 130), vol. III, ed. by James Hogg (Salzburg: Institut für Anglistik und Amerikanistik, Universität Salzburg, 1995), pp. 87–95

Offenberg, Adri K., 'The Chronology of Hebrew Printing at Mantua in the Fifteenth Century: A Re-Examination', *The Library*, 6th ser., 16 (1994), 298–315

Olivieri, Achille, 'Merenda, Apollonio', *DBI*, 73 (2009), 639–43

O'Neil, Mary, 'Magical Healing, Love Magic, and the Inquisition in Late Sixteenth-Century Modena', in *Inquisition and Society in Early Modern Europe*, ed. and trans. by Stephen Haliczer (London: Croom Helm, 1987), pp. 88–114

Orlandi, Antonella, 'Donne nelle dediche', in *La donna nel Rinascimento meridionale: atti del convegno internazionale (Roma 11–13 novembre 2009)*, ed. by Marco Santoro (Pisa and Rome: Fabrizio Serra, 2010), pp. 383–92

Ossola, Carlo, *Dal 'Cortegiano' all''Uomo di mondo'* (Turin: Einaudi, 1987)

Paladino, Giuseppe, ed., *Opuscoli e lettere di riformatori italiani del Cinquecento*, 2 vols (Bari: Laterza, 1913–27)

Palermo, Massimo, *Il carteggio Vaianese (1537–39): un contributo allo studio della lingua d'uso nel Cinquecento* (Florence: Accademia della Crusca, 1994)

Pallecchi, Nicola, 'Una tipografia a Siena nel XVI secolo: bibliografia delle edizioni stampate da Simone di Niccolò Nardi (1502–1539)', *Bullettino senese di storia patria*, 109 (2002), 184–233

Paoli, Marco, *La dedica: storia di una strategia editoriale (Italia, secoli XVI–XIX)* (Lucca: Pacini Fazzi, 2009)

Papworth, Amelia, 'Pressure to Publish: Laura Terracina and Her Editors', *Early Modern Women: An Interdisciplinary Journal*, 12.1 (Fall 2017), 3–24

Parent, Annie, *Les Métiers du livre à Paris au XVI<sup>e</sup> siècle (1535–1560)* (Geneva: Droz, 1974)

Parent-Charon, Annie, 'À propos des femmes et des métiers du livre dans le Paris de la Renaissance', in *Des femmes et des livres: France et Espagne, XIV<sup>e</sup>–XVII<sup>e</sup> siècle*, ed. by Dominique de Courcelles and Carmen Val Julián (Paris: École des Chartes, 1999), pp. 137–48

Parker, Deborah, 'Women in the Book Trade in Italy, 1475–1620', *Renaissance Quarterly*, 49 (1996), 509–41

Pasero, Carlo, 'Marcello Scalini e la calligrafia del XVI secolo', *LB*, 35 (1933), 430–39

——— 'Sulla vita del calligrafo cinquecentesco Marcello Scalini (Scalzini) detto il Camerino', *Commentari dell'Ateneo di Brescia*, 133 (1934), 109–77

Pellegrini, Paolo, 'Vecchie e nuove schede sull'umanesimo mantovano', *Res publica litterarum*, 35 (2012), 80–121

Percopo, Erasmo, *Vita di Giovanni Pontano*, ed. by Michele Manfredi (Naples: ITEA, 1938)

Perini, Raffaella, 'Manoscritti gonzagheschi conservati presso la Biblioteca Comunale di Mantova', *Civiltà mantovana*, 105 (November 1997), 45–55

Perosa, Alessandro, ed., *Giovanni Rucellai ed il suo Zibaldone*, vol. I, *'Il Zibaldone quaresimale'* (London: Warburg Institute, 1960)

Pesenti, Tiziana, 'Dinslaken (Dinslach, de Islach, de Dislach, Dedislach), Gaspare (Gaspare Alemanno da Colonia)', *DBI*, 40 (1991), 167–69

Petrella, Giancarlo, '"Ad instantia d'Hippolito Ferrarese": un cantimbanco editore nell'Italia del Cinquecento', *Paratesto*, 8 (2011), 23–80

Petrucci, Armando, *Writers and Readers in Medieval History: Studies in the History of Written Culture*, ed. and trans. by Charles M. Radding (New Haven: Yale University Press, 1995)

——— ed., *Il libro di ricordanze dei Corsini (1362–1457)* (Rome: Istituto storico italiano per il Medio Evo, 1965)

Petrucci, Franca, 'Cresci, Giovanni Francesco', *DBI*, 30 (1984), 668–71

Peyronel Rambaldi, Susanna, *Una gentildonna irrequieta: Giulia Gonzaga fra reti familiari e relazioni eterodosse* (Rome: Viella, 2012)

Piccolomini, Alessandro, *Cento sonetti*, ed. by Franco Tomasi (Geneva: Droz, 2015)

Piéjus, Marie-Françoise, *Visages et paroles de femmes dans la littérature italienne de la Renaissance* (Paris: Université Paris III Sorbonne Nouvelle, 2009)

Piscini, Angela, 'Domenichi, Ludovico', *DBI*, 40 (1991), 595–600

Pitacco, Francesca, 'La repromissione di dote di Francesca Lucrezia Giunti e la bottega veneziana di Aldo Manuzio il Giovane', in *Intorno al Polifilo: contributi sull'opera e l'epoca di Francesco Colonna e Aldo Manuzio*, ed. by Alessandro Scarsella, Miscellanea marciana, 16 (Venice: Biblion, 2001), pp. 217–38

Plaisance, Michel, *L'Accademia e il suo principe: cultura e politica a Firenze al tempo di Cosimo I e di Francesco de' Medici* (Manziana: Vecchiarelli, 2003)

Plebani, Tiziana, *Il 'genere' dei libri: storie e rappresentazioni della lettura al femminile e al maschile tra Medioevo e età moderna* (Milan: Franco Angeli, 2001)

Pomata, Gianna and Gabriella Zarri, eds, *I monasteri femminili come centri di cultura fra Rinascimento e Barocco: atti del convegno storico internazionale, Bologna, 8–10 dicembre 2000* (Rome: Edizioni di Storia e Letteratura, 2005)

Porqueddu, Chiara, *Il patriziato pavese in età spagnola: ruoli familiari, stile di vita, economia* (Milan: Unicopli, 2012)

Portioli, Attilio, 'Giacomo Galopini prete e miniatore mantovano del secolo XV', *Archivio storico lombardo*, 3rd ser., 11 (1899), 330–47

Premoli, Orazio, *Fra' Battista da Crema secondo documenti inediti: contributo alla storia religiosa del secolo XVI* (Rome: Desclée, 1910)

Primhak, Victoria Jane, 'Women in Religious Communities: The Benedictine Convents in Venice, 1400–1550' (unpublished doctoral thesis, University of London, Warburg Institute, 1991)

Prizer, William F., 'Isabella d'Este and Lucrezia Borgia as Patrons of Music: The Frottola at Mantua and Ferrara', *Journal of the American Musicological Society*, 38 (1985), 1–33

—— 'Secular Music at Milan during the Early Cinquecento: Florence, Biblioteca del Conservatorio, MS Basevi 2441', *Musica Disciplina*, 50 (1996), 9–57

—— 'Una "virtù molto conveniente a madonne": Isabella d'Este as a Musician', *Journal of Musicology*, 17 (1999), 10–49

—— 'Wives and Courtesans: The Frottola in Florence', in *Music Observed: Studies in Memory of William C. Holmes*, ed. by Colleen Reardon and Susan Parisi (Warren, MI: Harmonie Park Press, 2004), pp. 401–15

Procaccioli, Paolo, ed., *Lettere scritte a Pietro Aretino*, 2 vols (Rome: Salerno Editrice, 2003–04)

Pullan, Brian, 'The Conversion of the Jews: The Style of Italy', *Bulletin of the John Rylands Library*, 70 (1988), 53–70

Quilici, Piccarda, 'Legature di corte italiane', in *Il libro a corte*, ed. by Amedeo Quondam (Rome: Bulzoni, 1994), pp. 239–72

Quondam, Amedeo, *'Questo povero Cortegiano': Castiglione, il libro, la storia* (Rome: Bulzoni, 2000)

Rabitti, Giovanna, 'Matraini, Chiara', *DBI*, 72 (2008), 128–31

Ragionieri, Pina, ed., *Vittoria Colonna e Michelangelo* (Florence: Mandragora, 2005)

Ranieri, Concetta, 'Vittoria Colonna: dediche, libri e manoscritti', *Critica letteraria*, 13 (1985), 249–70

Ray, Meredith K., *Margherita Sarrocchi's Letters to Galileo: Astronomy, Astrology, and Poetics in Seventeenth-Century Italy* (New York: Palgrave Macmillan, 2016)

—— *Writing Gender in Women's Letter Collections of the Italian Renaissance* (University of Toronto Press, 2009)

Reardon, Colleen, '*Veni sponsa Christi*: Investiture, Profession and Consecration Ceremonies in Sienese Convents', *Musica Disciplina*, 50 (1996), 271–97

Rebecchini, Guido, *Private Collectors in Mantua, 1500–1630* (Rome: Edizioni di Storia e Letteratura, 2002)

Refini, Eugenio, 'Reappraising the Charlatan in Early Modern Italy: The Case of Iacopo Coppa', *Italian Studies*, 71 (2016), 197–211

Regan, Lisa K., 'Ariosto's Threshold Patron: Isabella d'Este in the *Orlando furioso*', *Modern Language Notes*, 120 (2005), 50–69

Renier, Rodolfo, 'Codici dell'Arcadia', *GSLI*, 11 (1888), 299–301

Rhodes, Dennis E. and Michele Feo, 'Sul tipografo Simone di Niccolò Nardi da Siena', *Studi medievali e umanistici*, 3 (2005), 29–46

Riccomanni, Cesare, ed., *Miscellanea letteraria pubblicata nell'occasione delle nozze Riccomanni-Fineschi* (Turin: Vercellino, 1861)

Richardson, Brian, 'Advising on Women's Conduct in Renaissance Paratexts', in *Conduct Literature for and about Women in Italy, 1470–1900: Prescribing and Describing Life*, ed. by Helena Sanson and Francesco Lucioli (Paris: Classiques Garnier, 2016), pp. 225–39

—— 'Improvising Lyric Verse in the Renaissance: Contexts, Sources and Imitation', in *Cultural Reception, Translation and Transformation from Medieval to Modern Italy: Essays in Honour of Martin McLaughlin*, ed. by Guido Bonsaver, Brian Richardson and Giuseppe Stellardi (Cambridge: Legenda, 2017), pp. 97–116

—— *Manuscript Culture in Renaissance Italy* (Cambridge University Press, 2009)

—— 'Memorializing Living Saints in the Milanese Convent of Santa Marta in the Late Fifteenth and Early Sixteenth Century', in *Nuns' Literacies in Medieval Europe: The Antwerp Dialogue*, ed. by Virginia Blanton, Veronica O'Mara and Patricia Stoop (Turnhout: Brepols, 2017), pp. 209–25

—— *Printing, Writers and Readers in Renaissance Italy* (Cambridge University Press, 1999)

Rifkin, Joshua, 'Munich, Milan, and a Marian Motet: Dating Josquin's "Ave Maria . . . virgo serena"', *Journal of the American Musicological Society*, 56 (2003), 239–350

Roberts, Ann, *Dominican Women and Renaissance Art: The Convent of San Domenico of Pisa* (Aldershot: Ashgate, 2008)

Robin, Diana, *Publishing Women: Salons, the Presses, and the Counter-Reformation in Sixteenth-Century Italy* (University of Chicago Press, 2007)

Rogers, Mary and Paola Tinagli, *Women in Italy, 1350–1650: Ideals and Realities. A Sourcebook* (Manchester University Press, 2005)

Romanato, Mikaël, 'Per l'edizione della *Gelosia del sole* di Girolamo Britonio', *Italique*, 12 (2009), 33–71

Romei, Giovanna, 'Dolce, Lodovico', *DBI*, 40 (1991), 399–405

Ross, Sarah Gwyneth, *The Birth of Feminism: Woman as Intellect in Renaissance Italy and England* (Cambridge, MA: Harvard University Press, 2009)

Rossi, Carla, *Il Pistoia: spirito bizzarro del Quattrocento* (Alessandria: Edizioni dell'Orso, 2008)

Rossi Parisi, Matilde, *Vittoria Farnese, duchessa d'Urbino* (Modena: Ferraguti, 1927)

Rouse, Mary A. and Richard H. Rouse, *Cartolai, Illuminators and Printers in Fifteenth-Century Italy: The Evidence of the Ripoli Press* (Los Angeles: UCLA Research Library, 1988)

Ruscelli, Girolamo, *Dediche e avvisi ai lettori*, ed. by Antonella Iacono and Paolo Marini (Manziana: Vecchiarelli, 2011)

—— *Lettere*, ed. by Chiara Gizzi and Paolo Procaccioli (Manziana: Vecchiarelli, 2010)

Russell, Camilla, *Giulia Gonzaga and the Religious Controversies of Sixteenth-Century Italy* (Turnhout: Brepols, 2006)

Saba, Agostino, *Federico Borromeo e i Mistici del suo tempo: con la vita e la corrispondenza inedita di Caterina Vannini da Siena* (Florence: Olschki, 1933)

Salzberg, Rosa, *Ephemeral City: Cheap Print and Urban Culture in Renaissance Venice* (Manchester University Press, 2015)

—— '"In the Mouths of Charlatans": Street Performers and the Dissemination of Pamphlets in Renaissance Italy', *Renaissance Studies*, 24 (2010), 638–53

—— 'Masculine Republics: Establishing Authority in the Early Modern Venetian Printshop', in *Governing Masculinities in the Early Modern Period*, ed. by Susan Broomhall and Jacqueline Van Gent (Farnham: Ashgate, 2011), pp. 47–64

—— '"Selling Stories and Many Other Things in and through the City": Peddling Print in Sixteenth-Century Florence and Venice', *Sixteenth Century Journal*, 42 (2011), 737–59

Sampson, Lisa, 'Performing Female Cultural Sociability between Court and Academy: Isabella Pallavicino Lupi and Angelo Ingegneri's *Danza di Venere* (1584)', in *Chivalry, Academy, and Cultural Dialogues: The Italian Contribution to European Culture*, ed. by Stefano Jossa and Giuliana Pieri (Cambridge: Legenda, 2016), pp. 107–22

Sanson, Helena, *Women, Language and Grammar in Italy, 1500–1900* (Oxford University Press for the British Academy, 2011)

Santagata, Marco, *La lirica aragonese: studi sulla poesia napoletana del secondo Quattrocento* (Padua: Antenore, 1979)

Santore, Cathy, 'Julia Lombardo, "somtuosa meretrize": A Portrait by Property', *Renaissance Quarterly*, 41 (1988), 44–83

Santoro, Caterina, *Gli offici del comune di Milano e del dominio visconteo sforzesco (1216–1515)* (Milan: Giuffrè, 1968)

Santoro, Marco, 'Imprenditrici o "facenti funzioni"?', in *La donna nel Rinascimento meridionale: atti del convegno internazionale (Roma 11–13 novembre 2009)*, ed. by Marco Santoro (Pisa and Rome: Fabrizio Serra, 2010), pp. 371–82

—— *Uso e abuso delle dediche: a proposito del 'Della dedicatione de' libri' di Giovanni Fratta* (Rome: Edizioni dell'Ateneo, 2006)

Sartori, Claudio, 'Una dinastia di editori musicali: documenti inediti sui Gardano e i loro congiunti Stefano Bindoni e Alessandro Raverii', *LB*, 58 (1956), 176–208

Savoldelli, Gianmaria and Roberta Frigeni, *Comin Ventura: tra lettere e libri di lettere (1579–1617)* (Florence: Olschki, 2017)

Savonarola, Girolamo, *Prediche sopra i Salmi*, ed. by Vincenzo Romano, 2 vols (Rome: Belardetti, 1969–74)

Scandola, Massimo, '"Dell'officio della scrittora": fra fides e custodia. "Monache scrivane" e notai a Verona nei secoli XVII e XVIII', *Scrineum Rivista*, 10 (2013), 259–312, www.fupress.net/index.php/scrineum/article/view/13697

Scarpati, Claudio, 'Le rime spirituali di Vittoria Colonna nel codice vaticano donato a Michelangelo', in *Invenzione e scrittura: saggi di letteratura italiana* (Milan: Vita e Pensiero, 2005), pp. 129–62

Schibanoff, Susan, 'Botticelli's *Madonna del Magnificat*: Constructing the Woman Writer in Early Humanist Italy', *PMLA*, 109 (1994), 190–206

Scholderer, Victor, 'Printing at Venice to the End of 1481', in *Fifty Essays in Fifteenth- and Sixteenth-Century Bibliography*, ed. by Dennis E. Rhodes (Amsterdam: Hertzberger, 1966), pp. 74–89

Scott-Warren, Jason, *Sir John Harington and the Book as Gift* (Oxford University Press, 2001)

Sedini, Domenico, *Marco d'Oggiono: tradizione e rinnovamento in Lombardia tra Quattrocento e Cinquecento* (Milan: Jandi Sapi, 1989)

Seidel Menchi, Silvana, *Erasmo in Italia 1520–1580* (Turin: Bollati Boringhieri, 1987)

'Le traduzioni italiane di Lutero nella prima metà del Cinquecento', *Rinascimento*, 2nd ser., 17 (1977), 31–108

Sestini, Valentina, *Donne tipografe a Messina tra XVII e XIX secolo* (Pisa and Rome: Fabrizio Serra, 2015)

Sforza, Ippolita Maria, *Duchess and Hostage in Renaissance Naples: Letters and Orations*, ed. and trans. by Diana Robin and Lynn Lara Westwater (Toronto: Centre for Reformation and Renaissance Studies, 2017)

*Lettere*, ed. by M. Serena Castaldo (Alessandria: Edizioni dell'Orso, 2004)

Shemek, Deanna, *Ladies Errant: Wayward Women and Social Order in Early Modern Italy* (Durham, NC: Duke University Press, 1998)

Shepard, Alexandra and Phil Withington, eds, *Communities in Early Modern England: Networks, Place, Rhetoric* (Manchester University Press, 2000)

Sherman, William H., *Used Books: Marking Readers in Renaissance England* (Philadelphia: University of Pennsylvania Press, 2007)

Simoncelli, Paolo, 'The Turbulent Life of the Florentine Community in Venice', in *Heresy, Culture, and Religion in Early Modern Italy: Contexts and Contestations*, ed. by Ronald K. Delph, Michelle M. Fontaine and John Jeffries Martin (Kirksville, MO: Truman State University Press, 2006), pp. 113–33

Smith, Helen, *'Grossly Material Things': Women and Book Production in Early Modern England* (Oxford University Press, 2012)

'Women and the Materials of Writing', in *Material Cultures of Early Modern Women's Writing*, ed. by Patricia Pender and Rosalind Smith (Basingstoke: Palgrave Macmillan, 2014), pp. 14–35

Smith, Lesley, '*Scriba, Femina*: Medieval Depictions of Women Writing', in *Women and the Book: Assessing the Visual Evidence*, ed. by Lesley Smith and

Jane H. M. Taylor (London: British Library; University of Toronto Press, 1996), pp. 21–44

Solerti, Angelo, *Vita di Torquato Tasso*, 3 vols (Turin: Loescher, 1895)

Sonzini, Valentina, 'Il sistema delle dediche nella produzione degli Osanna: le donne Gonzaga nella storia della stampa cinquecentesca mantovana', in *Donne Gonzaga a corte: reti istituzionali, pratiche culturali e affari di governo*, ed. by Chiara Continisio and Raffaele Tamalio (Rome: Bulzoni, 2018), pp. 417–29

Sorelli, Fernanda, *La santità imitabile: 'Leggenda di Maria da Venezia' di Tommaso da Siena* (Venice: Deputazione di storia patria per le Venezie, 1984)

Sorio, Bartolomeo, ed., *La teologia mistica* (Verona: Eredi di Marco Moroni, 1852)

Spierling, Karen E. and Michael J. Halvorson, eds, *Defining Community in Early Modern Europe* (Aldershot: Ashgate, 2008)

Spini, Giorgio, 'Bibliografia delle opere di Antonio Brucioli', *LB*, 42 (1940), 129–180

Spufford, Peter, *Handbook of Medieval Exchange* (London: Royal Historical Society, 1986)

Stabile, Giorgio, 'Borri (Borro, Borrius), Girolamo', *DBI*, 13 (1971), 13–17

Stampa, Gaspara, *The Complete Poems: The 1554 Edition of the 'Rime', a Bilingual Edition*, ed. by Troy Tower and Jane Tylus, intro. and trans. by Jane Tylus (University of Chicago Press, 2010)

Stevens, Kevin M., 'New Light on Andrea Calvo and the Book Trade in Sixteenth-Century Milan', *LB*, 103 (2001), 25–54

Stjerna, Kirsi, *Women and the Reformation* (Oxford: Blackwell, 2009)

Stoddard, Roger, *Marks in Books, Illustrated and Explained* (Cambridge, MA: Houghton Library, 1985)

Stoop, Patricia, 'From Reading to Writing: The Multiple Levels of Literacy of the Sister Scribes in the Brussels Convent of Jericho', in *Nuns' Literacies in Medieval Europe: The Kansas City Dialogue*, ed. by Virginia Blanton, Veronica O'Mara and Patricia Stoop (Turnhout: Brepols, 2015), pp. 47–66

—— 'Nuns' Literacy in Sixteenth-Century Convent Sermons from the Cistercian Abbey of Ter Kameren', in *Nuns' Literacies in Medieval Europe: The Hull Dialogue*, ed. by Virginia Blanton, Veronica O'Mara and Patricia Stoop (Turnhout: Brepols, 2013), pp. 293–312

Stras, Laurie, 'The *Ricreationi per monache* of suor Annalena Aldobrandini', *Renaissance Studies*, 26 (2012), 34–59

Strocchia, Sharon T., 'Abbess Piera de' Medici and Her Kin: Gender, Gifts, and Patronage in Renaissance Florence', *Renaissance Studies*, 28 (2014), 695–713

—— 'Learning the Virtues: Convent Schools and Female Culture in Renaissance Florence', in *Women's Education in Early Modern Europe: A History, 1500–1800*, ed. by Barbara J. Whitehead (New York: Garland, 1999), pp. 3–46

—— *Nuns and Nunneries in Renaissance Florence* (Baltimore, MD: Johns Hopkins University Press, 2009)

'Sisters in Spirit: The Nuns of Sant'Ambrogio and Their Consorority in Early Sixteenth-Century Florence', *Sixteenth Century Journal*, 33 (2002), 735–67

'Taken into Custody: Girls and Convent Guardianship in Renaissance Florence', *Renaissance Studies*, 17 (2003), 177–200

Strunck, Christina, ed., *Medici Women as Cultural Mediators, 1533–1743* (Milan: Silvana, 2011)

Stumpo, Elisabetta, 'Rapporti familiari e modelli educativi: il caso di Cristina di Lorena', in *Le donne Medici nel sistema europeo delle corti XVI–XVIII secolo: atti del convegno internazionale, Firenze, San Domenico di Fiesole, 6–8 ottobre 2005*, ed. by Giulia Calvi and Riccardo Spinelli, 2 vols (Florence: Polistampa, 2008), I, 257–68

Szépe, Helena K., 'Bordon, Dürer and Modes of Illuminating Aldines', in *Aldus Manutius and Renaissance Culture: Essays in Memory of Franklin D. Murphy*, ed. by David S. Zeidberg (Florence: Olschki, 1998), pp. 185–200

Tabarelli, Costanzo, *Documentazione notarile perugina sul Convento di Monteripido nei secoli XIV e XV* (Perugia: Deputazione di storia patria per l'Umbria, 1977)

Talbot, Michael, '*Ore italiane*: The Reckoning of the Time of Day in Pre-Napoleonic Italy', *Italian Studies*, 40 (1985), 51–62

Tarabotti, Arcangela, *Lettere familiari e di complimento*, ed. by Meredith Kennedy Ray and Lynn Lara Westwater (Turin: Rosenberg & Sellier, 2005)

Tarbin, Stephanie and Susan Broomhall, eds, *Women, Identities and Communities in Early Modern Europe* (Aldershot: Ashgate, 2008)

Tasso, Bernardo, *Rime*, 2 vols (Turin: RES, 1995)

Tasso, Torquato, *Lettere*, ed. by Cesare Guasti, 5 vols (Florence: Le Monnier, 1852–55)

Taurisano, Innocenzo, *I Domenicani in Lucca* (Lucca: Baroni, 1914)

Taylor, Bruce, *Structures of Reform: The Mercedarian Order in the Spanish Golden Age* (Leiden: Brill, 2000)

Terracina, Laura, *Discorsi sopra le prime stanze de' canti d'Orlando furioso*, ed. by Rotraud von Kulessa and Daria Perocco (Florence: Cesati, 2017)

Thornton, Dora, *The Scholar in his Study: Ownership and Experience in Renaissance Italy* (New Haven: Yale University Press, 1997)

Tinto, Alberto, *Annali tipografici dei Tramezzino* (Venice and Rome: Istituto per la collaborazione culturale, 1968)

Tippelskirch, Xenia von, *Sotto controllo: letture femminili in Italia nella prima età moderna* (Rome: Viella, 2011)

Tissoni Benvenuti, Antonia, 'Il mondo cavalleresco e la corte estense', in *I libri di 'Orlando innamorato'* (Modena: Panini, 1987), pp. 13–33

Tomas, Natalie, 'Eleonora di Toledo, Regency, and State Formation in Tuscany', in *Medici Women: The Making of a Dynasty in Grand Ducal Tuscany*, ed. by Giovanna Benadusi and Judith C. Brown (Toronto: Centre for Renaissance and Reformation Studies, 2015), pp. 58–89

Toniolo, Federica, 'Livres et images de femmes à la cour des Este à Ferrare', in *Livres et lectures de femmes en Europe entre Moyen Âge et Renaissance*, ed. by Anne-Marie Legaré (Turnhout: Brepols, 2007), pp. 311–24

Tordi, Domenico, *Il codice delle Rime di Vittoria Colonna, Marchesa di Pescara, appartenuto a Margherita d'Angoulême, Regina di Navarra* (Pistoia: Flori, 1900)

Toscano, Gennaro, 'La collezione di Ippolita Sforza e la biblioteca di Alfonso duca di Calabria', in *La Biblioteca reale di Napoli al tempo della dinastia aragonese: Napoli, Castel Nuovo, 30 settembre–15 dicembre 1998*, ed. by Gennaro Toscano (Valencia: Generalitat Valenciana, 1998), pp. 251–67

'Livres et lectures de deux princesses de la cour d'Aragon de Naples: Isabella de Chiaromonte et Ippolita Maria Sforza', in *Livres et lectures de femmes en Europe entre Moyen Âge et Renaissance*, ed. by Anne-Marie Legaré (Turnhout: Brepols, 2007), pp. 295–310

Toscano, Tobia R., *Letterati corti accademie: la letteratura a Napoli nella prima metà del Cinquecento* (Naples: Loffredo, 2000)

'Per la datazione del manoscritto dei sonetti di Vittoria Colonna per Michelangelo Buonarroti', *Critica letteraria*, 45 (2017), 211–37

Tramarin, Davide, 'With Pen or Brush: Traces of Women in Fifteenth-Century Italy', in *Invisible Cultures: Historical and Archaeological Perspectives*, ed. by Francesco Carrer and Viola Gheller (Newcastle upon Tyne: Cambridge Scholars Publishing, 2015), pp. 97–114

Trevisani, Filippo, ed., *Andrea Mantegna e i Gonzaga: Rinascimento nel Castello di San Giorgio. Catalogo della mostra* (Milan: Electa, 2006)

Trexler, Richard C., 'Le Célibat à la fin du moyen âge: les religieuses de Florence', *Annales: Économies, Sociétés, Civilisations*, 27 (1972), 1329–50

Tuohy, Thomas, *Herculean Ferrara: Ercole d'Este (1471–1505) and the Invention of a Ducal Capital* (Cambridge University Press, 1996)

Turba, Giuseppe, 'Galeotto Del Carretto tra Casale e Mantova', *Rinascimento*, 2nd ser., 11 (1971), 95–169

Tylus, Jane, 'Early Modern Women as Translators of the Sacred', *Women Language Literature in Italy*, 1 (2019), 31–43

Valdés, Giovanni di, *Alfabeto cristiano: dialogo con Giulia Gonzaga*, ed. by Benedetto Croce (Bari: Laterza, 1938)

Valdés, Juan de, *Alfabeto cristiano, Domande e risposte, Della predestinazione, Catechismo*, ed. by Massimo Firpo (Turin: Einaudi, 1994)

van Orden, Kate, *Music, Authorship, and the Book in the First Century of Print* (Berkeley: University of California Press, 2014)

Vecce, Carlo, 'Petrarca, Vittoria, Michelangelo', *Studi e problemi di critica testuale*, 44 (April 1992), 101–25

Veneziani, Paolo, 'Cartolari, Baldassare', *DBI*, 20 (1977), 804–06

Vignali, Antonio, *Dulpisto*, ed. by James W. Nelson Novoa, http://parnaseo.uv.es/lemir/textos/dulpisto.pdf

Vigri, Caterina, *Le sette armi spirituali*, ed. by Antonella Degl'Innocenti (Florence: SISMEL-Edizioni del Galluzzo, 2000)

Villa, Alessandra, *Istruire e rappresentare Isabella d'Este: il 'Libro de natura de amore' di Mario Equicola* (Lucca: Maria Pacini Fazzi, 2006)

Wagner, Bettina, ed., *Aussen-Ansichten: Bucheinbände aus 1000 Jahren* (Wiesbaden: Harrassowitz, 2006)

Walker, Claire, 'Recusants, Daughters and Sisters in Christ: English Nuns and Their Communities in the Seventeenth Century', in *Women, Identities and Communities in Early Modern Europe*, ed. by Stephanie Tarbin and Susan Broomhall (Aldershot: Ashgate, 2008), pp. 61–76

Wardrop, James, 'The Vatican Scriptors: Documents for Ruano and Cresci', *Signature*, n.s., 5 (1948), 3–28

Watson, Andrew G., *Catalogue of Dated and Datable Manuscripts c. 700–1600 in the Department of Manuscripts, British Library*, 2 vols (London: British Museum, 1979)

Watson, Rowan, 'Manual of Dynastic History or Devotional Aid? Eleanor of Toledo's Book of Hours', in *Excavating the Medieval Image: Manuscripts, Artists, Audiences. Essays in Honor of Sandra Hindman*, ed. by David S. Areford and Nina A. Rowe (Aldershot: Ashgate, 2004), pp. 179–95

Weaver, Elissa, *Convent Theatre in Early Modern Italy: Spiritual Fun and Learning for Women* (Cambridge University Press, 2002)

Welch, Evelyn, 'The Art of Expenditure: The Court of Paola Malatesta Gonzaga in Fifteenth-Century Mantua', *Renaissance Studies*, 16 (2002), 306–17

Welch, Evelyn S., 'Between Milan and Naples: Ippolita Sforza, Duchess of Calabria', in *The French Descent into Renaissance Italy, 1494–95: Antecedents and Effects*, ed. by David Abulafia (Aldershot: Variorum, 1995), pp. 123–36

*Shopping in the Renaissance: Consumer Cultures in Italy 1400–1600* (New Haven: Yale University Press, 2005)

Whalley, Joyce Irene, *The Art of Calligraphy: Western Europe & America* (London: Bloomsbury Books, 1980)

Whitthoft, Brucia, 'The Hours of Isabella di Chiaromonte', *Harvard Library Bulletin*, 18 (1970), 298–307

Wieck, Roger, *Time Sanctified: The Book of Hours in Medieval Art and Life*, with essays by Lawrence R. Poos, Virginia Reinburg and John Plummer (New York: George Braziller in association with the Walters Art Gallery, 1988)

Wiesner-Hanks, Merry E., 'Women's Economic Role', in *Women and Gender in Early Modern Europe*, 3rd edn (Cambridge University Press, 2008), pp. 101–37

Williams, Abigail, *The Social Life of Books: Reading Together in the Eighteenth-Century Home* (New Haven: Yale University Press, 2017)

Woudhuysen, H. R., *Sir Philip Sidney and the Circulation of Manuscripts 1558–1640* (Oxford: Clarendon Press, 1996)

Zaja, Paolo, 'Marinelli (Marinella), Lucrezia', *DBI*, 70 (2008), 399–402

Zappacosta, Guglielmo, *Studi e ricerche sull'umanesimo italiano (testi inediti del XV e XVI secolo)* (Bergamo: Minerva Italica, 1972)

Zappella, Giuseppina, *Il ritratto nel libro italiano del Cinquecento*, 2 vols (Milan: Editrice Bibliografica, 1988)

Zardin, Danilo, *Donna e religiosa di rara eccellenza: Prospera Corona Bascapè, i libri e la cultura nei monasteri milanesi del Cinque e Seicento* (Florence: Olschki, 1992)

'Libri e biblioteche negli ambienti monastici dell'Italia del primo Seicento', in *Donne, filosofia e cultura nel Seicento*, ed. by Pina Totaro (Rome: Consiglio Nazionale delle Ricerche, 1999), pp. 347–83

'Mercato librario e letture devote nella svolta del Cinquecento tridentino: note in margine ad un inventario milanese di libri di monache', in *Stampa, libri e letture a Milano nell'età di Carlo Borromeo*, ed. by Nicola Raponi and Angelo Turchini (Milan: Vita e Pensiero, 1992), pp. 135–246

Zarri, Gabriella, 'Blessed Lucia of Narni (1476–1544) between "Hagiography" and "Autobiography": Mystical Authorship and the Persistence of the Manuscript', in *The Saint between Manuscript and Print: Italy 1400–1600*, ed. by Alison K. Frazier (Toronto: Centre for Reformation and Renaissance Studies, 2015), pp. 421–45

*Figure di donne in età moderna: modelli e storie* (Rome: Edizioni di Storia e Letteratura, 2017)

'From Prophecy to Discipline, 1450–1650', in *Women and Faith: Catholic Religious Life in Italy from Late Antiquity to the Present*, ed. by Lucetta Scaraffia and Gabriella Zarri (Cambridge, MA: Harvard University Press, 1999), pp. 83–112

*Libri di spirito: editoria religiosa in volgare nei secoli XV–XVII* (Turin: Rosenberg & Sellier, 2009)

'Memoria individuale e memoria collettiva: gli scritti di Lucia da Narni († 1544) e la loro conservazione', in *Memoria e comunità femminili: Spagna e Italia, secc. XV–XVII*, ed. by Gabriella Zarri and Nieves Baranda Leturio (Florence: Firenze University Press; [Madrid]: UNED, 2011), pp. 73–86

'Novizie ed educande nei monasteri italiani post-tridentini', *Via spiritus*, 18 (2011), 7–23

*Recinti: donne, clausura e matrimonio nella prima età moderna* (Bologna: il Mulino, 2000)

*La 'religione' di Lucrezia Borgia: le lettere inedite del confessore* (Rome: Roma nel Rinascimento, 2006)

*Le sante vive: profezie di corte e devozione femminile tra '400 e '500* (Turin: Rosenberg & Sellier, 1990)

Zarri, Gabriella and Nieves Baranda Leturio, eds, *Memoria e comunità femminili: Spagna e Italia secc. XV–XVII* (Florence: Firenze University Press; [Madrid]: UNED, 2011)

Zonta, Giuseppe, ed., *Trattati d'amore del Cinquecento* (Bari: Laterza, 1912)

# Index

convents (cont.)
  S. Brigida al Paradiso (Birgittine), 105–08,
    164, 165, 184
  S. Caterina al Monte (Augustinian), 110
  S. Giuliano (Dominican), 181
  S. Iacopo di Ripoli (Dominican), 102,
    141–43, 179–81
  S. Lucia (Dominican), 103–04, 181
  S. Monaca (Augustinian), 110
  S. Onofrio (Franciscan), 163
  S. Orsola (Franciscan), 185
  S. Pier Maggiore (Benedictine), 100
  S. Verdiana (Vallombrosan), 110
  S. Vincenzo d'Annalena (Dominican), 181
  SS. Girolamo e Francesco (Franciscan), 185
Foligno:
  S. Lucia (Franciscan), 118–19
Genoa:
  Scala Coeli (Birgittine), 108–09, 177
Lucca:
  S. Domenico (Dominican), 104–05, 109
  S. Giorgio (Dominican), 104–05, 110,
    183
Mantua:
  Corpus Domini (S. Paola) (Franciscan), 98
Milan:
  S. Maria Maddalena del Cerchio
    (Humiliati), 161–62, 164, 184
  S. Marta (Augustinian), 119–26, 226
  S. Paolo Converso (Angelic Sisters), 97 n. 24
Naples:
  S. Francesco delle Monache
    (Franciscan), 27
Orvieto:
  S. Chiara (Franciscan), 159
Perugia:
  S. Agnese (Franciscan), 165
  S. Antonio di Padova (Franciscan), 165,
    170–71
  S. Maria di Monteluce (Franciscan), 113–18,
    170–71, 183, 227
Pisa:
  S. Domenico (Dominican), 160, 183, 184
Pontassieve:
  S. Maria di Rosano (Benedictine), 176–77
Prato:
  S. Niccolò (Dominican), 7, 109
Rome:
  S. Cosimato in Trastevere (Franciscan),
    99 n. 33
  S. Susanna (Cistercian), 147
Sassari:
  S. Chiara (Franciscan), 163
Siena:
  Ognissanti (Dominican), 146

S. Abundio (Gesuate), 174–75
S. Marta (Augustinian), 174–75
S. Niccolò (Franciscan), 146
Venice:
  S. Andrea della Zirada (Augustinian), 82
    n. 171
  S. Croce della Giudecca (Benedictine), 113
  S. Francesco della Croce (Franciscan), 101
  S. Maria della Celestia (Cistercian), 144
  S. Maria Maddalena alla Giudecca
    (Augustinian), 144
Verona:
  S. Spirito (Benedictine), 100
Vicenza:
  S. Corona (Dominican), 147
  S. Maria Maddalena (Augustinian), 147
*see also* nuns
Coppa, Iacopo, 30–31
Corboli, Aurelio, 133
Cornaro, Federico, 21
Cornelia, suor (Siena), 174
Correggio, suor Barbara da, dedication to, 67
Correggio, Gian Galeazzo da, 212–13
Correggio, Niccolò da, 207, 211–13, 222
Corsini, Caterina, 153
Corsini, Giovanni, 153
Corso, Rinaldo, 39, 68
Cortesi, Tedheria, 131
Cosmico, Niccolò Lelio, 207–08
Costa, Margherita, 19–20
Cox, Virginia, x, xvii, 17
Cresci, Giovan Francesco, 91, 98
Cristina, suor (Perugia), 183
Cristofano Fiorentino (l'Altissimo), 189
Croce, Giulio Cesare, 187–88
Cromberger, Juan, 228
Cucchetti, Giovanni Donato, 51 n. 116
Cueva, Maria Anna de la, dedication to, 16,
  40
Cuini, Vittoria, 128
Cyrus, Cynthia, 228

Dalla Noce, Agostino, 139
Dallasta, Federica, 159
dalle Vieze, Cesare, 201–02
da Mula, Marco Antonio, 1 n. 1
Daniello, Bernardino, 37 n. 85
Dante Alighieri:
  language, xviii
  works owned by women, 199, 204
Da Ponte, Aurelia, 133
Da Ponte, Giulia, 169
Da Ponte, Pacifico, 133
Darnton, Robert, xii–xiv, xv, 149
D'Atri, Iacopo, 203, 208, 209, 217

Lightning Source UK Ltd.
Milton Keynes UK
UKHW021943260123
416044UK00019B/161